China's Political System

China's Political System provides a concise introduction to the political, economic, and social factors that determine China's government. Highly respected specialist June Teufel Dreyer offers expert analysis of the challenges facing China's economic, legal, military, social, and cultural institutions while examining the historical context and current trends. *China's Political System* asks readers to think about the broader problems of governance and modernization in China and their global implications by comprehensively showing how the past and present impact leaders, citizens, ethnic minorities, and policies.

New to the Tenth Edition:

- the first text to incorporate results from the Nineteenth Party Congress and Thirteenth National People's Congress
- includes a new chapter on developments under Xi Jinping
- considers the effects of slowing economic growth on politics and society
- addresses recent Chinese assertiveness in military and foreign policy.

The tenth edition of *China's Political System* continues to provide all of the tools professors need to introduce their students to Chinese politics in ways that are informed, accessible, and intriguing.

June Teufel Dreyer is Professor of Political Science at the University of Miami, Coral Gables, Florida, a past commissioner of the congressionally established U.S.–China Economic and Security Review Commission, and a fellow of the Foreign Policy Research Institute. She is the author of *Middle Kingdom and Empire of the Rising Sun: Sino–Japanese Relations Past and Present* (Oxford University Press); *China's Forty Millions: Minority Nationalities and National Integration in the People's Republic of China* (Harvard University Press); editor of *Chinese Defense and Foreign Policy* (Paragon House) and *Asian-Pacific Regional Defense* (Paragon House), and co-editor of *U.S.–China Relations in the 21st Century* (Lexington) and *Contemporary Tibet: Politics, Development, and Society in a Disputed Region* (Routledge).

'June Teufel Dreyer is among the most internationally respected experts on China. This book convincingly demonstrates why. It has been and will continue to be a must-read for generations of students, scholars, and the general public.'

Jing Sun, *Associate Professor,*
University of Denver

'June Teufel Dreyer's latest edition of *China's Political System* continues the high standard that has been evident in each previous edition. In a crowded field of textbooks on Chinese politics, the two areas that distinguish the best books are comprehensiveness in terms of the coverage of important topics and material that is not only up-to-date but will not become dated quickly. Dreyer has succeeded admirably on both counts, with the high quality of the new chapter on The Era of Xi Jinping and the discussion of the results of the Nineteenth Party Congress, making this the best textbook on Chinese politics currently on the market.'

Stanley Rosen, *Professor of Political Science,*
University of Southern California

'Dreyer expertly examines and provides a comprehensive, up-to-date overview of the internal and external pressures and changes and continuities that have propelled political, social, and economic developments in contemporary China. From the republican era and the rise of the Chinese communists to post-Mao reforms and China's globalization, Dreyer surveys events, peoples, institutions, and policymaking and their implications within China and for the world.'

Roselyn Hsueh, *Associate Professor, Temple University*

'Comprehensive and accessible, *China's Political System* provides a clear overview of the complex political and social issues facing contemporary China. The text offers a solid foundation for students who are encountering China for the first time.'

Kerry Ratigan, *Assistant Professor, Amherst College*

Tenth Edition

China's Political System

Modernization and Tradition

June Teufel Dreyer

Routledge
Taylor & Francis Group

NEW YORK AND LONDON

Tenth edition published 2019
by Routledge
711 Third Avenue, New York, NY 10017

and by Routledge
2 Park Square, Milton Park, Abingdon, Oxon, OX14 4RN

Routledge is an imprint of the Taylor & Francis Group, an informa business

[First edition published by Palgrave Macmillan 1993]
[Ninth edition published by Routledge 2016]

Library of Congress Cataloging-in-Publication Data
Names: Dreyer, June Teufel, 1939– author.
Title: China's political system : modernization and tradition / June Teufel Dreyer.
Description: Tenth edition. | New York, NY : Routledge, 2018. | Includes
    bibliographical references and index.
Identifiers: LCCN 2018003725 | ISBN 9781138501515 (hardback) | ISBN 9781138501522
    (pbk.) | ISBN 9781351385824 (epub) | ISBN 9781351385817 (mobipocket/kindle) |
    ISBN 9781315144399 (Master) | ISBN 9781351385831 (WebPDF)
Subjects: LCSH: China—Politics and government—1949–
Classification: LCC JQ1510 .D74 2018 | DDC 320.451—dc23
LC record available at https://lccn.loc.gov/2018003725

ISBN: 978-1-138-50151-5 (hbk)
ISBN: 978-1-138-50152-2 (pbk)
ISBN: 978-1-315-14439-9 (ebk)

Typeset in Sabon LT Std
by Apex CoVantage, LLC

To the memory of my parents
Anna Elizabeth Waldhauer
Paul Albert Teufel

CONTENTS

ILLUSTRATIONS

FIGURES

TABLES

MAPS

PREFACE

As the People's Republic of China approached the seventieth anniversary of its founding, Chinese patriots had much to be proud of. A country that had been poor and war-ravaged in 1949 was now the world's second largest economy—first by some measures, had developed formidable military might, and was unequivocally accepted as one of the world's preeminent powers.

At the same time, major problems loomed with the potential to undermine these successes. Domestically, communism was moribund as an ideology, and the Chinese Communist Party had lost its legitimacy in the eyes of many of the PRC's citizens. Economic growth was slowing amid uncertainty about where it might level off. There were questions about how healthy the reported economic growth rates were: increases in gross domestic product do not necessarily translate into increased productivity. Moreover, growth had been accompanied by a widening of income inequality and increasing social instability. Corruption was endemic in the economic and political systems. Pollution filled the air of many urban areas and poisoned the waterways.

Although most people appeared content to enjoy the benefits of increasing prosperity, vocal minorities of farmers, workers, and ethnic minorities voiced their dissatisfaction with the status quo. Harsh punishments were meted out to dissidents, not infrequently in trials that seemed to violate the provisions of the country's constitution. Better laws were passed but not always enforced. A party which had come to power on behalf of the rights of the workers and the peasants seemed to have turned its back on them. While the slogan "serve the people" remained, party and government leaders seemed now to fear the people: surveillance, aided by artificial intelligence technology, has been tightened in a way that was scarcely imaginable in George Orwell's day.

Externally, foreign nations worried that their economies might be swallowed by the Chinese juggernaut, and complained that Beijing was manipulating the country's currency to create trade imbalances in China's favor. They also voiced concern about the motives behind rapidly rising defense budgets when the PRC faced no external threat, objected to Chinese efforts to dominate disputed areas in the South China and East China seas, and protested against cyber spying that was shown to have originated in China. Foreign analysts began to question their initial assumption that economic pluralism would lead inexorably to political pluralism and an evolution toward liberal democracy. In some areas, the Chinese system had become more rather than less oppressive. Moreover, the state also strengthened its control over the economy to some degree.

Whether the genuine achievements of the seven decades can be continued is a question much debated by scholars of China, both domestic and foreign. The present problems could represent no more than the growing pains of a greater and more powerful state. At the other extreme, they could portend the collapse of the current system. Or the country could be caught in a middle-income trap.

The genesis of the first edition of *China's Political System* grew out of my own efforts to understand how the communist government of China, having only recently, in the long sweep of Chinese history, come to power, could transform an impressive ancient civilization into an impressive industrialized socialist or, more recently, authoritarian quasi-socialist, state.

My aim has been to describe and analyze China's political system, taking as *leitmotif* the efforts of successive leaderships to harmonize elements of the country's unique indigenous culture with formulas for industrialization and modernization that originally evolved in the West. The nineteenth-century paradigm "Chinese learning for the essence; Western learning for practical use" resonates with Mao Zedong's injunction to "walk on two legs"—the modern and the traditional—as does Deng Xiaoping's search for "socialism with Chinese characteristics," and Xi Jinping's "China Dream" with "In Search of Wealth and Power." Over the past half century, these and related themes have become prominent in Chinese politics. As the leadership of the People's Republic shifted emphasis from revolutionary ideals to the more mundane but perhaps even more challenging business of governing, and from a socialist, planned economy to a semi-market-based system, the question of how much of its communist heritage it should retain has had to be addressed as well. Elements of retraditionalization coexist with trends toward modernization and globalization.

The intended audience for *China's Political System* is upper-level undergraduates specializing in political science and history or simply interested persons who want to learn more about China. The author hopes that this will be an enjoyable experience. Academic jargon has been minimized.

New to This Edition

The tenth edition has been updated to include the following:

- significant political and military developments through early 2018;
- policy changes since the Nineteenth Party Congress and Thirteenth National People's Congress
- recent legal and economic developments and statistics based on the latest (2017) edition of the *China Statistical Handbook*;
- expanded coverage of changing relationships among central, provincial, and local governments;
- a new chapter on the Xi Jinping era;
- the impact of enhanced citizen participation in the political process;
- effects of the decelerating economic growth rate.

Features

A summary of the different ways in which Chinese politics and history have been analyzed is followed by brief overviews of the traditional Chinese system, its breakdown, and the rise of communism, followed by a more detailed treatment of the characteristics and major events of the communist era. Because politics has permeated virtually every sphere of Chinese society since 1949, an analysis of how politics has impinged on these different spheres forms the major building blocks of the text—economics; the legal system; the military; literature, art, and journalism; and so forth. Although the list of topics that might be considered is long, the academic semester is limited, and hence the number of chapters has been set at fifteen—approximately one for each week of the average semester. Resisting the urge to be encyclopedic has meant not providing separate chapters for topics that some might prefer, such as ideology, human rights, and the role of women, which are treated as sub-themes in other chapters. A concluding chapter integrates these different areas, assesses the successes and failures of the Chinese communist system, and outlines possible scenarios for the future. Suggestions for additional reading—limited to five titles, on the advice of my editor—appear at the end of each chapter.

ACKNOWLEDGMENTS

The author very much appreciates the advice of many people. In addition to Evelyn Fazio, who suggested the first edition, these include, in alphabetical order, Routledge editors Jennifer Knerr, Maria Landschoot, Natalja Mortensen, and Ze'ev Sudry and fellow China-watchers Jerome Cohen, the late Edward Dreyer, Ed Friedman, Baogang Guo, François Godement, Cheng Li, Shending Li, Perry Link, Stan Rosen, Jim Seymour, and Suisheng Zhao, as well as several anonymous reviewers. Stephen Halsey generously provided the cover photograph, with its image of the restoration of a venerable pagoda against a background of new construction and a setting sun perfectly capturing the interplay of modernization and retraditionalization that provides the book's theme. I have also greatly profited from the collective discussions of several e-mail groups. Thanks also to those of you who responded to my call for suggestions for future editions. Please continue to send them: my e-mail address remains jdreyer@miami.edu.

JUNE TEUFEL DREYER
CORAL GABLES, FLORIDA

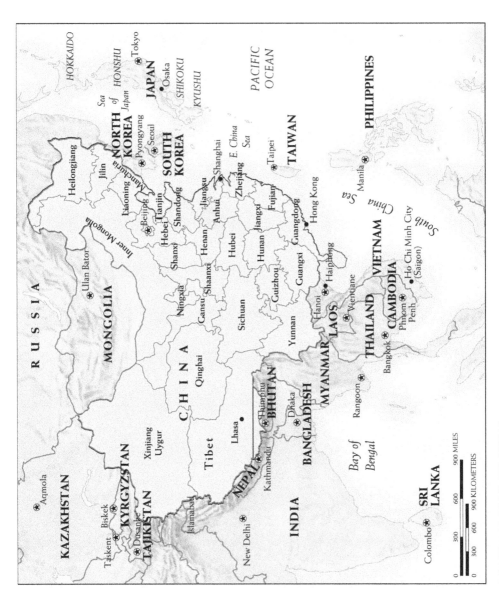

POLITICAL MAP OF CHINA.

CHAPTER 1

Introduction

Modernization and Chinese Civilization

As inheritors of the world's oldest continuous civilization, the Chinese can be justly proud of their achievements. Early creation of a written language, development of elaborate techniques of silk weaving and wet rice cultivation, and invention of the compass and gunpowder are but a few of the more outstanding of these accomplishments. Thus, the Chinese had good reasons for feeling secure in their image of themselves as the Middle Kingdom, *Zhongguo*, or that entity at the fringes of which the less favored groups of humanity existed.

The arrival, beginning in the sixteenth century, of Westerners who desired trade and wanted to spread their religious beliefs was therefore seen as an unwelcome intrusion into the peace and harmony of the empire. The Chinese government summarily rebuffed Western overtures, since it was obvious that ignorant barbarians could not contribute significantly to the well-being of the Celestial Empire and might even cause genuine harm. The Westerners, however, were persistent. They defeated the Chinese with relative ease in a series of armed confrontations, beginning with the Opium War of 1839–1842.

This posed a problem for the heretofore self-confident Chinese elite. Because there are no universally accepted criteria by which to measure aesthetic values, it is easy to reject another country's culture as inferior. Military superiority, however, can be judged on the battlefield, and in this area the Middle Kingdom proved decidedly deficient. Continued military inferiority jeopardized the survival of both the empire and its esteemed culture. It therefore became a matter of great importance to the Chinese government to build the country's defenses to the point where Western intrusions would no longer need to be feared.

One solution which occurred to a number of people was that China should learn the barbarians' military secrets in order to use them against the enemy. In addition to seeming perfectly reasonable, this solution could be—and was—rationalized by calling upon the authority of China's first and leading military strategist, Sun Zi. Writing in the fourth century B.C., Sun Zi had advised, "Know yourself, know your enemy, win ten thousand battles." At the same time, however, this precept raised a fundamental dilemma in the minds of many of the intelligentsia: Could one sustain the belief in the superiority of one's own civilization while borrowing from another's? If so, how much could be borrowed before one's own culture was lost? What actually was the essence of what one might call "Chineseness"? And, faced with a stark choice between saving one's culture at

1

the risk of sacrificing the empire to the barbarians or of sacrificing one's culture in order to save the empire from the barbarians, what should the decision be?

These and other related questions were heatedly debated by some of China's most brilliant minds. Initially, most of them deemed it acceptable to borrow military techniques only. This type of imitation was not unprecedented. Several times in the past, the Chinese had copied barbarian ways of war. The idea of fighting from horseback, as opposed to using horse-drawn chariots, had come from China's nomadic neighbors to the north. At a somewhat later date, the stirrup, which enabled mounted warriors to shoot backward, was adopted from Turkic invaders. Nevertheless, even in this area, borrowing from foreigners had been quite limited.

Western military techniques, however, were more elaborate. Their acquisition required, among other things, the creation of factories, foundries, and a system of raw material procurement on a much larger scale than had ever been attempted before. The desirability of adopting these, too, was eventually rationalized, as epitomized by the late nineteenth-century slogan "Chinese learning for the essence [*ti*]; Western learning for practical use [*yong*]." Unfortunately, certain difficulties emerged in putting this *ti–yong* ideology into practice. For example, the establishment of the factory system entailed fundamental changes in social organization. Its needs for a mobile labor force, specialized production, and the like necessitated major modifications in the Confucian family system, the educational curriculum, and many other areas. Western learning, it was later discovered, had an essence of its own.

By the end of the nineteenth century, a new generation began to reject many aspects of the Confucian tradition that most earlier Chinese thinkers had considered to be the essence of their civilization. Sun Yat-sen, an iconoclast, a Christian, and a medical doctor, sought to strengthen and modernize China in ways he considered compatible with the characteristics of the culture. The philosophy (or, more properly, ideology) that Sun attempted to substitute for Confucianism was the Three Principles of the People: People's Nationalism, People's Democracy, and People's Livelihood. He explicitly stated that his inspiration had been Abraham Lincoln's government "of the people, by the people, and for the people."

The imperial government was overthrown in 1911, a victim of its own ineptitude as well as of the revolutionaries' efforts. Sun, however, died before the movement he founded, which came to be known as the Kuomintang (KMT, or Chinese Nationalist Party), could come to power. His successor as head of the KMT, Chiang Kai-shek, was able to wrest control of the central government from a variety of warlords and almost immediately restored large elements of Confucianism to official ideology. Nevertheless, China remained poor and weak in relation to the Western powers and Japan. Within a few decades, the KMT government fell—the result of a combination of its own internal weaknesses, a bloody and draining war with Japan, and a communist insurgency.

One reason a number of Chinese intellectuals found communism appealing as a solution to their country's problems is that it purported to be a scientific, culturally neutral process that would occur naturally during the course of historical development. In other words, adopting communism did not have to be understood as borrowing something from the West. That its creator, Karl Marx, was very definitely a Westerner who drew most of his examples from the Western experience, and, in fact, believed that history had "gone to sleep" in Asia, was conveniently overlooked. To these intellectuals, the Bolsheviks' seizure of power in Russia indicated that communism might be relevant to China. The Bolsheviks' success had refuted Marx's contention that the communist revolution would occur first in a highly industrialized society; perhaps, then, it could happen in China as well. Even so, applying an ideology based on an appeal to industrial workers in an overwhelmingly peasant-based society like China's necessitated a fundamental reworking of Marxism.

Mao Zedong was well aware that even a theory purporting to be culturally neutral must come to terms with the culture in which it operated. As early as 1938, he declared:

> A communist is a Marxist internationalist, but Marxism must take on a national form before it can be applied. There is no such thing as abstract Marxism, but only concrete Marxism. What we call concrete Marxism is Marxism that has taken on a national form, that is, Marxism applied to the concrete struggle in the concrete conditions prevailing in China and not Marxism absolutely used.

Later, Mao declared that it was necessary to "make the past serve the present and foreign things serve China."

The way in which Mao sought to deal with the Chinese cultural context involved a bitter attack against *official,* or high culture, and a glorification of the culture of the *masses* or low culture. The term for official, *guan,* became one of opprobrium; the bureaucrats of the People's Republic of China (PRC) are called by a different name: *ganbu* or cadres. History was revised to emphasize the contributions of ordinary folk. Thus, a placard on the Ming tombs near Beijing focused on just how many of the masses toiled in the construction of the tombs rather than on the grandeur of the emperors buried there. And folk art, such as paper-cutting, was praised and encouraged, while art forms associated with the upper classes, such as richly embroidered silks and delicate paintings on gilt, were criticized. The distinction between high and low cultures was not clear-cut, however, and backward thoughts and practices were not confined to the upper classes. Hence, choosing which items from China's past to serve China's present was not easy. There were sharp disagreements over which elements to keep and which to discard, and several changes in the official party attitude occurred.

As for making foreign things serve China, Marx provided little help. He was primarily a theorizer and had few concrete suggestions about how to make his theories operational in the day-to-day administration of a state. For guidance in this area, Chinese communists looked to the example of the first, and for several decades the only, communist state, the now-defunct USSR. What they received were Leninist and Stalinist interpretations of Marx that had been influenced both by the worldviews of the Soviet leaders and by their perceptions regarding the needs of the Soviet Union. Even in the early years of the PRC, Mao Zedong and other leaders cautioned against blindly copying the experience of the USSR and urged adapting the Soviet experience to Chinese reality. But, since the Soviet Union was the PRC's only important ally and aid donor in these early years, it was almost inevitable that the Soviet model would be closely imitated.

A realization of the limitations that the experience of the relatively sparsely populated and capital-intensive USSR would have for the densely populated and labor-intensive PRC was an important reason for the Great Leap Forward of 1958. This daring socioeconomic break with the Soviet model attempted to modernize the PRC by making use of China's advantages, such as its abundant labor power, and certain traditional techniques, such as herbal remedies and acupunctural medicinal approaches. The culture of the masses was lauded to a much greater degree, with some elements of what had been regarded as acceptable heirlooms from the past now hastily discarded. The Great Leap Forward's message was radically egalitarian. It tried to implement Marx's definition of communism: "from each according to his ability, to each according to his need." Lacking incentives to work hard, however, too many people discovered ways to work less. For these and other reasons, production levels fell and, almost immediately, the country was plunged into yet deeper poverty and weakness. Production dropped to levels that prevailed during the early years of the communist government but with a substantially larger number of people among whom to divide what was produced. Millions died of hunger or malnutrition-related diseases. This particular effort to implement a Chinese version of modernity had failed disastrously.

By 1962, after many of the Great Leap Forward's more ill-advised measures had been reversed or modified, the PRC regained its pre-Great Leap Forward production levels. Returning along with recuperating production levels, however, were some of the phenomena that had induced Mao to begin the Great Leap Forward: greater disparities in income levels, officials using their positions for financial gain, marriages contracted for economic reasons, traditional superstitious practices, and gambling. The latter three, though definitely part of traditional culture, were clearly not acceptable in making the past serve the present.

In 1966, Mao unleashed the Great Proletarian Cultural Revolution, another massive effort to purge the country of Soviet, other Western, *and* traditional influences. In its zeal to purify the country of both foreign and decadent old influences, the Cultural Revolution radicals had to make some odd compromises. For example, totally reworking Chinese opera to remove "decadent" themes, including banning traditional musical instruments, meant performing it to a piano accompaniment. When asked how this fitted in with purging the culture of decadent Western elements, Madame Mao replied, "We have liberated the piano."

The Cultural Revolution's message, like that of the Great Leap Forward, was egalitarian and strongly anti-hierarchical, but to an even greater degree. Those who dressed better or ate better than others were believed to have been affected by Western bourgeois liberal or Soviet revisionist poison. Many people became the targets of brutal attack. Normal work activities were seriously disrupted in some areas, though the overall effect on production was not nearly as much as that during the Great Leap Forward. Social and political problems, however, were far greater. Although the violence of the Cultural Revolution had abated by late 1968, many of its policies remained for a number of years thereafter.

Mao's death in 1976 led indirectly to Deng Xiaoping's accession to power and the repudiation of many of Mao's more radical policies. Deng's "second-generation leadership" abandoned Mao's emphasis on class struggle and social transformation in favor of creating prosperity for society as a whole. (His reputation as an anti-ideological pragmatist had been the cause of Deng being purged during the Cultural Revolution.) Deng immediately announced that his priority was to modernize China and that his method would be to proceed on the basis of "seeking truth from facts." By modernization, Deng appeared primarily to mean industrialization and the attainment of higher living standards for the population. While explicitly acknowledging the need for greater personal freedom and pluralism in the decision-making process, Deng appeared to regard these as necessary in order to give people incentives to work harder rather than because he believed in freedom as a value in itself. Similarly, Deng announced that he would support the introduction of the rule of law, which is normally considered to be another concomitant of democratization in the West. His rationale, however, was less civil libertarian than a result of his belief that a legal system was necessary to resolve disputes, both between people and among businesses, before the wheels of production could turn smoothly. Modernization was not to be construed as slavish copying of the capitalist states but, rather, as a process of building "socialism with Chinese characteristics."

No precise definition of socialism with Chinese characteristics has ever been given. While stating that he had no intention of abandoning socialism, Deng was explicit that it was acceptable to be rich, as long as one became rich through one's own diligence and hard work rather than by inheriting wealth or getting it through speculative activities or personal connections. Moreover, he added, it was not necessary for everyone to become rich at the same time. Deng, like so many of his country's previous leaders during the past century and a half, was in search of wealth and power—a common slogan of nineteenth-century reformers—for his country: He sought to make China equal or superior to the Western states in a manner that was compatible with Chinese reality. Unlike the nineteenth-century reformers, Deng did not proclaim the necessity to select the best from East and West. But his policies, which included that of the Open Door to the West, encompassed importing advanced scientific and technical equipment and sending Chinese students abroad to acquire the ability to produce and improve upon this equipment. Although Deng's final goal of a prosperous, economically modernized China was not unlike that of Mao, the two men differed in important ways. Faced with making a choice between equality and prosperity, Mao had a tendency to favor equality, and Deng prosperity.

Under Deng, the profit motive was restored. Factories were allowed to retain their earnings beyond a certain amount to be paid to the central government, and peasants were allowed to sell on the free market whatever they raised beyond a fixed quota to be delivered to the government. Given these opportunities, a number of people prospered to a degree that would have been unimaginable only a few years before. A wider variety of consumer goods appeared in the stores, and the country's gross national product began a period of rapid growth. At the same time, however, other people were left behind. Sometimes, this was because they were inept farmers or indifferent workers. Often, however, it was because they were not able to take advantage of the new opportunities due to factors beyond their control. Farmers who held poorer land or could not procure adequate supplies of seed and fertilizer might actually become poorer regardless of how hard they worked. In addition, the state's investment policies favored coastal areas, on the sound assumption that these were the places that would most readily produce a quick return on investment capital. But at the same time, these policies discriminated against residents of the PRC's vast and more needy hinterland.

The new policies also generated inflationary pressures, to the detriment of those who lived on fixed incomes. These included the large number of state employees as well as students and the elderly. While businesspeople and farmers could increase prices to keep up with the rising cost of living, these other groups could not. Those who prospered under the new system were the envy of those who did not, and jealousy—the red-eye disease, as Chinese call it—became more prominent. When Deng deemed it acceptable for some to become rich before others, he had tacitly sanctioned others to become poorer. In order to increase the PRC's efficiency and prosperity as a whole, unprofitable factories and businesses would be allowed to go bankrupt. The system of guaranteed employment could no longer be sustained, he declared. "The iron rice bowl" was to be broken. Understandably, people worried about the disappearance of their safety net.

At first, these concerns were expressed privately and hesitantly. As the decade wore on, however, citizens began to take advantage of the less stringent controls over freedom of expression, a loosening that Deng considered necessary to provide economic incentives. Letters to the editors of newspapers, journal articles, and even protest marches became more common. Concerned with rising levels of civil disorder, Deng seemed to back away from earlier promises of liberalization and advanced the theory of neo-authoritarianism, meaning that the PRC needed firm guidance from above in order to continue its development. Partially obscured by the shock and horror of the Chinese government's brutal suppression of the demonstrations in 1989 was the message that large numbers of the PRC's citizens were dissatisfied with important elements of Deng's plan to build socialism with Chinese characteristics. There was widespread agreement about what was wrong with the present model, but little consensus on what should replace it.

After the 1989 demonstrations, the government made a number of adjustments to economic policy in an attempt to deal with the people's grievances while at the same time restricting their ability to express their concerns. It also blamed the unrest on a small handful of counterrevolutionaries who had been misled by foreign bourgeois liberalism. This was followed by a major propaganda effort

to convince people that such Western concepts as the separation of p
theory of checks and balances, and human rights were inappropriate to
A number of Chinese disagreed, feeling that only when China adopted such co
cepts would it be able to become a strong and prosperous power. Although much
about China had changed in the past 150 years, these debates were remarkably similar in tone and substance to those of the nineteenth century. The
ti–yong argument was again advanced: One cannot have Western-style economic
development (the practical manifestations) without the underlying freedoms (the
essence) that make economic development possible.

Coexisting with desires for more freedom, however, were profound feelings of uneasiness over the culture of materialism that Western capitalism was
believed to have brought with it. Some people turned to religion, including faiths
of Western origin, for solace. Others looked back into the Chinese past for guidance. There was renewed interest in both Buddhism and Confucianism as alternatives to Western commercialism. Having observed the deficiencies of Marxism
as the motivating force for modernization, some intellectuals began to search the
past for ways to insert a uniquely Chinese element into the Chinese revolution.
As these developments were taking place, Jiang Zemin chose to press forward
with economic reforms. For a variety of reasons, some of which were international and beyond Jiang's control, these reforms proved difficult to implement.
His successor, Hu Jintao, fared no better, with current leader Xi Jinping finding
progress equally difficult. A dissonant chorus of advice, ranging from those nos-
talgic for Maoism to advocates of popular direct elections, is emboldened when
economic difficulties occur.

As the legitimization of Marxism disappears, some people feel it is all the
more important to emphasize the Chinese nature of the Chinese revolution. This
same revolution aimed to destroy China's feudal culture, however, so it is unclear
how this can be done. Proponents argue that unless some way is found, the Chinese value system will be established on a dry streambed or a trunkless tree. The
search for a formula that will permit the modernization of the PRC in a manner
compatible with Chinese reality continues.

This book examines efforts to achieve modernization in the Chinese context. There are, to be sure, a variety of different opinions on what constitutes
modernity. Several of these theories of modernization, and their implications for
the Chinese case, are discussed in some detail in subsequent chapters. Briefly,
some individuals concentrate on the end goals of modernization, such as control
over destiny, individual autonomy, and the acquisition of material goods. Others,
including all the leaders of the PRC thus far, would define modernization more
narrowly, in terms of increased levels of industrialization and higher standards
of living. Yet a third group favors a broader definition, including additional factors, such as the commercialization of agriculture, increased urbanization, the
spread of mass literacy and improved education, the development of mass communication, and promotion based on merit. As people acquire a new sense of
being able to influence their own destinies, they will demand a larger share of
political power, and the modernized system will accommodate these demands.

iction

ader definition, believing that in practice it is extremely
strialization and higher living standards in the absence of
alture, urbanization, mass literacy, mass communications,

Theo.   f Analysis of Chinese Politics

In recent years, far more sources of information have become available to foreign analysts. Even so, there is much that we do not know. The restricted nature of the dissemination of information in the PRC has caused problems for the analysis of its political decision making. Typically, when examining political systems, analysts use a model that describes the society to be examined as an *environment*. Individuals who are resident therein are influenced by the environment in various ways and respond to it accordingly. They may have concerns or grievances that they wish to be addressed. An effective way to do this is to aggregate these demands through the formation of interest groups. These demands are termed *inputs* and are presented to the government, which has the job of *conversion* of the demands into decisions, which are termed *outputs*. The legislature writes laws, the executive carries them out, and the judiciary settles disputes arising in connection with the impact of the laws on those affected. These outputs then affect the environment through the *feedback loop*. Here, they may give rise to another set of inputs. For example, significant numbers of people in a given country may become dissatisfied with the cost of medical care. Interest groups representing them lobby, or bring inputs, to their parliament, which converts the demands into new health care regulations. This will change the health care environment, sometimes leading to new problems and new kinds of dissatisfactions. The feedback of these dissatisfactions results in the aggregation of new demands on government, and the law may be further modified.

Attempting to apply this scheme of analysis to Chinese politics yields very unsatisfactory results, particularly during the Maoist era. To start with, it is difficult to identify the interest groups. One may assume that they are similar to those in societies we are more familiar with: workers, farmers, doctors, the elderly, ethnic minorities, and so forth. Entities that the Chinese communist government calls *mass organizations* were established soon after the PRC was founded. Groups such as women, workers, peasants, writers, and doctors each have their own mass organization. These organizations, however, are very tightly controlled by the government specifically so that they support the agenda developed by the Chinese Communist Party (CCP) rather than articulating demands that would benefit their own memberships. The Chinese Medical Association does not demand that health care fees be raised, for example, and Chinese trade unions urge their members to work diligently to create national prosperity rather than calling for shorter working hours or better pension plans. Hence, these organizations have not functioned very well as interest groups.

Similar difficulties arise in applying other parts of the model described above. The Chinese party and government structures can be described in detail (and are, in Chapter 4), but how decisions are made remains a mystery. Politburo meetings are not televised except on ceremonial occasions, and politburo members do not give interviews about the differences of opinion that arise in their discussions. The memoirs of elderly or deceased leaders are sometimes published but, with the exception of those recorded surreptitiously by former Chinese president Zhao Ziyang while he was under house arrest and contrarian views expressed by his nemesis, former premier Li Peng, they have a suspiciously unreal tone and follow the current party line scrupulously, no matter what period in the past the writer is discussing. Who, then, decides how much money and attention will be allocated to which sectors of the society? In the absence of more specific information, foreign analysts sometimes resort to ambiguities, such as "the party has decided." The CCP, however, is a large and unwieldy organization—as of 2017 it had 89 million members, so the party as such does not really decide anything. Other analysts write as though the country's leader makes all the decisions, as in "Xi Jinping plans to re-redesign the structure of central government." The PRC is a huge country, though, with many problems calling for resolution each day. No one person can actually make all these decisions. *The party* and *Xi* are used here as shorthand: meaningful in the general sense, but potentially misleading unless one realizes that there is a great deal more to the decision-making process than is embodied in these names alone.

Because we do not know a great deal about the internal workings of Chinese politics, people have been obliged to make educated guesses on the basis of the facts available to them. Particularly during the early years of the communist regime when hard facts were much scarcer than they are at present, analysts resorted to such tactics as looking at photographs of the National Day parade and other ceremonial occasions to see who stood next to whom and who was missing. Sometimes, this indicated that someone had fallen out of favor (he was standing further from the center of the leadership group than before) or had been purged (he was not present on the parade's reviewing stand at all). Differences of opinion often arose over what one might conclude from this. If, for example, several people who were associated with leftist causes were missing for a long period of time, analysts expected that to be correlated with the implementation of moderate policies in the country.

This, however, would be unusual. More typical was that if *one* person whom China-watchers *thought* was associated with a particular policy would not be seen in public for perhaps a month or two, one might conclude that he had been purged. On the other hand, and given the advanced ages of many leaders in the PRC, it was also plausible that he had died of natural causes. This, too, had its pitfalls, since the dearly departed might suddenly reappear in apparent good health. He or she may have been recuperating from a non-life-threatening disease, escaping Beijing's less-than-salubrious climate for a while, or conducting a discreet investigation in the provinces. Sometimes, analysts were able to corroborate their hunches with gossip from within China, but even here they remained on shaky ground. Like many countries in which citizens do not trust their news media, the PRC has a lively and vivid gossip network. Frequently, however, it turns out to be wrong: The then-octogenarian Deng Xiaoping was unreliably reported to be dead at least three times in the 1980s—and one time to have been the victim of a bloodless *coup d'état* by the military organization he commanded. He died in 1997 of natural causes.

Dating from the time that Deng allowed greater access between China and the outside world, more sources have become available. Some foreigners were, and are, granted access to Chinese archives and other data. Journalists and scholars have been able to establish contacts with knowledgeable individuals who are willing to share their opinions. The Chinese press itself now expresses diverse opinions, albeit carefully and at risk of official sanctions.

Both in the past, when data were scarce, and in the present era of multiple sources, there have been a variety of different views about the PRC. When people start out with different basic assumptions, no matter how impeccable their processes of reasoning and how clear the facts, they are apt to reach different conclusions. These differing basic assumptions account for many of the disagreements among China-watchers. In addition, analysts differ in the particular angle from which they approach Chinese politics—economic development, for example, being more important to some and human rights considerations to others. Essentially, there have been three periods in the analysis of PRC politics. The first set of theories was fostered during the earliest years of the communist government; the second by the events of the Cultural Revolution; and the third by Deng Xiaoping's reforms.

Theoretical Analysis in the Early Years of the PRC

Initially, the leading paradigm for the analysis of Chinese politics was the totalitarian model. A one-party (the CCP) state headed by a strong leader (Mao) imposes its ideology (communism) on the citizenry, which owes total and unswerving loyalty to it. Organizations that mediate between the citizen and the state, such as family, professional groups, or religion, are weakened, co-opted, or destroyed. The motivation behind this is to isolate the individual from any influence except that of the ruling party and its ideology. Decisions were believed to be made consensually within a basically harmonious party elite dominated by Mao. Differences of opinion within the elite were seen as shifting in response to specific problems rather than motivated by some other force.

A variant on this view, the *generational school,* argued that there was a common generational viewpoint based on shared personal and political experiences. Here, *generation* was defined not in terms of chronological age but in terms of the year in which an individual joined the communist party. Advocates of generational analysis divided the early history of the CCP into 12 periods, each characterized by a crisis—such as a KMT attempt at exterminating the CCP or the outbreak of war with Japan. Those who joined the party at such a time were assumed to be responding to the crisis, which would therefore predispose them to certain political outlooks. By seeing who joined the party during which period and checking this list against which generations hold which levels of positions in the leadership hierarchy, one may be able to predict policy interests and predispositions.

For example, the first two generations to have joined the communist party were almost all born and raised in the central Yangtze Valley provinces, came from peasant backgrounds, had very little formal education, and had not traveled much outside China. Hence, they were assumed to have xenophobic tendencies: suspicious of foreign powers, and probably against close relations with them, no matter how benign their intentions toward China appeared. The political focus of these generations was likely to be local or regional. Militarily, they would favor defending China by means of small-unit, irregular tactics, such as those provided by guerrillas and local militias.

By contrast, the third and fourth generations entered the party at a time of increasing specialization and division of labor between the party and the army as well as within the party and the army themselves. After November 1931, the party had a special school to train military officers. It also began to put more emphasis on technology and less on guerrilla tactics. The people who joined the CCP during this period came from a larger number of geographical areas compared with those of the first two generations. They tended to be better educated and were more likely to have traveled outside China. Adherents of the generational school of analysis saw them as being more oriented to the national scene than to local areas. They were likely to be less suspicious of people who were not from their own native place, more cosmopolitan, and more open to alliances with other countries. Thus, a shift from a leadership composed mainly of the first two generations to a leadership predominantly from the third and fourth generations should correlate with greater emphasis on professional specialization and more internationalist policies. Those who entered the CCP at the time of close relations between the PRC and the USSR during the 1950s and who studied in the USSR may be assumed to be pro-Soviet in their outlook. An important rationale for the United States' offering Chinese students educational opportunities in the U.S. has been that they will return to the PRC with a good impression of the country, which will aid Sino–American relations when these young people become leaders of their country.

In a general sense, there was a great deal to recommend this line of analysis. The first two generations did seem to have been more inward-looking than the third and fourth, although it may be argued that there were few alternatives available, given the fact that it was necessary to mobilize members—a local/regional task rather than an international one—during the early days of the party's existence. Later, the party's championing of the idea of resistance to Japan became a useful technique for drawing supporters. This may be construed as reacting to an opportunity rather than the result of a mindset conditioned by when one joined the CCP.

In addition, while some important members of the first-generation CCP ruling elite did come across as xenophobic and suspicious of foreigners, others did not. Mao—poorly educated, from the central Yangtze Valley, and not well traveled—has indeed been regarded as distrustful of the outside world and preoccupied with China's domestic concerns. This, however, did not preclude him from concluding an alliance with the Soviet Union in 1950 or from approaching the United States at the end of the 1960s. Again, circumstances, rather than a mindset, seem to have been operative. Moreover, it should not be forgotten that the other towering figure of the first generation, Zhou Enlai, was a consummate cosmopolitan. Since there will be people of different backgrounds and experiences belonging to each generation, there will not be unanimity among them. A persistent minority can sometimes change the views of the majority, and changing circumstances can alter political perceptions as well. Former Chinese premier Li Peng, who studied for several years in the USSR, may be seen as pro-Russian in some ways. However, it is not necessarily the case that study in a given country will create warm feelings about that country. One might come away from the Soviet Union having made some close friends there but, at the same time, convinced from firsthand observation that the country's political and economic systems were not worth emulating. Hence, analytical schemes that depend on knowing the percentages of high-ranking positions held by a given generational group can be misleading.

A generational form of analysis is still applied but in its post-Mao view refers to the period during which a particular leadership group holds power. Hence, the elite during the Mao years is considered to be the first generation, and, when Deng was paramount leader, to be the second generation. Jiang Zemin and his cohort constitute the third generation, Hu Jintao the fourth, and Xi Jinping the fifth. Although it is acknowledged that there may be differences of opinion among them, a common mindset is still assumed. For example, foreign commentary on the leadership that emerged following the 1989 Tiananmen incident dwelt on the officially released picture of eight octogenarians who were assumed to have similar views on the need to suppress dissent and rein in the economy. It predicted that not until these "eight immortals" passed from the scene could meaningful political change be expected. When the "immortals" did pass away, however, the hoped-for political changes did not materialize. Nor did these changes come with the third, fourth, or fifth generation, better educated and more familiar with the outside world though they were. Analysts now seem less sure about when, or even if, such changes may occur.

Yet another theory of analysis, the *strategic interaction school*, saw the crucial issue motivating Chinese politics as the PRC's struggle for great-power status. Strategic interaction analysts believed in the importance for the present day of China's humiliation in the nineteenth century by foreign powers, including the so-called unequal treaties that were forced on it and the territorial concessions that China was forced to make. Hence—and this represents a rather large assumption—China's main goal at present is to erase, or at least compensate for, that memory. Thus, China's behavior can be explained in terms of trying to gain the respect—even the fearful respect—of the great powers.

Although this school starts from a historically conditioned premise, the humiliations of the nineteenth century, specific cultural–historical factors actually play very little part in its analytical scheme. It assumes that China is a rational international actor, capable of making reasonable judgments about goals, and about the options and costs associated with those goals. China is also seen as having broad geographical constraints from which no government—be it communist, capitalist, or carnivorous in ideology—can escape. The country is, quite simply, viewed as aiming to attain the maximum political-military power status at the least cost. Implicitly, an important task of analysis for this school is identifying China's major enemy at a given time.

Much of this scheme of analysis is unobjectionable. Many of the founding members of the CCP did feel keenly the humiliations visited on their ancestral land by foreign powers, and one of their motivations was to build a China capable of withstanding external pressures. This has not been completely forgotten in more recent times. A series of meetings commemorating the 150th anniversary of the Opium War were held (not coincidentally, one suspects) on the first anniversary of the Tiananmen incident. Speakers used the occasion to denounce Western imperialism and blame China's humiliation on the fact that the communist party had not yet been founded. A politburo member opined that the significance of the Opium War was that it showed that opposing imperialism and loving one's country did not preclude learning things from foreign countries that are useful for China. Similarly, the speeches accompanying lavish ceremonies in remembrance of the seventieth anniversary of the victory of the Chinese people over Japan in World War II credited the CCP with a major role in its triumph while ignoring the role played by the U.S.

There are problems, however, in applying the strategic interaction scheme to the analysis of Chinese politics. One is that it provides no role for ideology and culture. Any government is assumed to act the same, weighing the options presented by its territorial imperatives in a cold, calculating manner in order to attain success in its international relations. That culture and ideology may shape the government's perception of what may be a sensible response to an event is not taken into account. For example, culturally conditioned concerns about possible loss of face may motivate the Chinese government to react in a manner that would strike the Finnish or Peruvian government as illogical.

Another conceptual problem with the strategic interaction school is that it assumes the country possesses what one might call a corporate personality. It may be convenient to say that "China" takes a certain action or feels a certain way, but to do so risks creating the image of a monolithic entity, neglecting the possibility that there are groups of Chinese who prefer one policy option and groups who favor another. For example, there is considerable evidence that Mao Zedong met substantial resistance to his plan in the late 1960s for rapprochement with the United States. A number of high-ranking officials were adamantly opposed to coming to terms with capitalism, arguing that the Soviet Union, for all its faults, was at least a socialist state and was therefore preferable to the United States as a strategic partner. Were American policy makers to assume, consonant with the strategic interaction analysis, that there was a corporate Chinese personality firmly in favor of leaning toward the United States, they might be seriously misled.

A third criticism of the strategic interaction school is that it gives too much weight to foreign policy. The average Chinese citizen, like her counterpart elsewhere in the world, is apt to be more concerned with wages, health care, and children's educational opportunities than whether her country receives proper respect within the United Nations. And the Chinese leadership has a great many domestic problems to cope with that preclude it from dealing exclusively, or even predominantly, with foreign policy matters.

In sum, the Chinese elite continue to be concerned with maintaining and enhancing what members consider to be their nation's rightful place in the world. This was seen in the outrage expressed when Beijing was not chosen as the site of the year 2000 Olympic Games, and in the importance the government placed on China becoming a founding member of the World Trade Organization. (Beijing was later chosen to host the 2008 games, and the PRC entered the World Trade Organization in 2002.) The generation that felt most keenly the humiliations visited on their country by external powers has passed away, and China has already succeeded in winning the respect of those powers. Nonetheless, the leadership has found that reminders of China's "century of shame" can evoke powerful patriotic emotions among the population when it wishes them to back a strong foreign policy stand.

Another commonly heard theory during this period, which continues to have adherents today, might be called the *China-is-China-is-China school*. It assumes that communist China's economic landscape, psychological mindset, and bureaucratic processes are basically the same as those of imperial China. The paramount leader is similar to the emperor in what he may or may not do: unlimited in many ways, but also constrained by his fellow old revolutionaries or, later, his fellow politburo standing committee members, who perform the function of nobles; his wife (who may have a political agenda of her own); and the bureaucracy, which is seen as behaving much like the mandarinate that preceded it. Parallels are found between Confucianism and communism, although adherents to the China-is-China-is-China school generally argue that ideology is of secondary importance: All Chinese governments will eventually act in a similar fashion because of the force of tradition and the necessity to deal with a large population, scarce arable land, and water-control problems.

There is a great deal to recommend this line of analysis. Mindsets developed over centuries are not erased by a revolution, and there are relatively few ways in which to allocate modest amounts of cultivable land to an enormous population in a manner they consider tolerable. Mao's personal physician reported that Mao read Chinese history books rather than Marx when preparing strategies. He referred to his time with the chairman as "life in Mao's imperial court," noting that Mao occasionally even referred to himself as the emperor. In planning to seize power following her husband's death, Mao's wife consciously saw herself as a latter-day embodiment of the powerful Empress Wu Zetian, even to the extent of ordering copies of the woman's gowns for herself.

Chinese citizens who are not members of the elite are also prone to finding parallels with the past. Even though ordinary folk knew nothing of Madame

Mao's gown-ordering, they frequently compared her to ambitious empresses of past dynasties. After she was purged, cartoons regularly depicted her in the embroidered gowns, elaborate hairstyles, and long fingernails of deceased royalty. Deng Xiaoping, however, was less frequently referred to as emperor, and even then, it would appear, the term was intended metaphorically rather than literally. Neither Jiang Zemin nor Hu Jintao was seen in imperial terms at all, though Xi Jinping's far more powerful leadership and growing cult of personality has invited comparisons with past emperors.

As for the policies thus engendered, it is unfortunately not always possible to clearly distinguish whether a policy is based on tradition or communist ideology. For example, the prosperity and well-being of the common people were important to both Confucius and Karl Marx. The problem with the China-is-China-is-China school is that, although there are similarities between imperial and contemporary China, the two are not the same. If accepted too rigidly, such parallels are misleading. In addition to the commonalities between Confucius and Marx, there are also significant differences. For Confucius, the peasant was the backbone of the empire; Marx spoke of "rural idiocy." Confucian philosophy aimed at the attainment of a Great Harmony, to be achieved by properly ordering relationships, with the emperor at the pinnacle of a gradually descending hierarchy, each member of which was to set an example for those below. Marx, however, championed egalitarianism. Confucius was unconcerned with the ownership of the means of production or the idea of progress. For Marx, in contrast, ownership of the means of production was the key to social, political, and economic dominance. His Great Harmony was to be achieved through violent revolution from below. And, in yet another contrast between traditional and modern-day China, the PRC leadership accepts the concept of national sovereignty, at least nominally. Failure to take these important differences between past and present China into consideration will limit the usefulness of one's analysis.

Theories Engendered by the Cultural Revolution

The view of a basically harmonious elite group implicit in the models described above was invalidated by the outbreak of the Cultural Revolution in the mid-1960s. As leaders, once believed to be united in the pursuit of a strong communist state, began to battle each other both verbally and physically, foreign analysts began to reassess their theories. *Factional models* gained credence. In Andrew Nathan's classic statement of this view, factions are based on clientelist ties. These are cultivated essentially through the constant exchange of goods and favors, and result in relationships that involve unwritten but nonetheless well-understood rights and obligations among faction members.

Factions are assumed to be incapable of building sufficient power to rid the political system of rival factions—and, therefore, to have little incentive to try to do so. The most important concern of a faction is to protect its own base of power while opposing accretions of power by any other faction. Because today's enemy may be tomorrow's ally, factional alliances cannot remain stable. It is therefore impossible for factions to make ideological agreement a primary condition for alliance with other factions. There is an ongoing struggle for office and influence: To stay in the game, factions must often cooperate with those with whom they have recently disagreed.

Nathan believes that pre-Cultural Revolution China did approximate the factional model, though conceding that lack of data makes it impossible to identify the faction leaders. He sees Mao Zedong's decision to launch the Cultural Revolution as breaking the rules of factionalism: By calling on students—the so-called Red Guards—to destroy the other factions, Mao was mobilizing new sources of power from outside the elite. The rest of the factional elite tried to resist Mao's extra-party offensive, demobilize the Red Guards, and restore the factional conflict system of the first 15 years of the regime. In essence, they succeeded. Following the defeat of the fourth mobilization of the Red Guards in September 1967, there was no longer any hope of using the Guards to purge the party center of factionalism.

Nathan critiques his own model, pointing out that it simplifies by considering only one of many constraints that mold behavior: the organizational constraint. Ideological and cultural constraints are ignored. Insufficient data make it impossible to decisively accept or reject the model even within the confines of the organizational sphere. Also, the model does not explain why people adopt a factional framework, how long they will adhere to it, or why they persist in disagreeing with one another at all.

A variation on Nathan's theory, the *central–regional school,* also emphasizes personal affiliations and loyalty in its analysis of Chinese politics. Adherents point out that despite the unifying force of the imperial institution and an elaborately conceived hierarchy of central government, China has nonetheless had a long history of localism. The capital city was far away, communications poor, and the imperial bureaucracy thinly spread. Typically, the cultural milieu that one related to was not China as a whole but rather, in descending order of importance, one's village, clan, and province. As habitués of Chinese restaurants already know, the various Chinese provinces have distinctive styles of preparing food. They also have very different artistic styles and musical traditions. Different dialects may actually be mutually unintelligible, even where the speakers live in close proximity to one another. The *minnan* and *minbei* tongues of Fujian province are probably the most striking example of this.

Chinese culture also includes a strong element of personal loyalty. One relates to one's superior on grounds of personal feelings rather than obeying because of the position that he or she holds. In turn, the superior takes care of one in terms of security and serves as a mentor in more than career terms. Superiors may, for example, help subordinates find a spouse or perform intermediary functions to settle a dispute that has nothing to do with the workplace.

Analysts who favor the central–regional school initially saw the Chinese communist military, the People's Liberation Army (PLA), as the framework within which these loyalties developed. In the process of coming to power, the Chinese communists developed five so-called field armies. Because the CCP's road to power was through the rural hinterland, and because Japanese and KMT armies occupied a number of contiguous areas, communication among the different field armies was sporadic. Hence, they essentially developed independently of each other, with relatively little interaction. There were few transfers of people from one field army to another.

For several years after the communist victory in 1949, China was divided into six regions for administrative purposes. In each of these regions a given field army predominated (one of the field armies controlled more than one region). When transfers occurred, people often moved from one field army to another in groups, thereby maintaining the previously existing loyalty network. The field army hypothesis sees political behavior in China as a balance-of-power process involving five major interest groups—the field armies—with the central elite acting essentially as a power broker.

This theory, too, seems to have some validity in explaining past political behavior. Lin Biao's rise to power at the time of the Cultural Revolution was accompanied by the promotions of a disproportionately large number of members of his Fourth Field Army and far fewer promotions for members of other field armies. After Lin's fall from power, many of those who had risen with him were purged, and a larger number of promotions for those from other field armies occurred. The balance of power among the field armies that had existed before the Cultural Revolution was essentially re-created following Lin's death in 1971. Central–regional theorists interpret these events as the Fourth Field Army trying to destroy the balance of power and to dominate the military–political hierarchy. Other field armies resisted what they perceived as an attack on their territories, combining to force Lin out and re-establish the balance of power.

The statistical evidence bolstering the field army interpretation, however, is not as clear-cut as it may initially appear. We do not know the field army affiliation of a large number of PLA commanders and commissars, and are not sure how to factor in the approximately 15 percent of those whose field army affiliation we do know who served in more than one field army. Occasional transfers of officers from one field army into the bailiwicks of others may be as easily explained on the basis of random selection processes as by a conscious effort to achieve a balance of power among the military regions.

Although a purge of high-ranking Fourth Field Army officers occurred after the fall of Lin Biao, a number of Fourth Field Army people retained their important posts, and several of those purged with Lin were from other field armies. The fact that the dismissals began at the top suggests that Mao and other leaders were more concerned with the loyalties of the military people at the central government level than at the regional level. Finally, however convinced one may be that the field army analysis is a satisfactory explanation of what happened during the Cultural Revolution, it is no guarantee that field armies remain reliable predictors of loyalty affiliations in the twenty-first century. Ties formed during the CCP's rise to power in the 1930s did not appear to closely bind officers who were born in the 1950s or thereafter.

Expanding the central–regional analysis beyond the military, Korean scholar Jae Ho Chung sees the central leadership in an ongoing struggle to contain centrifugal tendencies, even to the extent of imposing a single time zone on the continent-sized country. After Mao's death, many manifestations of this were criticized as "blind commandism" and removed, though the leadership continues attempts to find the proper balance between vertical control and allowing for local diversities. He concludes that, while Beijing is in charge, localities listen to it selectively. The central government must also mediate among regional factions with different needs and aspirations.

Another variant of factional analysis, the *political-cultural school,* holds that the central issue in the PRC's politics is China's struggle to assimilate Western technology without destroying its own cultural traditions. In a general sense, this is a problem faced by all developing countries: how to modernize and industrialize without Westernizing and losing their cultural "soul." The problem has been especially painful for China, however, as the country has been unusually proud of its own culture. Analysts who adhere to this scheme of analysis see China as sharply divided within itself among groups who differ from one another in the level and amount of what they are willing to accept from the West and in how much they feel must be rejected. There is conflict among the groups, and political-cultural analysts feel that this conflict explains a great deal of, if not most, Chinese political behavior.

There is some validity to this line of analysis. Even a cursory check of the Chinese communist press over past decades will reveal the existence of conflicts that are dichotomized in precisely this manner. There are frequent references to the "struggle between the two camps"—the "counterrevolutionaries versus the socialists," the "Maoists versus the revisionists," and so forth. Ideologues of the early 1990s accused Western countries of plotting to subvert China through a campaign of "peaceful evolution." Among those deemed to have been subverted were individuals considered to be far too Westernized. Some playwrights, for example, suggested that Chinese culture should be discarded and replaced with that of the West. One of their productions, *River Elegy,* is discussed in Chapter 12.

Analysts formerly referred to these disputes as the red-expert conflict, *red* being symbolic of those who adhere quite rigidly to ideology and *expert* referring to technocrats who are willing to borrow Western techniques to a significant degree. As Marxism faded, so did the use of the term *red*. The debate turned back toward the nineteenth-century dilemma of what to absorb from foreign countries and what of the Chinese tradition—however that is defined—to retain. Although redness has been replaced by traditionalism, as seen in how to define "socialism with Chinese characteristics," this basic dichotomy remains.

A difficulty in conceptualizing Chinese politics according to the political-cultural school is that it is often impossible to know whom to classify in which group. This is partly owing to lack of data and partly because the same people who have been classified by the Chinese media as belonging to one group may get shifted to another group a short time later. Sometimes, circumstances have led the person to change his or her position; sometimes, the party line will have changed, leaving the person on the wrong side of an issue. For example, during the Cultural Revolution, defense minister Lin Biao led the campaign to study the thoughts of Chairman Mao. He was lauded as a leading leftist and typically identified as "Chairman Mao's closest comrade in arms." Indeed, the constitution of 1969 named Lin as Mao's heir apparent. By 1971, however, Lin had been accused of trying to kill Mao, and the media referred to him as China's leading rightist. When queried on this apparently complete about-face, the media explained that Lin had been "left in appearance, right in essence." Later, when the party line shifted to being anti-leftist, Lin was again described as a leftist. Lin's case is just one instance, albeit the most spectacular example, of many. The important point is that giving people labels like left and right, or conservative and radical, has only limited value. These labels may not describe their behavior patterns, or even their political beliefs, in any meaningful way. Clearly, this limits the usefulness of the political-cultural school as a tool of analysis.

Yet another form of factional analysis is that of the *bureaucratic politics school*. For those who espouse this methodology, the crucial question is to identify which part of the PRC's bureaucratic organization has decisive power over the direction and scope of sociopolitical change. This may be a certain ministry, or one part of the armed forces, or some department within the party organization. The underlying premise of this line of analysis is that Chinese political behavior is the result of inter-organizational bargaining for budgets, status, and power.

This is certainly a phenomenon noticeable in other countries where more information is available, and it is highly likely that this type of competition exists within the PRC. The problem is that, given the information we have, it is very difficult to identify the major players in this bureaucratic bargaining game and the stakes for which they are playing. There is some evidence of jurisdictional disputes between ministries on various issues. For example, an especially vigorous crackdown on crime in the mid-1980s was rumored to be the result of a turf fight between the newly created Ministry of State Security and pre-existing public security forces over which of them could cope better with the rising crime rate. At best, however, these are vague clues, as opposed to analytical schemes. It would be helpful to be able to examine the relative shares of the budget allocated to each organization and department over a substantial period of time. Not having the necessary supporting data limits the usefulness of the bureaucratic politics school as a tool of analysis.

The *palace politics school* focuses almost exclusively on the issue of who will succeed to the top position within the Chinese leadership. It assumes an ongoing struggle among a number of people who wish to put themselves in line for the succession—or at least move themselves closer to it. Adherents see this struggle as personality oriented rather than rooted in policy disagreements, fighting within the bureaucracy, or based on geographic imperatives or generations. The players are individuals rather than groups, although they do form factions and advance their cause with the help of those loyal to them.

The PRC has endured a number of power struggles in the relatively short time since its founding. As the story of Lin Biao indicates, some of these have been quite melodramatic. Unlike several of the other schools discussed earlier, the manifestations of palace politics interactions are fairly easy to discern. It is difficult to try to position oneself for the succession to high office without attracting attention. Unfortunately, it is not usually possible to ascertain what would be more helpful to our understanding of decision making in Chinese politics: the manner in which these promotions are achieved. Even at the very top of the hierarchy, we do not generally know the loyalties of more than a few people. The lower one descends in the power structure, the more difficult this becomes. It also seems to be possible for some individuals to survive when not associated with the party line and without a strong power base. The classic example here is former premier Zhou Enlai, who over the years had taken many policy positions that were different from those favored by Mao. Zhou was never purged and was actively involved in the administration of the country until his death in 1976.

Because someone has been successful in positioning himself for the succession, however, does not necessarily mean he will actually succeed to the top position. Lin Biao was removed from the succession in 1971, Hua Guofeng in 1976, Hu Yaobang in 1987, and Zhao Ziyang in 1989. Hu Jintao, an heir apparent who actually did become party general secretary at the sixteenth party congress in 2002, seemed painfully aware of the danger of his position, avoiding interviews and keeping a scrupulously low profile. Realizing that he could be a target for other ambitious people, Hu's rare public statements were strongly supportive of his then superior, Jiang Zemin. Even so, some Chinese believe that Jiang created a Shanghai faction which acted to circumscribe or even usurp Hu's power.

In another melodramatic occurrence, Bo Xilai, heretofore regarded as well positioned for leadership, was suddenly removed from power in 2013 (see Chapter 6). In sum, knowing who has been a successful practitioner of palace politics does not allow us to predict China's next leader with any certainty.

Post-Mao Theories of Analysis

Deng Xiaoping's accession to power in the late 1970s brought a diminution of the extreme, overt manifestations of factional struggle. The abatement of strife was accompanied by Deng's introduction of major changes in the political and economic structure. Foreign scholars were given greater access to China and had more sources of information available to them. The combination of these factors again caused analysts to rethink their theories of Chinese politics. As the party moved toward the establishment of a market economy and away from ideological rigidity, scholars put forth a *pluralist* paradigm.

Adherents of this theory believe that as the totalitarian state establishes itself, the need for terrorism and mass mobilization subsides. Political competition then begins, albeit within a rather narrowly drawn system of political controls. The atomization of individuals is only a temporary phenomenon: Social groups, not necessarily the same as those that existed before the communist government come to power, arise, and begin to articulate and otherwise pursue their common interests. Their activities may not be organized in the same ways as are interest group activities in liberal democratic regimes, but they are based on group identities and interests nonetheless. The more a totalitarian system tolerates this pluralistic competition, the more group politics will pervade bureaucratic institutions, and the more originally totalitarian systems will approximate liberal regimes. Eventually, convergence may take place.

Those who favor this paradigm cite evidence that a *civil society* is emerging in China, in which citizens feel free to voice their dissatisfactions with party, government, and individual leaders. They form associations and groups that, while in general loyal to party and government, seek to press them for changes consonant with the agendas of their constituents. Economic development, and particularly the economic decentralization that fosters this development, is generally seen as crucial. People who have become accustomed to making their own economic decisions will soon demand to make political and social choices, since these are often closely intertwined with economic decisions.

The PRC's citizens have indeed become more publicly assertive in recent years, and groups such as students, workers, and farmers have sometimes protested against government policies. This was most conspicuous in the mobilization and deployment of groups around Tiananmen Square during the spring of 1989. As the government's brutal suppression of these demonstrations showed, however, democracy is not the necessary outcome of this assertiveness. Certainly, the political situation since the overthrow of communism in the Soviet Union does not give rise to optimism that democracy is a natural successor to authoritarianism.

Although adherents of the pluralist paradigm view incidents like the suppression of the 1989 demonstrations as no more than temporary setbacks in an inexorable march toward liberalism and a civil society, other analysts argue that fundamental differences exist within the society that make such an evolution unlikely. The theory of *communist neo-traditionalism* put forth by Andrew Walder agrees with adherents of pluralism that communist societies are characterized by competition and conflict at all levels and that people have a choice of means through which to pursue their interests. At the same time, this theory affirms the validity of two major features of the totalitarian model. First, neo-traditionalists agree that there are distinctive communist institutions that make organized control possible; second, they argue that these forms of organization shape patterns of association and political behavior in distinctive ways.

However, in contrast to the totalitarian emphasis on disincentives to resistance caused by fear and the absence of alternatives to the existing government and ideology, neo-traditionalism emphasizes the incentives offered for compliance. Walder notes that political loyalty is rewarded systematically: with career opportunities, favored treatment in the distribution of scarce resources, and such other favors that officials in communist societies are uniquely able to dispense. In addition, the enforcement of the party's ideology has the unintended, but important, consequence of creating a highly institutionalized system of patron–client networks. These associations are composed of party loyalists and activists who trade their support for the party in exchange for preferential career opportunities and other rewards. Social atomization is replaced by the development of instrumental personal ties. Through them, individuals circumvent formal regulations to obtain official approvals, housing, and other public and private goods controlled by low-level officials.

Neo-traditionalism disagrees with the pluralist view that the "real" political and social forces are group forces: The social network rather than the group is its main structural concept. Neo-traditionalists reject convergence theories, arguing that the evolution of Chinese communism will result in a historically new system of institutionalized clientelism—in effect, a neo-traditional pattern of authority based on citizens' dependence on social institutions and their leaders. Kenneth Lieberthal takes this line of analysis further, describing an already partially evolved model of *fragmented authoritarianism* involving policy making through protracted bargaining among the top leaders and their bureaucracies, particularly in the provinces. Through their control over personnel appointments, the military, and key economic resources, the central authorities are able to influence the behavior of cities and provinces. Still, the decentralization of the economy has given these lower levels a certain ability to resist the central authorities as well. Hence, analysis should focus on the relationship between the center and the provinces and localities.

It has also been suggested that analysis should supplement its studies of the relationship between the state and various social groups by considering how these groups relate to each other. For example, as entrepreneurs have seen their economic status rise and their ties to the state strengthen, workers' economic status has declined, and their ties to the state have weakened. This is apt to have profound effects in shaping the sociopolitical dimensions of the Chinese state.

More recently, some scholars have challenged the applicability of these theories for analyzing China, arguing for what is known as Chinese exceptionalism. To insist on paradigms developed largely, albeit not exclusively, for Western societies amounts to "methodological totalitarianism." Chinese politics cannot, they believe, be understood outside the frame of reference of Chinese culture, with its different variety of state–society and central–local relationships. Critics argue that China is hardly unique: Although every society has its particularities, the logic of comparative political theory is applicable to all, since, as a value-neutral scientific method of inquiry, it seeks to explore and explain general patterns and regularities. They suspect that the party-state propounds the theory of exceptionalism to lend credence to what amounts, in essence, to the party line. The ruling group has a clear vested interest in maintaining that Western-inspired democracy is unsuited to China, with its allegedly very different Confucian value system, and that a strong authoritarian leadership in the form of the Chinese Communist Party is needed to prevent the country from descending into chaos.

Conclusions

As we have seen, each of the theories discussed seeks to explain the formal and informal rules under which the Chinese leadership operates, how they organize themselves to deal with differences of opinion, how resources are mobilized in support of a given end, what benefits accrue to the winners, and what sanctions are meted out to the losers. Their emphases differ, encompassing history, culture, ideology, personal power struggle, organizational theories, and the supremacy of domestic or foreign policy factors. Some seem more relevant at a particular point in time than others; none seems to have been an accurate predictor for the entire post-1949 period. Although each theory has something to recommend it, none is without its deficiencies. No single model can explain elite political behavior sufficiently and one should be skeptical of analyses based exclusively on any one of them. No one method of analysis is perfect, but the various different factors that are collectively central to them provide us with a list of useful variables to bear in mind when examining Chinese politics. Indicators such as the relative balance between state and society and that between the central government and lower level units as well as leaders' family background, level of education, foreign travel, date of entry into the party, service in particular geographic areas and/or ministries, and long association with particular persons provide valuable data for analysis and the inherently imperfect art of prediction.

Suggestions for Further Reading

Jae Ho Chung, *Centrifugal Empire: Central–Local Relations in China* (New York: Columbia University Press, 2016).

Sujian Guo, ed., *Political Science and Chinese Political Studies: The State of the Field* (Berlin: Springer, 2013).

Zhenhua Su, Hui Zhao, and Jingkai He, "Authoritarianism and Contestation," *Journal of Democracy*, January 2013, pp. 26–40.

Andrew J. Walder, *Communist Neo-traditionalism: Work and Authority in Chinese Industry* (Berkeley: University of California Press, 1986).

Fengshi Wu, "Collective Identity and Civil Society Development: The Left, Right, and Neutral among Social Activists in China," *Taiwan Journal of Democracy*, December 2012, pp. 25–50.

CHAPTER 2

The Chinese Tradition

To understand the problems faced by Chinese modernizers, it is important to have some sense of the tradition that provides the focus for their efforts. Many members of the post-1949 leadership had vivid memories of imperial China. While they have passed on, even people who do not hold the empire in living memory have had to deal with its legacy. No chapter—indeed, no multi-volume work—can hope to cover the richness and complexity of Chinese civilization adequately. Here, we will simply outline a few of the important points to give students of present-day China a better feel for the context within which the leadership had to operate.

Basic Characteristics

First, China was *one of the earliest sites inhabited by organized groups of human beings.* In the cold, dry soil of the Yellow River basin in north China, archaeologists have discovered skeletal remains, tools, and pottery dating from Neolithic times. The rest of the area now known as China was inhabited by what would later be referred to as barbarians. This small, core group gradually spread out to take control of an area whose contours are roughly similar to those of present-day China. Migration generally occurred in a southerly direction, along cultivable river banks, rather than toward the less hospitable north, with the original inhabitants being either absorbed or driven into less fertile areas.

This raises the question of what characteristics set the Chinese—or, as they normally refer to themselves, the Han—apart from neighboring ethnic groups. One is that the Han possessed the sophisticated agricultural techniques necessary for *wet rice cultivation* and *silk production.* Ironically, due to marked climatic changes, neither practice can now be carried out in the areas in which they were originally developed. The Han also developed a sophisticated written language at an early date. Chinese may be the *world's oldest continuously used script.* Egyptian hieroglyphics were developed considerably earlier, about 3000 B.C., but fell out of general use in the third century A.D., and disappeared entirely in the sixth century.

The records of Chinese civilization are relatively good. *An early and sustained interest in history and chronology* is another characteristic that set the Han apart from its neighbors. India, for example, also developed a highly sophisticated civilization, but one that was relatively little concerned with chronology. Originally, some of the earlier parts of traditional Chinese history were thought to be legendary. An accidental discovery, however, indicated that at least one of these supposedly mythical dynasties, the Shang, actually existed (Map 2.1). In the 1920s, some Westerners noticed that a traditional medicine shop in north China was selling bones incised with Chinese characters. Although oddly rendered, the characters were still recognizable as their modern-day counterparts. Curious, the Westerners purchased the bones and began to study them. Extensive research and testing confirmed that the inscriptions dated from Shang times: about 1500 B.C. It seems unlikely that the existence of a still earlier dynasty, the Xia, will be confirmed.

Chinese chronologies have proved to be amazingly precise. They have been verified, for example, by checking the eclipses and sightings of comets mentioned in Chinese records against when mathematical calculations say they must have occurred. Halley's Comet was observed regularly in China from 240 B.C. onward, and may have been the comet recorded in 611 and 467 B.C. By 444 B.C., Chinese astronomers had calculated the length of a year to be 365¼ days, a remarkable achievement given the technology of the times.

Not simply accurate record-keepers, the Chinese also had a well-developed *theory of history*: the dynastic cycle, according to which, although

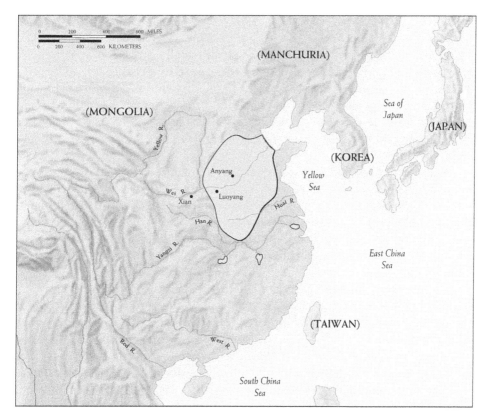

MAP 2.1A Bronze Age China during the Shang Dynasty (*c.* 1523–1028 B.C.)

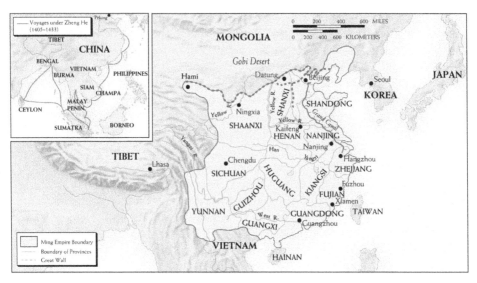

MAP 2.1B Ming Dynasty (1368–1644)

Note the tremendous expansion of territory as compared to that of the Shang dynasty (see Map 2.1A).

a golden age of perfection existed in the distant past, history was now cyclical. A dynasty is set up by a moral man in order to rectify existing evils. The ruler basically rules through presenting an example of virtue to be emulated by his people, and the person who is best qualified to rule is the one who is most moral. The first few emperors will fit this example, working very hard. After that, decline will begin to occur: Emperors will become more pleasure-loving and less virtuous.

A restoration, or mid-course correction, is possible. Eventually, however, the moral quality of the rulers will decline again, and the dynasty will deteriorate still further. Portents such as the appearance of comets, plagues of insects, drought, floods, and barbarian invasions are the indicators of the onset of decay. Those who are unjustly ruled will raise rebellions, and, when the quality of the emperor is poor enough, one of them—presumably through a rebellion led by the most moral man—will succeed. Its leader will found a new dynasty.

Unfortunately, in China as elsewhere, the existence of a theory influences one's perception of reality. In this case, the theory of history provided a mold for the writing of history: The last emperor of a dynasty was always portrayed as bad. There was also a belief that a short, brutal, and efficient dynasty would be succeeded by a longer, benevolent one. The dynasty became the unit of history, and most dynasties had a separate official volume devoted to them, with administrative organization, major personalities, and events recorded in meticulous detail. There are at least 24 of these dynastic histories, depending on how many one chooses to accept. These histories were typically compiled by the scholar-elite of the succeeding dynasty (see Table 2.1).

TABLE 2.1 The Chinese Dynasties

Five Emperors (mythical)	
Xia (mythical)	ca. 1994–ca. 1523 B.C
Shang (or Yin)	ca. 1523–ca. 1028 B.C.
Zhou	ca. 1027–256 B.C.
Qin	221–207 B.C.
Western (Earlier) Han	202 B.C.–9 A.D.
Xin	9–23
Eastern (Later) Han	25–220
The Three Kingdoms	220–265
Shu, 221–263	
Wei, 220–256	
Wu, 222–280	
Western Jin	265–317
Eastern Jin	317–420
Former (Liu) Song	420–479
Southern Qi	479–502
Liang	502–557
Chen	557–589
Northern Wei	386–535
Eastern Wei	534–550
Western Wei	535–556
Northern Qi	550–577
Northern Zhou	557–581
Sui	590–618
Tang	618–907
Five Dynasties and Ten Kingdoms	907–960
Later Liang, 907–923	
Later Tang, 923–936	
Later Jin, 936–947	
Later Han, 947–950	
Later Zhou, 951–960	
Liao	907–1125
Northern Song	960–1126
Xixia	990–1227
Southern Song	1127–1279
Jin	1115–1234
Yuan	1260–1368
Ming	1368–1644
Qing	1644–1911

Philosophy was also an important element of the Chinese tradition. From about 500 to 300 B.C., there was a period of vigorous debate among various schools of thought, known as the Hundred Schools era. The name is not to be taken literally: The Chinese, who used the decimal system from earliest times, are using hundred as a convenient shorthand for a large number. Two millennia later, Mao Zedong employed the idea of contending philosophies in a brief attempt at allowing people to express their true opinions on the best form of government. He encouraged his compatriots to "let one hundred flowers bloom, let a hundred schools of thought contend."

One of these schools was called *Confucianism*, after the Westernized name of its founder, Master Kong. His prescription for the well-ordered society included emphasis on hierarchical relationships: children subordinate to parents, wife to husband, subject to ruler, and so forth. The kingdom is the family writ large, with the emperor as father to his people. The Confucian ruler was a sage-king, a highly moral man whose exemplary behavior would inspire the people whom he ruled to emulate him. Confucius's ideal was the multi-generational family living together under the same roof, with its members paying respect to their common ancestors. Performance of these and other rites was important to Confucius, leading some foreigners to refer to Confucianism, somewhat misleadingly, as ancestor worship. Confucius was also strongly pro-agriculture and anti-commerce, regarding entrepreneurs as exploiters of what the labor of the peasantry produced. He also believed in "graded love," wherein one was expected to care more deeply for those people nearest one in the family and less so for those more distant. Confucius's notion of law was similarly hierarchical, with different rules for different classes of people.

Another school was *Mohism*, named for its founder, Mo Zi. The Mohists were more egalitarian in outlook, sounding much like modern-day advocates of democracy on many issues. They envisioned a state organization that measured everything in terms of its utility to all people. Mohists vehemently objected to aggressive war, though they produced skilled warriors and impressive tactics for defensive conflicts. They called for simplicity and frugality on the part of all people. Universal love, by which they meant equal regard for all other human beings, was also a central tenet, and one in sharp contrast with the Confucian outlook. Laws were to apply equally to all people. Mohists wanted the responsibility for power placed in the hands of the most able people, whom they expected to act according to the desires of the masses. However, they did not specify the mechanisms through which this might be done. Mo Zi was greatly honored in his day, and his teachings were no less influential than those of Confucius. Nonetheless, the school seems to have died out by the first century A.D.

A third school, the *Daoists*, believed (and still believe, as the school has a number of adherents even today) that a well-ordered society must be in harmony with The Way (*dao*). They hold that nature dictates all, and that the way to order life is to do nothing contrary to nature. Striving for power and material goods is to be eschewed, as is travel: The key to understanding The Way is within oneself. According to one Daoist sage, the ideal situation is to sit in one's own village listening to the barking of the dogs in the next village, but never to visit that neighboring village. Intensely quietistic, Daoists meditate in order to search for The Way. An often-quoted Daoist slogan advises that "the best form of action is inaction"; a Daoist ruler would accomplish everything by doing nothing.

Legalists, with the eminent Lord Shang as their principal spokesperson, insisted that the well-ordered state depends on a clearly enunciated rule of law that the state must enforce regardless of who may commit a crime. They advocated posting the laws of a city outside its gates so that all who entered would be aware of proper standards of behavior. In contrast to Confucius's image of the sage-king eliciting proper behavior from his subjects by providing them with a role model, the Legalists did not expect the people to do good by themselves. Rather, the ruler would, through the use of rewards and punishments, make sure that they would do no wrong. Legalist philosophy provided the guiding principles for the Qin dynasty (221–207 B.C.). Although Chinese tradition does not remember the Qin fondly, the system of governmental organization and criminal law for the next 2,000 years was basically of Legalist derivation.

The *Logicians*, or School of Names, vigorously debated the meaning of absolute versus relative terms. Despite an intense and ongoing interest in philosophy, China never developed a system of logic. In fact, the very name in use today, *luoji*, is borrowed from the West. But the logicians seemed to be groping toward a system of logic, as exemplified in the "Discourse on the White Horse" by its leading practitioner, Long Gongsun. Its main proposition asserted that "a white horse is not a horse," indicating the realization that adding the adjective *white* qualified the universal concept *horse*. The Logicians believed that only when names had been properly defined could any proper system of government and laws be set forth.

Yin–yang theory provided China with a cosmology. *Yang*, originally meaning sunshine, came to represent masculinity, activity, heat, brightness, dryness, and hardness, whereas *yin* was associated with the moon, femininity, passivity, cold, darkness, wetness, and softness. The interaction of these two primary principles was believed to produce all the phenomena of the universe. Yin and yang are complementary so that when one extreme is reached, the other principle begins to assert itself. The greatest of successes contains within itself the seeds of its own destruction, just as the sun at midday is on the verge of giving way to night. The diagrammatic representation of the yin–yang interaction is depicted on the present-day South Korean flag. Yin–yang theorists were concerned with divining the future through interpreting the configurations of the so-called eight trigrams, each one made up of combinations of three divided or undivided lines. They also devised prescriptions for good health through eating certain foods, some classified as hot and others as cold. Yin–yang principles had a brief popular revival in the United States during the 1960s.

Various folk religions incorporating other forms of geomancy also flourished during the Hundred Schools era. One popular belief was that the *feng shui*, or spirits of the winds (*feng*) and water (*shui*), had to be placated; otherwise disaster would ensue. A shaman would be brought in to determine the best site for a building or a grave in order to make sure that ill fortune would not befall those who commissioned the structure.

Buddhism is not properly a part of the Hundred Schools, as it arrived in China somewhat later, in the second century A.D. But, because it contended for power with the others, it is appropriate to consider Buddhism with them. Unlike the other schools, which are indigenous to China, Buddhism had its origins in India. Although many different sects of Buddhism exist, there is general agreement among them that human suffering arises from the individual's ignorance of the nature of things. From this ignorance comes the craving for and clinging to life, which binds the individual to the eternal wheel of life and death. Through enlightenment comes emancipation, or *nirvana*. This search for nirvana is essential to Buddhism.

Eventually, Confucianism won out over its rivals and became accepted as the state philosophy. However, in the process, it was fundamentally influenced by the other schools. For example, yin–yang symbolism was absorbed by Confucianism. Elements of Buddhism and Daoism figure prominently in the neo-Confucianism that emerged during the Song dynasty (960–1279 A.D.), and feng shui was incorporated as well. In addition to borrowing elements from other philosophies, Confucianism was not exclusivist. One could be a Confucian scholar, take time out for Daoist contemplation, and also be a practicing Buddhist. This basic tolerance did not hold true for all faiths, as will be seen later.

It is important to remember that Confucianism is not a religion in the usual sense of the word. Its concerns are with statecraft and with the proper relationships among human beings. Heaven is mentioned only once, when one of Master Kong's disciples states that heaven hears as the people hear and heaven sees as the people see. As a philosophy, it is unconcerned with the supernatural or with life after death. Confucius is revered as a great teacher rather than worshipped as a god.

The Governmental Structure of Traditional China

The governmental structure that arose out of these debates over statecraft and ethics was impressive in its degree of centralization and attention to the problems of administration. Its apex was the emperor, who theoretically reigned supreme. In reality, his decision-making powers were constrained by a number of factors, including the force of tradition, his own Confucian education, and the rest of the court structure.

The court structure included the empress and her family, who sought to have their members appointed to important and lucrative positions and might even try to seize the throne. There were also a large number of concubines, who similarly tried to advance themselves and their families through using their charms on the emperor. Providing the emperor with an heir was an excellent way to enhance one's status in court, although it often caused problems for one's relationships with the empress and other concubines. There was also typically a large eunuch population within the palace compound. In order to make sure that the imperial sons and heirs were really the children of the emperor, only castrated males were permitted in the parts of the palace where women lived. Because eunuchs were allowed substantial freedom of movement, which the palace ladies were not, a eunuch and a palace lady might ally for mutual benefit. The eunuch would provide the palace lady with information crucial to the advancement of her career in return for material and status benefits if she succeeded. Eunuchs could—and sometimes did—lead the imperial heir into a life of dissolution, opening the way for another woman's son to be named heir apparent. They might also administer poison to their lady's rival or to the rival's son.

The imperial bureaucracy was an elaborate hierarchy staffed by those who had passed the civil service examinations. From the fourteenth century onward, the pinnacle of the bureaucracy was the so-called Six Boards, corresponding to ministries in contemporary bureaucracies. Their respective administrative purviews also sound contemporary: The Board of Personnel granted civil service appointments to those who passed the examination system; the Board of Revenue collected taxes; the Board of Rites supervised the examination system, state festivals, and government-sponsored schools; the Board of War appointed military officers from the ranks of those who had passed the separate military examination system; the Board of Punishment provided the court system; and the Board of Works was in charge of building, irrigation, and "the produce of mines and marshes"—mostly salt, which was a government monopoly.

A seventh entity, the Censorate, was a uniquely Chinese institution. It existed to criticize the other organs of government, including the emperor. Censors had to be extremely courageous; they received no immunity by virtue of their position. Some were flogged to death by order of the ruler who was angered by their complaints. Others might receive the gift of a silken cord or a lump of raw opium from the emperor, thus conveying the imperial desire that they commit suicide. That so many censors were willing to take these risks speaks highly both for them as individuals and for the system that produced them.

Local government also had a well-articulated structure. Below the central government were the provinces. By the eighteenth century, there were 18 provinces in China proper; since then, more have been carved out of border districts that originally had other forms of administration. Provinces were divided into prefectures, which were in turn divided into counties, townships, and villages or hamlets. The county level was normally the farthest down that the imperial bureaucracy reached. By the time of the Qing dynasty (1644 A.D.), a typical county might contain several hundred thousand people. Supervising so many people, spread over a wide area, with roads that were often few in number and poor in quality, and without modern communications, was exceedingly difficult. The county magistrate had a staff of assistants, but they were far too few to actually administer the area under their jurisdiction. The county magistrate therefore had to seek the help of prominent local people and organizations.

In effect, then, the magistrate governed by supervising the local power structure, which was not part of the imperial bureaucracy. There was a tendency to preside passively, intervening only when it seemed absolutely necessary. Should the magistrate deem the situation important enough to do so, a number of measures were at his disposal. These ranged from dispensing informal advice, to calling in military forces to maintain order or gain compliance with imperial commands. The local worthies on whom the magistrate relied were typically members of a class known as the *gentry*. They were people of some wealth and social cultivation. Sometimes they were wealthy and, therefore, able to provide a son or sons with an education so that they might succeed at the examination system. Or they might be an originally poor family with a bright son who had managed to pass the examinations, become an official, and make his family wealthy. The informal hierarchy of elders that every village had was another set of people with whom the magistrate had to coordinate and work.

Yet another organization that might help the administration at the local government level was the *baojia*. In good Confucian fashion, the head of every household was responsible for the conduct of his family members. Since families tended to be large and multi-generational, this was a substantial responsibility. Every 100 households formed a *jia*, with one head of household designated as head, and every 10 *jia* formed a *bao*, again with a designated head. Each of these was responsible to those above him in the hierarchy for the conduct of those below him. Although the incumbents could be punished for breach of responsibility, none was paid for his efforts. This informal mutual security system did not always work: If one can be punished for something one's subordinates do, there are essentially two choices. First, one can try hard to keep potential troublemakers in line. Second, one can try to conceal what the troublemaker does. Often, the second choice proved to be easier than the first.

Concealment was also the hallmark of the secret societies. These groups had fanciful names, such as the Triads, the Yellow Turbans, the White Lotus, and the Fists of Righteous Harmony. Members were initiated in an elaborate ceremony that included such mystic rites as chanting, dancing, and animal sacrifice. They claimed a Robin Hood role, but tended to finance it by running Mafia-like protection operations. Secret societies were adept at resisting whatever aspects of central authority they did not like, such as tax increases. Not confined to particular local areas, they often had branches in other counties and provinces. When angered at imperial actions or mismanagement they might stage large rebellions. Secret societies were influential in toppling several dynasties.

Bandit groups operated in similar fashion, preying on travelers or demanding protection money from merchants and peasants. The larger their numbers, the more noticeable they became, and sometimes the magistrate was compelled to use force to deal with them. Imperial officials had no doctrine of hot pursuit, nor did they have any real incentive to resort to it: Bandits chased out of one magistrate's bailiwick became someone else's problem. Bandits thus preferred to operate from border areas, which had several advantages. First, they were far from the county seat and the magistrate's dwelling. Second, roads in border areas tended to range from sparse to nonexistent, and the bandits had the advantage of knowing the terrain. Third, should the pursuing force get too close, the bandits could quickly flee into another administrative area. Members of secret societies and bandit groups led lives of high adventure and, as a result, became a favorite topic of vernacular novelists. Mao Zedong, an avid reader of such novels in his youth, would later use some of the bandits' techniques in overthrowing the Chinese government of his day.

Faced with the enormous task of governing a large area with limited resources, the county magistrate tried to accommodate the informal power structure so that it would look to his superiors as though his district were peaceful and prosperous. In accordance with Confucian philosophy, lack of peace and prosperity would indicate that the magistrate was not setting a virtuous example. As a result, he might be removed. The upper levels of the bureaucracy were not completely unaware of these factors, but they had their own superiors to answer to. Various devices were tried to reduce the collusion between the magistrate and the local power structure. One method was periodic transfers. Another was the law of avoidance, whereby a magistrate was never posted to the area from which he came so that his judgment would not be compromised by Confucian obligations to take proper care of his family members. Even so, this did not prevent the local power structure from being able to circumvent or modify central government directives with reasonable frequency: The empire was too large, and the bureaucracy too small, to exact complete compliance. In the words of a popular Chinese saying, "Heaven is high, and the emperor is far away."

The resulting system of local government, though very informal, was surely not democratic, as the power structure was governed by rigid norms of authority and status. It was not even true decentralization, since all local power was conditional on the approval of higher levels. Nor was it really local autonomy, because a higher level of government could intervene if it decided to do so. It would probably be most accurate to say that basic-level traditional Chinese government was an operating arrangement, undertaken largely for reasons of administrative efficiency and conservatism, in which local authorities were encouraged to control their own areas, provided they did so effectively and without violation of imperial requirements. Gentry and other wealthy individuals, large clan groups, merchant and crafts guilds, and even secret societies could thus exercise great power over their subordinates and members. Possibly they could even influence the magistrate. But their power could go only so far as a direct challenge to the magistrate's power. At this point, a higher level would have to be brought in to deal with that challenge.

Although the bureaucracy could be almost nonexistent at the local level, it was quite top-heavy. There were many officials in the capital city, few of them with intimate knowledge of conditions in the countryside. For this reason, the bureaucracy tended to be out of touch with the people, a problem that the Chinese communists would later take considerable pains to rectify. In common with bureaucracies everywhere, it also had a tendency toward rigidity, with consequent stultifying effects on society. In the Chinese case, a major contributing factor to this rigidity was the imperial examination system.

The Examination System

From the time of the Tang dynasty (618–907 A.D.) onward, Chinese officials were selected on the basis of a competitive civil service examination. Candidates were tested on how well they had memorized the Confucian classics and internalized the code of ethics embodied therein. The tests were given on several levels of difficulty and, in many major cities, at special examination halls consisting of a series of individual cubicles. The applicant brought his own food—he might be there for three days—and was provided with a passage from the classics and a standard writing brush and ink. The cubicle was then sealed, leaving the candidate to write an essay on the passage in his best literary style under eight headings, referred to as legs. Every effort was made to prevent cheating, with monitors supervising the cells. The applicants' papers were copied before being submitted to the examiners lest the examiners be unduly influenced by the candidates' calligraphy. Those few who passed—less than 1 percent of the Chinese population—gained enormous prestige.

The examination system had a number of advantages. First, it produced intelligent officials who had thoroughly internalized the Confucian ethic. Second, it provided the people, including those who did not pass, with an orthodox belief system that was important for the management of the empire. Third, the system rewarded merit, providing a channel of social mobility for the ambitious, including commoners, that was based on widely accepted moral principles rather than on wealth, birth, brute force, or royal whim.

The examinations had disadvantages as well, many of them recognized by high-ranking officials who had succeeded within the system. One Song dynasty (960–1279 A.D.) statesman strongly urged that the principles of astronomy, ancient and modern laws, and political economy be included in the examinations. He and others criticized the excessive emphasis on memorization and the writing of couplets. In later times, the term *eight-legged essay* became a synonym for rigid, banal, stereotyped, and irrelevant. The degree of equality the examination system provided was also less than perfect: Despite the existence of a number of ways in which a poor child could gain access to education, the children of the wealthy were more likely to have better teachers and better environments for learning. Women were completely excluded from the competition. Nonetheless, the creation of the examination system was a remarkable achievement, especially when one considers how the various political entities of Europe were being governed at the time of the Tang dynasty. Despite its imperfections, the examination system served China well for many years.

Literature and Art

China produced art of great variety and subtlety that was prized far beyond its borders. Examples have been found in several areas of the Roman Empire. Somewhat later, Chinese pottery began to be exported to Indonesia. During the eighteenth and nineteenth centuries, a vogue for chinoiserie swept through Europe and the United States. Traditional China also produced a number of fine novels on topics ranging from the ribald to the introspective.

Interestingly, there is no tradition of literary and artistic protest. China produced no equivalent of *The Vision of Piers Plowman*, with its biting critique of status differentiations, or Hieronymus Bosch, whose paintings satirized corruption within the established church. Aesthetics were virtually monopolized by the scholar-official class, who painted and wrote poetry essentially as hobbies.

Society held those who painted for a living in low esteem: Culture was the triumph of the amateur ideal over that of professionalism. According to the *Analects*, Confucius said that "the accomplished scholar is not a utensil." It is worth noting that the great flowering of vernacular drama in China occurred during the Yuan dynasty (1260–1368 A.D.), when the Mongols suspended civil service examinations for 78 years. The theater became a way for the literati to compensate for their waning social prestige and wounded pride. To be sure, one can find examples of literature being used for protest purposes. For the most part, however, the elite protested through the established political channels—oral and written protests to the emperor—while the lower classes expressed their grievances by rebelling.

The Role of Law in Traditional China

Confucian teachings also influenced the legal system of traditional China. As noted earlier, Confucius did not believe in a uniform code of justice for all. A gentleman was assumed to be guided in his conduct by knowledge of the correct moral principles (*li*), while only the uneducated needed punishments (*fa*). Note that education, not birth, is the basis of gentility. Since differences were believed to be inherent in the nature of things; only through the harmonious operation of these differences could a fair social order, the Great Harmony, be achieved.

The idea of law as relative to one's status rather than as an absolute standard produced some rules that sound strange to Western ears. For example, how many bearers a person could have for his sedan chair was regulated by law, as was how much jewelry, and with what designs, could be worn. It was never possible to enforce these laws completely, however; nor was punishment ever completely done away with, even for high-ranking officials. There are instances of ministers being put to death, possibly on the reasoning that if their conduct were too outrageous they could no longer be considered gentlemen. More commonly, officials who fell from favor were reassigned to posts on the periphery of the empire. While they retained official status, this was actually a form of exile. As mentioned previously, there were also ways to suggest that an official commit suicide—which he generally did.

The influence of Confucian views on the importance of family was also reflected in the legal system. Crimes against family members were punished more heavily than those against outsiders, with patricide regarded as the ultimate horror. While the notion of the imperial system as a family writ large, with the emperor as the father of his people, is in most respects a reasonable and workable one, it did cause certain problems. Confucius never made clear what should happen when loyalty to one's family conflicted with loyalty to the emperor. The situation was not supposed to arise, since the desires of one's parents were not supposed to conflict with one's official duties. Unfortunately, such situations did arise—and with some regularity. The system tried to minimize these conflicts using various techniques. The law of avoidance, whereby officials were not to be posted to their family seats, has already been mentioned. In addition, the law provided that officials be granted leave for observance of the elaborate mourning rites demanded by Confucianism—a year in the case of a deceased father—which involved wearing special clothing, eating only certain foods, and preparing an elaborate funeral ceremony.

These codes notwithstanding, most matters were never brought to courts of law at all. There was no concept of what the Western world knows as torts: In order to bring a legal action, one had to accuse someone of a crime. The system recognized parents' authority to control and punish their children, and disputes between family members were settled in accordance with an individual's status within the kin group.

In addition to the notion that disputes should be settled within family or clan rather than consigned to the judgment of strangers, there was another important reason that most disputes were not brought to the courts: to do so was an expensive and risky venture. Bribery was the accepted way to influence one's case. Frequently, the county magistrate served as judge, and even if he were scrupulously honest, his various subordinates would have to be paid in order to persuade them to present the case: The magistrate had many other matters to attend to. This practice of payments, known as "squeeze," existed at all levels of government. Since it was understood that the bureaucrats involved had inadequate salaries and obligations to their own families, squeeze was not considered to be corruption unless the fee was exorbitant.

As to law in the higher sense, there were no guarantees against the exercise of imperial power. Government could initiate, regulate, adjudicate, and repress as it saw fit. Elites had a *moral* obligation to provide just and responsive government, but there were no constitutional or legal safeguards to back up this obligation. Enforcement depended upon, first, the bureaucratic recruitment process, which was supposed to ensure that only men of superior virtue would be chosen, and second, the bureaucracy's own supervisory system. The latter was really a case of self-regulation: Bureaucrats would have to agree to remove one of their numbers whom they believed was not exercising his responsibilities properly.

The traditional political system was essentially free to accumulate and exercise total power, although, to its great credit, it never made the fullest use of this right. An elaborate system of checks and balances was developed despite the absence of a constitutional framework. This system aimed not at safeguarding human rights but at preventing one faction or group of bureaucrats at the imperial court from annihilating the other. These informal checks and balances were sanctioned by custom, not law. This arrangement did not preclude one individual from seizing power, but it greatly increased the difficulty of anyone actually doing so.

Although people at the highest levels of leadership were expected to conform to a rigid moral code, they seemed relatively indifferent to what went on at the lower levels so long as there was peace. Efforts were made to indoctrinate the population at large with the Confucian ethic through such means as sponsoring public lectures, ceremonies, and schools to teach filial piety, respect for elders and superiors, peaceful and industrious conduct, and observance of the law. However, neither the efforts made nor the results achieved were especially impressive. In the vast countryside, people were generally neither positively loyal to the existing government nor actively opposed to it, but simply concerned with the problems of their own daily lives.

The Military

By 500 B.C., China had produced one of the world's greatest military strategists, Sun Zi, whose *Art of War* is even now required reading in military academies worldwide. However, with a few salient exceptions, most notably the Yuan (Mongol) dynasty, the military was not held in high regard in imperial China. A popular saying was: "As one does not use good iron to make nails, one does not use good men as soldiers." If the ruler were virtuous, the people would be prosperous and content, and there would be no need for a strong military. If the people were not prosperous and content, then the ruler must be at fault, and it might be necessary to make changes at the top. Hence, the army tended to be strong at the beginning of a dynasty, having been used to overthrow the previous incumbents. It would then be allowed to decay because it was no longer needed. Some military presence was considered necessary at all times owing to the need to deal with barbarian incursions. There was no navy to speak of, since China was attacked from the sea only by occasional pirates. Even then, the strategy adopted was often simply to move the coastal population inland.

Scholar-officials tended to dominate military command functions, especially during periods of dynastic decline, and always did their best to undercut military officers, who were usually not literate. This can be seen as another manifestation of the belief in the supremacy of amateurism over professionalism, but it was more than this as well. There was a tendency for the official class to want to wrest control of all areas that might rival their influence. This same tendency is noticeable in the campaign the scholar-officials waged against the impressive sea voyages of the early Ming dynasty (1368–1644 A.D.). These expeditions were run by eunuchs, who gained a great deal of imperial favor through the voyages. Ultimately, the scholar-officials succeeded in stopping them completely.

The Barbarian Problem

The term *barbarian* is used here to mean any non-Han Chinese group that interacted with the Han. Some of these groups were relatively cultivated, although most were not. The Han referred to them by a variety of terms, many of which had pejorative connotations. Unlike the Han, a number of these groups had great respect for the military and produced some formidable fighting forces. This was particularly true of northern groups, such as the Uygurs, Kazakhs, and Mongols. Members of these groups did not accept Confucian precepts, so the Han could not expect that the presence of a virtuous ruler on their own throne would deter the barbarians' depredations. A military force had to be maintained in order to deal with them.

Various techniques were devised to deal with the barbarians in order to minimize the need for battle. One was to buy them off through such devices as conferring official titles, with salaries, that entailed responsibility for ensuring peace in their areas. Another was to play one group off against another, a stratagem known as "using barbarians to control barbarians." This did not, however, prevent the barbarians from making alliances with each other against the Chinese.

On occasion, barbarians conquered all or part of Han China and established their own dynasties. This was accepted to the degree that the conquerors accepted Chinese cultural norms and assimilated themselves to Confucian precepts. The Yuan dynasty, founded by Mongols who strenuously resisted adapting to the existing system, was short-lived, and most Chinese regard it as unsuccessful. In contrast, the Manchus' Qing dynasty, whose leaders displayed considerable ingenuity in functioning as Confucian rulers while avoiding assimilation, lasted more than twice as long and, until its last half-century, was far better regarded.

Foreigners could even command Chinese armies in battle, as did An Lushan, a Sogdian, during the Tang dynasty, and Frederick Townsend Ward, an American, in the nineteenth century. Culturalism rather than nationalism characterized the Chinese empire: Birth and race mattered less than one's willingness and ability to conform to accepted standards of ethics, behavior, and dress.

Interpretations of Chinese History

The question of how to characterize this impressive and complex society then arises. One view, that of Karl Marx, is that of China the unchanging. In his words, history went to sleep in Asia. This is untrue. Artistic styles, technology, administrative techniques, and even Confucian philosophy were modified over time. Change may have come more slowly than in certain periods of European history, but there definitely was change.

A second view was held by Marxists, disciples of Karl Marx who applied his categories for Western society to China. This involves a historical progression from primitive communism, wherein small hunter-gatherer groups share the results of their foraging, to a slave society, in which some groups conquer others and use them in forced labor. Eventually, slave societies evolve into feudal societies, which are characterized by land that is held in fiefs and serfs who are bound to the land through oath and lack of other alternatives. Industrialization then occurs, leading to the bourgeois–capitalist stage of society, in which workers are exploited by capitalists, who monopolize ownership of the means of production. The workers rebel and inaugurate socialist society, in which they collectively own the means of production. The final stage, communism, is achieved when allocation depends on "from each according to his ability, to each according to his need." At this point, the state will have become unnecessary and will simply wither away.

It is interesting to compare Marx's theory with China's reality. Unfortunately, hunter-gatherer groups cannot be expected to leave written records. Although the stage of primitive communism may well have existed, it cannot be proved. During the Shang dynasty (*c.* 1523–*c.* 1028 B.C.), from whence our earliest records come, slavery does seem to have existed, as indeed it did during the Han and certain other periods. However, the presence of slaves does not characterize a society as a slave society unless a major portion of society's work was done by them. This was never the case in China.

Feudal society definitely did exist, though before the time the Hundred Schools contended. A noble class arose who were responsible for raising armies from among their serfs, rode in chariots, wore armor, and had an elaborate code of ethics that has been compared to chivalry. And, just as in Western feudalism, the king was rather weak *vis-à-vis* a coalition of his nobles. Feudal society, however, was already in an advanced state of decay by the time of the Hundred Schools period, in the latter part of the Zhou dynasty (*c.* 1027–256 B.C.). Throughout Confucius's writings, there are laments that the rules of etiquette are being ignored.

The next dynasty, the Han, began to institute bureaucracy. Nobles were paid in rice for their service to the state rather than being granted fiefs. Land began to be bought and sold. As a result of these developments, China could no longer be called feudal. Yet, if Marx's categories of development are to be applied to China, feudalism should have been succeeded by the bourgeois–capitalist stage. It was not—as even Marxists agree. There are a few indicators, they argue, that China may have been developing a bourgeois–capitalist society. One can see the slow rise of a money economy. A proto-banking system also developed, wherein money could be held on deposit in one city and drawn upon elsewhere. This enables Marxists to conclude that China went through a relatively long period—almost 2,000 years—of being "semi-feudal." Marxists also argue that China was on the verge of entering the bourgeois–capitalist stage when Western imperialism intruded, destroying what they call the sprouts of capitalism in order to colonize the country.

A third view is that Chinese society is an example of Oriental despotism, sometimes also referred to as *hydraulic society*. Devised by a German scholar, Karl Wittfogel, this view argues that of all the factors necessary for successful cultivation of crops in a preindustrial society, only water (as opposed to temperature and surface) can be controlled through human effort. The need for irrigation and flood control means that a large quantity of water must be channeled and kept within bounds. Dikes must be built and maintained, canals dredged regularly, and information relevant for navigation compiled and distributed. This can be done only through the use of mass labor. Moreover, the labor force must be coordinated, disciplined, and led. Effective water management requires an organizational web that covers the whole—or, at a minimum, the dynamic core—of the country's population. Timekeeping and calendar making are likewise essential for the success of hydraulic economies: Crops must be planted, irrigated, and harvested within fairly narrow periods of time. Systematic observation, careful calculations, and dissemination of results are needed. Hence, China needs a strong central government.

In consequence, those who control this network of laborers, calculators, and disseminators are well positioned to wield supreme political power. The resulting regime will be decisively shaped by the leadership and social control required by hydraulic agriculture. The state will be stronger than the society, and those outside the ruling apparatus are essentially enslaved to it. This contrasts sharply with multi-centered societies such as existed in medieval Europe and Japan, and with their modern democratic incarnations, where the need for water control was never so crucial.

In those other societies, Wittfogel argues, the state was effectively checked and restrained by other strong and competing organizations, such as the religious establishment, craft and merchant guilds, and private owners of land and industrial capital. Such political systems offer vastly greater protection to the individual and also provide a basis for adaptive and progressive social change. By contrast, the fate of hydraulic societies such as China is apt to be slow stagnation. Critics have charged that Wittfogel's analysis overemphasizes the importance of water control. They point out that the emperor and his officials viewed the collection of taxes, the administration of justice, and the conducting of annual sacrifices to heaven and earth as matters of far higher priority.

A fourth view is that China became modern during the midpoint of the Tang dynasty, about 850 A.D. This is known as the *Naito hypothesis,* after Naito Konsan, the Japanese scholar who first articulated it. As previously discussed, the term *modernization* can be defined in a number of ways. Naito's major criterion is that of social mobility: In a modern society one rises through merit, as opposed to inheriting one's status. This did actually happen in the mid-Tang dynasty, thanks to the widespread institutionalization of the examination system during that period. At about the same time, one begins to find military leaders who had been common soldiers of peasant background, as opposed to the aristocratic warriors who predominated in feudal society. Vernacular literature also spread, supplementing Confucian treatises and Buddhist sutras. The position of the commoner improved.

There is no doubt that all these phenomena took place, as Naito points out. However, one may argue that China did not necessarily become modern because of them. A bureaucracy chosen by merit does not in itself confer modernity on a state. According to Max Weber, the eminent sociologist of bureaucracies, the hallmark of modernity is functional specificity: Bureaucrats have specific tasks, such as supervision of engineering projects and preparation of the state budget. The first group would have been trained in bridge building and dam construction; the second in accounting. This ran counter to the primacy of amateurism over professionalism in the Chinese bureaucracy. The examination system trained generalists, not specialists. What it tested was the candidate's ability to expound on the Confucian classics, not his ability to build public works or analyze statistics.

One should point out, however, that there is a consensus that nineteenth-century Great Britain was a modern state. Yet its bureaucrats were also trained as generalists: A background in Greek and Latin classics was considered to be excellent preparation for future leaders.

Another argument against the Naito hypothesis is that whereas modernity includes the ability to rise through merit within a hierarchy, success in the Chinese bureaucracy was heavily dependent on whom one knew. Assuming a person was able to rise within the official hierarchy, he was also supposed to help those who passed the examinations in the same year, and their children as well. A counterargument is that the phenomenon of promotion on the basis of connections, whether one's own or one's relatives and their friends', is scarcely unknown in modern Western societies, and the perception of obligation to help members of one's peer group is the very essence of the "old school tie" in Britain and the *Burschenschaft* in Germany. The crucial element that kept China from modernity is less likely to have been the absence of a modern bureaucracy than the country's lack of industrialization.

Implications for Industrialization

The question of what factors are necessary for the industrialization of a country has been carefully examined by a number of social scientists, and not surprisingly there is less than total agreement among them. As summarized by sociologist Barrington Moore, a standard list of prerequisites for industrialization includes:

1. capital from the sale of commercially marketable agricultural surpluses that can be invested in manufacturing;
2. legal codes to protect businesses and their personnel;
3. the concept of progress;
4. a positive attitude toward science;
5. geographic mobility in order to take advantage of manufacturing and other opportunities as they arise.

As we have seen, Confucianism was a rich and varied tradition. There were different interpretations of the classics over the years, and the original philosophy absorbed elements from other philosophies and religions. However, regardless of time or dynasty, Confucianism had a pro-agriculture, anti-commercial bias. Peasants were considered to be the producers of wealth—that is, food. Merchants were regarded as nonproductive parasites on society: dishonest folk who sought to make a profit out of other people's work through such schemes as buying at a low price at one time of year or in one area and selling at higher prices at another time or place. Neither Confucius nor his disciples saw any value in the entrepreneurial function.

Those states that have succeeded in industrializing have done so by harnessing capital derived from a commercially marketable, agricultural surplus to manufacturing purposes. The Confucian attitude toward merchants and their activities made this virtually impossible. The socially sanctioned outlet for money derived from the sale of produce was investment in land. The goal was gentry status, not merely through possessing substantial landholdings but also by passing the examination system or having a son or close relative do so.

In addition to being anti-commerce, Confucius was not favorably disposed to the rule of law as we know it; hence, no codes that could regulate business transactions developed. Merchants did exist, the Confucian attitude toward them notwithstanding, but they could not protect themselves to a sufficient extent to be able to compete with officialdom. Business activities were inhibited by the need to pay bribes or taxes, often to the point of unprofitability.

A third basic ingredient of industrialization, the concept of progress, was also absent in traditional China. There was no motivation to strive toward a better age. Confucius perceived the golden age as in the past, during the period that preceded the Warring States era (443–221 B.C.). History after this golden age was seen as a series of cycles, as in the dynastic cycle. The virtue of rulers and the prosperity of the country would wax and wane in the manner depicted by yin–yang symbolism. Change certainly took place, but it was not regarded as a good thing in itself—and the ultimate perfectibility of the society was not expected. The aim was not progress but harmony, as represented by the Chinese character for king: three horizontal lines, representing heaven, earth, and man, joined by a vertical stroke through the middle (王). The king, through his virtue, aligns heaven, earth, and man in equilibrium.

Science, the fourth prerequisite for industrialization, was regarded as unimportant and unnecessary. As is well known, the Chinese made some remarkable discoveries, including the compass and gunpowder, many years before they were invented in the West. In medieval times, their shipbuilding techniques were far superior to those of the West. These skills made long voyages possible, of which those of the early Ming dynasty are the best known. Confucius was not opposed to science, but he viewed exploration and invention as trivial: It was more important to cultivate one's moral virtue.

Confucius's emphasis on the veneration of ancestors also inhibited geographic mobility. It was incumbent on one to keep up the ancestral graves, and the village occupied an almost mystical point of reference for its inhabitants. This did not prevent some Chinese from venturing far and wide: Prosperous Chinese merchant communities grew up in such places as Cambodia, Singapore, and Indonesia many hundreds of years ago. Generally speaking, however, Chinese tradition did not encourage geographic mobility, and even those who migrated great distances often set aside funds to ensure that their earthly remains would be sent back to the ancestral village for proper burial.

Confucianism might, of course, have adapted to industrialization. One could easily look at medieval Europe, with its religiously mandated prohibition against lending money at interest and fatalistic belief that because human misery was divinely ordained nothing could be changed, and conclude that Christianity must permanently prevent industrialization. Such adaptation, however, did take place in Europe, leading to speculation about why this did not occur in China.

An intriguing hypothesis for China's slow technological development, presented by scholar Mark Elvin, is that progress was held back by a *high-level equilibrium trap*. According to Elvin's theory, through a number of interlocking causes, the input–output relationships of the late traditional economy had assumed a pattern that was almost incapable of change through internally generated forces. In both technological and investment terms, agricultural productivity per acre had nearly reached the limits of what was possible without industrial-scientific inputs, and the increase in population had therefore steadily reduced the surplus product above what was needed for subsistence. A falling surplus per head meant a reduction in effective demand per person for goods other than those needed for bare survival (see Figure 2.1). Pre-modern water transport was close to a similar ceiling of efficiency, and few possibilities existed for increasing the demand for goods by reducing transport costs.

For these technological reasons, the rising price of food during periods when population pressure on land was becoming severe could not induce a higher output of grain except through migration and the opening up of new land. Migration did take place. It was the chief means whereby the Chinese economy grew in quantitative terms, but there was almost no qualitative change. If the huge size of the traditional economy had any implications for technological change, they were probably negative. Any significant change in input–output relationships would have involved enormous amounts of materials and goods. For example, Britain's consumption of raw cotton tripled between 1741 and the early 1770s, when effective machine spinning of cotton fiber first began. For China to have tripled consumption in a 30-year period would have been beyond the cotton-producing ability of the entire eighteenth-century world.

With a falling surplus in agriculture and, hence, falling per capita income and per capita demand; with cheapening labor but increasingly expensive resources and capital; and with farming and transport technologies so good that no simple improvements could be made, the rational strategy for peasant and merchant alike argued not for labor-saving machinery but for economizing on resources and fixed capital. Large but nearly static markets did not tend toward creating the systemic bottlenecks that might have prompted technological creativity. Merchants dealt with temporary shortages by using cheap transport more creatively. This is the essence of the *high-level equilibrium trap* explanation.

A related theory called *involutionary commercialization,* advanced by Professor Philip Huang, also hypothesizes that China's large population was a major factor in the country's failure to modernize. With the size of farms shrinking as population pressure grew, peasants turned to commercialized crop production and handicrafts, which required much more intensive labor input than grain production. Total output value grew, but at the cost of lower marginal returns per workday. Peasants marketed not for capitalist profit, which could have been reinvested, but for sheer survival, and economic growth was not accompanied by economic development.

Figure 2.1 illustrates the effects of a quasi-ceiling in late traditional Chinese farm technology. The solid line shows potential output for a given input of labor

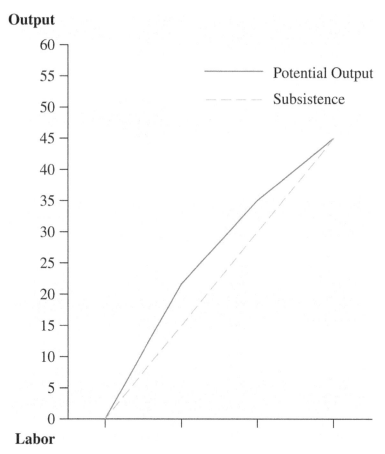

FIGURE 2.1 High-level Equilibrium Trap

Source: Adapted from Mark Elvin, *The Pattern of the Chinese Past* (Stanford, CA: Stanford University Press, 1973), p. 313.

using the best pre-modern methods; the dotted line shows the proportion of output needed for the subsistence of a given labor force. With land being constant, potential surplus shrinks, first relatively, and then absolutely, as the labor force grows. At the farthest end of the chart, adding inputs no longer results in increased output. This trap can be broken out of only through the use of industrial-scientific inputs.

Conclusions

To briefly summarize the many points touched on in this chapter: First, the opinions of some Marxist-influenced analysts notwithstanding, China was not feudal in the usual sense of the word, nor had it been for almost two millennia. Second, there was a great deal of social mobility in traditional China—in fact, an unusual amount for a pre-modern society. Hard physical labor and diligent study had raised a number of paupers or their sons into the official class. Third,

China was not unchanging, although changes tended to come slowly and within the context of tradition. Fourth, history was perceived as cyclical rather than as marching progressively onward. Fifth, the Chinese state was culturalistic rather than nationalistic. Acceptance into the society depended less on an individual's ethnic background than on his ability to assimilate Confucian principles. Sixth, the imperial bureaucracy was hierarchically arranged and subdivided according to function, but did not extend down to the level of local government. Seventh, the individual was subordinated to his or her family group. The empire was conceived as a family writ large, with the emperor as a benign, if authoritarian, father. Eighth, scholars, administrators, and even the emperor himself were expected to follow an ethical rather than a legal code of conduct. Western-style individualism and the supremacy of law never became established, nor did the personal freedom under law as represented by Western civil liberties and institutions of private property. It should be noted that legal safeguards of personal liberty are relatively recent even in the West, and still far from perfect. Ninth, traditional China was based on noncommercial agriculture and ruled by a powerful bureaucracy. Although politically centralized, China was economically decentralized. Its structures were sanctioned by customs and ethical beliefs rather than by religion or law. When traditional China lived up to its ideals it was a relatively good system.

Suggestions for Further Reading

Sarah Allan, "Erlitou and the Formation of Chinese Civilization: Toward a New Paradigm," *Journal of Asian Studies*, vol. 66, no. 2 (March 2007): 461–486.

Mark Elvin, *The Pattern of the Chinese Past* (Stanford, CA: Stanford University Press, 1973).

L. Carrington Goodrich, *A Short History of the Chinese People*, 3rd edn (New York: Harper, 1959).

Stephen R. Halsey, *Quest for Power: European Imperialism and the Making of Chinese Statecraft* (Cambridge, MA: Harvard University Press, 2015).

Jonathan Spence, *The Search for Modern China* (New York: W.W. Norton, 2013).

CHAPTER 3

Reformers, Warlords, and Communists

The New Invasion

By the nineteenth century, China was not a society that was living up to its ideals. Tax assessments remained fixed while the population expanded rapidly, meaning that the monies available for public works diminished. Poor management led to popular discontent and domestic rebellion became a problem. As noted in Chapter 2, these were important indicators of a downturn in the dynastic cycle. When the West, newly commercially developed and eager for markets, arrived and demanded trade privileges that Chinese officialdom had no desire to grant, the Westerners were seen as a third indicator of dynastic decline: barbarian invasion.

Despite their odd appearance and the fact that, unlike most other barbarians, they had arrived by sea, Westerners were not at first seen as a serious threat. Minor concessions were granted, as they had been to other barbarians in times past. It was believed that foreign countries could not get along for a single day without tea and rhubarb, so His Majesty graciously bestowed the privilege of acquisition on them. Since the articles the Westerners brought in return were considered toys—elaborate clocks, for example—that were not needed by the Celestial Empire, China could simply cut off this privilege should the barbarians become too demanding. Officials downplayed the possibility of military threat. Among other misconceptions it was believed that the barbarians' ships could be set on fire by soldiers applying torches to the vessels' waterlines.

While the imperial government saw itself as benevolently acceding to some of the annoying demands of these inferior beings, Westerners chafed under what they regarded as arrogant behavior and petty restrictions. These became increasingly irritating. Trade was confined to one small area, and they could not communicate directly with the imperial government. Western merchants and their governments made a number of requests, including the opening of ports to trade, access to China's hinterland, and the right to station an ambassador in the capital city. From the Beijing government's point of view, the barbarians had become too demanding. Particularly upsetting was their preferred method of payment for Chinese goods: opium. The drug was not new to China: It was raised domestically and used medicinally. Addiction existed, but on a relatively small scale.

This changed dramatically with the arrival of foreign opium. More and more Chinese smoked ever larger amounts. In addition to its deleterious effects on the health of the population, foreign opium caused financial problems for the government: A large net outflow of silver meant less prosperity, more unrest, and a greater likelihood of rebellion—a further slide down the slippery slope of dynastic decline.

The foreign intruders refused entreaties to stop shipping opium, pointing out that China also produced it and that if they were to do so, demand would simply be served by domestic sources. In 1839, an imperial commissioner at Guangzhou (Canton) seized nearly three million pounds of British raw opium and flushed it out to sea. Urged on by irate merchants, London dispatched a fleet whose modern, steam-driven vessels and long-range guns quickly destroyed Chinese defenses. This was the most decisive defeat the Qing (Manchu) dynasty had ever received, though worse were yet to come. The settlements ending the Opium War of 1839–1842 gave the foreigners substantial concessions in trade, tariffs, right of residence, extra-territoriality, most favored nation status, and redress for damages. Britain was also given Hong Kong island. These were the first of the so-called unequal treaties, discussed in Chapter 1.

After signing, however, the Qing court delayed compliance, trying the patience of the British and French governments. Jointly seizing on a fairly minor incident in 1856 to recommence hostilities, they marched on Beijing, forcing the emperor to flee. The 1860 Treaty of Beijing—actually a series of treaties, since through the most favored nation clause, other nations participated in concessions won by the victors—constituted the second set of unequal treaties. After more than two decades of trying to ignore the barbarians, the court at last realized that something would have to be done.

The Self-strengthening Movement

Its first response held that the empire's difficulties had occurred because of declining adherence to Confucian tradition. A return to those principles would arrest decay, strengthen the empire, and enable a midcourse correction to the dynastic cycle. This was the basis for the Tongzhi restoration of 1862–1874. *Tongzhi*, meaning "unified government," is the reign title of the emperor who ruled during these years.

The Tongzhi restoration was conceived of as a self-strengthening movement to be conducted within the parameters of Confucian tradition. Although there were differences of opinion among officials on precisely what to do, most agreed that it would be acceptable to borrow Western military techniques. Traditional China's pre-eminent military strategist, Sun Zi, had written, "know yourself, know your enemy, win ten thousand battles" and, as previously noted, the Chinese had occasionally borrowed military techniques from barbarians in the past. One would study the Westerners in order to defeat them.

The slogan of the self-strengthening movement was "Chinese culture [*ti*] for the foundation, Western learning for practical use [*yong*]," as has been discussed in Chapter 1. There is no doubt that a great many things were accomplished during the Tongzhi restoration:

- the Grand Canal and some lesser canals that had been allowed to silt up, essentially through mismanagement, were dredged and reopened.
- a new and generally successful tax was instituted to ease the government's revenue problems. Called *likin,* a tax of one-thousandth, it was too small to make avoidance worthwhile and so proved easier to collect than other taxes.
- new, regionally based armies and navies were founded, funded by customs revenues and *likin.* Efforts were made to recruit literate gentry as officers and healthy young peasants as volunteers. Arsenals and shipyards were founded, again on regional bases, to supply the new armies with better weapons. Officers of the new armies were warned against corrupt practices, such as padding the payrolls with the names of deceased or nonexistent soldiers and keeping the money that should have been paid to their actual troops.
- a school for the study of foreign languages was set up.
- a coal-mine was opened.
- a proto-foreign office was set up. None had existed before, as all other countries were considered too inferior to warrant it.
- army officers were sent to Germany to study military science.
- a group of students was dispatched to the United States to study at Yale University.

Despite all these efforts, the Tongzhi restoration as a whole was a failure that contrasted starkly with the success of Japan's comparable effort. China's neighbor to the east had felt the pressure of the West even later than China. It was much smaller than China, was much poorer in natural resources, and had a similarly Confucian bias against commerce. Large parts of Japanese culture, including the written language, had been borrowed from China. Although it was not widely recognized at the time, some of Japan's apparent disadvantages also had advantageous aspects: Being smaller meant that new ideas and new technologies could be disseminated more quickly than in China's far-flung domains. In addition, because the Japanese had borrowed major parts of their culture from China, they were psychologically less averse to borrowing from the West.

Beginning in 1868, several years later than China, Japan's Meiji restoration had raised the country to major power status within a few decades. In 1894/1895, Japan easily defeated its much larger neighbor, which symbolically marked the failure of China's program.

Why did the Tongzhi restoration fail while the Meiji restoration succeeded brilliantly? One theory is that the Chinese program aimed at a genuine restoration, whereas the Japanese were, in essence, cloaking a revolution in traditional garb, the better to obtain compliance. In this view, trying to make China into a strong, modern nation through restoring Confucian principles was doomed to failure, because Confucianism was incompatible with the requirements of a modern nation. It was not even nationalistic but rather cultural. Other factors, such as anti-commercialism, the relatively low regard with which technology and practical matters in general were held, and the belief that the golden age lay in the past, have been discussed in Chapter 2.

The Tongzhi restoration did attempt some genuine changes, carefully rationalized as being compatible with tradition, and therefore cannot be too starkly contrasted with the Meiji restoration on this matter. It was how the reforms worked themselves out that was crucial, and here many of them were rejected definitively, portending the certain defeat of the self-strengthening movement. For example, officials understood well the necessity of efficient communications for administrative purposes, as can be seen in their great concern for maintaining the speed of the traditional courier service, but rejected the means for even faster communication. When foreigners suggested building railroads and telegraph networks to do so, the officials replied that the existing system was fast enough for them. The only reason to send messages more quickly would be to facilitate commercial transactions and, since commerce was despicable, there was no need for railroads or telegraphs.

After being repeatedly refused permission to build a telegraph, a foreign consul suggested building one that would connect only treaty ports, in order to circumvent the official objection that the telegraph system would adversely affect China. At the same time, however, building the system in this way would reduce much of its value to China. The consul was eventually permitted to proceed with construction—provided that all the lines were immersed in water and all the terminals were on ships.

The steamship company that had been established as part of the self-strengthening movement failed dismally. Set up under the principle that merchants would run the company under official supervision—a concession to the prerogatives of the official class as well as a recognition of the inferior position of the commercial class—it performed quite well at first. However, the company failed financially when its initial profits, which should have been reinvested, were used instead to buy land or unproductive goods. Confucius would have approved, but Adam Smith would not.

The Tongzhi restoration's educational mission failed as well. After the students had been at Yale for a few years, they were sent to meet with the newly appointed supervisor of the mission. When the boys were ushered into his presence, they failed to perform the *ketou* (kowtow) of deference, as called for by traditional manners. Taking this as an indication that studying Western ways had caused them to neglect Chinese tradition, the supervisor arranged to have the mission recalled.

The common theme of these examples is that borrowing from the West was considered acceptable so long as it did not interfere with Chinese tradition. Unfortunately, this attitude *did* interfere with China's self-strengthening. In actuality, unswerving adherence to tradition was in itself untraditional. Chinese tradition had never been rigid and unbending, changing somewhat—albeit slowly—in response to the needs of the time. Neither manners nor technology remained the same from dynasty to dynasty. Tradition was not an imperative "we must" but rather a guide: "How could a reasonable person do otherwise?" Thus, insistence on blindly following tradition actually ran counter to Chinese tradition.

Confucianism could certainly have adapted. Dramatic changes have occurred in other ideologies through such means as heretical thinkers who provide radical reinterpretations of the official canon or people who reason that if the great founder of the philosophy were alive today, she or he would surely have spoken differently. Possibly the shock of discovering how different the West was—and how great an adaptation China would have to make—was a factor in the inability of the leadership to adapt. Had a smaller amount of borrowing been called for, the adaptation might have taken place. This takes the problem back before the Qing dynasty, to the turning inward of China after cessation of the sea voyages of the early Ming. Had China kept in better contact with the rest of the world, adaptation could have taken place more gradually. Responsibility for this lies with the official class.

Another factor lay in the dynastic leadership—or lack thereof. The Tongzhi emperor came to the throne as a child of 5 years old, succeeding his incompetent father. Although nominally in charge during the restoration that bears his name, the real ruler was his mother, Cixi. Originally a lower ranking concubine, the empress dowager had been the only palace lady to bear her sickly master a male child. Cixi was intelligent, competent, and utterly ruthless—a set of qualifications generally believed to be shared by many highly successful world leaders. However, the empress dowager had to expend most of her energies fighting off plots against her. In terms of dealing with foreigners and the problems they presented, she was at a further disadvantage: Being a woman, Cixi was unable to leave the palace and therefore had to get most of her information from eunuchs. But, under a Qing law imposed some years before in order to curtail the eunuchs' power, they too were prohibited from leaving the palace grounds. Although eunuchs did have considerably more freedom of movement than the empress dowager, there were real limitations on their ability to provide the information she needed for proper decision making. What they did tell her was often biased in terms of their own interests as well.

China's defeat in the Sino–Japanese War was a devastating blow. One problem was that China's navy was composed of several different, regionally based naval fleets without a unified command. In addition, widespread corruption had diverted large sums of money meant for naval modernization. The empress dowager herself had ordered a marble boat to be constructed on the lake of her summer palace outside Beijing. Whatever the decisive factor, however, the Sino–Japanese War put an end to the idea of reform through Confucianism. With China's weaknesses further exposed by this humiliating defeat, a number of foreign powers, including England, France, Italy, Germany, Russia, and Japan, began demanding concessions. Years of effort to improve China's situation had thus resulted in making it worse.

Reform and Revolution

While the first generation of reformers had been full of confidence and almost arrogant about their chances of success, the second generation was less certain.

Most of them felt strongly that China would have to be saved at all costs, even if it meant drastically changing or discarding Confucianism. This change of priorities marks an important step away from culturalism and toward nationalism. Some also began to blame China's problems on the fact that non-Han Chinese occupied the throne.

One of the most interesting of the second-generation reformers was a scholar named Yan Fu. Reading and translating the works of many Western philosophers into Chinese, he originally aimed at a compromise between Western thought and that of traditional China. Yan was struck by Herbert Spencer's theory of social Darwinism, which applies Darwin's concept of survival of the fittest to nations. Spencer's ideas seemed most relevant: Many Chinese scholars during the last quarter of the nineteenth century did entertain doubts about their country's survivability. Eventually, Yan Fu came to the rather devastating conclusion that the Confucian system could not be preserved and that, in fact, there was a fundamental flaw in the entire *ti–yong* dichotomy: Western civilization contained an essence (*ti*) of its own, of which the coveted items for practical use (*yong*) were manifestations.

As is common during times of widespread dissatisfaction with the status quo, those who wanted change fell into three broad categories: reformers, reactionaries, and revolutionaries.

The Reformers

The most famous of the reformers was Kang Youwei (1858–1927). After passing the first level of the imperial examination system while still quite young, he became passionately interested in Western studies, especially science. He then began writing to the emperor about the need for reform.

After Tongzhi's death in 1874, Cixi chose her husband's 6-year-old nephew to succeed him. He reigned as the Guangxu emperor (1875–1908), though functioning as little more than her puppet during his childhood. As time went on, the empress dowager gradually took less interest in the affairs of government, and Guangxu gained in stature. The emperor, perhaps flattered, since it was quite unusual for people to pay so much attention to him as opposed to his aunt, agreed to receive Kang in person, a rare privilege.

Kang's technique for reforming China was to entirely reinterpret Confucius, describing the great sage as a progressive and dismissing as forgeries those ancient writings that conflicted with his point of view. Kang's plan was to find support for Western ideas within the Chinese tradition so that traditional Chinese, who would otherwise be unable to accept ideas from the West, could do so with a clear conscience.

In 1898, Kang managed to persuade the emperor to promulgate a daring set of reforms. Called the "Hundred Days Reforms"—because they were in effect only for that period of time—they included:

- *a revamp of the examination system.* Questions were to be chosen from current problems rather than from the Confucian classics.

- *the establishment of a bureau of agriculture, industry, and commerce in Beijing.* This was aimed at fostering and coordinating the sectors that would provide the basis for creating greater prosperity for the country.
- *the abolition of sinecure positions.* There were a number of these at the time. The official in charge of grain transportation, for example, had no responsibility for transportation, and the official in charge of the salt monopoly had no salt fields to supervise.
- *the establishment of a regular foreign office.* This would succeed the proto-foreign office set up under the Tongzhi restoration.

Unfortunately, Kang had persuaded only the emperor of the wisdom of these reforms. The empress dowager, the nobles, and the officials, including those who controlled military power, had never even been consulted about the changes, much less consented to them. Seeing their status threatened by Kang's reforms, these influential groups agreed that both Kang and the emperor would have to be dealt with. Rumors of Guangxu's ill health began to circulate, and the empress dowager, professing great reluctance, stepped in to conduct government affairs again. Helped by a leading military commander Yuan Shikai, she effected a *coup d'état*. Although Kang escaped to Japan, a number of his followers were executed. Guangxu was put under the equivalent of house arrest, and the reforms were rescinded.

The Reactionaries

The failure of the Hundred Days Reforms weakened the reform movement while strengthening the more extremist forces of ultraconservatism and revolution. The ultraconservatives made their move first. Many Qing officials began to support, at least tacitly but sometimes openly, a violently xenophobic movement. The literal translation of the movement's Chinese name, *Yihetuan*, is "Fists of Righteous Harmony," but Westerners referred to its practitioners as Boxers because the ritual calisthenics they practiced somewhat resembled shadow-boxing.

The Boxers' leader believed he had received a command from the Jade Emperor, a Daoist deity, to kill all foreigners. They stalked and murdered Western missionaries, Chinese Christians, and foreign officials, often horribly mutilating them. The empress dowager played a delicate game: encouraging the Boxers covertly while publicly deploring their actions.

In 1900, the Qing government declared war on the foreign powers, and the Boxers laid siege to the foreign legation sector in Beijing. After two difficult months, the siege was lifted by an allied force from eight foreign nations. Its arrival forced Cixi, dressed as a peasant, to flee from the capital in a crude cart. Through no fault of her own, the empress dowager had not been outside the imperial palace since she was a teenager. The condition of the Chinese countryside therefore came as a shock. This experience, the death of many prominent ultraconservatives, and the humiliating settlement exacted by the foreign powers left Cixi with little choice but to institute reforms.

Over the next few years, many of the reforms that Kang Youwei had called for, including the establishment of a regular foreign office and the abolition of many sinecure positions, were instituted. The examination system, in both its civil and military forms, was ended altogether. Traditional Confucian academies were converted into Western-style universities, and students were encouraged to go abroad to learn. Provinces were told to establish Western-style military academies to train officers rather than, as in the past, recruit them through the military examination system. A Ministry of Education and a Ministry of Police were established. However, the reforms may have come too late. In 1908, realizing that her end was near, Cixi had the Guangxu emperor poisoned and arranged for yet another small child to assume the throne. She died the next day. In 1911, the dynasty itself fell.

The Revolutionaries

Sun Yat-sen, leader of the forces of revolution, was born to a poor family in Guangdong province, not far from Hong Kong, in about 1866. His elder brother went to Hawaii as a common laborer, prospered, and sent for his sibling. Enrolled in one of the most expensive and prestigious Western-style schools in Honolulu, young Sun excelled in English and declared his intention to become a Christian. Unhappy with the conversion, his brother sent Sun home, where Sun promptly destroyed the idols in the village temple. After this scandalous act of civic desecration Sun's father packed him off to Hong Kong, where he formally became a Christian and earned his medical degree. He also began to advocate the overthrow of the Qing.

In 1894, shortly after the outbreak of the Sino–Japanese War, Sun founded his first revolutionary society, the *Xingzhong Hui*, or Revive China Society, with some friends. The society advocated establishing schools to educate the masses, newspapers to help them become good citizens, and industries to improve their standard of living. Among those who joined were a financially successful American-educated Chinese businessman named Charles Jones Soong and his wife. Sun Yat-sen later married one of the Soong daughters.

The revolutionaries tried to smuggle arms and dynamite into China from Hong Kong but failed. Sun managed to escape not only this but several other efforts to apprehend him. He began to travel around the world raising money, mainly from among overseas Chinese communities, to support the revolution. In 1897, Qing secret agents caught Sun in London and imprisoned him in the Chinese legation there, pending the Qing government's authorization of the money for his passage back to certain death in China. Ironically, the very inefficiency that Sun railed against saved his life. While the wheels of Qing bureaucracy creaked slowly, Sun convinced a chambermaid that he would be executed because he was a Christian, and she agreed to get a message to one of his former medical school professors. Finding the British government uninterested in interfering with internal Chinese affairs, the professor turned to London's yellow press. Their sensationalized story of a persecuted Christian, to whose plight Her Majesty's government was utterly indifferent, created sufficient official embarrassment that Sun was eventually released. The incident also made him a celebrity.

Sun continued his fund-raising activities and refined his ideology. In 1905, he founded a new organization, the *Tongmeng Hui*, or Alliance Society, which was later to become the Kuomintang (KMT), or Nationalist Party. It had four slogans: Drive out the Manchus, recover China for the Chinese, establish a republic, and equalize landownership. Sun described his country as a "sheet of loose sand," with the individual particles rolling over each other in response to external forces. His new organization was intended to cement these pieces together in order to form a counterforce capable of resisting these forces.

In 1911, in the Yangtze River port of Wuhan, one of the Tongmeng Hui's homemade bombs exploded by accident. With the location of their arsenal thus revealed, society members had to fight to protect themselves. This provided the spark for the overthrow of the Qing dynasty: As news of the Wuhan uprising spread, it roused others to action in many different parts of the country. Sun himself was on a fund-raising trip in the United States at the time, and learned about the revolution from a newspaper.

The Qing court turned for help to Yuan Shikai, the general Cixi had used to put down the Hundred Days Reforms in 1898. However, the court, fearing that Yuan had become too powerful, had dismissed him in 1909 on totally specious grounds of ill health. The general therefore had little incentive to rush into the fray, and informed the court that unfortunately his ill health prevented him from commanding armies. Meanwhile, Manchus were being massacred throughout China. After extensive bargaining with both the court and the revolutionaries, Yuan Shikai exacted his compromise: The Republic of China was founded, with himself as president.

The 1911 revolution was better at tearing down than building up. The abolition of the traditional examination system had meant the end of the scholar-official class that had provided such an important support for the dynasty and undermined the basis of the gentry class, which had been an important factor in the stability of China's vast rural areas. This left a virtual administrative vacuum in the countryside. In addition, students now attended Western-style universities in China's major cities. This outflow of intellectuals meant less understanding of the problems of China's rural areas—which then constituted about 90 percent of the country—than had been the case before. The gap between the Westernized city dweller and the Chinese peasant widened, compounding the problems of government.

The connection between civilian government and the military had deteriorated as well. The professional officers turned out by the new provincial military academies founded by the empress dowager's decree were more likely to feel loyal to their regional commanders than to the central government.

While peasants raised their crops in much the same way that their ancestors had, intellectuals gathered in university common rooms and urban teahouses to discuss ideologies. Sun Yat-sen's infant KMT could not provide a check on Yuan Shikai, who grew increasingly autocratic, even attempting, unsuccessfully, to make himself emperor. Yuan died in 1916, ushering in a period of warlordism as various military leaders vied with each other to succeed him.

The most obvious characteristic of warlordism is war, with capturing Beijing as the prize. Since Beijing had been the imperial capital, control of it conferred a certain prestige as well as access to such of the central government machinery as was still functioning. Moreover, because foreign nations had decided to regard whoever was in charge of the government in Beijing as the legal government of China, the incumbent received international legitimacy as well as customs revenue and better access to foreign loans. However, contracting these loans had the simultaneous effect of increasing both China's already large foreign debt and the pressures that foreign governments could put on the country. Foreign governments were not, of course, confined to dealing with the person in charge of Beijing, and they often had contacts with, and made loans to, several warlords. Since one of the charges leveled against the Qing was that it capitulated to foreign pressure, the new situation was not only no improvement, but actually regressive.

Warlordism was regressive in other ways as well. It was by nature divisive, thereby weakening the strength of the country as a whole. It was a distinct disincentive to production and commerce. For example, taxes might be levied at each section of a road controlled by a different warlord. Several warlords were competent governors with carefully thought-out plans for their areas, including literacy programs, economic development schemes, sanitation codes, and strict regulations against opium smoking, gambling, corruption, and even littering. However, the warlord era was not good for China as a nation.

While the decade following the 1911 revolution was unsatisfactory from the point of view of solving many of the problems on the revolutionaries' agenda, it was an exciting time intellectually. Translations of many of the West's leading political philosophers became available, and heated discussions took place about how relevant their theories were to China. In addition, Chinese who had studied abroad returned, contributing their observations and experiences to the discussions.

World War I and Its Aftermath

The outbreak of World War I was at first beneficial to China. Factories in its major cities expanded to meet increased demand from the belligerent countries and, preoccupied with the war effort, Western powers eased their pressures on China. Unfortunately, however, Japanese pressure increased markedly without the West to intervene on its behalf. Many of China's new industries were Japanese owned and managed. In 1915, Tokyo presented the Chinese government with a long list known as the Twenty-One Demands, which indicated that it had far greater ambitions than factory ownership. If implemented, they would have made China into a quasi-colony.

Chinese intellectuals were impressed by Woodrow Wilson's Fourteen Points, especially those promising self-determination and the return of territories seized by force. When it began to look as though the Allies would be victorious, China joined them in a declaration of war, sending a large number of laborers to Europe to aid in the war effort. This exposed a number of young Chinese, including future leaders Deng Xiaoping and Zhou Enlai, to Western influences. Allied victory was expected to mean, at the very least, the return of the area in Shandong province that China had been forced to lease to Germany.

The merits and drawbacks of differing social and political systems were debated in a number of newly founded journals. Neither capitalism nor communism had much initial appeal, the latter because Marx himself had felt it inappropriate for any but the most developed countries. Anarchism had many advocates—including, at one point, the young Mao Zedong. Most intellectuals were sympathetic to socialist ideas, particularly the moderate forms espoused by eminent British philosopher Bertrand Russell, and John Dewey, an American known for his advocacy of pragmatism. Echoing this message, prominent Chinese intellectual Hu Shi advocated the slogan "more study of problems and less talk of isms."

The feelings of hope and optimism that pervaded this period received a rude shock on April 30, 1919, with the announcement of the terms of the Versailles Treaty that formally ended World War I. Rather than returning Shandong to China, the treaty awarded it to Japan, which had also been on the victorious side in the war and claimed Shandong as its prize. Chinese patriots were horrified to learn that their country's delegate had acquiesced in this abomination, undoubtedly because he felt unable to do anything else: The Japanese had already taken Shandong from the Germans in 1914. Yet another shock was finding out that, during the war, the Chinese government had secretly agreed to most of the humiliating Twenty-One Demands Japan had presented it with in 1915. The Versailles Treaty destroyed the faith that many of the new intelligentsia had placed in the West.

On May 4, 1919, several thousand students demonstrated in Beijing. A scuffle with police ensued, with some injuries resulting. One student subsequently died of his wounds, setting off a nationwide strike in which the students were joined by merchants and other members of the new urban middle class. Work strikes, anti-government harangues, and boycotts of Japanese goods continued for six weeks; Japanese nationals were accosted and beaten. Finally, on June 12, the Chinese cabinet resigned. If the Versailles Treaty had disillusioned Chinese intellectuals about the West, the May Fourth movement showed them what a group of dedicated activists could accomplish. The May Fourth generation was a generation in revolt against many aspects of its culture, and the movement had effects in a number of fields, including a renewed attack on the Confucian family system and an impetus toward the vernacular written language. It also resulted in a rejuvenated KMT and in the founding of the Chinese Communist Party (CCP). Since the KMT and the CCP were to coexist, usually not peacefully, in differing but always complicated relationships for many years, it is important to understand these interactions as well as the plans that each had for China.

The Kuomintang

While Yuan Shikai's successors vied for power in northern China, Sun Yat-sen's KMT supporters made their way to Guangzhou, capital of Sun's home province of Guangdong and contiguous to Hong Kong. There they set up a provisional military government, with Sun as generalissimo. At this point, the KMT government did not look very different from those of the warlords elsewhere in China, except that Sun had no military experience. Factionalism within the party made it difficult to accomplish anything. Sun, though a superb orator, lacked basic organizational skills and had become increasingly irritable with dissent. The KMT's future looked none too bright.

Following the Bolshevik Revolution in 1917, the new Soviet government began to cast about for ways to help spread world revolution, and Sun Yat-sen came to its attention. Certain of his ideas, such as the primacy of economic relations, and his frequent references to the need to improve the livelihood of the common people, sounded properly socialistic. Representatives of the Communist International (Comintern) made initial overtures to several warlords, including Sun. Comintern representative Adolph Joffe subsequently conferred at some length with Sun, seeing immediately that what the KMT needed was reorganization. The Soviets offered to provide it.

After some negotiation, the Sun–Joffe Manifesto was signed in January 1923. In it, Sun recognized the desirability of friendship with, and help from, the Soviet Union. Joffe acknowledged that there was no necessary connection between Soviet help and the adoption of communist ideology. Members of the CCP were to join the KMT as individuals, in the so-called Bloc Within of what was to be the First United Front.

Within a month, the USSR began to supply Sun Yat-sen with money and arms, and Comintern advisers were reorganizing the KMT along Leninist lines. Fundamentally, this involved reconstituting the KMT so that it could be the one party ruling a one-party state, while also taking Sun Yat-sen's ideas into account. What emerged is known as the five-*yuan* system, in which the familiar Western-style triad of legislature, executive, and judiciary is supplemented by an examination yuan and a control yuan. The examination yuan was to supervise a modern civil service examination and the control yuan was to investigate improprieties in government, much as the censorate had done in imperial China.

Sun and his supporters wrote a new constitution that gave Sun almost dictatorial powers. However, his actual power continued to be contingent on the loyalty of various military groups. Soviet advisers suggested founding a military academy to train loyal officers so that there would be no need to rely on warlord, regional, or mercenary troops. The Whampoa Military Academy duly came into existence. Its first commander was Sun's deputy, Chiang Kai-shek; somewhat later, Zhou Enlai was appointed political commissar.

The Comintern representatives also provided public relations advice. Sun was already an excellent speaker, able to present complex, abstract ideas in a nonacademic way that audiences found spellbinding. The Comintern representatives simply worked at packaging his message better. In book form his *San Min Zhu Yi* (Three Principles of the People) became the bible of the KMT; set to music, the Three Principles provided the Republic of China with its national anthem. The book itself is somewhat disorganized and illogical, partly because it is a faithful reflection of Sun's somewhat disorganized and illogical thought. Derived from a series of lectures in 1924, the manuscript was rushed immediately into print before its contradictions had been reconciled: Getting the book out quickly seemed more important.

The Three Principles are people's nationalism, people's sovereignty, and people's livelihood; Sun explicitly linked them with Abraham Lincoln's government by the people, of the people, and for the people. Before the 1911 revolution, Sun had used nationalism to mean opposition to the Manchu government, whom he blamed for China's problems. His advocacy of a "real" Chinese—that is, Han—government represented an important step away from the culturalism—i.e. adherence to Confucian norms—that had characterized the Chinese tradition. Sun's precept was ethnically based and closer to Western nationalism.

After the fall of the Manchu dynasty, Sun changed the content of people's nationalism to mean opposition to foreign imperialism. Incredibly, he tried to scare the Chinese into nationalist consciousness by predicting that the country would die out for lack of population. People's sovereignty would be achieved by introducing the rights of initiative, referendum, and recall so that people could check the excesses of government. Unfortunately, the processes of initiative, referendum, and recall are rather difficult for the general public to organize, and are not considered very successful in the West where they were invented.

People's livelihood is the principle in which Sun appears closest to left-wing thought; yet he was no Marxist, explicitly rejecting the idea that material forces determine history. He also characterized Marx as a social pathologist rather than as a social psychologist, observing that Marx described the evils of the capitalist system rather than the capitalist system itself. Sun believed that capitalism should be reformed, not destroyed. The Three Principles of the People—their specific interpretations somewhat revised to soften the criticisms of Marx—and Sun himself are held in esteem in China today.

Sun Yat-sen died in 1925 and was succeeded by Chiang Kai-shek, who used his position as head of the Whampoa Military Academy to mobilize support for his leadership. The Whampoa clique, as it came to be called, would form the core of Chiang's support throughout his tenure on the mainland. Chiang proceeded to inaugurate the Northern Expedition, a military campaign aimed at bringing all of China under KMT rule (Map 3.1). This it did, at least in the formal sense. In December 1928, the KMT took control of Beijing, thereby becoming the acknowledged legitimate government of China, but victory had been obtained at a cost, which was to infinitely increase the problems of governance. While some warlords had been conquered, others had simply been co-opted, with Chiang designating them governors of the provinces they had ruled. This meant that they retained a great deal of autonomy from the KMT central government and Chiang, thereby weakening the authority of the KMT. In addition, in the course of the Northern Expedition, Chiang had definitively ended his united front with the communists, who as a result became a party in overt opposition.

This expedition, from 1926 to 1928, unified, at least nominally, most of China under the Nationalist (Kuomintang) government of Chiang Kai-shek,

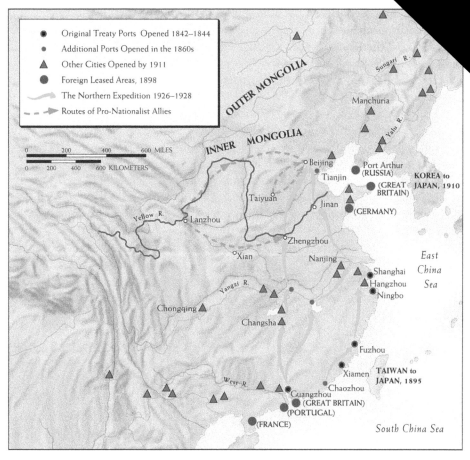

MAP 3.1 The Northern Expedition of the Kuomintang

inaugurating the Nanjing decade. Semi-autonomous co-opted warlords continued to exercise power on the periphery.

Chiang also jettisoned large portions of the more left-wing aspects of KMT ideology and rehabilitated Confucius. In 1928, Chiang ordered his military officers to spend their leisure time studying the Confucian classics. Confucius's birthday became a national holiday, and Confucian temples received government protection. In 1934, Chiang inaugurated the New Life Movement, based on Confucian virtues that were updated to link their abstract concepts to twentieth-century goals, including injunctions against eating noisily, spitting, smoking, and bad posture as well as admonitions to kill rats and flies, be punctual, and use native products. The KMT also tried to revive the gentry class so that it could back up central government directives and influence the common folk to comply. In yet another effort to assist in local control, the *baojia* system was revived.

Although a loyal disciple of Sun, Chiang was a very different person. Born in 1887 to a prosperous salt merchant family in Zhejiang, he had a classical

by study at a Japanese military academy. Whereas Sun turally and linguistically, among China, Hong Kong, Japan, ted States, Chiang had relatively little knowledge of foreign ot traveled much abroad. He was not, however, a tradition-nineteenth-century traditionalists had been, being an enthu-ndustrialization and railroad building. The main centers of KMT support were in large industrial cities and included China's newly emerging middle class. Chiang also made considerable use of foreign advisers.

Like Sun Yat-sen, Chiang had married a daughter of Charles Soong. Unlike Sun, Chiang was not a Christian, although he converted in deference to the wishes of his bride and her family, and thereafter attended church services regularly. The attractive and articulate Soong Mei-ling, a graduate of Wellesley College's class of 1917, played an important role in interpreting the West for her husband and in interpreting the KMT in the West. Nonetheless, Chiang Kai-shek's ideas were formed much more within the Chinese tradition than were Sun's. The failures of the KMT government on the mainland are unconnected to these expressions and formulas. Indeed, the KMT moved its five-yuan government, Confucian precepts, and industrialization strategy to Taiwan, where modernization within a steadily changing tradition enjoyed great success. If Chiang's eclectic blend of the old and new cannot directly be credited with this success, neither can his formula be said to have hindered it. The mandate of heaven was not to belong to the KMT for very long before it passed to the Chinese Communist Party.

The Communist Road to Power
The Early Years: 1919–1923

The founding of the Chinese Communist Party (CCP) resulted from the convergence of two events: the victory of the Bolsheviks in Russia in 1917, and the rising wave of nationalism in China in the wake of the Versailles settlement in 1919 (see p. 56). Most intellectuals considered Marxism inapplicable to China because the country's proletarian class was so small. Some, however, argued that China was actually a part of the world proletariat, since foreign imperialists were exploiting the Chinese people in a manner similar to the way capitalists exploited their own workers. Conveniently, the Chinese term for proletariat, borrowed from the Japanese, translates as "propertyless class" and, therefore, could be applied to the many peasants who did not own the land on which they worked.

The fact that Marx described his developmental scheme as scientifically based and culturally neutral was also appealing. Chinese who felt both humiliated by the West and disgusted with its behavior had no desire to borrow from it. Marx, by contrast, was highly critical of the political and economic systems of the West. He argued that what appear to be *national* characteristics are, in reality, the characteristics of *bourgeois* society. Abolishing capitalist rule would open the way for the emergence of a common proletarian culture in which the exploitation of one group by another simply would not occur. Moreover, Marx promised immediate results, which seemed far more preferable to the time-consuming gradualism advocated by people like John Dewey. An apocalyptic revolution would sweep away problems. In addition, the founding of the Soviet Union in what had been regarded as one of Europe's most industrially backward areas—and much of whose land area was located in Asia—seemed to indicate that China could have such an apocalyptic revolution, despite its lack of indus-trialization. A number of prestigious intellectuals became attracted by a Marxist solution for China's problems, as were several less prestigious figures, including a young clerk at the Beida library named Mao Zedong.

Mao was born in 1893 to a rich peasant family in Hunan. His strict father sent him to a Confucian academy for a traditional education. Resistant from the outset, young Mao hid bandit novels behind the Confucian texts and read those instead. He also refused to consummate the marriage his father, following tradi-tional practices, had arranged for him. One of Mao's earliest writings, prompted by the suicide of a young woman who chose suicide rather than an arranged mar-riage to a man she did not love, concerned the evils of the traditional family sys-tem. He was also intensely concerned with the plight of his country, and devoted much thought to discovering the reasons for China's weakness. Another of his early writings castigates the traditional distaste for physical labor. A lifetime of indolence, Mao argued, creates weaklings; a nation of weaklings is a weak nation. In the wake of the Bolshevik Revolution and the May Fourth Movement, Mao found in Marx a quick solution to strengthening China.

The suddenness of the conversion of this group had important implications for the future development of communism in China. Its members had never sys-tematically studied Marxism. Early Chinese communists were thus quite unlike European and Russian Marxists, who typically spent years studying and debating the fine points of Marxist theory before they decided to participate in the kinds of activities indicated by the communist worldview. The group around Chen and Li first became committed to a course of action to effect a Marxist-style revolution; only later did they accept even the basic assumptions of the Marx-ist worldview—for example, Marx's internationalism. Communism's appeal to Chinese intellectuals was that it provided an immediate solution for *China*. In addition, since its members had no strong attachments to Marxist formulations, they found it relatively easy to change these formulations to fit the needs of the Chinese situation. This gave Chinese communism a certain amount of flexibility, but would later lead to debates on what was orthodox and what was not: One person's idea of creative adaptation of the sacred texts may be another person's definition of revisionist heresy.

Initially, this was not a major problem: On July 1, 1921, 12 people arranged to meet quietly in Shanghai's French quarter, where they were less likely to be harassed by the Chinese authorities. Here, the CCP was formally founded, with delegates arguing about such questions as whether to cooperate with the bour-geoisie and, if so, how much. They reached a consensus that the party should work toward the eventual achievement of a dictatorship of the working class but must be prepared to cooperate with other parties during a transitional period of unspecified length, and to give immediate priority to the organization of trade unions in China. The members also agreed to make full use of the experience and example of the Soviet Union.

The Period of Soviet Control: 1923–1931

Initial efforts at first seemed promising: Railway workers proved enthusiastic converts, and other unions were founded at Anshan, China's largest iron works, and elsewhere. Hence, the signing of the Sun–Joffe Manifesto in January 1923 came as an unpleasant shock. Its provisions for a united front between the CCP and the KMT seemed to undermine the party's previous successes. The blow was not appreciably softened by Comintern advisors telling the CCP leaders that they would not actually be surrendering the CCP's independence, since party members were to join the KMT only as individuals. They continued to regard the united front decision as both unnecessary and unwise.

Subsequent events made the Comintern's decision seem wiser. One warlord brutally suppressed a railway strike, while another broke the powerful Beijing–Hankou Railway Workers' Union. Many of the strikers were killed, and those union organizers who survived were arrested. The Chinese labor union movement entered a period of decline.

The uneasy "Bloc Within," or First United Front between the KMT and CCP, continued until 1927, with the Soviet leadership maintaining that after Chiang Kai-shek and his bourgeois-democratic party had served their purpose—the unification of China—they would be discarded. In Stalin's metaphor, Chiang Kai-shek would be squeezed out like a lemon and dumped into the dustbin of history. Chiang, however, was well aware of these plans, and when the Northern Expedition reached Shanghai, it became clear that *he* intended to place the *CCP* in the dustbin. Aided by the Green Gang, a secret society heavily involved in the Shanghai stock market, Chiang very nearly succeeded. A "white terror" of frightening proportions was unleashed in China's urban areas: Those suspected of having any communist sympathies risked immediate execution. Among the victims was Mao Zedong's beloved second wife.

It was no longer possible to pretend that a united front existed. In a cruel irony, the Comintern removed the CCP leader, alleging he had "misunderstood" the policy of the united front. His replacement was ordered to stage uprisings in the cities: Stalin had discovered a "revolutionary upsurge" in China that would allow the CCP to carry on urban insurrections without the cooperation of the KMT. This course of action was even more unrealistic than the united front, since the CCP did not have an army. In fact, it was Stalin who had ordered that they should not have an army, although there appears to have been no disagreement within the CCP on the matter. Its members associated militarism with the warlords, whom they considered their—and China's—enemies.

Armed uprisings were duly carried out in various areas. An insurrection at Nanchang, the capital of Jiangxi province, in August 1927 marked the first organized use of military force by the communists. A second occurred in Shantou, on the south China coast. Mao Zedong was actively engaged in these activities, but with a very different focus. His aim was to take advantage of increasing peasant discontent with landlords and officials rather than, as envisioned by Marx, working with the urban proletariat. Mao led the so-called Autumn Harvest uprising in his home province of Hunan. None of these efforts succeeded, with the Comintern holding Mao responsible.

The final failure was that of the Canton (Guangzhou) Commune in December 1927. Not having uniforms, party members distinguished themselves from their enemies by wearing red kerchiefs or armbands. After realizing they were losing, the communists ripped off these identifying badges and threw them away. Unfortunately, the red dye that had run out of the kerchiefs and armbands proved almost impossible to get off their skin. Government troops tore open people's jackets to check for stains and bayoneted those who did not pass the test.

The Canton uprising received worldwide press coverage and was a failure of such magnitude that Stalin was forced to reconsider the party line. Rather than take responsibility for the debacle himself, Stalin chose to blame the CCP leader he had chosen, accusing him of "putschism." His replacement, one of the few CCP members who actually had a proletarian background, was ordered to establish an urban base but failed, and was, like his predecessors, removed from office. The brutality of the "white repression" had made it very dangerous for workers to even express sympathy for the communist cause, much less overtly support the CCP. Moreover, the party leadership had failed the workers cruelly. The KMT was itself making reforms, including supporting the organization of trade unions. Communists castigated these as "yellow" unions designed to distract the proletariat's attention from preparing for the revolution that alone could save it. Workers, however, viewed the unions as a safer way to press for more benefits. Meanwhile, party membership had dwindled to about 15,000. A small dedicated urban hard core met in highly secret groups in industrial cities.

The Jiangxi Soviet: 1931–1934

Following the failure of the Autumn Harvest uprising, Mao withdrew to a remote area on the border between Jiangxi and Fujian, where he founded what would later come to be known as the Jiangxi soviet. It was precisely the setting of the bandit novels that had so intrigued Mao as a boy. Here, Mao established a rural base area. He was aided by a ragtag army led by Zhu De, a reformed opium addict with some military training. Zhu and Mao cooperated with bandits and secret societies, some of whose members agreed to serve in what was then known as the Red Army.

Both base area and army began to grow, with the growth of the army directly related to the expansion of the base area. It was during this time that Mao articulated his philosophy that political power grows out of the barrel of a gun, adding that the party must always control the gun instead of the gun controlling the party. At Jiangxi also, Mao began to work out the principles that would later become known as People's War. Acting on traditional Chinese wisdom that "the army is the fish and the people are the water; the fish cannot swim without the water," Mao tried to enlist the entire population in support of the military. The military was to pay a fair price for anything it took from the people; harassment of civilians could be, and sometimes was, punished with death. The techniques of guerrilla war were developed, with slogans such as "enemy advances, we retreat; enemy retreats, we pursue."

The rudiments of administration were set up: government offices, schools, and medical facilities. While the soviet's constitution proclaimed it a democratic dictatorship of the proletariat and peasantry, in reality the CCP monopolized power, with not even the semblance of a coalition. In addition, its proletariat was confined to village artisans and handicraftsmen.

A radical-sounding land reform law was also less than it seemed. Landlords and rich peasants managed to retain political authority by declaring their loyalty to the new regime. Hence, they were able to control the implementation of land reform, either completely avoiding the confiscation of their land or arranging to have the best land allocated to themselves. This did not satisfy the poor peasants, whose continuing demands led to repeated redistributions. More than once, the government had to stop a redistribution in order to save crop production. The Jiangxi soviet exerted relatively tenuous control over the scattered mountain areas that were nominally under its jurisdiction.

Mao's soviet faced external problems that were just as troublesome as those of internal management. There was a great deal of interference from the CCP's politburo in Shanghai, which was concerned with maintaining a link, however tenuous, with the proletariat in whose name the revolution was to be fought. The Comintern had conferred the CPP leadership on a group of people known as the "Returned Student" group or "the Twenty-Eight Bolsheviks": young party members who had studied at Moscow's Sun Yat-sen University. Mao and his supporters considered this group to be almost as out of touch with Chinese reality as their Soviet mentors and tried to ignore them as far as possible. In 1932/1933, Chiang Kai-shek's repression forced the Central Committee to move its headquarters from Shanghai to the Jiangxi soviet. Some of the Returned Student group received influential positions there, consonant with Mao's tendency during this period to absorb rather than eliminate rivals. However, their leader, Mao's chief nemesis within the group, was sent back to Moscow as China's delegate to the Comintern.

The Central Committee's relocation to the Jiangxi soviet marked a formal end to the CCP's urban link and also a sharp drop in the degree of the USSR's control over the CCP. The claim to an urban base, and the degree to which the Soviet Union exercised control over the communist movement in China, had been weakening for some years. Comintern advisers lamented that, despite their best efforts, what had started out as a proletarian revolutionary movement had degenerated into a typical Chinese peasant rebellion. Such disillusionment with the CCP led Stalin to refer to the Chinese communists as "margarine communists" or "radish communists": red on the outside but white within.

To summarize the important events of the Jiangxi period: First, it saw the development of the technique of building up rural base areas from which to begin the takeover of China and the abandonment of the technique of urban insurrection to achieve this end. Second, a regular army was created to aid in this task. Third, the CCP became increasingly independent of ideological direction from the Soviet Union. Fourth and finally, Mao Zedong rose to a position of de facto pre-eminence in the CCP although he was not yet formally acknowledged as its leader.

The Long March: 1934–1935

Chiang Kai-shek had not forgotten about the communists who had fled to the countryside. In addition to trying to eradicate CCP cells in urban areas, he attempted to encircle and destroy the rural soviets. What began as one encirclement campaign in November 1930 grew into five, with the first two being fairly perfunctory. Partly, this was because the KMT had underestimated the CCP. But the KMT was also riven by factionalism, and its co-opted warlords, wanting to protect their own troops, did not always obey Chiang's orders. The third encirclement campaign, in 1931, may well have succeeded had the Japanese not chosen this moment to step up their pressure on China.

After assassinating the KMT-affiliated warlord of northeast China, the Japanese army seized the three northeastern provinces and, in 1931, set up a puppet kingdom called Manchukuo (Manchu country). The Qing emperor who had been deposed in 1911 was enthroned as its ruler, but was surrounded by Japanese advisers. In response, Chiang withdrew his troops from Jiangxi and moved them to Shanghai. An all-out war with Japan seemed imminent. Knowing that he had no chance to win a confrontation with the superbly trained and highly motivated Imperial Japanese Army, Chiang succeeded in avoiding war, though at the cost of damaging his image. Chiang's decision had been correct in that it avoided unnecessary bloodshed, but it angered many patriots who were already hypersensitive to the humiliations of foreign pressures on China. Chiang argued that the Japanese were but a disease of the skin, whereas the CCP represented a more serious, internal problem. He also reasoned, correctly, that the Japanese and the Americans would eventually go to war and that the United States would prevail, thereby curing the skin disease. Hence, Chiang turned his attention back to the communists and prepared for a fourth encirclement campaign.

Meanwhile, there were differences of opinion within the CCP on how to cope with the encirclement campaigns. Mao's preferred tactics of highly mobile guerrilla warfare predominated in the first three campaigns, and were blamed for the near-annihilation of the Jiangxi soviet during the 1931 campaign. During the fourth encirclement campaign, CCP military leaders advocated a strategy of defense beyond the borders of the soviet, as opposed to Mao's technique of trying to lure the enemy deep into his territory and attacking its troops there. This turned out to be ill advised, since it intruded on the turf of a number of landlords and turned them against the communists. Whereas their attitude had previously been that the KMT and CCP were equally bad, the landlords now decided to support the KMT. During the fifth encirclement campaign, Chiang adopted a strategy of building blockhouses in an ever-tightening circle around the soviet, and it was landlord control of the *baojia* system that provided the manpower to build these blockhouses. As the blockhouse strategy began to succeed, the Jiangxi soviet experienced acute shortages of medicine, cloth, kerosene, and even salt. However, as the KMT's net grew tighter, it became apparent that the blockhouses were not being built in a complete circle according to plan. Here again, the piecemeal way in which the KMT had unified China inhibited its strategy. To the east and north of the Jiangxi soviet, units who were loyal to the KMT built blockhouses as ordered. But areas to the south and west of the Jiangxi soviet were controlled by warlords who wanted to overthrow Chiang. They built no blockhouses and kept their military forces concentrated in county seats.

This gap in the blockhouse circle allowed the communists to break out, abandoning the Jiangxi soviet and beginning the arduous trek across China that is known to history as the Long March. In October 1934, an estimated 100,000 men and 35 women, one of them Mao's pregnant third wife, crossed Jiangxi province and entered Hunan. Later communist writings have glorified the march, describing participants' courageous struggle against strong resistance. They also allege that the reason for the march was to fight Japan. Foreign scholarship, however, indicates that about 70 percent of the troops deserted relatively early on, and that it was fear of annihilation by the KMT rather than a desire to fight Japan that motivated the Long March.

Efforts at mythologizing the Long March notwithstanding, the fact that even a small percentage of the group survived represents a triumph over adversity. The KMT's efforts at annihilation were a minor part of the CCP's problems. Chiang Kai-shek needed to be concerned with keeping up the strength of his own troops *vis-à-vis* potential warlord rivals, and he therefore tried to destroy the Red Army with minimal involvement of his own units. In several instances, warlords who likewise did not wish to weaken themselves by fighting the communists simply withdrew and allowed the Long Marchers to pass through. However, other hazards awaited the CCP. The march had begun in October and passed through wild, mountainous terrain during the coldest months of the year. The locals were generally not hospitable. Often, they were members of ethnic minorities who had been pushed into marginal lands by the expansion of the Han Chinese state (see Chapter 2) and were quite resentful of the Han. The marchers were set upon by Yi snipers with rifles, had boulders rolled down on them by Tibetans as they filed through narrow mountain gorges, and were attacked by skilled Muslim cavalrymen who despised infidels.

The progress of the Long March was further impeded because its leaders had no clear destination in mind (Map 3.2). Having failed in an attempt to link up with another, smaller soviet in northern Hunan province, the march turned west to Sichuan. In January 1935, the exhausted survivors decided to rest in a desolate

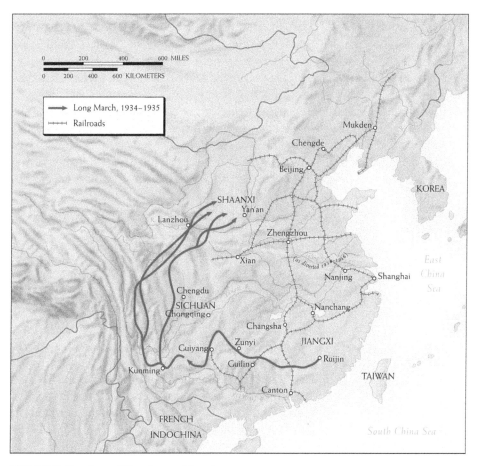

MAP 3.2 Routes of the Long March

area of Guizhou province called Zunyi. It was here that Mao Zedong, whose career had suffered as a result of the poor results his military strategy had yielded in 1931, called for an enlarged conference of the CCP's politburo. Supported by several of the party's important military figures, he emerged as the dominant figure in the politburo. The Zunyi conference was the great turning point in Mao's career. Although the wisdom of his decisions would sometimes be challenged, he remained the party's dominant figure until his death in 1976.

Finally, in October 1935, almost exactly a year after the Long March began, an emaciated band of between 7,000 and 10,000 persons straggled into northern Shaanxi, where a small communist base area centered in the city of Yan'an already existed, We have no accurate statistics on how many died en route and how many deserted, but even accepting the higher number of arrivals at Yan'an would amount to less than 10 percent of those who left Jiangxi a year before. Since the total includes some people who became impressed with the communists en route and joined the Long March while it was in progress, the number of original marchers was even smaller.

The Xi'an Incident: 1936

The area the communists entered had been the cradle of Chinese civilization 2,000 years earlier as well as home to three major dynasties. Since then, however, the region had fallen into decline. Severe erosion had destroyed forest land, leaving a thick layer of fine, yellow loess soil. Rainfall was sparse and sporadic. Having no lumber to build houses, people lived in caves hollowed out of loess. The soil was so light that it rose in clouds when disturbed by a passing cart or animal. Those areas where traffic was frequent had become canyons just the width of the vehicles that traversed them, with walls that might reach 40 feet in height. Travelers described the scene as yellow as far as the eye could see: hills, roads, rivers, and houses. There was even a persistent yellow haze in the air.

Already desperately poor, the people of Shaanxi province were suffering from a famine when the Long March arrived in October. At that point, it would have been too late to plant crops even under the best of circumstances; hence, the emigrants' first winter was enormously difficult. Even the most optimistic observer could not have predicted a bright future for the Yan'an base area.

Both the inhabitants and their technology seemed primitive, even by comparison with rural Jiangxi. Peasants required much more indoctrination before they could begin to understand the party's message. One propagandist recalled his frustration in trying to explain the concept of exploitation to bewildered people who insisted that was the way things had always been and always would be. Dedicated party members managed to reconstitute the institutions of government of Jiangxi: schools, a military academy, health care facilities, and social clubs. A campaign to confiscate landlords' land began, though the communists cooperated with other elements in the local power structure, including secret societies. Meanwhile, Chiang Kai-shek was making plans for a sixth encirclement campaign.

Largely, it would seem, to save themselves, CCP leaders had been trying to convince local warlords that it would be best to reconcile their differences in order to fight the Japanese. Most receptive to this message was Zhang Xueliang, son of the warlord whom the Japanese had killed in the process of setting up their client state of Manchukuo: he wanted to avenge his father's death and recoup the lost territory. China's students and intellectuals were also very much in favor of mounting a strong resistance to Japan, as were those who, for vested interests of their own, found Chiang's unwillingness to attack Japan a convenient issue through which to criticize him.

On December 4, 1936, Chiang Kai-shek flew to Xi'an, the capital of Shaanxi, to supervise the attack on the communists. On December 12, he was kidnapped. Some of the details, such as whether the CCP colluded in planning the kidnapping, are murky. Certainly Zhang and the party had common cause, and certainly the CCP was involved in the negotiations with the KMT over Chiang Kai-shek's release. These were complicated: Chiang had a number of rivals within the KMT who had no particular desire to see him return.

After several weeks of intense bargaining, Chiang was released, returning to his capital at Nanjing on Christmas Day 1936. He had agreed to cease his attacks on the communists, to guarantee their "democratic rights," to summon a broadly based conference to unite for "national salvation," to make immediate preparations to resist Japan, and to improve the people's livelihood. The CCP in turn agreed to stop its armed insurrections aimed at overthrowing the KMT, to rename the workers' and peasants' democratic government it had set up at Yan'an as a special region of the Republic of China, to place the Red Army under the jurisdiction of the National Revolutionary Army, to discontinue its policy of confiscating landlords' land, to join in the anti-Japanese united front, and to institute a democratic system based on universal suffrage in the areas under its control.

The Second United Front: 1936–1941

Thus began the period known as the Second United Front. Since the anti-Japanese war effort involved a joint effort between the KMT and the CCP but not individuals from one party joining the other as had been the case with the First United Front, it is also called the Bloc Without. However reluctantly, Chiang Kai-shek had been placed at the head of a movement to resist Japan.

The CCP immediately renamed its soviet the Shaanxi-Gansu-Ningxia (Shaan-Gan-Ning) Special Region of the National Government, and party members expanded their organizing activities in the parts of those three provinces encompassed by the region. Other names were changed in order to conform to the concept of the united front: The Red Army was renamed the Eighth Route Army to indicate that it was now part of the KMT military system. Remnants of forces left behind in central China when the Long March began formed the New Fourth Army. The Red Army Academy became the Resist Japan Academy. Social clubs, previously called Lenin Clubs or Workers' Clubs, now became Salvation [from Japan] Rooms.

In addition to reducing Chiang Kai-shek's attacks against it, the Xi'an settlement had other positive effects for the CCP. Patriots applauded the party's initiative to organize resistance to Japanese pressures, and many Chinese students made the long journey to Yan'an to participate in the resistance movement. The need to resist seemed all the more pressing when, in 1937, Japan began full-scale war against China. The horrific cruelty of the Japanese assault, which aimed at reducing civilian resistance, was documented by foreign photographers and played an important part in mobilizing world opinion on the side of China.

At a more mundane level, the party's agreement to modify its land redistribution plans enabled it to reach out to a wider spectrum of the population. CCP functionaries experimented with, and gained expertise in, the techniques of household registration and tax collection. They were also able to provide the base area with a stable currency, an achievement that would later prove crucial. The population of the Shaan-Gan-Ning base area grew rapidly, from an estimated 600,000 in 1938 to about 1.5 million in 1944. As in the Jiangxi soviet, military power proved to be the spearhead for party expansion. Since high-ranking CCP leaders typically held leading military positions as well, the issue of whether the party controlled the gun, or vice versa, was moot. The majority of these leaders had no formal military education, but gained valuable on-the-job training in this hostile environment of landlords—some of whom had their own armies—plus the KMT and the Japanese.

The Xi'an agreement did nothing to allay the distrust that the CCP and KMT had for each other, and each seemed more concerned with countering the other than with fighting the Japanese. For example, by 1938, the Eighth Route Army had moved into Shandong province, beyond the territory the KMT government had assigned to it, and the New Fourth Army began organizing the population in the Jiangsu–Zhejiang–Anhui area, which was also beyond the scope of the agreement. Chiang Kai-shek became increasingly concerned, with adverse effects on the functioning of the united front.

Meanwhile, the CCP began functioning as a legitimate government. While Shaan-Gan-Ning was not the party's only base area, it was the only one where conditions were stable enough to allow the CCP's programs to be carried out with any consistency. Other areas, often located behind Japanese lines, had to be concerned with survival as a first priority. These bases took general direction from Yan'an but, since they had only minimal ability to communicate, exercised a significant degree of autonomy.

The techniques of *mass mobilization*, already seen in earlier CCP efforts to organize workers and, subsequently, peasants, were further developed and refined during the Yan'an period. Partly because of Leninist influence and partly because of the persecution to which it had been subjected, the CCP was a secretive, elite organization. Yet it wanted to encourage popular participation in its programs. One of the ways in which this was done was to create *mass organizations*, structured to channel the energies of specific groups within the population. There were, for example, a women's group, a youth organization, and peasant and merchant federations. The goal was to have the entire population, including the lowest levels, involved in and supportive of CCP programs.

The first of the party's programs to be carried out after the formation of the united front was *elections*. These had enormous significance, both domestically and internationally. Even before the 1911 revolution, many Chinese intellectuals had come to believe that powerful nations were democratic nations and that holding competitive elections was an important component of democracy. Foreign observers were impressed that a communist party would encourage and permit free elections, thereby contributing to the impression that CCP members were communists of a different—and infinitely preferable—sort.

The election law called for universal, direct, equal suffrage by secret ballot to all those over 16 years of age, regardless of social class. Rhetoric stressed Sun Yat-sen's Three Principles of the People rather than Marxist–Leninist class struggle. Mass organizations were encouraged to nominate and campaign for their candidates. Discussion meetings were held in the villages and townships, with the aim of getting people to discuss local issues and state their opinions. For peasants who had never participated in elections before (indeed, some of them had never even heard of the concept), this was an important educational technique.

Actual balloting took place in an atmosphere resembling a county fair. Since the electorate was largely illiterate, options other than a secret ballot were devised, including dropping beans into jars that had been placed behind the candidates' backs. However, the government thus elected was not the sole decision-making authority. It shared that responsibility with the party, the bureaucracy, the military, and mass organizations in a manner that assured that the party's voice would be the decisive one. Although the process was far from that of an ideal democracy, most observers credited it with being a remarkable achievement under the circumstances.

Land redistribution was another important part of the party's program during the Yan'an period. Under the provisions of the united front, this had to be done in a restricted fashion. It had been agreed that the lands of all anti-Japanese soldiers and those involved in anti-Japanese activities would not be confiscated. Hence even large landlords could escape redistribution by having one son enlist in the Red Army. Nor did the party's program deal with the issue of rationalizing landholdings. Households might own a number of widely scattered plots which took time and energy to commute to and limited the utility of machines that might be better used in a larger, consolidated plot. The party's program neither improved productivity nor prevented an elite group from re-emerging. Nonetheless, the measures taken seem to have been relatively popular with the peasantry, while at the same time not alienating members of the local elite whose support and talents the party wished to retain.

Control of *education* aimed at getting the party's message across to a large number of people as well as teaching them skills that would facilitate economic development. Although the number of primary schools increased greatly after 1937, nearly all were in district capitals. The pupils tended to have families who could afford to send them there, and the curriculum was not really relevant to rural life. Parents viewed education for their children as desirable, but perceived success as having the children become officials and moving out of the village rather than bringing their new skills home with them.

The party attempted to deal with these problems through a series of experiments in popular education, operating on the principle of "management by the people, with government assistance." This shifted the responsibility from party officials and professional teachers to village leaders and grassroots activists, who presumably knew better what was needed and what techniques would work. Night schools, half-day schools, and winter schools—to take advantage of the slack season for peasants—were set up. A *xiaxiang* (to-the-village) movement sent some of the educated youth who had come to Yan'an for patriotic reasons to the villages to teach the peasants. Equally important from Mao's point of view was that these educated urban youth develop an appreciation of the problems that 90 percent of China's population faced. The new schools were also expected to help overcome the gap between urban and rural areas and between mental and manual labor.

As the Yan'an base area grew, so did differences of opinion that Mao worried would weaken party control. His solution, a *zhengfeng*, or rectification, campaign, would become the forerunner of larger, more spectacular mass movements after the founding of the PRC. Peasant activists who were almost exclusively concerned with rural reorganization and urban intellectuals whose primary motivation was anti-Japanese had to be brought together under a common program if the party were to succeed. Since knowledge of Marxism was not widespread and such expertise as existed was concentrated at the higher levels of the party, much study was required.

The several thousand people who participated in the *zhengfeng* were divided into small groups and given documents to study. Many of these were written by Mao or contained interpretations of Marx that he favored. Understanding that blind adherence to party directives would have been counterproductive, Mao sharply criticized those who studied Marx and Lenin as religious dogma, asking his listeners, rhetorically, how they could tell the difference between dogma and dog shit. Dog shit, he answered, was useful; it could fertilize the fields. But dogmas were of no use at all.

Another of Mao's concerns was to make the theory of Marxism relevant to the Chinese situation. If theory could not be put into practice, he argued, then something was wrong with the theory, and it would have to be revised. While agreeing that a communist is a Marxist internationalist, Mao insisted that Marxism had to take on a national form before it could be applied. Calling explicitly for "the sinification of Marxism," he ordered "an end to writing eight-legged essays on foreign models." He rejected the notion of literature and art for the sake of literature and art, stating that all art and literature had a class character. Proletarian art and literature should motivate the masses to struggle to change their environment.

Yet another technique developed during the Yan'an period was the concept of the *mass line*. No matter how successful a *zhengfeng* campaign might be in uniting leaders on the basis of correct views, it would mean little if the masses were not brought along in this consensus. Fundamentally, the motivation behind the mass line was anti-bureaucratic: Cadres were warned not to divorce themselves from the common people and their concerns. "Commandism"—that is, giving orders rather than persuading people to do the right thing—was to be avoided. Again, education played a pivotal role. Occasionally, the masses might not want to behave in a proper manner. ("It sometimes happens that the masses objectively need some reform but are not yet subjectively awakened to it and willing or determined to bring it into effect.") With time and indoctrination, they would adopt the proper view.

The significance of the Yan'an era is that it provided the party with experience in actually administering a territory. This was an enormous benefit, and one not commonly available to movements that seek the overthrow of an existing regime. Techniques of taxation, allocation of resources, education, and popular participation were developed and refined. Although Yan'an provided a blueprint for the future development of China, it would later be charged that Mao Zedong had become too rigidly attached to the "lessons of Yan'an" and was unwilling to face the fact that techniques, which had worked well in the

1930s and 1940s, had become counterproductive by the 1960s and 1970s. Nonetheless, the Yan'an spirit is part of the founding myth of Chinese communism, and continues to be honored, particularly during periods of ideological and economic uncertainty.

Compared to its relative lack of success during the Jiangxi period, the stunning success of the CCP at Yan'an has led to speculation on the reasons. One explanation is that the communists were better able to appeal to the patriotic spirit of the peasantry than the KMT. The CCP was helped immeasurably in this endeavor by the tremendous cruelty that characterized the Japanese occupation, and also by the fact that the Japanese were more firmly ensconced in the areas of north China, near the communist base areas, than they were in the areas of south-central and south China, to which the KMT had fled. Thus, the party was able to win over the peasantry in the course of the struggle against Japan. An alternative explanation downplays the nationalism of the peasants, crediting instead the appeal of the party's economic reforms. The two explanations are not mutually exclusive. It is possible that some people responded primarily to the CCP's anti-Japanese message, others to its economic program, and still others to both.

While both foreign journalists who visited Yan'an and post-1949 communist historiography generally portray Mao's leadership and accomplishments during the periods of the Long March and Yan'an soviet in glowing terms, later scholarship tends to focus on his shortcomings. Some accounts describe Mao as a heartless tyrant who needlessly sacrificed his own followers. Since over 70 years have passed since the events, the truth is difficult to ascertain.

Civil War and Victory: 1941–1949

The united front remained nominally in force during the war with Japan, despite serious tensions. In 1939, for example, 300 communist guerrillas who moved into Shandong in violation of the Xi'an agreement were massacred, presumably on Chiang Kai-shek's orders. The presence of the New Fourth Army in central China also concerned KMT leaders. In January 1941, Chiang ordered it to withdraw north of the Yangtze. When, after a month, the army did not, KMT troops attacked, killing more than 3,000 of its members. Cooperation between KMT and CCP against the Japanese, which had been minimal at best, became still more perfunctory. Following what came to be known as the New Fourth Army Incident, Chiang ordered a cessation of subsidies that had been paid to the communist government under the united front agreement and began a blockade of the Yan'an base area.

An American diplomat residing in China's wartime capital of Chongqing noted that the news of Japan's attack on Pearl Harbor in December 1941 was celebrated as a holiday by both CCP and KMT leaders, since it meant that now the United States would declare war on—and, presumably, defeat—their common enemy. This, of course, left the two more free to fight each other. The United States, now formally fighting on the same side as China, gave Chiang Kai-shek's government substantial sums of money to assist it in fighting Japan. Much of the aid apparently found its way into the pockets of high-ranking government officials, who lived well despite the poverty surrounding them. By contrast, foreign observers commented on the relatively egalitarian conditions that characterized the Yan'an base area.

Meanwhile, the population suffered horribly under the Japanese occupation. Imperial forces had a ready answer to the CCP's slogan that the people were the water and the army the fish: Drain the pond. The "three alls"—kill all, burn all, destroy all—were ruthlessly applied in areas where the Japanese met resistance. Those not killed might be marched long distances away from their homes to serve as forced laborers and prostitutes or become the subjects of grotesque medical experiments. However, no matter how efficient, ruthless, and well trained, the emperor's troops could not be everywhere at once, China is much larger than Japan, with a much bigger population, and Japanese troops had to fight in numerous other areas of the Asian-Pacific hemisphere. Often unnoticed, communist organizers, especially in north China, were able to move into areas where the Japanese were absent. They reinstituted the *baojia* system as part of this effort.

The use of hitherto secret atomic bombs against Hiroshima and Nagasaki brought Japan's surrender more quickly than most people had expected, causing certain difficulties for the change of power in China. Chiang Kai-shek ordered the Japanese to surrender to his representatives rather than to those of the CCP, and had the Americans transport his troops to the north, where the KMT had only a minimal presence, to do so.

The USSR, also on the winning side and, for reasons of geographic proximity, the first Allied power on the scene, managed to delay this process. Moscow also ordered its troops to dismantle whatever they could find of value in Manchuria, home of China's most advanced heavy industry, and bring it to the Soviet Union. Much of this industry had been built by the Japanese. The Soviets also turned over huge stocks of Japanese weapons to the CCP. Now the civil war was on in earnest.

Chiang, again using American transport, moved his troops into north China. His predilection for choosing the commanders who were most loyal to him, rather than the commanders who were most competent to direct battles against the communists, proved unwise. The KMT did enjoy some successes. In 1947 it captured Yan'an, thus formally bringing an end to the Yan'an period. But it also lost several key battles, along with large quantities of American-supplied weapons and vehicles. The morale of KMT troops suffered badly.

Inflation compounded the KMT's problems. A common phenomenon at the end of wars, when pent-up purchasing power seeks to buy scarce consumer goods, dealing with it requires the kind of strong, united, and scrupulously honest government that the KMT was not. Strenuous efforts by some dedicated and honest officials to damp down inflation proved futile. Runaway inflation is apt to disadvantage urban areas most seriously, since rural areas can more easily conduct barter exchanges in food and other crucial commodities. Unfortunately for the KMT, urban areas had provided its original base of support, and that support now slipped away. Meanwhile, the CCP, ensconced in its largely rural base areas, was relatively little affected. CCP morale had never been higher, and several KMT-affiliated warlords defected to the communist side. One of these was the general in charge of Beijing. His switch in allegiance was of great import, both strategically and symbolically.

On October 1, 1949, Mao Zedong rode through the streets of Beijing in a captured American jeep and, ascending the rostrum at Tiananmen Square, proclaimed the founding of the People's Republic of China. Although a number of battles remained to be fought in southern China, the end of the civil war was foreordained. The mandate of heaven had passed to the Chinese Communist Party.

Suggestions for Further Reading

Edward L. Dreyer, *China at War* (London: Longman, 1995).

Elisabeth Köll, *From Cotton Mill to Business Empire: The Emergence of Regional Enterprises in Modern China* (Cambridge, MA: Harvard University Press, 2003).

Harold Z. Schiffrin, *Sun Yat-sen and the Origins of the Chinese Revolution* (Berkeley: University of California Press, 1970).

Benjamin Schwartz, *Chinese Communism and the Rise of Mao* (Cambridge, MA: Harvard University Press, 1951).

Jay Taylor, *The Generalissimo: Chiang Kai-shek and the Struggle for Modern China* (Cambridge, MA: Belknap Press, 2009).

CHAPTER 4

PRC Politics Under Mao: 1949–1976

Consolidation of Power: 1949–1955

Mao Zedong was under no illusions that the revolution had been won when the Chinese Communist Party (CCP) took power on the mainland: He explicitly compared the founding of the People's Republic of China (PRC) to the first step on a new Long March. Victory had come more quickly than even the optimists had predicted. During the later stages of the war, the communist troops' main challenge was not fighting the Kuomintang (KMT) troops, who were in full retreat, but running after them. Some soldiers referred to this jokingly as "the battle with the feet." Still, CCP leaders were aware that they had not won the hearts and minds of the majority of the population. The next few years would be characterized as the party's efforts to legitimize its power.

A first step was establishing the organs of government. In the fall of 1949, the CCP convened a meeting of more than 1,200 "persons from all strata of society" called the Chinese People's Political Consultative Conference (CPPCC). In addition to CCP members, delegates included representatives of assorted patriotic associations and minor political parties, including the China Democratic League and the KMT Revolutionary Committee. The latter had broken away from the main body of the KMT some years earlier in protest against some of the KMT's policies. Also attending were several warlords; a few former members of the KMT; prominent lawyers, doctors, and professors; social workers; artists; members of ethnic minorities; and religious leaders. There appear to have been two criteria for receiving an invitation to the CPPCC. First, the invitees had to be influential with a sizable number of people, either since, like the warlords, they held a great deal of power, or since, like the religious leaders and the professional experts, they were highly respected. Second, candidates had to agree with the idea of social change. Given the economic and social chaos in China at the time, this second criterion was not difficult to meet.

The rationale for this type of meeting is to be found in a creative adaptation of Marx, called "On the New Democracy," that had been written by Mao several years before. In it, Mao argued that since China was still colonial and semi-feudal, its principal enemies were imperialism and semi-feudal forces. Thus, all other forces, even the bourgeoisie, should unite against these enemies in a democratic dictatorship of several revolutionary classes under the leadership of the proletariat. Under such an arrangement, China would be able to pass through the bourgeois–democratic phase called for by Marx while simultaneously preparing the conditions for the socialist revolution. The CPPCC would serve as the vehicle to initiate this dictatorship.

The CPPCC, its disparate composition allowing the CCP's carefully organized voice to dominate, passed a document called the Common Program. This would function as a proto-constitution until elections could be held and a more legitimate constitution agreed upon. The program declared that China was a democratic dictatorship of four classes: workers, peasants, petty bourgeoisie, and national bourgeoisie. The petty bourgeoisie included such people as tradesmen, peddlers, and owners of small shops. The national bourgeoisie comprised persons of more substantial means who were considered patriotic: They had not collaborated with the Japanese or been suborned by any other foreign power.

Under the leadership of the working class and the CCP, the People's Democratic Dictatorship would suppress the lackeys of imperialism: landlords, bureaucratic capitalists, and KMT reactionaries. Those who could be reeducated would be dealt with leniently; those who could not, or would not, would be dealt with ruthlessly. The CPPCC also adopted a flag whose symbolism reflected this class structure: red, with four small gold stars, representing the four classes, surrounding the large gold star of the CCP. The design of the flag has sometimes also been described as the large star representing the dominant Han nationality and the smaller stars standing for the more important minority groups—Tibetans, Mongols, Manchus, and Muslims.

The decision to include the bourgeoisie in the coalition allowed the adoption of parliamentary forms, since China was judged to be in the bourgeois–democratic phase of the revolutionary process. It also provided the theoretical basis for a new united front. Unlike the two previous united fronts, this was composed of several different *classes* instead of an alliance between the CCP and the KMT. Its job was to promote the unity of all the people against the "non-people," this latter category comprising big landlords, capitalists, and those who had collaborated with foreigners. Although democratic in theory, this alliance was to be under the dictatorship of the workers and peasants in the institutional form of their party, the CCP.

Class labels were assigned, with a certain amount of arbitrariness, to everyone. Many bourgeois who considered themselves very patriotic may have cooperated with foreigners, sincerely believing that what they were doing was good for China as well as for themselves. One person's judgment of patriotic cooperation might be another person's verdict of treasonous collaboration. In addition, a number of peasants had a landlord or person of some wealth in their background. As one peasant about to be assigned a bad class label argued poignantly to party officials, given the fact that marriages entailed the payment of expensive bride prices from the groom's family and the provision of dowries by the bride's family, the sort of really poor peasant family favored by communist propaganda would have been unable to arrange a match and was apt to have died out as a result.

To make matters worse, class labels were not only assigned for life, they were hereditary as well. This caused problems when the children of bad classes wished to get married, apply for jobs, or seek educational opportunities. Such hereditary designations cannot be considered Marxist, since if a person no longer controls the means of production, he or she cannot be considered a member of the exploiting class. They do not even seem to be properly Maoist, since, as we have seen, Mao emphasized the value of persuasion and education in molding socialist attitudes. Hereditary class designations are decidedly anti-modern—in fact, feudal. As time went on, they were increasingly irrelevant to the Chinese context, as former landlords became the exploited class and party members took charge of the means of production, albeit on behalf of the collective, and prospered thereby. Why, then, did the CCP not undertake a new class analysis? Clearly, it was because this would risk alienating its main supporters.

Meanwhile, the party set about creating unity among those it had designated "the people." A series of mass campaigns was begun in order to build popular enthusiasm behind a common cause. The first was a 1950 campaign to "Resist the United States and Aid Korea." In addition to allowing the leadership to support its socialist brethren in North Korea and castigate its chief enemy, the United States, the theme was an excellent one in terms of building a sense of national unity against an external threat. As previously mentioned, many Chinese had stronger loyalties to clan, village, and province than to the nation. This made it difficult to coordinate responses to external aggression. Unity and patriotism would allow the leadership to give concrete form to the society that Sun Yat-sen had described as a sheet of loose sand.

This campaign, and others like it, took place in a celebratory atmosphere. Workers received time off to attend and were given small flags to wave; children in brightly colored costumes performed traditional dances. The military paraded to the accompaniment of bands. Stirring speeches were punctuated with firecrackers and concluded with a display of fireworks. The new symbols of loyalty were much in evidence: The national flag and large pictures of Mao Zedong.

Other, less dramatic efforts at unity were also undertaken. The party attempted to impose a common spoken language—standard Mandarin, which the new regime, understandably having no desire to honor the Mandarins, referred to as "the national language" or "common speech" in official documents. China is a land of many dialects, some of them mutually unintelligible even when the groups who speak them live in close proximity. Attachment to one's dialect may indicate localist sentiments; hence, imposing a standard that everyone was required to learn was one way of breaking down local barriers.

The party also took charge of printing and distributing mass-circulation magazines and newspapers, using a written language that was closer to actual spoken Chinese than the literary language that had been used by the official class. This had been one of the demands of the May Fourth generation. Publications written in this "new" form were much easier to read; hence, the party's message could be absorbed more easily. Since the magazines and some of the newspapers were distributed nationwide, they also contributed to unity. At least in theory, Chinese all over the country would be reading the same things. The plethora of currencies that had existed in China before the communist takeover was standardized as well.

A second mass campaign, which began a few months later, had the counterrevolutionaries as its main focus. Secret societies and anti-communist groups were searched out and, to the extent possible, destroyed. The non-people were identified, brought to mass meetings, and struggled against. Repentance might save one, but there were nonetheless a number of executions after the mass meetings had assessed guilt. Drug dealers, war profiteers, big landlords, pimps, and prostitutes were among the victims. Efforts were made to be more lenient with the less culpable, who may have been forced into their illicit trades through poverty. There were programs to train beggars and prostitutes for other professions, and cold-turkey rehabilitation for drug addicts. The methods were crude but effective. Official sources indicate that more than 800,000 executions took place; other estimates run up to 10 million. Party leaders defended the process as necessary: "A revolution is not a dinner party," and "To make an omelet, one must break some eggs." Meanwhile, a generally successful effort was made to convince people that the new government was *for* the people.

The third major campaign, begun in 1951, is known as the *sanfan*, or "three antis": anti-corruption, anti-waste, and anti-bureaucracy. Its main targets were the cadres—as the CCP called officials, in preference to the old term for bureaucrat that they despised—of party and state organs. There was concern within the ruling elite that a number of opportunists had joined the CCP when its victory was assured, with the motive of profiting themselves and their careers rather than because they sincerely believed in the party's goals. Other party and state cadres, they worried, had become corrupted by the new opportunities that supervising activities in postwar China offered. The *sanfan* aimed at purging party and government of careerists.

At first, outside observers viewed the campaign through the perspective of the eighteenth-century revolution in France: The Chinese revolution was devouring its own children. Later, opinion changed, and the *sanfan* came to be seen as a manifestation of party health rather than as sickness. The attack on deviations and weaknesses within its own ranks was regarded as increasing CCP strength and discipline. A few months later, in January 1952, a *wufan* or "five anti" campaign began, with the bourgeoisie as its target. The *sanfan* had revealed that most party and government corruption occurred in agencies that dealt with economic matters and had ties to the bourgeoisie. Hence, it was decided to attack them as well. The targets of the five anti campaign were bribery, tax evasion, fraud, theft of government property, and theft of state economic secrets. Since the two movements overlapped so closely, both in time and targets, they are sometimes referred to as the *sanfan–wufan*, or "three-anti–five-anti" campaign.

Also during its first years in power, the party worked hard to restore the economy and bring it under party control. This included ending inflation, rebuilding and expanding the infrastructure, instituting land reform, and preparing for collectivization. These will be discussed in detail in Chapter 7. It is important to remember, however, that changes in the political party line were often made with economic goals in mind.

Establishing the Organs of Power

For the first few years after the communist takeover, China was divided into six large regions under the administration of Military Administrative Committees, later to be known simply as Administrative Committees. Since China is so large, and since communications at the time were quite primitive, organizations such as these made sense in terms of allowing the CCP to consolidate its power. Some evidence indicates that the leadership was worried about the existence of centrifugal forces within these large areas. For example, two regional leaders were removed on the grounds that they had colluded to set up "independent kingdoms"—meaning bureaucracies that could evade Beijing's control—but precisely how far the central leaders thought these regional power holders intended to go has never been made clear. Although central–regional tensions were a concern during this period, we have too little information to assess how serious a problem they were.

Consonant with the concept of a people's democratic dictatorship, the communist party is, and has been, the only meaningful party in China since 1949. Also in line with a people's democratic dictatorship, a complete state apparatus was set up after basic-level elections were held in 1953 and a constitution ratified in 1954. Thus, there are two parallel hierarchies, the party and the government, with interlocking memberships (Figures 4.1 and 4.2). This type of structure is quite different from the Western concept of political parties competing for control of the organs of government. Westerners, noting the overlap in leadership positions at the top of the hierarchy—leading government offices are almost always held by leading party members—are often puzzled by the apparent redundancy of the system. The answer to why two organizations exist where one would seem adequate is that the party is supposed to provide spiritual and ideological input for policies, while the government executes the policies by working out the administrative details thereof and supervising the routine decisions that follow on from them. The party's will is to be supreme.

Although given no formal decision-making role in either party or government hierarchy, the military has been a key political actor as well. However, as will be seen in Chapter 9, the dividing line between military and non-military in the PRC was not sharply drawn during the Maoist period. Since members of the elite frequently held leading positions in party, government, and military simultaneously, or moved from positions in one hierarchy to another and back again, there was little possibility that the military, as a discrete institution, could exercise influence over the party or the state.

Chinese political institutions were modeled on those of the former Soviet Union, but were not exact duplicates. The PRC has nothing comparable to the

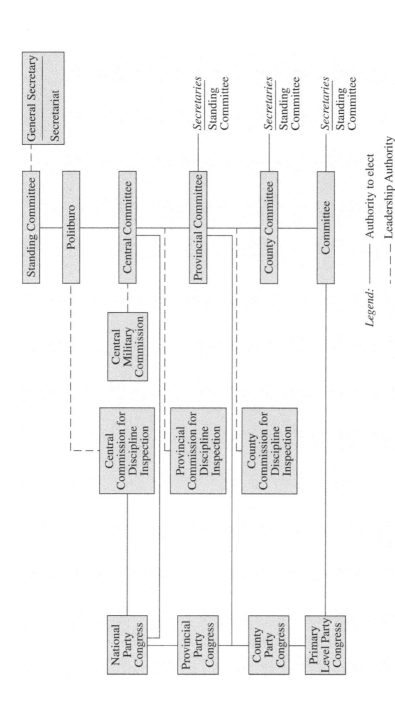

FIGURE 4.1 Organization of the Chinese Communist Party

Source: Adapted from the Constitution of the Chinese Communist Party, 1982.

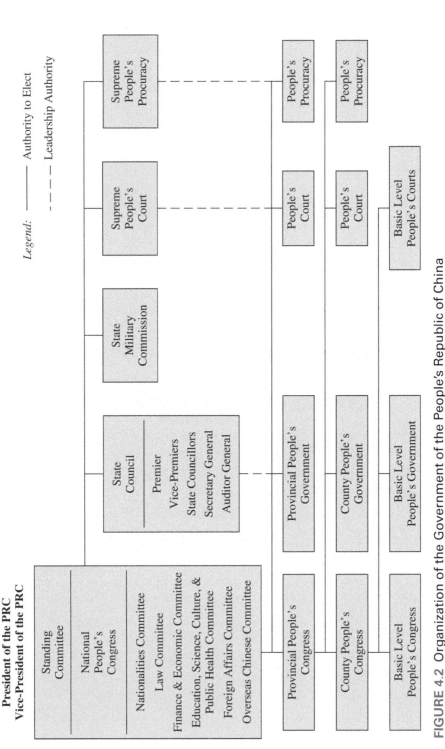

FIGURE 4.2 Organization of the Government of the People's Republic of China

Source: Adapted from the Constitution of the People's Republic of China, 1982.

USSR's Soviet of Nationalities, and China's constitution, unlike the USSR's, does not allow the PRC's constituent units the right to secede.

The highest organ of state, at least in theory, is the National People's Congress (NPC). It is empowered to enact laws, ratify treaties, and select the president and vice-president. NPC members are influential within their communities and, like candidates at every other level of the state hierarchy, are individuals who are considered acceptable to the party. It is not necessary that they belong to the CCP, although many do. The NPC has no fixed size, though typically there have been 2,000 to 3,000 members. In recent years, the NPC has become more assertive (see Chapter 6). Nonetheless, its unwieldy size, plus the fact that it meets infrequently, means that power is delegated. There is a Standing Committee of the NPC with perhaps 150 members, which is still relatively large for interactive debate. It meets fairly frequently, seemingly to explain party policy to the more important non-party officials.

The organ that performs most administrative work is the State Council, headed by a powerful premier assisted by several vice-premiers. Again, there is no fixed number of vice-premiers. The various ministries and commissions are responsible to the State Council. Below the central government, in descending order of importance, are four tiers. Thirty-four provincial-level governments include five autonomous regions (which have very little actual autonomy: see Chapter 13) with substantial ethnic minority populations; four large cities that report directly to the central governments; the two special administrative regions of Hong Kong and Macau; and Taiwan, which the PRC claims but does not control and which functions as an independent nation. On the second level are over 300 prefectural-level administrative units. Below prefectures there are nearly 3,000 counties and county-level cities. The lower tier comprises about 40,000 towns and townships. Except at the prefectural level, all have political structures similar to that of the central government. Although prefectural-level cities and so-called autonomous prefectures have government organizations and people's congresses, regular prefectures have administrative agencies instead.

The party hierarchy is more important. A National Party Congress—again, a very large body: Over 2,000 at the most recent Nineteenth Party Congress—elects (at least in theory) a central committee. The committee has no fixed size, although it currently has over 200 full members, who vote, and a somewhat lesser number of non-voting alternates. The Central Committee has a secretariat, selected from among its members, which in turn supervises the descending hierarchy of provincial party and municipal party committees, and so on down to basic-level party organizations.

Central Committee members, in theory, choose a politburo of perhaps 15 to 25 members, and it in turn selects approximately 5 to 9 of them as members of the Politburo Standing Committee (PBSC). Currently, the PBSC has seven members. These individuals, and particularly the PBSC chair, are considered the most powerful people in China. The chair, who has in recent years served as president of China and chair of the Central Military Commission, can exercise enormous authority. How much is somewhat dependent on his personality: Hu Jintao appeared to be first among almost-equals, with decision making seeming to occur through coalition formation among PBSC members, while Xi Jinping has virtually monopolized decision making in his person.

The process by which lower levels elect higher levels, who in turn make decisions to be passed down the hierarchy, is called democratic centralism. In reality, individuals are chosen rather than elected in free competition, with higher levels choosing members for lower levels, rather than vice versa. Although all congresses in China claim to be organs of popular political power, only the basic-level congresses are directly elected by the people. Other levels are formally elected by the level immediately below.

Following the establishment of the institutions of state power, the CPPCC did not pass out of existence but remained as the organ of the united front. Typically, the party congress will meet first, and changes, which will have been formulated earlier by the politburo Standing Committee, will be ratified with little debate. The NPC will then convene and endorse the party congress's decisions, as will the CPPCC. Recently, the latter two have been meeting almost simultaneously.

The relative stability of party and government organs during the past several decades belies the political battles that have swirled around them. From 1956 to 1977, no party congress served its full five-year term, and neither did any of the central committees appointed by the party congresses. The Eighth Central Committee, by contrast, served almost eight years beyond its term. On the government side, the NPC did not even convene in 13 of the first 30 years it was formally in charge, and did not meet for one entire 8-year period between 1966 and 1974. One head of state, Liu Shaoqi, whose term would have officially ended in January 1969, was deposed in October 1968, not by the NPC, which was the only organ legally entitled to do so, but by a plenary session of the party central committee, which did not have a quorum. In 1976, Hua Guofeng was appointed prime minister and Deng Xiaoping removed as deputy prime minister, even though both of these were government positions, by the *party* politburo, with no attempt at constitutional legitimization. Deng later returned to power and, in 1985, retired several members of the politburo at a party conference, apparently because he feared the opposition of the constitutionally designated body, the party central committee. From 1989 onward, Deng, the universally acknowledged paramount leader of China, held *no* leadership position in party *or* government. In the 1990s, procedures gradually became more regularized.

The party made considerable efforts to draw the average individual into the political process. Mass organizations were founded, just as they had been in Yan'an. These included a Communist Youth League, a trade union federation, a women's organization, and a medical association, to name just a few of the more prominent. To reach the individual on a still more personal level, small study groups were instituted. In the rural areas this was done through the production team, and in urban areas through the *danwei*, or work unit. These were further broken down into *xiaozu*, or small groups, of 8 to 15 people. Based on the model developed at Yan'an, the most common form of the *xiaozu* was the political study group, in which members engaged in long discussions about study materials under the guidance of a group leader. Under the rubric of "criticism and self-criticism," members were required to express their views individually, criticize themselves, and submit to the criticism of others in the group.

The *xiaozu* was useful to the party in a number of ways. First, it gave cadres a forum through which to personally transmit party policy to the average citizen. Second, it placed policy changes in the context of face-to-face discussion, enhancing the possibilities for personal persuasion. Third, because the *xiaozu* normally consisted of people who lived near and worked with each other, it could exercise strong pressures for conformity within the group. Since group conformity was highly valued by Chinese tradition, the CCP could use this predilection to its advantage in gaining unanimous acceptance of policy changes. Fourth, the small group could give individuals a sense of participation in the political process, as well as provide a channel of information for the party on those individuals who showed stubborn or deviant tendencies. Finally, the small group was a method of strengthening the weak vertical integration of Chinese society—the leadership's ability to mobilize popular sentiment behind its policies being an important means of giving structure to the heretofore loose sand society described by Sun Yat-sen.

All of this assumes that the group functions according to plan. It did not always do so. Cadres complained of "individualism" and "particularism" among small-group members who stubbornly resisted accepting an unpopular party policy. Many people were also simply bored: while physically present at the meetings, they tuned out the content of the discussions. Even the politically unsophisticated could comprehend that they were being manipulated. Moreover, long periods of time spent in political study meant less time to spend in economically profitable activities. Frustrated cadres often resorted to behavior referred to in party documents as "formalism" and "commandism." By 1956, there was a noticeable trend toward ritualism rather than true participation in the small groups. The device became moribund in the post-Mao period.

The Hundred Flowers Period: 1956–1957

During the first few years following liberation, there was fairly broad agreement within the Chinese population on goals, and the party did a reasonably good job of implementing them. Railroads were rebuilt and irrigation systems made functional again. The cities, which had been short of food, were better supplied. Inflation was halted and the currency revalued. Land reform was carried out.

By about 1955, however, tensions and stresses had begun to emerge. The mass collectivization of agriculture, handicrafts, private commerce, and industry had proved to be not nearly as popular as land reform. A much larger number of people perceived themselves as disadvantaged by the collectivization than during land reform, and made their views known in a variety of ways. A repression campaign against certain writers led to a decline in both the quality and quantity of what was written, to the dismay of party leaders.

Mao Zedong realized that these tensions existed and was concerned to do something about them. Elsewhere in the communist world following the death of Stalin, popular discontent had boiled over into rioting in several areas. The Chinese leadership seemed to agree with analyses made elsewhere that an important cause of these outbursts was that dissension had been repressed for too long.

The Hundred Flowers campaign was Mao's attempt to ease the tensions within Chinese society. In May 1956, he made a speech that included the phrase "let a hundred flowers bloom; let a hundred schools of thought contend." The second half of the slogan is a reference to the numerous philosophies that vied for pre-eminence in the Warring States period 2,000 years before. The "hundred flowers" metaphor seems to have been coined by Mao himself, based on his conviction that criticism would strengthen socialism, since, in the end, truth wins out. In the course of debate, more people will become convinced that socialism is true precisely because the controversies will have forced them to think carefully about various options. This sounds remarkably like ideas advanced by the British utilitarian philosopher John Stuart Mill, though there is no evidence that Mao was familiar with Mill's writings.

Mao's speech was made to a group of party leaders and was never published. What we know of it comes from references to the speech that appeared in the Chinese press. These references indicate that there were limits within which free speech was to be encouraged. Pornography was explicitly forbidden, as were attitudes such as "The moon in America is rounder than the moon in China" and "Let's all play mah-jongg and to hell with state affairs." The underlying assumption was that differences of opinion would not be serious because they would be examples of what Mao referred to as "non-antagonistic contradictions"—that is, those which do not need to be dealt with by coercive means—among the people.

At first, the result of this call for debate was a deafening silence. A well-known anthropologist hinted at the reason with an oblique reference to fear of "early spring weather," which encourages buds to bloom but is quickly followed by a frost that kills the flowers. In February 1957, Mao made another speech, again not published at the time. Quotations and excerpts that appeared in the press indicate that this second effort went considerably further in encouraging freedom of speech. Backed up by party pressures, it began to yield results.

Initially, the criticism was mild. Intellectuals asked for a larger role for the CPPCC and democratic parties, and for the right to import more foreign periodicals that were relevant to their work. Later, the citizenry became bolder, indicating that it now interpreted the still-unpublished second speech as sanctioning freedom of expression. Criticism escalated in ways that the leadership found shocking. Students at China's leading university, Beida, designated a particular wall as the place to vent their feelings and covered it with "big-character" posters that were highly critical of the party. A Tianjin engineer complained that the communists had promised China a revolution but gave it no more than a change of dynasties. A journalist wrote that the party had quickly become estranged from the masses and that most of its members were "flatterers, sycophants, and yes-men." A professor pointed out that Marx and Lenin had constantly revised their theories and opined that they would not be pleased to learn that people with petty bureaucratic minds—that is, the CCP leaders—were applying their doctrine so rigidly.

Peasants complained that the cooperatives were no good and demanded their land back. Workers proclaimed that the wage system was irrational and voiced their annoyance at being required to "volunteer" to work overtime without pay. Some people even said that they had been better off under the KMT. Ethnic minorities advocated splitting off from China and founding independent states.

This was not the kind of criticism the party had anticipated. Rather than helping to create unity, it seemed to be inciting disunity and centrifugal forces. Mao's February 1957 speech, entitled "On the Correct Handling of Contradictions among the People," was finally published, but some passages appear to have been added. Among other things, it noted that certain criticisms were no longer to be considered as fragrant flowers: They had been reclassified as noxious weeds in the garden of socialism. As antagonistic contradictions, they would have to be uprooted and destroyed.

The frosty weather that would kill the hundred flowers began in June 1957 and took the form of yet another mass campaign. Known as the anti-rightist campaign, it had identified more than 300,000 people as "rightists" by the end of the year. Many of China's brightest and most dedicated intellectuals were among them. Rather than being encouraged to use their skills in economics, engineering, and astrophysics to help develop China, their careers were ruined. Jail, reform through labor, or banishment to rural areas (the latter being to acquaint them with the "real" China, thus enabling them to understand the nation better, while breaking down the sharp distinction between city and countryside) were among the punishments meted out. Promising futures were destroyed, and families split. Some who had been branded rightists divorced, or were divorced by, their spouses in an effort to minimize the stigma on the rest of the family. Others committed suicide, often after being struggled against and tortured; a few were executed.

Could the Hundred Flowers campaign have been cleverly contrived to ferret out malcontents? Initially, foreign analysts felt that it had not. They believed that party optimists, including Mao, were genuinely convinced that the campaign would solidify a unified population behind the party and ratify its plans for collectivization. By contrast, ideological hard-liners within the party would have had real doubts about the wisdom of this course from the beginning, and would have reminded the optimists of this when criticism escalated. Mao responded by espousing the hard-line position, rewriting his speech and allowing it to be published. Unity would then be obtained by weeding out the dissident "rightists."

However, later analysis cites a presumably authentic document indicating that the Hundred Flowers campaign had an entrapment motive all along. In a letter circulated to higher party cadres in mid-May 1957, Mao stated:

> Things are just beginning to change. The rightist offensive has not yet reached its peak. [The rightists] are still very enthusiastic. We want to let them rage for a while and climb to the very summit.

The Great Leap Forward and Its Aftermath: 1958–1961

Among the more radical members of the leadership, a number of factors converged to create a mood of impatience with the status quo. The Hundred Flowers campaign seemed to disprove the idea that China could move gradually toward communism, with people's attitudes moving inexorably toward acceptance of socialist goals. Furthermore, there was increasing dissatisfaction with the speed at which progress was taking place. Grain production in 1957 had risen only 1 percent *vis-à-vis* a population growth of 2 percent. Collectivization had been introduced in 1955/1956, and there were concerns that staying too long at this intermediate stage might make it harder to advance to true communism.

There was also a growing realization of the limitations that the Soviet model had for China. After the PRC was founded, the USSR sent a number of advisers to China to assist in fields as varied as economics and ethnology. Although there is no evidence that these advisers attempted to rigidly apply inappropriate Soviet experiences to the Chinese situation, they had an understandable tendency to think in terms of the categories and procedures they knew best. Because labor shortages were characteristic of the USSR, whereas labor surpluses were more typical in China, the Soviet tendency to substitute capital for labor did not work well in the PRC. Chinese leaders wished to put the country's huge population to work in order to increase production. Consistent with Mao's long-standing belief that Marxism must be made compatible with the society to which it was applied, the Great Leap Forward would implement communism in a way that was compatible with Chinese characteristics.

There was also a growing conviction that China's problems should be attacked by levels larger than cooperatives and villages. The leadership was additionally concerned with the growth of bureaucracy, believing that increases in production were being held back by a morass of officially generated red tape. As well, new status differences were becoming evident. These were antithetical to the egalitarian ideas with which the party had come to power. A separate but related factor was Mao's deeply felt desire to reduce differences between the city and the countryside. This is believed to reflect both Marx's views and Mao's own background.

Particularly in his earlier writings, Karl Marx had been very much concerned with reversing the alienation of man from the product of his labor, which the specialization that was inherent in the factory system had caused. In the communist society which he envisioned, someone could be a craftsman part of the day and, by turns, a fisherman, hunter, and literary critic at other times. Mao Zedong, as well as many non-Marxist Chinese of this era, had for many years been concerned with the urban–rural gap in their own country. Mao seems to have felt the gap particularly keenly. The product of a rural upbringing, he had been looked down on by various CCP leaders, including the Returned Student group, because of both his relative lack of sophistication and his emphasis on the peasants. They had referred to him disparagingly as a *tugong*, or "earth/dirt communist." Mao believed strongly that there should not be a dichotomy between the ideologically pure—that is, communists—and the technocrats, who were assumed to be infected with bourgeois ideology: China needed people who were "both red and expert." The Great Leap thus contained a radically egalitarian message.

Mao was also convinced that international forces were favorable to a bold step forward at this time. In October 1957, the Soviet Union launched Sputnik, the world's first satellite, and made breakthroughs in intercontinental ballistic missile technology earlier that same year. Mao, who often wrote poetry and was fond of using poetic metaphors in his speeches, commemorated these developments in a heavily publicized speech fraught with symbolism, arguing that "the east wind is prevailing against the west wind." He urged all progressive forces, including the Soviet Union, to take advantage of these favorable developments and march boldly onward.

Not surprisingly, the vehicle chosen to seize the moment was a mass campaign—in this case the Great Leap Forward. Precisely how the Great Leap was decided upon has been the subject of much scholarly controversy. One analyst notes that Liu Shaoqi, whose bureaucratic orientation and sober nature made him a very different personality from Mao, delivered the speech that started the movement, although Liu would later be identified as having opposed the Leap. A second scholar argues that Liu supported the movement, but for completely different reasons than Mao: Whereas Mao believed in the power of unleashed mass energy, Liu had organizational reasons for believing that the Great Leap could succeed. He also wanted to support Mao for reasons of self-interest. Mao's physician opined that we may never know what part the major actors played in formulating the Leap, since Mao's lieutenants, including Liu, displayed sycophantic enthusiasm, which may have masked their true feelings.

The early stages of the Great Leap Forward involved experiments with larger scale units of organization during the agricultural slack season in winter 1957/1958. Several cooperatives were encouraged to work together on projects such as dam building and other water control work. The idea was to rely on local people and resources in preference to asking for state aid. Photographs of thousands of peasants scraping out tons of earth with crude shovels, and even rice bowls, in order to build dams appeared in newspapers in China and around the world. Outsiders' image of China changed from one of a sheet of loose sand to that of an army of ants, attacking enormous problems through group organization and sheer force of numbers. One author even called his study of Mao

Emperor of the Blue Ants, the color being a description of the caps, jackets, and pants that nearly all Chinese wore during this period.

In industry, hortatory slogans appeared on factory walls, urging the workers on to new goals. At first, these were realistic: For example, "Overtake England in steel production in 15 years" was a plausible target. Although the PRC's steel production in 1957 was well below that of Great Britain, Chinese levels were rising while Britain's output remained essentially the same. Britain is also a much smaller country than China. Hence, the PRC could reasonably be expected to draw even with England within 15 years. However, the slogan's time frame was progressively reduced from ten years to five and even, in a couple of areas, to three. The slogan "More, better, faster, and cheaper" appeared everywhere. A visiting Soviet scientist recalled seeing such a banner over the door of a maternity hospital where, given China's enormous population, he found it especially inappropriate.

There was also an intensification of a campaign, begun somewhat earlier, to send young urban intellectuals (defined at that time as those who had graduated from at least junior middle school) to the countryside to "take root, flower, and bear fruit." Known as the *xiaxiang*, or "sent-down" youth, they were expected to share their intellectual knowledge with the peasants, while at the same time learning agricultural techniques that would enable them to raise more food for China. This fitted well with Mao's desire to reduce the differences between city and countryside. In general, however, it did not fit well with the desires of either peasants or urban youth. Although it would have been dangerous to protest publicly, peasants resented having thrust upon them large numbers of youth who were unused to hard physical labor and ignorant of farm work. Conversely, the *xiaxiang* youth tended to abhor the rigors of country living and farm chores, and to miss both their families and the amenities of city life.

Another slogan associated with the Great Leap Forward is "walk on two legs," with one leg representing the modern—for example, heavy industry with its need for expensive machinery or, in the health field, up-to-date Western medical procedures—and the other leg representing the traditional: labor-intensive spinning and weaving techniques in the textile industry and traditional Chinese medicine in the health field. The scientific method and research projects of all sorts were castigated as bourgeois. Correct political views and peasant wisdom were extolled; "bourgeois scientific objectivism" was ridiculed.

In August 1958, large-scale agricultural units, called communes, were formed by combining several cooperatives. The economic implications of these communes will be discussed in detail in Chapter 5. Politically and sociologically, the communes entailed enormous changes. Backyard blast furnaces were intended to teach peasants the rudiments of industrial techniques, thereby helping to reduce the differences between city and countryside, and also to solve the problem of transporting steel to rural areas. This had been a problem due to poor transportation networks in the countryside. There was also an attack on private property: Peasants had to give up not only their private plots but even, in many cases, their personal possessions such as wristwatches and jewelry.

Work points as a measure of income were abandoned in favor of the communist formula "from each according to his ability, to each according to his need." In addition to its appeal to ideological orthodoxy, this formula would free bookkeepers from the need to record work points so that they, too, could spend more time in the fields. People were to eat in mess halls so that they did not have to waste time cooking and, incidentally, so that the state could control how long they spent at meals. Theoretically, there would also be less waste if one cooked in large quantities. Housewives were to be freed from working at home by providing nurseries for their children so that they, too, could become productive. Old people were to enter "happiness homes for the aged." In some areas, there were direct attacks on the nuclear family: even married workers were to live in dormitories segregated by sex.

New agricultural techniques were mandated as well, including the use of a double-wheeled, double-bladed plow, planting seeds more closely together and deeper than before, and utilizing land heretofore regarded as unsuitable for crops. While a few brave individuals protested the folly of some of these ideas, most had been cowed into silence by the anti-rightist campaign. This was the very antithesis of the mass line and a negation of the party's slogan "from the masses to the masses."

For a time, the enthusiasm of the Chinese people seemed unbounded. There were stories of activists who arrived at work "on the backs of green frogs" (at first break of day), of elderly and sick people who toiled for 18 hours in the fields to show their love for Chairman Mao, and of agricultural production that tripled the previous year's harvest. Such tales did not last for very long. The resolution on setting up communes was introduced on August 29, 1958; by October, reports began of party officials meeting to discuss "certain problems" that had arisen in the course of the Great Leap Forward.

The November issue of the party's theoretical journal *Red Flag* contained an article entitled "Have We Already Reached the Stage of Communism?" It may be fairly described as an exercise in how to sound enthusiastic about the Great Leap Forward while actually trying to damp down enthusiasm. After some discussion, the author concluded that "we" have not yet reached communism, and that therefore it would be appropriate to modify the practice of "from each according to his ability, to each according to his need" to what he called the "half-supply" system of "from each according to his ability, to each according to his work." The real reason, of course, was that most people had reacted to the previous formulation by not working very hard. Some had responded to unreasonable pressures by passively resisting; others engaged in active sabotage by destroying property and killing their animals rather than turn them over to the state. The government, having been told of bountiful harvests, reasoned that it could collect more in taxes, and did so. Grain thus collected sat in warehouses while those who had raised it starved or were reduced to cannibalism.

In December, it was announced that Mao would not stand for re-election as chairman of the PRC, though he retained his top party post. The stated reason was that he wished to spend more time in theoretical study and writing. The actual reason appears to have been that the failures of the Great Leap Forward had increased the power of a less ideologically hard-line faction within the party. Liu Shaoqi took over the post vacated by Mao, and the Wuhan Resolution, introduced by the party central committee that month, in addition to calling for "doing away with blind faith," established definitively that China was in the stage of socialism rather than communism, and confirmed the half-supply system.

This and subsequent directives dismantled much of the Great Leap Forward. For example, mess halls were reduced in size and told to improve the variety of food they served. Their clients often had to spend so long commuting from their jobs to the mess halls that any economies gained from serving large numbers of people were negated by peasants having less time to work. The decision of whether to leave children permanently at nurseries was left to parents, who were guaranteed the right to bring their children home with them at any time. No elderly person was to be forced to enter a "happiness home"; if she or he wished to stay with relatives who were amenable to the arrangement, the state would not interfere. People were also to be guaranteed the right to eight hours' sleep each night. Private plots were returned, along with the right to keep a few pigs and chickens. The unit of accounting was no longer to be at commune level but at that of the brigade—that is, the former cooperatives, where it had been before the Leap began. Not long after, it devolved still further, to the level of the team.

Liu's replacement of Mao as head of the PRC government did not end dissension within the elite. Although it was officially announced that the chairman had resigned because he wanted more time to think and write, Mao was extremely annoyed with Liu. According to Mao's physician, he had been angry with Liu Shaoqi and Deng Xiaoping since mid-1956, holding them responsible for propagating principles that were anathema to him at the Eighth Party Congress in September of that year. These principles included: (1) supporting the idea of collective leadership; (2) removing Mao Zedong's thought as the country's guiding ideology; and (3) criticizing Mao's "adventurism." The physician believed that Mao spent the next decade trying to reverse these principles, ultimately launching the Cultural Revolution to do so. The descending economic spiral continued to exacerbate differences of opinion among them, and in August 1959, at a party meeting held at Lushan, it was officially admitted that many of the accomplishments claimed for the Great Leap Forward were false. The defense minister, Marshal Peng Dehuai, chided Mao for his role in planning the Leap. Although Peng had meant his remarks as constructive criticism, the angry chairman sacked Peng for his candor, replacing him with Marshal Lin Biao. Mao, however, remained a low-key presence during the following several years.

Remedial measures could not bring immediate improvement. Crop damage cannot be undone overnight, and depleted animal populations, particularly in the case of large animals who have few offspring, take several years to recover. There were problems internationally as well. China's repudiation of the Soviet model, and Mao's urging the Soviet Union to take a stronger ideological line had angered the Soviet leadership. In 1960, the USSR withdrew its advisers, many of whom took their plans and blueprints with them, leaving scientific research projects incomplete and factories half-built.

Even the weather was uncooperative. Some areas suffered from drought. others from floods, typhoons, and plagues of insects. Although some people saw this as the equivalent of the seven biblical plagues and others as a manifestation of the mandate of heaven, there were man-made causes as well. One reason for the plague of insects was a prior mass campaign against sparrows that had killed many other types of birds as well, thereby removing the natural predators of various types of insects. Some floods were caused by the collapse of dams and dikes that had been poorly built by people unskilled in construction techniques.

Bourgeois expertise, whether red or not, began to seem desirable again. In terms of Max Weber's paradigm for modernization, the Great Leap's attack on specialization and expertise was antithetical to the modernization which the leadership hoped to achieve. Indeed, it appears as a Luddite attack on modernization, with disastrous effects for society. In this parlous state, the value of redness paled by comparison to the value of expertise. It was just such a realization that must have prompted the party secretary-general of the time, Deng Xiaoping, to remark, "It does not matter whether it is a black cat or a white cat, so long as it catches mice"—that is, so long as the economic system meets the population's needs, it does not matter whether it is communist or capitalist. With actual physical survival at stake, people resorted to desperate measures. Survival, rather than ideological orthodoxy of any sort, was the imperative of the time.

The years 1959 through 1961 are known as the "three lean years." There were widespread shortages of nearly everything: food, clothing, fuel, and even paper. An African student at a Chinese university recalled his surprise at seeing an otherwise demure young lady lift her skirt high above her waist before sitting down. He later discovered that, because the cloth ration was so low, she was trying to make the garment's thin cotton material last for another year. The party's rationing system is credited with preventing many more deaths than the famine might otherwise have led to. Years later, official sources admitted that 8 million people had died of causes related to the Great Leap Forward. Unofficial sources estimated the figure at between 12 and 20 million. Whatever the actual number, the CCP, having expended years of effort attempting to win the loyalty of skeptics and the uncommitted, had lost considerable prestige with the masses in whose name it claimed to govern.

The Socialist Education Movement: 1962–1966

By 1962, production levels had returned to their pre-Great Leap Forward levels, and in October the party central committee met, with Mao Zedong appearing in a more prominent role than he had for some time. The meeting's official communiqué contained references to class struggle, "opportunistic ideological tendencies within the party," and "the spontaneous tendency toward capitalism." The situation that lay behind these rather abstract words became clearer when the Taiwan government released a series of documents obtained by infiltrating frogmen-commandos into a commune near the Fujian coast. Called the Lianjiang Documents after the commune from which they were obtained, they describe a situation believed to be fairly typical of the early 1960s in China.

The documents revealed the existence of considerable concern with so-called unhealthy tendencies, among which were the following:

- a "spontaneous tendency toward capitalism," meaning that peasants preferred to make money on their own rather than on behalf of the collective;
- relaxed social controls that had allowed gambling, speculative activities, and abandonment of farmlands;
- revived "feudal practices," including religious observances, marriages contracted for economic reasons, spiritualist scams, and even sorcery;
- a decline in cadre morale, with cadres complaining that the efforts necessary to fulfill their responsibilities far exceeded the rewards, and many wanting to resign;
- cadre misappropriation of public funds for private use.

The next several years saw a major effort to correct these unhealthy tendencies and reintroduce socialist orthodoxy through another mass campaign, the Socialist Education Movement.

One measure adopted in the campaign was to send groups of higher level cadres to the countryside. This reflected concern that cadres' isolation from the masses they allegedly served had caused many of the country's present problems. By living and working with the common people, cadres could better understand them and, therefore, deal with difficulties more effectively. By early 1963, preliminary results of the experiment were summarized, and the Socialist Education Movement began to take shape as a systematic campaign.

In May 1963, the party issued a document known as the Draft Resolution of the Central Committee on Some Problems in Current Rural Work or, more simply, the First Ten Points. It called for the formation of Poor and Lower Middle Peasant Associations to oversee management at the commune and brigade levels and to carry out the "four cleans"—cleaning up of accounts, granaries, properties, and work points. At the same time, however, the associations were told to avoid interfering in routine administrative affairs. In practice, the distinction between intervening to find corruption and not interfering with routine administrative affairs was difficult to make. In order to coerce cadres to spend more time in production and less time on administrative work, the number of work points they could claim for the performance of administrative tasks was greatly reduced—to 1 or 2 percent from 4 percent or even, in extreme cases, 10 percent. Cadres were also given minimum numbers of days they needed to spend in productive labor, ranging from 60 for county-level cadres to 180 for those at the brigade level.

The following two years saw successive attempts to refine this effort to reimpose ideological orthodoxy without harming production. In September 1963, the central committee issued what came to be known as the Later Ten Points, and, in June 1964, the Eighteen Points. This was followed in September 1964 by the Revised Draft of the Later Ten Points, and by the Twenty-Three Points in January 1965. These and other documents caused no small amount of confusion. As mentioned earlier, people remained bewildered by the scope of activities of the Poor and Lower Peasant Associations. They were also unable to distinguish between legitimate sideline occupations, which the party approved of as a way to increase production, and "spontaneous capitalist tendencies," which the party condemned.

What *is* clear from a careful reading of these successive documents is the leadership's growing pessimism that the unhealthy tendencies could be corrected quickly: Longer and longer time frames were proposed. A hardening of the class line was also noticeable, with a greater tendency toward viewing problems as antagonistic (requiring struggle and violent methods to resolve) rather than non-antagonistic (capable of solution through persuasion and education). There were hints that the errant lower level cadres had protectors at higher levels. In 1964, a new "politics takes command" campaign was introduced, and the People's Liberation Army (PLA) was held up as a model of political and ideological virtue for all Chinese to emulate. The cult of Mao study began to be propagated nationwide, soon reaching fever pitch. At the same time, the targets to be struggled against began to be found at higher and higher levels in the party and government hierarchies. Although there is no direct link between the Socialist Education Movement and the convulsive Cultural Revolution that followed it, the latter can be seen as a logical extension of the former.

The Cultural Revolution: 1966–1976
The Years of Upheaval: 1966–1969

In November 1965, a young party official from Shanghai named Yao Wenyuan published a scathing article that is usually taken to mark the beginning of the Cultural Revolution. Yao attacked a historian-playwright, Wu Han, for "using the past to ridicule the present" in his works (see Chapter 12). This was followed by attacks on another writer, Deng Tuo, with whom Wu had collaborated on a column called "Three Family Village" for the newspaper *Beijing Daily*. The two men also contributed to a magazine called *Front Line*. Since most of the PRC's newspapers and periodicals, including these, did not circulate outside China, nonresidents had never seen the material being criticized. One article in the "Three Family Village" series was entitled "Great Empty Talk." It complained that "some people," since they are experienced in public speaking, can talk endlessly on any subject; yet, after they have finished, nobody can remember what it was they said. The column warned that if this technique of empty talk were taught to the younger generation, and if experts in it were cultivated among youth, things would go from bad to worse. The authors said that, to illustrate their point, they would take the example of a "neighborhood boy" who imitated the expressions of great poets and had written many great empty talks, including:

> The heaven is our father; the sun is our governess
> The east wind is our benefactor; the west wind is our enemy.

The neighborhood boy was unquestionably Mao, while the great empty talk referred to party propaganda in general. Meanwhile, the cult of Mao study was escalating, with the study of his thoughts being credited for all sorts of accomplishments, from operating on cancerous tumors to raising watermelons, to winning table tennis tournaments.

At the same time, all other culture, both Western and traditional Chinese, became suspect for its bourgeois and/or feudal content. Chinese opera was considered as tainted as Bizet and Wagner. Hence "The East Is Red," a song praising Mao, became one of the few safe things to sing; the country's real national anthem ceased to be heard. Books other than the works of Mao disappeared from bookstores. A pocket-sized selection of Mao's quotations, chosen by defense minister Lin Biao and bound in red plastic, became a runaway bestseller albeit in the near-total absence of any competition. Its small size allowed the Little Red Book to be kept conveniently visible on one's person as a symbol of loyalty, and even held aloft and waved on appropriate occasions. Another useful talisman was the Mao button, a small metal pin embossed with the image of The Great Helmsman which could be pinned on one's jacket. Since these came in a variety of shapes and designs, some people took to pinning on several dozen badges at a time, hoping for a multiplier effect on this evidence of their loyalty to the chairman.

While it was possible to view Yao's attack as directed against the opinions of a few disgruntled intellectuals, his sally was actually a great deal more than that. In addition to being a historian and playwright, Wu Han was vice-mayor of Beijing. Deng Tuo was a secretary of the Beijing Party Committee, and the *Beijing Daily* and *Front Line* were official publications of the Beijing Party Committee. The hint made in the course of the Socialist Education Movement that officials at higher levels were protecting ideologically deviant subordinates now had concrete referents. The attacks which curiously—or so it seemed at the time—were led by the official military newspaper, *Liberation Army Daily*, then moved on to ask who was behind the "black gang" of Wu Han and Deng Tuo. No answer was given, although it was noticed that Peng Zhen, the mayor of Beijing and a ranking member of the party politburo, had not been seen in public or otherwise heard from in several months.

Nor had Mao been seen in public. In the West, rumors circulated that he might be dead or very sick and that the deification campaign had been plotted by those who hoped to succeed him. These rumors apparently convinced the chairman that he should appear in public. Mao chose to return to the city of

Wuhan in July 1966 for a swim in the Yangtze River. The real intent of the swim was to demonstrate Mao Zedong's health, although the official account went a bit far in claiming that the portly, chain-smoking 73-year-old had covered 9 miles in 65 minutes, thus breaking all world records by a wide margin. Mao was, moreover, in no particular hurry: He was described as having stopped several times along the way to teach other swimmers some new strokes. Suspicious foreigners also speculated that the official photograph might have been contrived: the chairman's face did not look wet and the angle at which his head met the water did not seem proper. Since the press release quoted several of those present as saying "our respected and beloved leader Chairman Mao is in such good health," those who initially suspected that Mao was ill were now convinced that he was near death.

In August, Mao called out the Red Guards, young people tasked with enforcing revolutionary purity. Guards were to be the children of the so-called five pure classes: workers, poor and lower middle peasants, soldiers, party officials, and revolutionary martyrs. Mao wrote a big-character poster calling on activists to "bombard the headquarters" of established authority and struggle against the power holders who were following the capitalist road. There was a clear implication that Liu Shaoqi, the man who had displaced Mao as head of government in the wake of the Great Leap Forward, was the chief capitalist roader. In addition to attacking established authority, the Red Guards were admonished to attack the "four olds": old ideas, culture, habits, and customs. In order to "exchange revolutionary experiences," they were encouraged to travel as well.

Seemingly instantly, Red Guard groups fanned out all over China. Millions decided that Beijing was the proper place to exchange revolutionary experiences, jamming transportation systems and causing health and sanitation problems. Others who had been sent to the countryside in past years felt that revolutionary experiences could best be exchanged by returning to the families and urban areas from whence they came. Hundreds of thousands returned to already crowded Shanghai and other major cities.

Possible ulterior motives notwithstanding, the young Guards proved extremely zealous. Among their demands were that blood banks draw their supplies only from those of pure class background, that Tiananmen (Gate of Heavenly Peace) Square be renamed East Is Red Square, and that traffic light colors be reversed so that red, the color of revolution, could signify "go" rather than "stop." In accordance with Mao's orders, the Guards did indeed drag out many power holders. The proof of their decadent capitalist leanings was often little more than possession of foreign liquor or a penchant for meals comprising a large number of dishes. Any association with the Soviet Union, whose leaders were believed to have perverted true Marxism–Leninism, was also very dangerous. Liu Shaoqi and a number of others were declared "revisionists" (as opposed to Mao, who was declared a genius for creatively adapting Marxism to the Chinese context). Liu was also castigated as "China's Khrushchev," after the despised leader of the Soviet Union. The Guards also ransacked museums and religious institutions, destroying their contents—all egregious manifestations of the "four olds"—and generally made a nuisance of themselves.

The Red Guards were far from homogeneous or united. While the idea that they should be of pure class background fitted well with the campaign against the "four olds," since the "olds" were associated with the overthrow of the old feudal–bourgeois classes, children from bad family backgrounds protested at their exclusion from the movement. How, they wondered, could one be "red by birth"? Mao's original mandate had, in effect, asked the children of power holders to purge the power holders. When it became clear that the struggle was not producing the desired results, he began to use the children from impure backgrounds against party leaders whom he held responsible for the Red Guards' erroneous line. Hence, two different kinds of Red Guard organizations existed. Although both professed unswerving loyalty to Mao, one was more likely to defend the established power holders than the other.

At the elite level, power shifted from the party organization to a group called the Cultural Revolution Small Group, with Yao Wenyuan, several other Shanghai radicals, and Mao's wife Jiang Qing as prominent members. Jiang, who had been active in left-wing theatrical circles in Shanghai during her youth, had become involved with Mao at Yan'an. Shortly thereafter, the wife who had made the Long March with him was sent off to Moscow "for her health." Since the USSR's capital was not known for either its salubrious climate or the excellence of its medical facilities, she, like Mao's defeated rival Wang Ming, was undoubtedly sent there to get her out of the way. It was rumored that there was considerable discomfort within the Yan'an leadership with this situation and that, in return for their acquiescence, Jiang had had to promise to stay out of politics. Her activities during the Cultural Revolution have been interpreted as motivated by revenge. In addition to the Small Group and the party organization, the PLA, led by defense minister Lin Biao, emerged as a powerful actor. The significance of the attacks in *Liberation Army Daily* and of Lin's editing the little book of Mao's quotations thus became more apparent.

By the late summer of 1966, the principle of "free mobilization of the masses" was adopted: Elite factions, having reached a stalemate in their conflict with each other, drew in the masses, using official ideology to do so. Both party and government bureaucrats and the Small Group maneuvered to achieve control over the mass organizations. For ordinary citizens, mass involvement meant that all sorts of long-suppressed, latent tensions in society rose to the surface. Tens of millions of people who had been socially conditioned by the party's previous mass campaigns responded enthusiastically, and the Cultural Revolution entered a new, more radical phase. No longer did possession of the Little Red Book and Mao badges, or a documentary record that one had been supportive of the party and Chairman Mao, necessarily protect one. Enemies could—and did—claim that the accused was mounting an outward show of support to conceal the disloyalty within. They referred to this behavior as "waving the red flag in order to oppose the red flag." The atmosphere of the Cultural Revolution was militantly egalitarian: Anyone who had had authority over anyone else could be accused of being a corrupt power holder. A large number of people were tortured or driven to suicide. Liu Shaoqi died when, gravely ill, he was denied medical care. Party secretary-general Deng Xiaoping's son, driven to jump out of a window by his Red Guard tormentors, was crippled for life; Deng himself was tortured and removed from office.

In January 1967, the Small Group succeeded in establishing the Shanghai Commune based on the real or imagined model of the Paris Commune during the French Revolution. It was intended to emphasize the spontaneity of the masses without cadre participation but, unfortunately for the radicals, the commune proved unworkable. Chaos ensued as radicals in other areas tried to copy the Shanghai example. Premier Zhou Enlai, who had emerged as leader of the party/government faction, gave the impression of being unconcerned with whether radicals or conservatives seized power, so long as production could proceed normally. Production was definitely not proceeding normally at this time, with railroad traffic disrupted and factories becoming battlegrounds for rival groups of workers. By February, Zhou seemed to have convinced Mao to opt for a more moderate policy. The formation of new bodies called revolutionary committees, which would assume both party and state functions, was ordered. The CPPCC and its functions were not mentioned. As the organ of the united front, which radicals had attacked since it represented collaboration with impure classes, the CPPCC simply disappeared. Revolutionary committees were to be composed of a three-way alliance of representatives of the revolutionary masses, revolutionary cadres, and revolutionary PLA members.

Radicals, believing that the emphasis on regularizing production meant selling out their principles, referred to this period as the "February Adverse Current," and began their counterattack in mid-March. Several other shifts were to occur in what became a power struggle among the Small Group, the PLA, and a group of bureaucrats around Zhou Enlai. Although Mao's sympathies appeared to lie with the radicals, he was not above curbing their activities when it seemed wise, and went to great lengths to publicly show his affection for Lin Biao. The two were photographed arm-in-arm, with the caption describing Lin as "Chairman Mao's Closest Comrade in Arms." Zhou Enlai seemed to have formed a coalition with Jiang Qing's radicals, despite their ideological and policy differences. He protected the Small Group against the PLA, perhaps because he wanted to maintain the balance between the two, with himself as mediator. In return, the Small Group restrained the Beijing radicals from attacking Zhou.

As time went on, the PLA gained power over the Small Group. Mao gave the military authority to use force against any attempt to seize its weapons and told it to unify the various warring factions. Lin Biao was designated Mao's heir apparent. With at least the façade of peace being made among some of the factions, revolutionary committees were set up in 1967 and on into 1968. On July 31, 1968, Mao sent a gift of mangoes to a workers' group stationed at Qinghua University, thereby symbolizing his support of the workers in their factional struggle with the students. The PLA moved onto campuses to maintain order. Thus, the violent phase of the Cultural Revolution came to an end.

In October, the central committee—or what was left of it—met. Its major decision was to expel Liu Shaoqi from the party and from all his posts in party and government. The draft of a new party constitution was also agreed upon. Formally accepted in April 1969, it contained an unusual article designating Lin Biao, by name, as Mao Zedong's successor. Approximately half the politburo could be considered Lin's supporters; even his heretofore politically inactive wife became a member. The Small Group was also prominently represented. Mao and Zhou Enlai were members as well.

At the middle and lower levels of the power structure—provincial level and below—a number of old cadres who had originally been targets of the Red Guards returned to, or remained in, positions of importance. They had neither forgotten nor forgiven their erstwhile tormentors. The "revolutionary masses," on behalf of whom the Cultural Revolution had allegedly been waged, were, at best, admitted selectively to the lowest levels of power, where they were kept under the careful surveillance of those whom they had accused of revisionism and of taking the capitalist road. Some of them were actively persecuted.

If the Great Leap Forward had been antithetical to modernization, the Cultural Revolution was still more so. Its attacks on specialization and routinization of procedures ran directly counter to the modernization paradigm. While it may be argued that Mao opposed bureaucratism rather than bureaucrats and elitist snobbery rather than specialization per se, it proved very difficult in practice to uncouple one from another.

Although falling considerably short of its goals, the Cultural Revolution had a number of other consequences. Rather than establishing greater egalitarianism, the revolution simply replaced many long-serving leaders with new leaders, dubbed "helicopter people" for their rapid ascent upward. The relationships of authority were destroyed in some areas and badly weakened in others. The party and certain ministries had all but ceased to function. Meanwhile, the role of the military in general, and of Lin Biao in particular, had been greatly enhanced. Production had declined, though the drop was by no means as precipitous as during the Great Leap Forward. There were drastic effects on the educational system (see Chapter 10), and both foreign and traditional influences on culture were sharply reduced. What would take the place of institutions that had been damaged or destroyed was not yet clear. A large number of lives and careers had also been damaged. Miraculously, some people emerged from the Cultural Revolution with their faith in the party intact. However, many others blamed the country's leadership for what had happened, thereby further weakening the CCP's legitimacy.

Reconstruction: 1970–1976

As the turmoil of the Cultural Revolution subsided, a rebuilding process began. The year 1970 saw the revival of party organs. Revolutionary committees remained, but functioned as governmental bodies, replacing the people's congresses. Foreign policy also began to return to normal, with diplomats again being posted abroad.

Behind the scenes, a fierce power struggle raged within the disparate coalition that survived the holocaust. The main contenders were Lin Biao and his faction within the military; the Cultural Revolution Small Group, including Jiang Qing, which had its power base in Shanghai; and the less ideological party and government bureaucrats around Zhou Enlai. The prize was survival—and also the succession to Mao. Mao Zedong's health had been the subject of speculation for some years. The fact that he did not show up at several Red Guard rallies in late 1967 was considered noteworthy enough that Jiang Qing, who attended in his place, had seen fit to tour Tiananmen Square in a jeep, announcing repeatedly through a bullhorn that Chairman Mao was in "robust" health. Whatever the truth of this, Mao seemed to decline during the early 1970s; visiting foreign dignitaries were summoned from their beds in the middle of the night or plucked from visits to the Great Wall by helicopter in order to take advantage of Mao's lucid moments. Although Mao's sympathies lay with the Small Group ideologues, he did not automatically side with them.

The first victim of the power struggle was Lin Biao, who made no public appearances after June 1971. He was later officially declared dead in a plane crash that occurred in Mongolia in September of that year. Lin was allegedly fleeing to the Soviet Union—China's arch-enemy at the time—after his plot to kill Chairman Mao was discovered. The "official" story exists in a number of versions, with several discrepancies among them that have never been resolved. Nor is there a convincing explanation of why Lin would want to kill an ill man whom he was constitutionally designated to succeed. Many analysts believe that Lin was actually removed by his rivals Zhou and the Small Group, possibly with the help of non-Lin-affiliated factions of the PLA. Whatever the circumstances, Lin was deleted from the power equation, and more than 130 of his subordinates also disappeared. The succession struggle now had only two major contenders: Jiang Qing's Shanghai hard-liners, and Zhou Enlai's less ideological bureaucrats.

The Tenth Party Congress, held in August 1973, saw the rehabilitation of some leading pre-Cultural Revolution bureaucrats, including former party secretary-general Deng Xiaoping. Regarded as Premier Zhou's leading protégé, Deng quickly regained positions of prominence, including the directorship of the PLA's general staff department and a vice-premiership. A number of military men also re-emerged. Generally from field armies that were different from Lin's, they had opposed the Cultural Revolution. These rehabilitations represented victories for Zhou Enlai and for military leaders outside of the Fourth Field Army.

At the same time, the Cultural Revolution Small Group began to fight back hard, launching a mass campaign to "Criticize Lin Biao and Confucius," in which Confucius was widely understood to mean Zhou Enlai. The main charge against "Confucius" was that he was a "restorationist"—that he wanted to return China to its pre-Cultural Revolution state. Zhou, a master manipulator whose methods were often so subtle that their full extent may never be known, countered the Small Group's attack in various ways. Always outwardly friendly to Jiang Qing, he suggested that she contact an American woman to write her biography. Jiang did so, discussing matters that her enemies later used against her, alleging that she had confided state secrets to foreigners. Satirical cartoons appeared that depicted Jiang Qing as, among others, the empress dowager Cixi. The implied commonality was that both had usurped the prerogatives of leadership that rightfully belonged to their husbands.

Another method used by the radicals, who realized that they had few supporters in the military, was to build up the militia as a counterweight to the PLA. Militia units functioned as vigilante units in a number of cities, enforcing a left-wing line. Meanwhile, Zhou's group cultivated the PLA. As head of its general staff department, Deng Xiaoping was well positioned to do so.

In the end, the relative health of senior leaders rather than clever planning determined the succession, at least in the short run. Zhou Enlai, who had been suffering from a particularly painful form of cancer for several years, died in January 1976. Always eclipsed by Mao's cult of personality, Zhou was nonetheless genuinely beloved by millions of Chinese. His loss was deeply mourned by huge numbers of average people, though, one imagines, by no one more so than his now-vulnerable protégé, Deng Xiaoping. On the next observance of the traditional Chinese festival of *Qingming*, or the sweeping of the graves, in April, Zhou's supporters flocked into Tiananmen Square with floral wreaths commemorating their deceased hero. There was also a large demonstration in favor of Deng and, allegorically, against Mao. According to the official, pro-Maoist account, demonstrators shouted that the people had had enough of "Emperor Qin Shi Huang," the autocratic, egotistical emperor of the Qin dynasty, and made various "counterrevolutionary" and "rightist" demands. Foreign observers confirmed that the demonstrators had denounced Emperor Qin Shi Huang—Mao—and that they had demanded democracy.

At the height of the demonstration, an estimated 100,000 people were in the square. Although the sincerity of the pro-Zhou Enlai sentiment is not in doubt—many of the mourners were openly weeping—it is quite plausible that the demonstration was suggested by Deng for reasons of self-interest. If so, the plan backfired. "The party"—presumably meaning the Cultural Revolution Small Group—sent the militia and some public security and PLA units into Tiananmen Square to suppress "the counterrevolutionaries." This they did: Several people were killed, and a large number were injured. Deng was blamed for instigating the demonstration and stripped of all his party and government posts. His removal from the succession cleared the way for the Shanghai-based Gang of Four to take over. However, to nearly everyone's surprise, this did not happen: Mao Zedong apparently decided to entrust the succession not to the ideologues but to Hua Guofeng, who did *not* belong to either the reform or the hard-line group. He had been a party secretary in his and Mao's native province of Hunan. According to Hua—conveniently the only person present in the room at the time—the terminally ill chairman called Hua to his bedside and wh him, "With you in charge, my heart is at ease."

Mao's health continued to deteriorate. On July 28, 1976, one of hist most devastating earthquakes hit the Tianjin-Beijing area of northeast China claiming many hundreds of thousands of lives. Its occurrence seemed portentous. In classical Chinese, one does not use the usual character for death to describe the passing of an emperor. The proper ideograph depicts the fall of a mountain and means "cataclysm" or "earthquake." A few weeks later, on September 9, Mao died.

Suggestions for Further Reading

Jeremy Brown and Paul Pickowicz, eds, *Dilemmas of Victory: The Early Years of the People's Republic of China* (Cambridge, MA: Harvard University Press, 2007).

Susan V. Lawrence and Michael F. Martin, *Understanding China's Political System* (Washington, DC: Congressional Research Service R41007, March 23, 2013).

Roderick MacFarquhar and Michael Schoenhals, *Mao's Last Revolution* (Cambridge, MA: Belknap Press, 2006).

Alexander Pantsov and Steven I. Levine, *Mao: The Real Story* (New York: Simon & Schuster, 2012).

Yisheng Yang, *Tombstone: The Great Chinese Famine* (New York: Farrar, Strauss, & Giroux, 2012).

CHAPTER 5

Deng Xiaoping and His Protégés: 1976–2012

Interregnum: 1976–1978

Hua Guofeng, having claimed Mao Zedong's mantle by virtue of his conversation with the dying chairman, was duty-bound to preserve Mao's legacy. He pledged himself to "support firmly whatever decisions Chairman Mao made, and to follow persistently whatever directives Chairman Mao gave." This pledge, referred to as "the two whatevers," would later cause Hua considerable discomfort.

Initially, however, Hua Guofeng's position seemed secure. In the confused and potentially volatile months before and immediately after Mao's death, Hua seemed to have at least the acquiescence, if not necessarily the enthusiastic support, of the major groups in the political spectrum. These included groups ranging from the far-left followers of the Gang of Four, led by Mao's widow Jiang Qing, to the furthest-right group, characterized by extremely bitter memories of the Cultural Revolution, whose most prominent member was Deng Xiaoping. In between were three factions representing different groups within the military and a group known as the Petroleum Faction that saw opportunities for developing the PRC's impressive fossil-fuel resources after a Middle East-based oil cartel had succeeded in raising world petroleum prices in the early 1970s.

Throughout all their interactions, an underlying issue was the principles under which the PRC would henceforth be ruled. Mao's death had meant the end of an era. Should the new era be a continuation of the old or involve a reassessment of the changes of the past and a radical break with Maoism? Those who adhered to the former view were frequently described as ideologues or hardliners. They wished to affirm Maoist radical values and methods. Those who preferred to break sharply with the Maoist past are generally termed reformers, even though the reforms they wished to institute, including reduction of state subsidies and greater personal accountability in production, will strike foreign observers as more like what would be referred to in the West as conservatism. Finally, there were a number of people who occupied various intermediate positions on the spectrum between ideological hard-liners and reformers, being in favor of some reforms under some circumstances. The origins of these groups and their interactions fitted well with the central–regional model introduced in Chapter 1, in both its native place and field army variants. The events also fitted neatly with the analyses of the bureaucratic politics and palace politics schools. Although foreign policy was of lesser importance than internal considerations during this period, arguments over the method by which China should acquire foreign technology and on which, if any, foreign powers to rely have overtones of the strategic interaction and political-cultural schools. A generational struggle between old revolutionaries and a younger group who had not endured their struggles was also occurring.

The reader will also notice a reassertion of traditional Chinese values, including the importance of family and patronage ties, which resonates with the China-is-China-is-China paradigm. In the sense that ideological differences did not preclude alliances among different groups, the factional model seemed to apply as well. Since the system now permitted a limited form of competition among those who favored different policies, one may also see an incipient form of pluralism. As predicted by the communist neo-traditional paradigm, political competition took place more within the institutional framework set up by the party than it did along Western-inspired models of interest group articulation. However, none of these analyses could have predicted what was to follow.

Hua's acceptability to various groups as a compromise candidate was in certain ways a liability rather than an asset: He was faced with reconciling often incompatible demands from across the political spectrum and risked being attacked from all directions by those whose requests he could not satisfy. For example, victims of the Cultural Revolution and other leftist-inspired attacks demanded a thorough repudiation of these policies and a reinstatement of their pre-purge status. At the same time, those who had profited by the campaigns strongly resisted attacks on the Maoist system, fearing that their own status would deteriorate.

At the time of Mao's death, the Gang of Four, concerned for its future at the hands of military leaders with whom it had previously dealt harshly, tried to take over, using the urban militia as its armed force. The military acted forcefully in support of Hua, easily defeating the militia. Less than a month after Mao's death, Hua arrested the Gang of Four. Saved from one group, he became more beholden to another. In July 1977, acceding to the wishes of leading military figures, Hua rehabilitated Deng Xiaoping. Understandably reluctant to reinstate the man whose place he had so obviously moved into the year before, Hua took this step only after Deng gave written guarantees of his support for Hua as Mao's successor and admitted his own mistakes. Deng was then restored to his former positions of member of the standing committee of the politburo, vice-premier of the State Council, vice-chair of the Central Military Commission, and chief of the PLA's general staff.

Pledges notwithstanding, Deng immediately began to undermine Hua's position. He revived the office of party general secretary, which had been defunct since Deng had held it at the outset of the Cultural Revolution. Deng then used the position to take over the responsibility, formerly exercised by Hua as premier of the State Council, of overseeing the implementation of politburo decisions. At the same time, Deng began moving his supporters from positions they held in the provinces to the central government in Beijing. One protégé, Zhao Ziyang, the first party secretary of Deng's native province of Sichuan, showed open contempt for Hua. Sichuan did not participate in praise of Hua and instituted agricultural policies that were quite different from those sanctioned by Hua.

In addition to moving his people from the provinces into the center, Deng consolidated power in areas where he and his former mentor, Zhou Enlai, had been strongest, such as the foreign ministry. He rehabilitated previously purged cadres, thereby earning the gratitude and, presumably, the allegiance of experienced and capable people. At the same time, Deng worked to purge or marginalize Hua's supporters. Hua tried to fight back, wrapping himself in the cloak of Maoist legitimacy and seeing that stories showing his love for the people and his ties with Mao appeared regularly in the official press. Observers noticed that he even began to comb his hair in the same style as Mao.

Deng's supporters retaliated, accusing Hua of attempting to create a cult of personality. They also ridiculed him for the "two whatevers," implying that Hua was incapable of more than slavish imitation of Mao. Moreover, they hinted strongly, Hua might have fabricated his alleged deathbed conversation with the chairman. Deng counterposed Hua's pledge to follow Mao's principles with a slogan of his own: "seek truth from facts." This derived from Mao's essay on the need to link theory with practice, which argued that when a theory did not prove consonant with practice, it was necessary to revise the theory. Apart from providing Deng Xiaoping with a cleverly indirect way to attack Hua, the slogan confirmed Deng's reputation as a pragmatist. Henceforth, he declared, practice would be the sole criterion of truth. Dogma was officially dead.

Finally, in December 1978, Deng decided to permit a degree of liberalization. Drawing his inspiration from a Qing dynasty poem that began "Ten thousand horses stand mute," he argued that the repressive atmosphere of previous years had stifled the population's creativity and desire to work hard. Deng proposed to allow the people to actually exercise the freedoms of expression that the constitution had, in theory, already given them. The populace responded with enthusiasm, writing wall posters that contained vigorous denunciations of policies and leaders with whom they disagree. Certain walls became gathering places for poster writers and those who wished to express their views orally. Known as "democracy walls," they sprang up in many cities. By far the most famous was in central Beijing, not far from Tiananmen Square. Because many of the people who gathered at these walls demanded the removal of precisely those power-holders whom Deng wanted to get rid of, his decision to permit greater freedom of speech proved to be an effective weapon.

By early 1979, with its aims largely achieved, the movement was gradually cut off. No longer content with criticizing past leaders, critics had begun to make adverse comments about the present elite, including Deng. Wall poster writers were first moved from central Beijing to a much less conveniently located park, ostensibly because they had been disrupting traffic. Although this was true, other government actions indicated that the leadership had more in mind than gridlock reduction. Poster writers were told to register their names and work units with public security personnel, who were to monitor activities in the park. A few months later, even this constricted avenue of expression was closed.

At the same time, the journals of dissent that had flourished during this period were ordered to cease publication; some of their authors received severe prison terms. The charges against them seemed contrived and implausible. For example, Wei Jingsheng was accused of having passed secrets on China's war with Vietnam to a foreigner. It was difficult to imagine how Wei, an electrician at Beijing Zoo, came to acquire military secrets. What was not controversial was Wei's outspoken advocacy of human rights and democratic reforms. He was sentenced to 15 years in prison. In 1980, the "four freedoms" clause, which allowed people to assemble, express their views, write wall posters, stage demonstrations, and—a fifth freedom—hold strikes, was removed from the PRC's constitution.

Some analysts have interpreted Deng's sponsorship of the democracy movement as cynically manipulative: a tool to be discarded once it had served its purpose. Others saw the crackdown not as evidence of a ruse but, rather, as an attempt to mold democracy into a less socially disruptive form. Yet a third view is that Deng was himself a reformer and in favor of democratic freedoms, but had acceded to the wishes of party conservatives who feared that the movement was getting out of hand.

Deng Ascendant

By the time the Third Plenum of the Eleventh Central Committee of the Chinese Communist Party (CCP) was held in December 1978, the extent to which Deng had been able to exert his influence was clear. With the cult of personality proscribed and Hua diminished in stature, Deng reintroduced a much more ambitious form of the Four Modernizations program that had originally been discussed some years earlier. It was revived by Hua soon after Mao's death, but after the Third Plenum, the program and its ambitious goal of bringing the PRC into the ranks of the more developed countries by the year 2000 became identified with Deng.

The primary focus of the Four Modernizations was economic and is discussed in Chapter 7. The sociopolitical ramifications of these economic reforms were, however, enormous. In order to encourage people to produce more, the leadership sanctioned economic incentives that would have been unthinkable under Mao. They were told that there was no shame in being rich, and, further, that it was all right for some people to become rich before others. Wealth could even be inherited. Agricultural goods could be sold in free markets, and productive factory workers could be awarded bonuses. Unproductive factories would be closed, with workers forced to find other employment. The media repeatedly warned people that the "iron rice bowl"—guaranteed employment regardless of job performance—would be smashed.

Intellectually rigorous examinations were reintroduced as the criterion for admission to universities. At the same time, the requirement for political reliability was quietly downgraded. Under the new regime, "redness" was to be less important than expertise. Rapid modernization would require knowledge of modern technology. To accomplish this faster, Deng announced an "open door" to the advanced countries of the world. Advocating measures that would have sounded familiar to proponents of the self-strengthening movement a century before, Deng announced that foreign trade was welcome, foreign technology could be purchased, and Chinese students would be sent to Western and Japanese universities. There were other innovations as well. Since increases in productivity would have a lesser effect if they had to be divided among a larger number of people, a stringent birth control policy was announced: The ideal family would have only one child, and no more than two was permitted.

In order to enlist the support of intellectuals, the Maoist characterization of them as "the stinking ninth category" was removed. No longer to be despised, experts' advice would be actively sought out. Major party and state ministries and commissions began to consult think-tank specialists. The whole concept of progress through class struggle, which had been so important to the Maoist variant of Marxism–Leninism, was explicitly repudiated. Henceforth, cooperation rather than confrontation was to be the driving force of progress. A new state constitution, promulgated in 1982, deleted the 1978 constitution's definition of China as a "dictatorship of the proletariat" and replaced it with a description of China as a "people's democratic dictatorship." This meant a return to the language used in the original 1954 state constitution.

Class labels such as capitalist and landlord, that had been awarded as long as 30 years ago and that had been hereditary, were removed. An investigation was promised into verdicts rendered during such mass campaigns as the anti-rightist movement of 1957 and the Cultural Revolution of the late 1960s; people discovered to have been wronged would have their verdicts reversed. Many famous figures, including former head of state Liu Shaoqi, were rehabilitated posthumously. Henceforth, verdicts were supposed to be delivered according to proper legal procedures. Because the legal profession had all but disappeared by the late 1970s, codes would have to be drawn up and people trained to implement them. The codes would also cover business practices, since foreign companies were understandably reluctant to trade with a country that did not provide them with any means of redress for such problems as delivery of substandard merchandise or failure to deliver goods at all.

Constitutional guarantees and procedures would also be extended to the electoral system. In marked contrast to the practice of the previous decade, party and state organs would now meet at their scheduled times. Members of these bodies were to be chosen by secret ballot. There would be more candidates than positions, although in lower level elections only, at least at first. This would be a first step toward competitive elections. The Chinese People's Political Consultative Conference was revived. As the organ of the united front, it had disappeared during the Cultural Revolution, when the whole concept of the united front came under attack for being tantamount to collaboration with bourgeois revisionism.

A separation was to be effected between party and government, and between party and military revolutionary committees, which had replaced the organs of party and government during the Cultural Revolution and then retained governmental functions after party organs reappeared, were phased out. Communes first lost their government functions and then were dismantled completely. They, as well as the revolutionary committees, were replaced by standard, pre-Cultural Revolution governmental bodies.

A new, more tolerant policy toward religion was announced. Services could again be held, and the government offered help in rebuilding churches, mosques, and temples that had been destroyed in the Cultural Revolution. It announced the creation of an institute for the study of religion and that it would subsidize a new edition of the Koran—the first to be printed, legally at least, in China since 1949. Policy toward ethnic minorities also became more tolerant.

While foreign observers described these changes as China's turn toward capitalism and democracy, Deng vigorously denied it, stating that his intent was to create "socialism with Chinese characteristics." What this meant was never explicitly stated, though the official media supplied a four-point summary, known as the Four Basic Principles, of the new orthodoxy:

1. acceptance of the leadership of the communist party;
2. adherence to Marxism–Leninism–Mao Zedong thought;
3. the practice of democratic centralism;
4. following the socialist road.

There are obvious problems with this definition. A great deal of content in Deng's new program was in direct opposition to Marxism, Leninism, and the thought of Mao. And how could one follow the socialist road when many of the directional signals appeared to be written in capitalist language? Other problems in operationalizing Deng's principles soon appeared. Economic *decentralization* had uncomfortable consequences for the *centralized* political leadership of the CCP, and promises for truly competitive elections at lower levels were contrary to the *practice* of democratic centralism. Although the *principle* of democratic centralism stipulates that lower level bodies should elect the members of higher level bodies, in reality it had been just the opposite. Now, when the higher levels persisted in picking all the candidates for lower level positions, vigorous protests occurred. Ambiguities and dissonances from reality notwithstanding, the Four Basic Principles constituted the definition of the new socialism and became the standard against which loyalty was judged.

The Legacy of Mao

The large number of changes from Maoist theory and practice, plus the rehabilitation of so many people, including Deng, who had suffered under him, inevitably raised the question of Mao's legacy. Deng apparently wanted an explicit repudiation of the chairman and was enthusiastically supported by many others who considered themselves victims of Mao's regime. Several moves were made in this direction. The Mao mausoleum was closed for several months in 1979, and stories appeared in the official press describing the hardships of the workers whose homes had been razed in order to build the edifice. In that it was clear to all who had given the order to build the Mao mausoleum, this had the effect of tarnishing Hua as well as Mao. In August 1980, the central committee issued a directive banning all personality cults of all leaders, dead or alive. Mao's and Hua's pictures were the only ones that were regularly hung in public places, and images of both rapidly disappeared from most offices and meeting halls. Several statues of Mao were dismantled, some of them toppled by angry crowds. There was no overt official sanction of such acts, but neither were the perpetrators punished, as would have happened only a few years before.

In November 1980, the Gang of Four was put on trial, with carefully edited excerpts of the proceedings made available for television broadcast. Its members were charged with executing policies that were widely believed to have had the backing of Mao. A defiant Madame Mao argued exactly this from the prisoners' dock. Characterizing herself as "Chairman Mao's dog," she described her role as barking when he told her to bark. Most politically aware Chinese seem to have understood the trial as an indictment of Mao. Foreign visitors who spoke with locals about the Gang of Four reported that they pointedly held up five fingers, the last digit representing the chairman as unindicted co-conspirator.

There were also people who strongly disapproved of the idea of destroying Mao Zedong's reputation. Some were ideological hard-liners who had been advantaged during the period when such policies had prevailed. Significantly, however, others had not. One elderly military officer who had been cruelly treated during the Cultural Revolution pleaded poignantly that removing Mao from his place of honor would leave young people with nothing to believe in, thus provoking the kind of crisis of confidence he had noticed in many countries of the West, despite the high level of material well-being they had achieved.

Eventually, a compromise was reached by declaring that Mao's record was 70 percent positive and 30 percent negative. His mausoleum reopened, with a chamber containing Zhou Enlai memorabilia added. Pictures of Mao were rehung in public places, albeit in lesser numbers than before. The study of his works resumed, but more selectively and with less fervor. No longer idolized, Mao was at least accorded a modicum of respect.

Political Realignment and Policy Readjustment

Politically, Deng Xiaoping moved steadily to consolidate his power. The same Third Plenum of the party's Eleventh Central Committee that introduced a new, more ambitious version of the Four Modernizations also saw the resignation of several potential rivals. As well, the plenum officially reversed the verdict on the Tiananmen incident of 1976, which had led to Deng Xiaoping's last purge.

Because Hua Guofeng had been minister of public security at the time of the incident, he might well have been indicted in 1980 along with the Gang of Four. Deng's price for not doing so was reported to be Hua's resignation.

Hua was replaced as premier by Deng's protégé, the former Sichuan party secretary Zhao Ziyang. Another Deng ally, Hu Yaobang, whose previous career had been concentrated in the Communist Youth League (CYL), took over as party general secretary. Deng Xiaoping himself took over Hua's position as head of the party's Central Military Commission. Deng then withdrew from his position as head of the PLA's general staff department and replaced himself with yet another old ally from his Second Field Army, Qin Jiwei. He had thus chosen to install his protégés in the top positions in party and government rather than taking either position himself. There was, however, no doubt who exercised ultimate decision making. Deng was referred to as "the paramount leader," a position that existed on no organization chart. Actual power at the top of the PRC leadership was therefore not synonymous with theoretical power, as indeed it had not been under the latter part of Hua Guofeng's time in high office either.

Deng then moved to discredit the Petroleum Faction by holding it responsible for concealing the capsizing of an oil-exploration rig in the North China Sea. Suspicions that the release of this information was politically motivated—the information was released a year after the event had occurred—were reinforced when the scandal was *not* blamed on the remnant poison of the Gang of Four, as virtually everything else at that time had been. A military faction leader was removed after a spate of PLA publications took a markedly different propaganda line from that espoused by Deng. Another military leader, Marshal Ye Jianying, was decidedly more difficult for Deng to deal with. Although privately defiant, he did not publicly challenge Deng. As Ye was also nearly 90 years old, Deng may have considered that time was on his side.

Having successfully neutralized his rivals, Deng found that some of his reforms were themselves causing problems. The "ten thousand horses" that had stood mute were definitely energized, but the flaw in Deng's reasoning was his assumption that the changes he introduced would cause all of them to rush forward in the desired direction. What actually happened was that while some did rush forward, others hung back or charged off in a number of different directions, and a few even butted heads with each other. In practice, economic decentralization often led to wasteful duplication, adversely affecting profits and sometimes leading to cutthroat competition. For example, five areas decided to build cigarette factories when only one was needed. From the government's point of view, too much money was being invested in the wrong kinds of projects: Localities typically decided to construct upscale guest houses rather than more needed facilities, such as fertilizer factories. Some areas refused to sell resources needed by others, preferring to use them locally, and also indulged in other market-fragmenting actions like imposing levies on trucks passing through. If selling vegetables brought more money than selling pigs, many independent producers switched to raising vegetables, resulting in shortages of pork. A policy that tried to limit families to just one child was most unpopular, particularly among the farmers who formed the great majority of China's citizens at that time.

Deng's judgment that it was acceptable to be rich and that it was all right for some to become rich before others led to increasing inequalities of income and a concomitant increase in jealousy—the "red-eye disease." Those with an entrepreneurial flair and a willingness to work longer hours than their fellows often became comparatively wealthy, but not without dangers to themselves. One woman's neighbors destroyed all the eggs she had planned to sell; another's broke the legs of her milk cows, forcing her to kill the cows herself. Still other newly prosperous people were victimized by cadres who exacted punitive "taxes." Moreover, not everyone who became rich did so as a result of intelligence and hard work. Some prospered because they were able to exploit family or other connections—the pervasive *guanxi*. Those who had access to vehicles and warehouses could buy items cheaply in one area, smuggle them to another, and hoard them until scarcity drove the price up to the profit margin they wanted. Regional income disparities were also widened by the new policies: Nature had endowed some areas with better resources than others.

Another focus of jealousy was the children of high-ranking officials. It was noted that they constituted a disproportionate number of those who were selected to study abroad and that Deng Xiaoping's own son was among them. When and if they decided to return to China, these privileged sons and daughters of the powerful frequently obtained positions with access to foreign currency and travel to coveted destinations. Often, such positions were connected with the PRC's newly founded foreign trading companies, where the children might receive lucrative bribes from companies desiring contracts or access to their influential parents. This aroused intense resentment from their peers, who considered themselves at least as well qualified, and often were. The individuals thus favored became known as princelings.

Many leaders became concerned with the rise of what they regarded as rampant materialism that led people to have little regard for other human beings. Examples that would support their claim abounded. A survey conducted at a Tianjin factory asked the question "What is your ideal?" A composite response went something like "I find revolutionary ideals hollow. Only visible and tangible material benefits are useful." On the other side of the spectrum from materialism, the reforms also generated idealism of a sort that made some leaders equally uncomfortable. In 1980 and 1981, a series of disturbances took place on college campuses in different parts of the country. The proximate cause was a local communist party decision to delete from the ballot the name of a student who was a candidate for local office in Changsha. Arguing that elections in which the party vetted the candidates were not free elections, large numbers of students began to protest. Their demands soon moved beyond reinstating the student's name on the ballot and toward more fundamental issues like human rights and democracy.

The promise to investigate past judgments and, if warranted, to reverse verdicts clogged the system. Enormous numbers of petitioners appeared. These included people who had been sent down to the countryside 10 or 20 years before and who were eager to return. When their demands were not dealt with quickly, they were likely to demonstrate in front of party or government offices and to publicly declare that they held their leaders responsible. Desperate to present their grievances to the leadership, a small army of peasants camped out in Beijing in the bitterly cold winter of 1979/1980. They also proved ready to talk with foreign reporters: Much to the annoyance of the elite, their pinched faces and sad stories were frequently featured by foreign news media.

Generally speaking, there was broad agreement within both the leadership and the public on what the country's problems were: inflation, corruption, nepotism, inefficiency, and low production levels. Where they disagreed was on how to deal with the problems. Leftists tended to hold the reforms responsible for the problems and to argue that recentralization of party and government controls was needed to curb these dangerous tendencies before chaos ensued. Reformers believed that many of the problems had arisen because the reforms had been partial: More reforms were needed. They added that to rescind them or to suppress people's right to criticize aberrations of the system would lead to worse problems and even chaos. Both groups favored the goals of the reforms, but leftists tended to be more fearful of the consequences thereof. They wanted to move more slowly on implementing the reforms while acting faster to correct problems they saw as caused by them.

One should be wary of differentiating too sharply between the two groups, since the specific circumstances of China's situation at any given point in time could persuade some people who had been in favor of rapid reforms to opt for a more moderate pace, or vice versa. Even the strongest pro-democracy activists were aware that many obstacles had to be overcome before they could bring about the sorts of sweeping reforms they favored. For example, in the mid-1980s, a young man who would become a prominent human rights activist during the 1989 demonstrations attempted to survey public opinion in rural Gansu province. He abandoned the effort after discovering that most peasants were unable to read, much less fill out his questionnaires. An interview with one of the richest and best-educated peasants in the area also yielded surprising results. Of course, said the patriarch with feeling, he knew who Chairman Mao was: the emperor. He had been a great emperor, and the new emperor, Deng, also seemed good. The peasant added emphatically that reform was good, and that he agreed with whatever the government did. Later, the frustrated interviewer told a fellow researcher that "if we gave these people the vote tomorrow, they would simply agree to surrender all their rights to the emperor."

The crisis of faith that some had feared would accompany a repudiation of Mao seemed to come about anyway. One small incident in 1981, involving a traffic accident between the mayor of Shanghai's limousine and a truck, may be indicative of attitudes toward authority. Seemingly indifferent to the matter of who was responsible for the crash, a crowd of bystanders quickly surged forward to form a barrier between the truck driver and the traffic police. In shouted consensus, they announced that a fitting punishment would be for the mayor to be crushed to death in his car. Reformers had, in essence, encouraged emancipation of the mind from the fetters of rigid and outworn dogma, but without providing a coherent new set of ideals. This, in turn, caused many to pursue selfish, materialistic goals, or, alternatively, to adopt Western notions of freedom and democracy. Increasing numbers turned to religion, whether imported or domestic, thus rejecting the party's atheistic stance.

Such tendencies worried the leadership, and its emphasis switched from reform to readjustment, aiming to correct the imbalances caused by previous reforms. A campaign against "spiritual pollution" began in October 1983 to try to counter rampant materialism. Excoriating the emphasis on money making, it also criticized those who had forsaken fine revolutionary traditions of plain living and austerity in favor of Western-derived notions of hedonism. These included long hair, gold jewelry, tight blue jeans, and sunglasses as well as interest in "vulgar" Western books, rock music, and pornography. The latter category was rather broadly interpreted and included material that Westerners might describe as merely bawdy, off-color, or even as art.

The protracted debate of the 1980s over how much to borrow from foreign industrialized states and how much to rely on China's indigenous resources and customs reminded many observers of the abortive self-strengthening movement of 100 years before. The twentieth-century debate about how to deal with distasteful customs and mores that accompanied foreign technology seemed to emphasize again what Yan Fu had pointed out in the nineteenth century: Western learning had an essence of its own, which proved impossible to separate from the practical uses to which China wished to put Western technology.

The campaign against spiritual pollution was not a success. Peasants, many of whom had been among the beneficiaries of Deng's encouragement of free-market policies, concluded that the new rhetoric was likely to portend a reversal of those policies. Their concern that they might be branded capitalists and persecuted, present ever since the new policies were introduced, grew. Those who had developed a fondness for Western clothing, hairstyles, and entertainment were loath to give them up. Foreign reaction ranged from amusement at all the sins for which Western influence was held responsible, to apprehension that China's open door might be about to close again. In that peasant concerns about the movement were having a detrimental effect on agricultural production, rural areas were exempted from the campaign against spiritual pollution only two months after it began. The campaign itself faded out a few months later, on Deng's orders.

Other problems addressed at this time included streamlining bureaucratic organs and the number of personnel who staffed them. Ambitious economic development plans had led to a proliferation of new offices and bureaus to oversee them. A great deal of redundancy and overlap existed among the different entities, causing lengthy delays in getting projects approved, turf fights, and various other inefficiencies. Some reform plans were thwarted by leftists, often elderly and poorly educated, who were entrenched in bureaucracy. No retirement age had been established for senior cadres, many of whom were in their seventies and eighties. Below them, a large number of capable people had remained unpromoted for decades, thus dampening their enthusiasm. Reduction in numbers and ages of personnel offered a way to solve some of these problems. Since the cuts could be arranged to fall disproportionately on opponents of Deng's programs, the drive could be used to reduce factionalism and ease the path of reform as well.

The Twelfth Party Congress in September 1982 established the Central Advisory Commission as a way to retire some elderly senior leaders with honor. The commission did absorb some of these, but not necessarily with the desired effect. Several individuals agreed to leave their current positions for the advisory group, but not until they were able to select their own successors. Typically, this was someone who could be expected to do his mentor's bidding, and the older leader therefore continued to rule from behind the scenes.

The handpicked successor was often the retiree's own son or daughter, thus swelling the ranks of the princelings and giving credibility to the arguments of critics of that faction. Some elderly leaders would not resign at all. These included Ye Jianying, Deng's erstwhile ally and more recent nemesis. In that more people who did not possess formal power continued to exercise real power, the creation of the Central Advisory Commission and various other schemes to induce the elderly to retire widened the gap between theoretical responsibility and actual authority.

The retirements caused other problems as well. In his zeal to reduce the average ages of office holders, Deng had passed over an entire generation in its sixties and late fifties, leading to grave disappointments and loss of morale. Moreover, a select group of Deng cronies, headed by Deng himself, remained at the center stage of power despite being in their late seventies or early eighties. A newspaper which suggested that Deng should set an example by resigning himself was promptly closed down. Deng had, in fact, made an effort to relinquish his position as chair of the Central Military Commission (CMC)—though he did not suggest leaving his seat on the politburo—in favor of his protégé Hu Yaobang. Since Hu was party general secretary, this would have placed the party's top military position in the hands of the person who held the highest position in the party, as had been the case while Mao ruled and also during the earlier part of Hua Guofeng's time in office. Arguing that Hu had no significant military experience, and apparently also believing that he lacked good judgment, PLA leaders were able to block the move. This resistance from the military represented a significant weakness in Hu's position. While Deng certainly retained ultimate decision-making power with regard to the military, he was busy with many more pressing aspects of the administration of China. The actual day-to-day running of the PLA was in the hands of the CMC's general secretary, Yang Shangkun.

The mid-1980s were characterized by some events that allowed the reformers to claim success for their program and by others that lent credence to the leftist critique thereof. For example, nominal personal income rose in 1985, but so did the inflation rate. Rising prices triggered panic buying, which in turn caused shortages. Shortages encouraged black marketeering, speculation, and smuggling. Many of these illegal activities were organized by cadres or their children, thus further eroding the ordinary citizen's faith in the leadership. An elaborate $1.5 billion foreign exchange scam was uncovered on Hainan Island, with the island's highest-ranking official serving as ringleader. Trying to recover the total amount would have crippled the island's economy. Punishments were relatively light, and therefore probably had little disincentive effect on others who might be contemplating similarly deft financial maneuvers.

The removal from office of the leftist propaganda chief who had headed the campaign against spiritual pollution cheered reformers, as did the results of a special party conference held in September 1985. Ten of the politburo's 24 members resigned, including the doughty Ye Jianying. In what was believed to be Ye's price for departing, his son, Ye Xuanping, was named governor of Guangdong province shortly thereafter. The senior Ye had been a member of the even more select standing committee of the politburo as well; his departure from that body meant that the standing committee now numbered five, with the reformers Deng Xiaoping, Hu Yaobang, and Zhao Ziyang having a slight numerical edge over leftists Chen Yun and Li Xiannian. Here again, however, there were doubts as to how much the reform faction had gained. The procedures involved in the resignations were quite irregular. According to the party constitution, the resignations should have occurred at a party congress, not at a conference whose members were invited at the discretion of the party leader. The implication was that Deng felt he lacked broad consensus within the party to make these changes.

A plenary session of the party central committee held immediately after the conference added six new members to the politburo, most of whom were younger and better educated than those they replaced. One of the newly appointed was Li Peng, a Soviet-educated engineer. Although Li, orphaned at an early age, was the adopted son of Zhou Enlai, the widespread popular affection for Zhou did not extend to Li. A leftist in most aspects, he was also a member of the princeling faction. The same plenary session also featured a highly unusual—because it was so public—debate between Deng Xiaoping and the leftist economist Chen Yun. Predictably, Deng made a speech praising the results of his reforms and noting the increases in living standards that had resulted. Chen followed by pointing out that the number of high-income households had been greatly exaggerated, and noting that the country's grain production had, in reality, gone down. In what is perhaps the most telling indication of the relative strength of the two sides, the official media printed both speeches in order of presentation.

The disagreements between those who were more in favor of reforms and those who were less so were also mirrored in a debate on the relevance of Marxism to present-day problems. Initially, Marx seemed to be losing ground. In October 1984, Deng Xiaoping observed that China need not fear "a little capitalist stuff," and on December 7, an unsigned commentary in the official party newspaper *Renmin Ribao* stated that "one cannot expect that the works of Marx and Lenin, written in their times, will solve the problems of today."

A few days later, however, the newspaper noted that it had made a mistake; the commentary should have said that the works of Marx and Lenin should not be expected to solve *all* of present-day China's problems. In March 1985, Deng stressed the need to heighten ideological vigilance lest the country's youngsters fall victim to capitalist ideas. Marx and Lenin had clearly regained official backing, with Deng's behavior interpreted as yet another of his tactical retreats in the face of criticism.

Infighting between reformers and leftists continued. Uncertainty about whether the system would move backward, forward, or stay the same caused problems as well. The nation's peasant-oriented newspaper repeated a favorite slogan of its constituency: "Fear neither waterlogging nor drought, but a change in the party's policies." Those who believed that they could make no predictions about the future were reluctant to invest in the present. Although such attitudes were understandable, they had a dampening effect on development. Officials also worried about the rising incidence of disorder, with the population increasingly unwilling to accept their directives. In widely different parts of the country there were soccer riots, anti-Japanese demonstrations, Turkic Muslim protests against nuclear testing in Xinjiang, and demonstrations against various official abuses of power. In 1986, a Beijing crowd estimated at 1,000 cornered a police vehicle, jeering at its occupants and threatening to overturn it. The rather minor incident that had sparked this confrontation—a policeman had slapped a motorcyclist in an argument over a traffic violation—suggested the existence of a more serious underlying hostility toward police authority.

At the end of 1986, large student demonstrations began at a university in Hefei, Anhui province. Despite an official attempt to suppress the news, the demonstrations quickly spread to many other areas, including Shanghai and Beijing. On January 1, 1987, Beijing students assembled in Tiananmen Square, defying both an explicit ban against demonstrating and the freezing weather. To further discourage the gathering, the police had sprayed water onto the huge square, transforming it into a slick sheet of ice. Among the students' demands were greater democratization in general and, specifically, the return of the "four freedoms" clause that had been deleted from the constitution in 1980. After several weeks of uncertainty, the demonstrations were put down.

Leftists saw the unrest as proof of their contention that granting political freedoms would lead to chaos and disruption. Hu Yaobang, with his background in the Youth League and his association with the reform group, was blamed for mishandling the demonstrations and resigned as party general secretary. A spate of anecdotes illustrating Hu's inept conduct in the office began to circulate. Some simply repeated previously known stories; others may have been fabricated. The common thread of the anecdotes reinforced the wisdom of PLA leadership in blocking Hu's appointment as CMC chair. Others of lesser renown were also relieved of their positions for complicity in the demonstrations. Among them was Fang Lizhi, the vice-president of the Anhui university where the demonstrations began. An eminent astrophysicist, he had also been vocal in support of democratization.

Deng's acquiescence in the dismissal of his long-time protégé Hu Yaobang was generally interpreted as yet another tactical retreat in the face of resistance. The commonly heard analogy was to chess: Deng had sacrificed a pawn, Hu, in order to save the king, himself, and his reforms. Subsequent events seemed to bear out this hypothesis. Leftists of all ages, and elderly leftists in particular, seemed to gain in power. A campaign against bourgeois liberalism was stepped up, and there was much talk about upholding the Four Basic Principles. Official pronouncements declared that adherence to the four principles had become "the central task of the political and ideological sphere." Deng himself sounded more leftist, calling, for example, for a restoration of the party's tradition of democratic centralism. He also spoke of "neo-authoritarianism," implying that steady progress toward economic development could best be ensured by a leadership with highly concentrated powers.

By April 1987, the tide had turned toward reforms. Deng again took the lead, telling a foreign visitor that a leftist tendency in the party was jeopardizing China's economic reforms. Zhao Ziyang, who had taken over Hu Yaobang's position on an acting basis, delivered several speeches with liberal overtones. In November 1987, the party's Thirteenth Party Congress confirmed Zhao as general secretary and made him first vice-chair of the CMC, an honor never bestowed on his predecessor. Deng Xiaoping, Li Xiannian, and Chen Yun resigned from the standing committee of the politburo on grounds of their advanced ages and collectively entered the Central Advisory Commission. This left Zhao as the only holdover from the previous standing committee. Although the new standing committee had a three-to-two leftist edge, it contained no open critics of reform. Reformers were prominently represented in the politburo as well. These included Hu Yaobang. Since Hu had been demoted by the leftists partially because they thought he had been too lenient in his treatment of the students, the students now saw him as the champion of their cause. The deliberations of the congress indicated that reforms would continue to be made.

The Seventh National People's Congress, meeting in March and April 1988, continued the mixed signals sent by the Thirteenth Party Congress. Its communiqué stressed that reform was China's central task. At the same time, two elderly leftists with military backgrounds, Yang Shangkun and Wang Zhen, were selected as president and vice-president of the PRC, respectively, and Li Peng became premier. Li's speech focused on coping with inflation and declining grain production, both standard leftist themes.

A few months later, Zhao Ziyang, apparently with Deng's backing, launched an ambitious retail price reform. While completely in line with the end goal of reducing state subsidies and moving toward a free market, the reform produced the worst inflation in post-1949 China. The official figure, 18.5 percent, is believed to be less than half the actual inflation rate, which some estimates placed at almost 50 percent. There were runs on banks, panic buying, and greatly increased social disorder. Deng characteristically opted for tactical retreat; Zhao, however, pressed on. During the summer, he presented the politburo with a daring proposal to end all state price controls within four to five years and, furthermore, proposed to devalue the currency in order to encourage the country's exports.

This scheme would have been ambitious under the best of circumstances. These were not the best of circumstances. Given the escalating inflation rate and level of popular discontent, Zhao's plan struck not only leftists but also some reformers as unacceptably foolhardy. Sources close to Zhao later explained that Deng had urged Zhao to do it, but shifted the blame to him when resistance was encountered. By the time of the Thirteenth Central Committee's Third Plenum in September, it became clear that price reform had been postponed indefinitely. Other solutions favored by leftists would be pursued: efforts to cut back on capital construction, recentralize decision making, and rectify ideology. Rumor had it that Zhao had been stripped of his responsibility for economic work. Despite official denials, Zhao's activities in the economic sphere diminished at the same time that leftists like Li Peng became more active. Official sources again spoke of the advantages of neo-authoritarianism, with its proponents envisioning Zhao Ziyang as the strong force guiding reform. Deng appeared to become increasingly worried about the consequences of his own reform program, and to be siding with the leftists. In the words of one disgruntled intellectual, Deng's admonition to seek truth from facts had been transformed to mean "seek truth from certain approved facts." Anti-Deng doggerel became increasingly common. One of the more popular ditties, sung to the tune of the hymn to Mao, "The East Is Red," went as follows:

> The west is red; the sun has set/A Deng Xiaoping has come
> He serves the privileged very well/And tells the rest to go to hell.

Such pressures seem to have convinced the leadership to respond by digging in its heels rather than giving in. Intellectuals resisted, calling for greater freedom for all and the release of political prisoners. Students spoke openly of a large demonstration to commemorate the seventieth anniversary of the May Fourth Movement in 1919. Protests in Tibet during March 1989, later alleged to have been instigated by the government, resulted in martial law being declared there. The atmosphere was rife with anticipation.

The Tiananmen Demonstrations, 1989

The sense that a time of reckoning was near may have convinced Hu Yaobang to come forward again. At a politburo meeting dedicated to the discussion of problems in education, Hu reportedly suffered a fatal heart attack while arguing with a leading leftist over greater state aid to the sector. This rumor seemed suspiciously tailored to fit the students' cause, though the important thing is that most of them appeared to believe it. Again flouting the ban on demonstrations, as they had in 1986/1987, thousands of them staged a sit-in at Tiananmen Square the night before Hu's memorial service. There was talk of founding unions for students and workers on the model of Poland's Solidarity movement. Similar demonstrations were held, and similar demands made, in many other Chinese cities.

Zhao Ziyang was on an official visit to North Korea, thus inadvertently helping the leftist cause. Premier Li Peng and President Yang Shangkun, who was concurrently general secretary of the CMC, met with Deng Xiaoping, who approved a hard line toward the demonstrations. On April 26, *Renmin Ribao* published an editorial prohibiting the protests, which were deemed counterrevolutionary. It warned that troops would be sent in, if necessary, to quell the "chaotic disturbances."

The students, who generally considered themselves patriotic remonstrators in the traditional Chinese sense of carrying out the duty of educated citizens to press the government to right existing wrongs, were upset and insulted by the April 26 editorial. A mass march of as many as 100,000 students surged into Tiananmen Square, meeting only token resistance from security forces. The students were supported by an estimated 1 million Beijing citizens, many of whom marched with them under the banners of their work units and made their own demands on the government. Newspaper reporters, for example, carried banners asking to be allowed to print the truth, thereby implying that they had been forced to print lies for the past 40 years. Party and government leaders were not pleased. Even more irksome was the fact that many banners were written in both English and Chinese, indicating that the demonstrators had a foreign audience in mind as well.

Placards denouncing inflation and official corruption joined those asking for freedom and democracy. Leaders were criticized by name, with Li Peng a favorite target. Deng Xiaoping also had a number of detractors, with one banner reading: "It doesn't matter whether it is a black cat or a white cat if it is a bad cat." The party's monopoly of power was criticized as well: One poster proclaimed that "absolute power corrupts absolutely." The students began a hunger strike in support of their demands, again attracting the rapt attention of the foreign media. By mid-May, the entire population of Beijing seemed to support the demonstrators.

Although the leadership tried to prevent news of the demonstrations from reaching other parts of the PRC, the U.S.-sponsored radio service Voice of America (VOA), which reported the events as they took place, drew a wide audience from all over China. Always acutely sensitive to foreign influence in Chinese politics, partially due to the experiences of the previous century, the leadership became very angry with both the VOA and the government that sponsored it. Chinese living abroad were also able to communicate foreign media reports to their friends and relatives in the PRC via telephone or the country's still rather few facsimile machines ("truth from fax," quipped one observer). In Hong Kong, where many citizens were apprehensive about the colony's scheduled reversion to PRC sovereignty in 1997, self-interest as well as ethical values led to strong support for the demonstrators' demands. To the annoyance of the PRC leadership, generous donations poured in from Hong Kong, Taiwan, and elsewhere.

Soviet general secretary Mikhail Gorbachev's visit to Beijing, which should have provided the Chinese leadership with a triumphant conclusion to the Sino–Soviet dispute, was disrupted. Since the logical, and more impressive, route from the airport to the Great Hall of the People was blocked by several hundred thousand protestors, Gorbachev's car had to be rerouted through dilapidated back streets. This sent a clear signal that the CCP's control over its people was tenuous, which could only weaken the Chinese leadership's bargaining position with Gorbachev. Infuriated, Li Peng and Yang Shangkun lectured an unrepentant group of students on their behavior.

Zhao Ziyang, having returned to China, attempted to play the intermediary between the protestors and the party leadership hard-liners, but his compromise proposal was rejected by the politburo. At midnight on May 19, the day after Gorbachev left China, Premier Li Peng chaired a nationally televised meeting of several thousand party, government, and military officials. He announced that, in accordance with Article 89 of the country's constitution, the government had decided to declare martial law in most of Beijing. Zhao Ziyang was the only member of the politburo standing committee not present on the platform. Symbolically, Zhao's place was occupied by PRC president and party Central Military Commission general secretary Yang Shangkun.

The next two weeks were characterized by behind-the-scenes maneuvering. Deng was reportedly using his powers of persuasion to enlist the support of several influential PLA leaders who objected to using military force against civilians. Yang Shangkun was also able to call upon units considered part of his loyalty network, the "Yang family village." Such activities left little doubt that the functioning of the modern Chinese state continued to be marked by a high degree of personalism.

Civilian resistance made it difficult for even those troops who wanted to enforce martial law to do so. Meanwhile, heat, exhaustion, and poor sanitary conditions in Tiananmen Square were rapidly depleting the ranks of demonstrators. In what seemed a desperate move to staunch the outflow, art students created a large styrofoam statue of a woman with a torch that they called the Goddess of Democracy. Set up in the square, the figure, which bore a marked resemblance to America's Statue of Liberty, attracted a large number of people. Foreign observers described the crowds as drawn more by curiosity than by a desire to join the protest. Nonetheless, leftists, already leery of foreign "bourgeois" influence, did not react well to the arrival of the statue. Finally, in the early hours of Sunday, June 4, the troops attacked. In full view of foreign television cameras, tanks smashed barricades, and soldiers fired into the crowds.

By morning's first light, the demonstrators were gone. The government claimed that only 300 were killed, none of them in Tiananmen Square itself; foreign and dissident Chinese estimates ranged into the low thousands. Whatever the actual count, it was small in comparison to those who died in the Great Leap Forward and Cultural Revolution. The significance of the Tiananmen incident of 1989 lies not in the numbers killed but in the symbolism of the event. The image of tanks rolling toward unarmed young people and ordinary citizens protesting injustice was horrifying. The party's already tenuous claim to represent the people was weakened still further. Demonstrations in other cities were also put down.

The failure of the Tiananmen demonstrators to achieve their goals weighed heavily on the survivors and their sympathizers, particularly after the victories of similar popular protests in the USSR and in Eastern Europe. They tended, probably unfairly, to blame themselves. The demonstrations in the PRC, by encouraging others to voice their grievances openly, may have resonated throughout the communist world. The Chinese situation was also different from that in the Soviet Union and Eastern Europe. Deng Xiaoping's personal ties with the military appeared to have been critical in winning over PLA leaders who were reluctant to move on the protestors. By contrast, Gorbachev had made many enemies within the Soviet military through years of budget cutting, and the Romanian military did not support Ceaucesçu. Poland, unlike China, had an organized opposition, the Solidarity movement, headed by the charismatic Lech Walesa. Factionalism within the ranks of the Chinese demonstrators was, however, a problem, and apparently no attempt was made to draw the peasants into the protest movement. Were the demonstrations to be held again today, the outcome might be very different. No subsequent leader had or has the depth of ties with the military and the personal authority that Deng Xiaoping enjoyed, and the peasantry, quiescent during the 1989 demonstrations, has become far more restive.

In the short run, the resolution of the demonstrations was a victory for leftists. The day after the Tiananmen incident, Deng appeared, surrounded by his octogenarian support group, most of them (President Yang Shangkun and Vice-President Wang Zhen being the exceptions) members of the Central Advisory Commission rather than holders of formal positions of authority. There seemed no better way to symbolize who was in charge in China: The PRC had not yet managed the transition from the revolutionary generation to the successor generation.

Zhao Ziyang was replaced as party general secretary by Jiang Zemin, a former Shanghai party chief. Like Premier Li Peng, Jiang was an engineer who had received training in the Soviet Union. Never very popular in Shanghai, Jiang may have come to the attention of party leftists because of his efficient suppression of the 1986/1987 demonstrations there. He had also fired the editor of a Shanghai newspaper known for its willingness to test the limits of government censorship. Shanghai people believed that Jiang had not worked very hard to obtain their city's fair share of resources allocated by the central government, which central government leftists may have regarded as a point in his favor. However, Jiang had presided over a number of reforms in Shanghai and could not simply be classified as a leftist.

Zhao was also deprived of his seat on the standing committee of the politburo, being replaced by Jiang Zemin. The policies China pursued for two years following the Tiananmen incident of 1989 were somewhat more to the left, but with certain important counter-trends. Initial fears that the open door to the outside world would be slammed shut were not borne out. The new leadership continued to value the skills that could be learned in foreign countries; it also continued to seek foreign investment and foreign tourism. Market reforms moved ahead, and stock exchanges were opened. Internally, however, the government became more repressive. Those who spoke out during the demonstrations were identified and apprehended. There were increased pressures toward ideological conformity, including a campaign to learn, yet again, from that selfless hero of the early 1960s, Lei Feng (see Chapter 9).

Domestically, the leadership continued to chart a course of economic reforms and political authoritarianism. Deng's well-publicized trip to areas of south China in early 1992 that had prospered through his reforms symbolized his decision to again speed up the pace of those reforms. In line with his wishes, the Fourteenth Party Congress, meeting in October 1992, called for the creation of a socialist market economy. The Western press immediately renamed this unusual hybrid "market-Leninism" (see Chapter 8). Deng Xiaoping and the surviving octogenarian leaders stressed the need for stability. The party congress abolished the Central Advisory Commission, though this did not guarantee that the members thereof, with their powerful network of connections and protégés, would no longer influence decision making.

Despite Deng's emphasis on rejuvenation, the average age of the Fourteenth Central Committee's members was up slightly, from 55.2 years in the Thirteenth Central Committee to 56.3. However, in the much smaller and more powerful politburo, this situation was reversed: The average age of its 20 full and two alternate members had declined from 68.6 to 62.5 years. Thirteen members had graduated from college, mostly in engineering and natural sciences, *vis-à-vis* only four in the previous politburo. The new politburo also had more of what might be called an external orientation: The foreign minister and minister of foreign trade became members, as did the heads of five coastal provinces and cities. Liu Huaqing, a military man loyal to Deng, joined the politburo's standing committee. Yang Baibing became a member of the politburo, though his formal ties to the PLA were severed at the same time that he was appointed (see Chapter 9). Deng's motive was apparently to ensure that his chosen successor, Jiang Zemin, would not be deposed by a member of the Yang faction of the military. Yang Shangkun resigned as president of the PRC; shortly thereafter, his position was assumed by Jiang Zemin. Since Jiang remained party general secretary and head of the military commission, he had thus concentrated much of the formal political power of the PRC in his person.

Although open challenges to party and government authority continued to be harshly punished, the citizenry became increasingly assertive. A number of Beijing voters protested at the slate of candidates offered to them in a 1991 local election by casting ballots for Zhao Ziyang, whose name was not listed. At the National People's Congress two years later, 11 percent of the delegates either voted against Premier Li Peng or abstained. Since the delegates had been chosen partly on the basis of their loyalty, their actions represented a stunning rebuke. In Beijing during the closing months of 1993, leading democracy activists formed a "Peace Charter" group that called on the CCP to accept a multiparty system or face the only other alternative: violent change. Its members were promptly arrested.

Not all protest was so overt. Although China's security apparatus was regarded as so ruthlessly efficient that escape was rarely thought of, much less attempted, 8 of the 21 June 4 dissidents on the government's "most wanted" list managed to flee to the West. Several years later, a cameraman with politically sensitive film was told by a public security officer, "I could arrest you, but what for? I'll get some praise, but I won't get rich. And then the situation will change. You will be exonerated and I'll be the one in trouble for having arrested you."

The radio call-in show, a new phenomenon with a potentially great impact on Chinese politics, appeared in a few urban areas. Callers showed remarkable frankness in criticizing local officials for poor performance of duty and in pointing out violations of laws. They suggested ways to better handle problems, from toll collection to garbage pickup. People were also more willing to protest, sometimes violently, when they felt that their grievances were not being addressed. Each year brought a new, record number of these disturbances. In the countryside, clan and religious leaders gained power at the expense of party organs. Power drifted away from the center, with regions and provinces becoming more important.

The Third Generation: China under Jiang Zemin

By the mid-1990s, Deng Xiaoping's public appearances had become increasingly rare. Chinese and foreigners alike speculated on whether Jiang Zemin, Deng's heir apparent, could survive his mentor's demise. Although his ability to act independently was surely constrained to some degree by Deng's presence, Jiang began to take a more active role in governance. He paid ceremonial visits to various areas of the country, talking with officials, peasants, workers, and ethnic minorities about their problems and successes. Mass media emphasized the need for stability and loyalty to the party center, with Jiang as its core. A powerful potential rival, Chen Xitong, head of the party apparatus in the city of Beijing, was convicted of corruption. And, in a symbolic assertion of his authority over the military, Jiang personally conferred promotions on generals.

In early 1997, Deng Xiaoping slipped into a coma; he passed away on February 19. Possibly because his death had been expected for so long, mourning was subdued, and power passed seamlessly to what was called the third generation. Mass media continued to emphasize the need for stability and loyalty to Jiang. Both themes had a defensive tone. Economic problems were looming. In 1996, for the first time, subsidies to state-owned enterprises (SOEs) were greater than the amount they remitted to the state treasury, and the deficit was projected to worsen. In a major speech to the Central Party School in May, Jiang proposed to reorganize SOE ownership, criticizing the left by name in the process of doing so. The Fifteenth Party Congress, held in September 1997, was regarded as an important test for his leadership.

The result was a qualified victory for Jiang. The central committee supported his request for a mandatory retirement age of 70, with the year of birth and the month of June rather than one's actual birth date being used for purposes of calculation. This allowed Jiang Zemin to remain as general secretary but forced his major rival, Qiao Shi, to retire. However, a man regarded as Qiao's protégé replaced him on the politburo standing committee. Admiral Liu Huaqing, in his eighties, also retired, meaning that there was no military representation on the standing committee. Li Lanqing, a vice-premier of the state council with special responsibility for education, filled the vacancy. The other members remained the same.

Jiang also failed to revive the position of party chair, a post he had hoped to assume. If, as alleged, Jiang was trying to create a Shanghai faction, his success was only partial. A number of Shanghainese thought to have Jiang's backing failed to receive enough votes to serve on the central committee. Only one of Jiang's "gang" was elected to the politburo, with his vote tally being one of the lowest. Jiang's fellow standing committee member Zhu Rongji was also from Shanghai, but because of his success in bringing a soft landing to China's overheated economy in the mid-1990s, Zhu was more often regarded as Jiang's rival than as a member of his clique.

The new standing committee comprised seven members, the youngest of whom, Hu Jintao, had been elevated to the standing committee in 1992 at an unusually early age. Hu was thus regarded as the front-runner to succeed Jiang. Members of the Fifteenth Central Committee, its politburo, and its standing committee were comparable in age to, though better educated than, those of the Fourteenth. Engineering was by far the best-represented profession, with foreign analysts predicting that this would lead the standing committee to seek pragmatic solutions to problems.

At the congress, Jiang spelled out in more detail the plan for economic restructuring which he had initially mentioned at the Central Party School. The Ninth National People's Congress, meeting in March 1998, decreed that 40 ministries would be reduced to 29 and half of the state bureaucracy's 8 million jobs eliminated. Skeptics noted that the PRC's numerous previous efforts to prune its bureaucracy had resulted in an initial reduction, after which numbers of cadres actually increased beyond the original levels. Plans also aimed at reorganizing the country's entire financial structure, including its banking system and investment institutions. State-owned enterprises were to be drastically restructured, privatized, merged, and, if all else failed, closed down.

The "Three Represents"

Following a brief effort to establish Jiang theory, Jiang fell back on the study of Deng Xiaoping theory as a method of achieving consensus. Treading very lightly on the subject, for obvious reasons, he added that his mentor's theories must not be applied too rigidly. In 2000, Jiang introduced a new formulation designed to leave his ideological stamp on history, the "Three Represents." The party, he claimed, represented the most advanced productive forces, the most advanced culture, and the fundamental interests of the broad masses of the Chinese people. Despite their innocuous sound, these words were political dynamite. For one thing, Jiang had not mentioned his mentor's Four Basic Principles. For another, the phrase "most advanced culture" seemed to signal greater openness to modern Western culture. Finally, and most explosively, the "most advanced productive forces" included the capitalists, entrepreneurs, and educated classes that Mao Zedong had so despised.

Those with leftist leanings were shocked: With millions of workers being laid off in the economic restructuring and peasant incomes declining, the party was, in effect, turning its back on the workers and peasants who had brought it to power, and associating itself with bourgeois capitalism. Jiang's supporters countered that his theory represented an important ideological breakthrough, since now the party would represent the interests of all the people. A disgruntled official rebutted with, "The theory is that the party can represent both the exploited and exploiters. How do you do that? Just because you say you do?" Nonetheless, the country's media praised the Three Represents extravagantly and often, advocating that they serve as guidelines for doing virtually everything from educational reform to modernizing the military.

•

Civic Organizations

By the mid-1990s, the number of non-governmental organizations (NGOs) had proliferated. In order to make sure that they do not escape control, all are required to register with the government. Some, however, manage to evade close supervision and behave with a degree of autonomy. Some do not register at all, and hence exist outside the law. One study of NGOs observed that, while they might evolve from "state corporatist" to "societal corporatist" modes of organization, high-status groups rather than ordinary people are likely to be the principal beneficiaries of the evolution. In addition, although some of these groups strongly favor the protection of individual liberties and democratic reforms, others advocate a variety of other positions, including strong leadership and the suppression of any sort of freedom of expression that could cause social instability. Even so, the central government, fearing loss of control, became concerned.

In 1998, Beijing passed more restrictive laws that disestablished a large number of NGOs for reasons that included redundancy, poor management, illegality, serious interference in social and economic order, and possession of a politically problematic nature. One of those which was disestablished was Falun Gong, a society combining meditative elements of Buddhism and Daoism with traditional Chinese breathing exercises and certain martial arts techniques. In late April 1999, more than 10,000 of its members quietly gathered outside the leadership compound of Zhongnanhai to request re-registration. Party and government appear to have been taken completely by surprise: The group's members had come to Beijing from many different parts of the country, eluding the surveillance techniques that are supposed to prevent such organized movements. Falun Gong's timing was also sensitive, coming exactly ten years after the Tiananmen demonstrations began. A crackdown resulted in the arrest and often brutal treatment of thousands of innocuous-seeming middle-aged and even elderly people, some of whom died as a result. Other religions were targeted as well. From the point of view of those who wanted to see a civil society emerging in the PRC, this represented regression.

Despite Jiang's concern with stability, a modicum of freedom was allowed. Both books critical of reform and books critical of the critics and demanding more reforms were tolerated. Prison conditions improved somewhat. Some high-profile dissidents, most notably Wei Jingsheng, were released. This did not necessarily indicate a softer attitude toward dissent, since the dissidents were freed so that they could seek medical treatment abroad. This had the advantage of ridding the PRC of high-profile potential troublemakers while simultaneously allowing American political leaders who championed their cause to claim that they had extracted a concession from their Chinese counterparts. Immediately after one set of dissidents is released, others may be arrested.

Under current regulations, NGOs continue to be restricted in various ways. They must have an official sponsor, defined as a government or party department or mass organization, which undertakes to monitor the NGO's activities. NGOs are required to present membership lists, and must have a certain level of funding, with all donations notarized. Under Hu Jintao, restrictions on receiving foreign funds were tightened. Organizations with similar agendas are not permitted to function within a given administrative region. They must be inspected annually, and can be de-registered for even perceived shortcomings. Many report being harassed in various ways such as having their water or electricity cut off. Some easing may be taking place: Beijing and Shanghai municipalities and the Shenzhen Special Economic Zone no longer require certain groups to have a sponsor organization, for example. Nonetheless, the government remains vigilant in approving and supervising NGOs.

Changing Central–Local Relationships

In the same timeframe, a fundamental restructuring of the relationship between the central government and its subordinate units was occurring. Scholars disagree on what this means for Beijing's ability to extract compliance with its orders. Some see provinces and localities as becoming more autonomous. Others point out that, despite having independent sources of revenue, even wealthier provinces and localities remain dependent on the center for budgetary subsidies. Since Beijing's ability to reduce or withhold such subsidies can result in serious budget shortfalls, it is an important lever in ensuring compliance. So, too, is the central government's ability to appoint and remove officials: Those regarded as loyal and reliable will have their careers advanced insofar as they obey Beijing's orders; those who do not will be removed.

Still, there are limits to the center's powers. Although officials tend to be very responsive to orders from their immediate superiors, they tend to be less responsive to superiors at successive levels above them. Individual officials must also operate within their local bureaucracies, which often have interests and goals that differ from those of the center. If local officials try too hard to enforce unpopular policies from higher up, they risk alienating their constituents; if they do not implement the policies, they may hurt their careers. The art of balancing these contradictory pressures often involves telling both sides what they want to hear. Quiet deviation and rule bending are less dangerous and more effective than outright defiance but, if discovered, can also have adverse consequences for the individuals involved.

Alternate sources of revenue, such as locally raised, illegal, taxes, can lower dependence on Beijing. To its dismay, the central government has discovered some villages, and even small cities, that operate quite autonomously from its control. While some of these so-called independent kingdoms are well run by what the media term their "local emperors," lack of supervision is conducive to the abuse of power and corruption. Imposing age and educational requirements to improve cadres' qualifications has a downside as well. It separates officials into two categories: promotable and terminal, with most of the latter found at lower levels of party and government. Knowing that their tenure in office is limited incentivizes terminal officials to take as many of the spoils of office as they feel they can get away with. Hence, the decreasing control of the state does not necessarily mean an evolution toward pluralist government or civil society.

The government's recentralization of the fiscal system, followed by the abolition of the agricultural and fee-for-services taxes (see Chapter 7), devastated local finances in many rural areas and led to the rise of entrepreneur cadres who, in charge of local businesses, feel less need to be responsive to central government demands. There has been talk of abolishing township governments, which would eliminate a great deal of expense but has significant disadvantages. In essence, this would mean that the reach of the central government would stop at county level, leading to a re-creation of the situation in imperial China. However, the PRC has many more people than imperial China, and they have come to expect more of their government than was true in imperial China. Moreover, the specter of the return of the roving bandits and secret societies of yore is not attractive; nor is the prospect of a new Maoist-type political insurgency movement.

At the lowest level of society, Deng's reforms also fundamentally changed the nature of central government control. The disbandment of communes led to a rapid erosion of the party's authority in rural areas. Crime rates rose, as did resistance to government policies such as tax collection and family planning. Certain tasks that the commune had taken care of were simply not being done. By the early 1980s, peasants in some areas began to experiment with various forms of self-government. The central government saw these as a way to re-legitimate its authority in rural areas, allowing it to maintain social stability and raise revenue. In 1987, the National People's Congress passed a provisional law on village elections, revising and extending it in 1998. All of the country's 730,000 administrative villages must now conduct direct elections every three years.

There have been both successes and problems in the implementation of this reform. Elections have provided a safety valve for peasants who feel angry and exploited. They have also introduced a standardized system of elections into a culture with very little prior experience in making political choices, thus fostering a new value system and awareness among peasants that they have some leverage in bargaining with party and government. On the debit side, cadres have sometimes refused to allow individuals to exercise their constitutional right to run for office. Those who know the law and insist on their rights may be arrested, charged with endangering national security, and sentenced to several years in prison. Clan organizations, mafia-style "black gangs," and quasi-religious leaders exercise powerful pressures in many villages. Vote buying occurs more often than the government would like. Still, there are also villages where the process works as it should, providing a valuable education in democracy.

Education in democracy is but a first step. There are few indications that village democracy is challenging the local power structure. Voters tend to select candidates who are acceptable to the local power elite, and, since corruption is often perpetrated by cadres at township or county level, it is difficult for even the most motivated village leaders to do anything to curb it. An author who was invited to one county to write about its economic successes described bureaucrats there and elsewhere as speaking two languages: standard mandarin and under-the-table deal making. He found that they ignored regulations and the central government's guidelines, concentrating instead on their own interests. The scores of defamation suits which aggrieved officials filed against the author were dropped after he presented evidence to back up his statements.

In urban areas, elections have been occurring on an experimental basis since 1999, when 12 pilot cities were allowed to choose positions on urban residence committees. These constitute the lowest level of state power in cities. As is the case with rural elections, these are sometimes reasonably democratic and at other times far from it. With regard to the latter, lists of candidates may, for example, be prepared by an election committee controlled by the municipal government. Sometimes the committees have achieved results of significant importance to their constituents, such as getting the government to improve sanitation collection, close down a noisy karaoke bar, or improve street lighting. The authorities also hope that the committees will help them in reporting on, for example, the presence of illegal workers or members of banned religious sects.

The path to reform is not linear, and there have been significant setbacks. Free-wheeling Shenzhen, the Special Economic Zone abutting Hong Kong, was chosen as the testing ground for a new municipal structure implemented in 2003. Government was to be divided into three divisions—policy making, execution, and supervision, replacing the traditional communist government structure that had no such division of power. Shenzhen officials, aware that the concept of the separation of powers is taboo, explicitly denied any similarity between this tripartite arrangement and the executive–legislative–judicial division that is common in Western governments. Nonetheless, the plan was quickly abandoned and replaced with a less ambitious plan that unfortunately failed to solve Shenzhen's corruption and other problems.

The party itself is undergoing an evolution. Hoping to reverse the trend of loss of party control by having more members, particularly at the lower levels of society, authorities staged a recruitment drive that raised the number of CCP members from 50 million in 1991 to 89 million in 2017. This still amounts to only slightly over 6 percent of the PRC's total population. Nor is it certain that the new recruits will help reimpose party control. Many join because they believe that membership will result in economic or political benefits to themselves rather than from ideological conviction. Younger and better educated than previous generations of members, they are unlikely to be as amenable to party discipline as their predecessors. By 2013, advocates for a smaller rather than a larger party became vocal. The CCP, they argued, should slough off opportunist members in order to return the party to its initial mission. Critics scoff that this is impossible. Be that as it may, party recruitment has slowed and entrance requirements tightened.

Another salient feature of Jiang Zemin's administration was a drive against corruption: The Strike Hard (*yanda*) campaign. Jiang's sincerity in doing so cannot be questioned—among other problems it causes, corruption means that less tax revenue reaches the central government treasury—but he was believed to have other motives as well. Arrested Beijing party leader Chen Xitong was not only corrupt but also one of Jiang's rivals: Critics pointed out that Jiang had numerous other associates who were equally corrupt but nonetheless had not been investigated. The campaign against corruption in Xinjiang and certain other ethnic minority areas seemed a thinly disguised excuse for intimidating those minorities who were unhappy with Beijing's rule. Another facet of the drive against corruption was Jiang's July 1998 order to the PLA to divest itself of its commercial empire. These efforts notwithstanding, corruption seemed to be becoming more rather than less entrenched in the political and economic system. Jiang came to power at a time of great difficulties for his country. Unlike his predecessors he had no revolutionary credentials, and was regarded as lacking both vision and charisma. The Chinese populace had become more overtly cynical, as exemplified by a bit of doggerel that could be heard in widely separated parts of the country:

Chiang Kai-shek led thieves and mugs; Mao Zedong led peasant thugs;
Deng Xiaoping led a corrupt crew; Jiang Zemin asks "What do we do?"

The common person's reaction to his plan to restructure the economy was no better:

Mao Zedong wanted us to *xiafang* [do manual labor in rural areas]
Deng Xiaoping wanted us to *xiahai* [jump into the sea of business]
Jiang Zemin wants us to *xiagang* [be laid off].

The Fourth Generation in Power

As the Sixteenth Party Congress approached in 2002, speculation grew in intensity. Five of the seven members of the politburo's standing committee—all save the outspoken Li Ruihuan and heir apparent Hu Jintao—would be ineligible to continue, since they were over 70 years of age. Should the transition to the fourth generation occur without major upheaval, this would be a milestone in CCP history as well as an important marker in the institutionalization of political power in the PRC. Yet the media's incessant praise of Jiang Zemin and his Three Represents, championed by the military, caused many to wonder whether the transition would actually take place.

In the end, Jiang did step down and, apart from Hu Jintao, so did all the other standing committee members. A rule change assumed to be motivated by factional interest lowered the maximum eligible age to 68, thereby mandating even Li Ruihuan's resignation. Hu assumed the title of party general secretary, though Jiang retained the position of chair of the party's CMC. Some argued that this could open a division between the party and the gun, and there was much talk of two centers of power, Jiang's and Hu's. Jiang's efforts to place himself among the great names of the party fell a bit short: The congress agreed unanimously to take "Marxism–Leninism, the thought of Mao Zedong, Deng Xiaoping theory and the Three Represents" as its guide to action, pointedly not attaching Jiang's name to his contributions. The congress also decreed that the Three Represents would be a guiding ideology which the party must uphold for a long time to come—that is, not forever, as appeared to be the case for Marx's, Lenin's, Mao's, and Deng's contributions. In his concluding report, Jiang announced the objective of creating a well-off (*xiaokang*) society by 2020. This task would, of course, fall to Hu Jintao to implement.

There were doubts about whether Hu, despite holding the position of party general secretary, would be able to wield the power associated with it. The unusually large new politburo standing committee had nine members—two more than its predecessor. Its increased size was believed to reflect the rivalry between Jiang's "Shanghai mafia," melding with the princeling faction, and Hu's power base, the CYL. Five or possibly six of them were regarded as allied with Jiang (see Table 5.1).

TABLE 5.1 Size of Politburos and Politburo Standing Committees, 12th–18th Party Congresses

Central Committee	Year	Politburo	Politburo Standing Committee
12th	1982	25	6
13th	1987	17	5
14th	1992	20	7
15th	1997	22	7
16th	2002	24	9
17th	2007	25	9
18th	2012	25	7

Source: compiled from *Beijing Review*, Xinhua.

The average age of the standing committee members was 61.1 years, about the same as that of the comparable group in the Fifteenth Party Congress. Curiously, no member was young enough to be considered as a member of the fifth generation and therefore as being groomed for a top position. The absence of military leaders, as in the previous standing committee, seemed to indicate the institutionalization of a norm that the military should not have formal representation at the highest levels of political decision making. All nine standing committee members had an engineering background, leading many analysts to conclude that they were technocrats and, therefore, predisposed to seek pragmatic solutions to problems. Others pointed out that China has many engineers who did not rise to high political positions: The members of the standing committee attained their pre-eminence not because they were pragmatic problem solvers but because they had survived numerous bureaucratic battles and factional strife. The educational backgrounds of members of subsequent politburos and their standing committees have become more varied, and current emphasis has been on analyzing their factional affiliations. Interest in red-expert explanations appeared to have ended.

Speculation about a Jiang–Hu rivalry reached a crescendo as the fall 2004 Fourth Plenum of the Sixteenth Central Committee approached. Jiang was rumored to want to serve his full five-year term, until 2007, as CMC chair. References to Deng Xiaoping voluntarily resigning the same position appeared in the press, as did a story about an entertainer believed to be romantically involved with Jiang demanding an exorbitant fee for performing in a poor city. Jiang's supporters responded in kind. In the end, Jiang relinquished the position, ending the uncomfortable two centers of power situation, at least in the formal sense. In what was regarded as another defeat for Jiang, his protégé, Zeng Qinghong, failed to receive the vice-chairship of the CMC. Shanghai–CYL rivalries continued. Hu's desire to weaken the Shanghai/princeling faction's power is believed to be the underlying reason that Shanghai party leader and politburo member Chen Liangyu was indicted on corruption charges and removed from office. Chen's replacement, Xi Jinping, was, however, a princeling whose father had close ties with both Deng Xiaoping and Hu Yaobang.

With Hu Jintao and his premier, Wen Jiabao, certain to receive approval for a second five-year term, attention during the run-up to the Seventeenth Party Congress focused on the selection of those who would succeed them in 2012. Hu was believed to favor Li Keqiang, who had been active in CYL work and, like Hu, was born in Anhui province. Surprisingly, Xi Jinping was selected before Li, and subsequently confirmed as vice-president at the Eleventh National People's Congress in March. This positioned Xi to take over as president in 2012. Xi's appointment to vice-chair of the CMC in 2010 solidified his prospects. Li, who was chosen next, was named vice-premier, and therefore the replacement for Premier Wen Jiabao.

Insofar as factional affiliations could be ascertained, the princeling group expanded its membership relative to those affiliated with the CYL and Shanghai group. Another prominent princeling was apparent rising star Bo Xilai, son of revolutionary leader Bo Yibo. Apart from Xi and Li, there was little generational turnover as compared with the Sixteenth Party Congress; the average age of the new standing committee was 62.

Members of the new politburo not only had more diverse educational backgrounds but were disproportionally from east China, as had been the case for several decades. Many had studied in Western countries and Japan, whereas previous leaders, if they had studied abroad at all, were likely to have done so in the Soviet Union or one of its client states.

In choosing the top officials of party and government, a fundamental motivation was believed to be to guard against any one leader or faction from dominating all the others. While a collective leadership has the advantage of preventing dictatorship, the need to obtain consensus is apt to inhibit any bold initiatives to implement the reforms that all parties agree are needed. Political infighting took the form of pressing Hu to deal with familiar issues centering on official corruption and social injustice, for which conservatives and progressives had different solutions. Reiterating familiar positions, conservatives argued that the socialist cause was being abandoned and urged policies that would alleviate the grievances of the workers and the peasants. Progressives countered that incomplete reforms were the underlying causes of social unrest and political crises, and urged more reform.

Hu appeared to be trying to find a middle ground between the two. Questioning single-party rule or advocating Western-style multi-party elections remained dangerous, but suggestions for reform included instituting formal checks on the party's power through a strengthened legal system and freer media. As the Eighteenth Party Congress approached, doubts emerged about Xi's abilities. During a visit to Mexico in 2009, Xi accused Western politicians of interfering in the PRC's domestic affairs. A few months later, in Pyongyang, Xi praised the glorious Korean War partnership between China and North Korea, angering South Korea. Chinese commentators began to express quiet concern about his diplomatic qualities. Xi's failure to receive the vice-chairship of the CMC at the fall 2009 party plenum reinforced the impression of doubts about his competence. These were not entirely erased when, at the fall 2010 party plenum, Xi did receive the vice-chairship that had eluded him the year before. Still, the evolution toward a more collective Chinese leadership seemed assured.

Conclusions

By the end of the first decade of the twentieth century, both the legitimacy and the organizational efficiency of the CCP had eroded badly, particularly in the years since the death of Mao Zedong. With the passing away of iconic revolutionary leaders and the routinization of governing procedures and social rituals, some of this was probably inevitable. However, some of these changes could not have been so easily predicted. Most notably they include the alienation of large numbers of people from the leadership caused by such upheavals as the anti-rightist campaign, the Great Leap Forward, and the Cultural Revolution.

Deng Xiaoping's reform movement caused a further, and more rapid, erosion of both the party's organizational efficiency and its legitimacy.

More than three decades of limited, piecemeal reforms weakened the integrity of the previous system while not replacing it with one that most people believe functions better. The previous system was relatively efficient at equitably distributing the products of scarcity; the new system has been less efficient at distributing the new wealth. It generated prosperity in some areas, but at the cost of producing great inequalities of income and status. Stability and predictability were undermined, leading to popular doubts about the competence of the party to manage either the economy or the political system. The June 1989 demonstrations were simply the most visible of a series of social disruptions caused by partial reform.

The Deng leadership staked its legitimacy on an ambitious economic program. Following several years of relative success, especially in the countryside, problems generated by the program threatened to overwhelm it. Deng's reforms appeared to be suffering from the law of diminishing marginal returns: the easy reforms—those that might be described as tinkering with the system without cutting deeply into the vested interests of powerful social and political groups— had all been tried. Although a thoroughgoing structural reform is regarded as crucial to future development, popular enthusiasm for further reform is low. Too many people fear the consequences; surveys indicate that most people prefer the Maoist iron rice bowl to an uncertain future. Jiang Zemin, in turn, staked his legitimacy on an effort to restructure the economy and end corruption. His success in both was limited, since the consequences of these reforms had sufficiently adverse short-term effects for so many people that they could not be fully implemented. Hu Jintao's plans to improve the quality of party and government services, and to move China toward the well-off society envisioned in Jiang Zemin's valedictory report, were praiseworthy, but accomplishments were meager. Critics charged that Hu and Wen represented a new style, not a new policy.

Suggestions for Further Reading

Joseph Fewsmith, "The 18th Party Congress: Testing the Limits of Institutionalization," *China Leadership Monitor*, no. 40, Hoover Institution, January 14, 2013.

François Godemont, "China's New Long March: *Ite Missa Est*," European Council on Foreign Relations (March 18, 2013).

Yingjie Guo, "Classes without Class Consciousness and Class Consciousness without Classes: The Meaning of Class in the People's Republic of China," *Journal of Contemporary China* (September 2012): 723–739.

Patricia Thornton, "The Advance of the Party: Transformation or Takeover of Urban Grassroots Society?," *China Quarterly* (March 2013): 1–18.

Jing Vivian Zhang, "Natural Resources, Local Governance, and Social Instability: A Comparison of Two Counties in China," *China Quarterly* (March 2013): 78–100.

CHAPTER 6

The Era of Xi Jinping

The Eighteenth Party Congress of 2012 may be said to symbolize the end of the Deng Xiaoping era. Whereas Deng had chosen not only Jiang Zemin as his successor but also Hu Jintao as Jiang's successor, Hu had not been able to arrange for his preferred candidate Li Keqiang to become CCP general secretary. An evolution toward collective decision making, policies arrived at through consensual processes, and the routinization of selection for top leadership positions appeared to have taken place. What transpired was quite different.

Political Drama before the Eighteenth Party Congress

As 2012 dawned, the fifth-generation succession seemed assured. However, a completely unexpected event in February—Chongqing's chief of police appearing at the U.S. consulate in Chengdu to request asylum—set in motion a major scandal that spelled the political demise of princeling Bo Xilai, hitherto regarded as well positioned to join the politburo standing committee (PBSC) and perhaps, in due course, to head the party and government. According to his chief of police, Bo had made great efforts to cover up his wife's murder of a British businessman with whom she was allegedly romantically involved. In what was believed to be a high-level political compromise, Bo himself was not accused of complicity in the murder, but only of massive financial corruption. Still, his political career was over.

Although Bo's much-resented egotism was a likely factor in his demise, so were ideological differences and factionalism. Bo's policies in Chongqing involved a leftist agenda that also included group singing of revolutionary-era songs and a crackdown on corruption that was viewed as being less than objective. His "red [songs]-black[anti-corruption]" policies were often contrasted with the reformist policies of Guangdong party leader Wang Yang as competing blueprints for the future: the Chongqing model versus the Guangdong model. Bo had been at odds with the Communist Youth League (CYL) faction for some time. After his disgrace, the pro-democratic reform premier Wen Jiabao publicly stated, though without specifically mentioning Bo's name, that reviving Maoist-era policies could lead to a return to the chaos of the Cultural Revolution.

As seen through the lens of factional analysis, members of the princeling/ Jiang Zemin group retaliated with an attack on CYL-affiliated Ling Jihua and his superior Li Yuanchao, also affiliated with the CYL, for attempting to cover up a high-speed car crash involving the death of Ling's son as well as that of a nude female companion, and severe injury to a second, partially clad, young woman. Netizens quickly remarked that Ling could not possibly have paid for the car, a Ferrari, from his salary. Western news agencies then revealed—almost certainly with the help of officials linked with the princeling/Jiang Zemin group—that Wen Jiabao's family had amassed huge wealth, thus damaging his image as a man of the people. Earlier in the year, similar revelations had appeared about Xi Jinping's family, again presumably aided by factional enemies.

The opening of the Eighteenth Party Congress was delayed twice. Shortly before it was due to open, Xi Jinping disappeared for nearly two weeks, giving rise to sensational rumors. When he reappeared, the official explanation, that he had been incapacitated by a back injury incurred while playing soccer, struck many as implausible.

In the end, the party congress and subsequent National People's Conference were held, with Xi confirmed as general secretary, president of the country, and head of the Central Military Commission (CMC), and Li Keping as premier. Hu Jintao, perhaps due to his political defeat, did not stay on as CMC chair, as had been rumored. Hence there would not be a reprise of the two centers of power situation of the first two years of Hu's time in office. The size of the standing committee was reduced to seven, with reformer Wang Yang not among them.

In another departure from the past, the holders of the portfolios of propaganda and security were not included in the PBSC, leading to speculation that the position of the latter had become too powerful. The average age of the members was 64.4, noticeably older than that of the Seventeenth PBSC. Also in contrast to the Seventeenth PBSC, and in a nod to central–regional theories of analysis, there are more members from inland provinces (see Table 6.1).

Table 6.1 Size of Politburos and Politburo Standing Committees, 12th–19th Party Congresses

Central Committee	Year	Politburo	Politburo Standing Committee
12th	1982	25	6
13th	1987	17	5
14th	1992	20	7
15th	1997	22	7
16th	2002	24	9
17th	2007	25	9
18th	2012	25	7
19th	2017	25	7

Source: compiled by author from *Beijing Review* and Xinhua

TABLE 6.2 Politburo Standing Committee CCP 18th Party Congress (in rank order)

Name	Position	Birthplace	Birth Year	Factional Affiliation
Xi Jinping	CCP General Secretary; CMC Chair; PRC President	Shaanxi	1953	Shanghai/princeling
Li Keqiang	PRC Premier	Anhui	1955	CYL
Zhang Dejiang	Chair, NPC	Liaoning	1946	Shanghai/princeling
Yu Zhengsheng	Chair, CPPCC	Zhejiang	1945	Shanghai/princeling, ties to Hu Jintao
Liu Yunshan	CCP Exec Vice-Secretary; PRC Vice-President	Shanxi	1947	ties to both Shanghai and Hu Jintao
Wang Qishan	Chair, CDIC	Shanxi	1948	Shanghai/princeling
Zhang Gaoli	State Council Vice-Premier	Fujian	1946	Shanghai/princeling

Source: compiled by author from Xinhua data.

In terms of factional analysis, the meetings were a clear victory for the princeling/Jiang Zemin group (see Table 6.2).

However, age limits would require all the PBSC members apart from Xi and Li to retire after the next party congress in 2017; thus the factional makeup of the Politburo as a whole, from which the new PBSC is normally promoted, would be more evenly balanced. Hence the CYL faction could conceivably regain its importance. Another factor to be considered was the importance of the party elders: for the first time since the founding of the PRC, China would have two former party general secretaries capable of exercising power from behind the scenes. Should the octogenarian Jiang Zemin be removed, Hu Jintao's influence might, it was speculated, prove influential in the next round of selections. In terms of policy implications, indications were that Xi intended to follow a conservative political agenda while implementing modest economic reforms.

Xi Takes Control

Confounding these predictions, Xi immediately assumed an assertive stance. Soon after assuming office he began to speak of a "China dream," of a strong military and economic power, and he also promulgated the "seven unmentionables": universal values, freedom of the press, civil society, citizens' rights, the party's historical errors, the capitalist elite, and judicial independence.

Aware of the obstacles that could impede his goals, Xi moved quickly to centralize power in his hands, earning the half-facetious epithet of "chairman of everything." Refuting the theory that China would continue to evolve toward rule by consensus decision making within the elite, he quickly assumed control of numerous policy "leading small groups," some of which, like the "Civil–Military Integration Leading Small Group," were newly founded. A national security commission that seemed as much aimed at internal social control as at external defense was also established. Premier Li Keqiang became all but invisible. In 2016, for example, Xi pre-emptively announced key economic decisions before the prime minister was able to deliver the government work report and budget.

A few months later, the party central committee bestowed on Xi the title of "core of the party leadership," with more than half of prime-time news that evening devoted to central committee members professing their fealty to him as Xi called for strict discipline and unconditional loyalty.

Announcing an anti-corruption campaign that would spare neither lesser figures ("flies") nor those at the pinnacle of power ("tigers"), Xi, through trusted ally Wang Qishan, pursued it vigorously, ensnaring more than a million party members in the campaign's first five years. Skeptics noted, however, that a disproportionate number of the tigers were Xi's rivals or potential rivals. One of these, Zhou Yongkang, was a former politburo member who oversaw the country's security apparatus and had been ranked the ninth most powerful man in China. He was sentenced to life in prison for accepting bribes and channeling lucrative contacts to family members and close associates.

In the defense sphere, General Xu Caihou, a former vice-chair of the Central Military Commission and politburo member and at one time considered to be among the country's top 24 leaders, was convicted of accepting massive bribes that included the sale of military ranks. Xu passed away from bladder cancer while awaiting trial, his party membership already rescinded and his assets seized. Many lesser, but nonetheless powerful, figures were also removed from power. Despite speculation over whether Xi's true aim was to end corruption or to purge those who might best be in a position to oppose him, the end result was to further centralize power in his hands.

As the China dream campaign was promulgated, a cult of Xi unfolded. Visitors to markets in Chinese cities noticed images of Xi on plates and other objects placed prominently in front of similar images of Mao, and even statues of the Buddha. Posters praising his "China dream" slogan, never explicitly defined but clearly implying a prosperous and powerful future for the country, also appeared with appropriate subtitles, such as "young people's dream is the China dream" near schools.

Ambitious economic plans, a *sine qua non* of achieving the China dream, accompanied these developments. In November 2013, the party's third plenum outlined a plan of proposed economic reforms aimed at increasing international competitiveness and efficiency by 2020.

The one-belt, one-road (OBOR) initiative aimed to establish a creatively re-imagined PRC-centered version of ancient silk routes, one of them over land, through Asia to Europe, and the other maritime, to Southeast Asia, Africa, and beyond. An Asian Infrastructure Investment Bank (AIIB), headquartered in Beijing, was founded to help finance the costs, with the PRC to provide major funding and 60-odd countries applying to join. Pursuant to this objective, Greece agreed to sell a 67 percent stake in the country's largest seaport to a Chinese company. China also expanded its presence in Gwadar, Pakistan, east of the Persian Gulf, and in Djibouti, on the strategically placed Gulf of Aden, construction began on China's first overseas naval base.

The March 2016 National People's Congress approved the country's thirteenth Five Year Plan, covering the years 2016–2020. Continuing past efforts to build a moderately prosperous society by the plan's end, its outline assumed a readjustment to what Xi has called the new normal, with growth no less than 6.5 percent during the period. Disparities in income levels were to be narrowed, all rural residents lifted out of poverty, and the distinction between the rural and urban populations removed. Improvements to education, health care, and public services were promised as well.

Left unsaid was whether sufficient funding could be found to underwrite the costs of these ambitious goals. A Middle Eastern analyst termed the effort "China's five year plan fantasy," pointing out that targets are much easier to set than to reach. Others noted that the government, while saying that it would allow the market to play a decisive role, was simultaneously pursuing heavy-handed industrial policy goals that would inhibit marketization. Burdensome security laws, information control, and ideological rhetoric would combine to work against the plan's commitment to innovation and entrepreneurship. Further, given the likelihood of resistance from powerful vested interests, effective implementation could not be assumed.

Pushback, Then Pullback

Within China, criticism was at first *sub rosa*—conversations among university professors with trusted friends, the occasional defacement of a China dream poster, an online cartoon which depicted a crown-wearing frog that resembled Xi at the bottom of a well and which was quickly removed by censors. Criticism became more open in the months before the meeting of the government's highest level organ, the National People's Congress, in March 2017.

Among the first signs that discontent was building was a post on social media by party member and real estate mogul Ren Zhiqiang. In response to Xi Jinping's directive that the media must protect the authority of the central party leadership and preserve the party's unity, Ren asked pointedly when the people's media had become the party's media, and objected strongly to "using taxpayer money to do things that aren't in service of taxpayers." His social media accounts were shut down, but not until a verified 37 million followers had read them.

Next came an essay on the website of the party's Central Discipline Inspection Commission (CDIC). Entitled "A Thousand Yes-Men Cannot Equal One Honest Advisor" and signed with the pen-name Lei Si, it pays homage to a phrase found in a Han dynasty historical document. The essay riffs on an ancient tradition known as patriotic remonstrance, in which the writer, at the risk of his life, alerts a powerful superior to missteps that should be corrected. For those who understood the allegory, the message was chilling: King Zhou of the Shang dynasty surrounded himself with people who told him what he wanted to hear instead of what he should hear, resulting in the fall of the dynasty in 1046 B.C. The CDIC, which plays a crucial role in the anti-corruption campaign, was headed by Wang Qishan, hitherto believed to be close to Xi. Hence speculation about his role in the post focused on the possibility of a rift between them.

In his closing speech to the National People's Congress, politburo standing committee member Yu Zhengsheng cited only two of the "four consciousnesses:" Ideology and the bigger picture. Those omitted were consciousness of the core and consciousness of consistency, both being understood to mean unquestioning obedience to Xi Jinping's directives. Further, Yu added a new consciousness: That of responsibility to one's job. Xi, who was present at the speech, was described as visibly displeased.

The next salvo was anything but elliptical. In an open letter dated March 16, a group describing themselves as loyal party members urged Xi Jinping to resign, charging that he had abandoned the party's tradition of collective leadership in the standing committee of the politburo and that due to his gathering of all power into his own hands and making decisions directly, the country was facing unprecedented problems and crises in all political, economic, ideological, and cultural spheres. Moreover, he was responsible for the emergence of an unfavorable international environment. The anonymous writers declared that, since Xi did not possess the capabilities to lead the party and the nation, he should resign from all his positions and allow the party's central committee and the people of the nation to select a virtuous leader capable of leading China into the future.

More was to come. An employee of the official state news agency Xinhua posted an open letter denouncing the increasingly tight media constraints "for triggering tremendous fear and outrage among the public," a message quickly deleted by censors. Next, the editor-in-chief of the often stridently nationalistic *Global Times* became involved in a public spat about the PRC's foreign policy with a former Chinese ambassador to France. Responding to an article urging the government to take a more assertive stance, the ambassador accused the editor of being ignorant of foreign affairs, and opined that being soft was more difficult and effective than being hard. The editor then counter-charged that this attitude showed all that was wrong with the country's foreign policy.

Revelations that members of Xi Jinping's family were heavily involved in an international financial scandal with a Panamanian law firm at its center bore directly upon Xi's role as a crusader against corruption. Efforts at censorship failed to prevent sarcastic commentary on social media, with Xi often referred to as "brother-in-law" in reference to the direct involvement of his sister's husband in the operation. In mid-April, in separate issues that appeared on the same day, the websites of two foreign magazines, *Time* and *The Economist*, were blocked after they ran cover stories accompanied by full-page pictures depicting the cult of Xi.

These rumbles of discontent ceased as quickly as they had begun. Analysts speculated that, although the standing committee of the politburo was dominated by people believed to be Xi Jinping's staunch allies, age limits would require all but Xi to retire by the next party congress, in fall 2017. While it was unthinkable that Xi would be prevented from being awarded a second five-year term, there was speculation that resistance from accumulated discontents would force him into a more consensual decision-making mode. This would validate the earlier predictions of foreign analysts that China is no longer the weakened, demoralized country Mao Zedong inherited in 1949, and hence is far less likely to accept the notion of a strong leader to solve its problems.

In the short run, at least, this did not happen. Under Xi, restrictions on the press and social media were tightened. In 2013, new regulations forbade journalists from undertaking any investigations not expressly permitted by the party's publicity (i.e., propaganda) department. State-sponsored China Central Television (CCTV) dropped or toned down its investigative and analytical programs. China's more adventurous newspapers such as Guangzhou's *Southern Metropolitan Daily* and *Southern Weekend* were silenced, with an editorial writer for the latter complaining that the press in his province had retreated into its darkest periods since the start of Deng Xiaoping's reform and opening up policies of the late 1970s. Journalists who had previously been simply dismissed when authorities deemed they had gone too far were now sent to prison. According to the Committee to Protect Journalists, China in 2017 incarcerated more journalists than any country except Turkey.

A particular area of concern in the party, and Xi's desire for control, are the social media. The big three—Baidu, Alibaba, and Tencent, known collectively as BAT—are, respectively, the country's largest search engine, e-commerce platform, and messaging and social media services. Both Baidu and Tencent have been investigated for alleged violations of cybersecurity as well as for their roles in promoting more unequivocally objectionable practices like gambling, addictive online gaming, and bogus medical treatments. Alibaba and Tencent have been approached to sell shares to the government, thereby enabling the party-state to participate in business decisions as well as, presumably, to receive dividend payments. Since these companies are world leaders in mobile payments as well as working with the government on artificial intelligence, the same tools that enable retailers to predict consumer behavior can be used to anticipate and deal with dissent. As mobile payments are increasingly replacing cash transactions, party and government's ability to track financial movement is enhanced as well.

In late 2017, new government regulations banned bitcoin, which was being used to circumvent a worrisome cash flow out of China. However, the ban did not seem to be effective. Those wishing to use the crypto-currency take cash to one of the country's underground money exchanges where they are provided with an anonymous bitcoin wallet. The only link between the bitcoins and the owner is an IP address, which can be hidden by using a Virtual Private Network or the TOR network, which bounces communications around a distributed network of relays in a number of different parts of the world, enabling the bitcoins to be connected to an overseas bank account.

For these and other reasons, powerful and politically well-connected real estate and financial tycoons also came under scrutiny. The Xi administration wants to avoid the rise of oligarchs who could threaten Xi's authority and subvert his reforms. The chairman of China's largest insurance company was detained without charges, the only explanation being a terse statement by his company explaining that for personal reasons the chairman was no longer able to perform his duties. A leading financier was seized from his Hong Kong hotel, taken across the border, and was not heard from for several months, when his trial began. One of the few to have commented publicly, from his luxury hotel suite in New York, stated, without producing evidence, that he possessed information involving corruption at the highest levels, including against the leader of the anti-corruption campaign Wang Qishan.

In these and other areas, the party and Xi are seeking to find a proper balance between encouraging the growth and innovation needed to enhance the country's prosperity, on the one hand without losing control, on the other. High-ranking party figures continued to be removed from office. Chongqing party head Sun Zhengcai was abruptly dismissed for failure to curb the "pernicious influence" of his predecessor Bo Xilai. Sun, who had been the youngest member of the politburo and therefore a likely candidate to succeed Xi in the Twentieth Party Congress, was later accused of vote rigging at both the Seventeenth and Eighteenth party congresses, along with two other already disgraced officials. Since Xi Jinping had emerged victorious on both occasions, analysts were puzzled by the nature of the allegations, but no details were revealed. What was clear was that yet another potential rival to Xi had been dismissed.

Another of Xi's initiatives involved weakening the Communist Youth League. Xi publicly criticized the CYL for chanting inane slogans and focusing on entertainment rather than on results. Its leading training ground for future CYL cadres, the China Youth University of Political Studies, also known as the Central School of the CYL, was reborn under a new name, the University of the Chinese Academy of Social Sciences, and placed under the control of the Chinese Academy of Social Sciences. The net result was to weaken the CYL to the extent that discussions of balances among factions, so prominent prior to previous party congresses, faded from analyses.

The Nineteenth Party Congress

Beginning in July 2016, more than a year before the Nineteenth Party Congress, surveillance became still tighter. According to a Canadian analysis based on China's most popular messaging app, Tencent's WeChat, censors blocked increasing numbers of words, ranging from those that might be construed as critical of party and government, to generic and neutral terms. While references to political infighting could be expected to trigger filters, even references to the anti-corruption campaign, the one belt one road initiative, and the "glass ceiling," referring to the lack of female representation at the highest levels, were blocked. Some observers speculated that Tencent may have been over-cautious in order to avoid reprimands from officials.

In the month before the congress was due to open, security in Beijing was tightened. All police leave was cancelled and thousands of additional security personnel were brought into the city to guard against "social instability." Veterans, who had several times in the past year protested their treatment since demobilization, were cautioned against doing so. Identification cards were checked not only in and near public buildings, but also at airports, subways, and train and bus stations. All Airbnb contracts were suspended, and drone flights prohibited. A film with a sensitive theme had its opening postponed. Heavy industry was ordered to scale back production to ensure blue skies, and funds were injected into the stock market to guard against fluctuations.

Despite the censorship, or perhaps in response to it, rumors abounded. Would the party constitution be amended, and if so, what would be the formula? Mao had been memorialized by having his "thoughts" added to Marxism–Leninism as the guiding philosophy of the CCP, while Deng's "theory" was added after his death. Neither Jiang Zemin nor Hu Jintao succeeded in having their names added to the constitution: Only their respective signature projects the Three Represents and the Scientific Outlook on Development.

Another much-discussed issue was whether the politburo standing committee would remain at seven, be increased to nine, as it had been under Hu Jintao, or decreased to five or six, as it had been in the early 1970s. In theory, a larger PBSC might mean more voices to take into consideration in order to arrive at a consensus. Conversely, a smaller PBSC might mean easier control for the party's general secretary. But it is also possible that, since they would be more powerful as individuals, few members could exercise more power against him.

Yet another topic of concern was age limits: the so-called "seven up, eight down" rule meant that those who were aged 68 or older were expected to step down from the politburo, since they would be past retirement age by the end of the current party congress. Wang Qishan, Xi's confidante and director of his anti-corruption campaign, was 68. Would the rules be skirted to keep him on? Moreover, with Sun Zhongcai's removal from the politburo along with three other members, no politburo member was of the proper age to be promoted to the standing committee, and therefore be a likely successor to Xi. Sun's successor in Chongqing, Chen Min'er, was young enough to meet the age requirement, but, unlike Sun, Chen was not a member of the politburo. In theory, he could be promoted to the politburo standing committee without prior service in the politburo, but this would be highly unusual. If the new standing committee contained no one young enough to succeed Xi, did that mean that Xi intended to stay on for an unprecedented third term, or even longer? Furthermore, how would the

Central Committee delegate votes? Would there be the kind of surprise that saw Xi Jinping eclipse Hu Jintao's protégé Li Keqiang?

The constitution was indeed changed, and both Xi's name and his thoughts were memorialized, thereby elevating Xi to a status equal to Mao Zedong and above not only his two immediate predecessors but even above Deng Xiaoping. The somewhat unwieldy addition reads: "Xi Jinping's thought on socialism with Chinese characteristics for the new era."

Wang Qishan did step down, as did all the other members of the PBSC except for Xi and Li. But their replacements included no one who, assuming that the seven up eight down rule continued to be observed, would be eligible to succeed Xi at the Twentieth Party Congress, thereby leaving open the question of his serving a third term. Some speculated that Chen Min'er, who was appointed to the politburo, might receive an unprecedented mid-term promotion into the PBSC, others that Xi's goal was to stay in power for life. New rules were instituted in response to allegations that there had been vote rigging in previous party congresses. It was said that "some comrades just ticked a ballot" unthinkingly, or

Table 6.3 Politburo Standing Committee CCP 19th Party Congress (in rank order)

Name	Position	Birthplace	Birth Year	Previous Experience
Xi Jinping	Party General Secretary, CMC Chair, PRC President	Beijing	1953	Party General Secretary, CMC Chair, PRC President
Li Keqiang	PRC Premier	Anhui	1955	PRC Premier
Li Zhanshu	Director, CCP General Office	Hebei	1950	Director, CCP General Office
Wang Yang	Vice-premier	Anhui	1955	Agriculture, foreign trade portfolios
Wang Huning	Director of Policy Research Office of CCP CC	Shanghai	1955	Professor of international politics, Fudan University, Shanghai
Zhao Leji	CDIC director	Qinghai	1957	Head of Central Committee's Organization Department
Han Zhang	CPPCC head	Shanghai	1954	Shanghai party head

Source: compiled by author from Xinhua data.

that they had been influenced by personalism and cronyism. The solution to this was to replace voting with a consultation system. There was no explanation of how consultation would take place, or how it would avoid the personalism and cronyism of the previous system.

The size of the PBSC remained at seven. Notable was their backgrounds: Whereas only a decade ago eight of the nine top party leaders had studied engineering or natural sciences—perhaps appropriate in an era where the focus was on industrialization—no one on the Nineteenth PBSC could be classified as a technocrat. Two had received degrees in political education; five others majored in management, philosophy, politics, and law. Although Xi Jinping studied chemical engineering as an undergraduate, he had never worked in the field, going immediately into party and government work following graduation and later pursuing a higher degree in Marxist theory and political education (see Table 6.3).

After the Party Congress

In a carefully staged piece of political theater, the new PBSC went from Beijing to the birthplace of the CCP in Shanghai where, with arms raised in salute, members pledged their loyalty to the party with Xi as its core. Fresh shipments of Xi's collection of speeches, *The Governance of China*, appeared in bookstores, often already gift wrapped for presentation. Said to have sold more than 6.6 million copies before the conference, it was soon to be accompanied by a second volume that would detail the practices of the Central Committee "with Xi as its core in uniting and leading the Chinese people to develop socialism with Chinese characteristics for the new era." Centers for the study of Xi's thought were founded at universities throughout China.

Some observers found parallels with the adulation surrounding Mao Zedong's Little Red Book of quotations at the time of the Cultural Revolution. When adding the cult of Xi to the contests for singing red songs that were being held in prisons and the campaign against "black" (corrupt) elements, they saw striking similarities to the "red-black" criticisms leveled against Bo Xilai.

The anti-corruption campaign continued unabated under its new director Zhao Leji, who quickly shared another "tiger," the former head of the China Cyberspace Administration and a deputy director of the party's propaganda department. A mock form of greeting began to be heard in Beijing:

Urban poor: "Have you found a place to live?"
Middle class: "Are your children okay?"
Upper class (communist business elite, red aristocracy, princelings): "The Communist Party Discipline Inspection Committee hasn't come for you yet?"
The 13th National People's Congress, which met in March 2018, named Wang Qishan vice-president of the PRC, where he is expected to play a leading role in trade negotiations with the United States.

A continuation of the assertive foreign policy that had characterized the previous several years seemed assured. Xi Jinping's address to the Nineteenth Party

Congress had mentioned China moving to center stage in international relations. Earlier, he had established a rapport with Russian leader Vladimir Putin, despite the latter's distaste for the role reversal which meant that Moscow was now junior partner to Beijing. China is an important customer for Russia's oil and gas. Putin stood next to Xi at the lavish military parade held to commemorate the seventieth anniversary of the end of World War II, as Xi had stood next to Putin at Russia's parade.

With regard to relations with the United States, Xi advocated a new type of great power relations, which some interpreted as a "G-2," i.e., the People's Republic of China and the United States jointly managing the world order. Others thought that Xi's goal was to make China the sole arbiter of international relations.

Regionally, Xi declared that Asian affairs should be managed by Asians, and that Asian security should be protected by Asians, which was widely construed as a strong suggestion that non-Asian states should not become involved. It was also clear that other Asian states were expected to conform to Chinese wishes. Southeast Asian nations had been lobbying for years to have the non-binding Declaration of Conduct on the disputed areas of the South China Sea replaced with a binding Code of Conduct. However, shortly after the congress concluded, the Chinese foreign ministry announced that the PRC was open to negotiations on a non-binding Code of Conduct, leaving open the question of whether the latter would be any more effective than the former had been.

At the same time, the foreign ministry replied to concerns in Taiwan and Japan about flights through the Miyako Strait and around Taiwan by announcing that they were part of a "new normalized training," and that "neighboring countries should be prepared for such changes." When, in response to missile threats from North Korea, the South Korean government announced that it would deploy the U.S. THAAD (terminal high altitude area defense) anti-ballistic missile system, Beijing imposed economic sanctions upon South Korea that included restrictions on tourism and the import of pop culture and cosmetics. Eventually, an uneasy and, in South Korea, controversial agreement was reached in which China lifted the economic sanctions while the Seoul government accepted Beijing's "three nos": Not to install additional THAAD batteries, not to participate in a regional missile defense system, and not to form a trilateral alliance with the United States and Japan. China asserts that THAAD radars could be used against the PRC.

Conclusions

For those Chinese who hope for an evolution away from authoritarianism and toward pluralism, the centralization of power that Xi has achieved represents a regression and a disappointment. They argue that a rapidly modernizing and internationally more powerful China needs to bring together those with different areas of expertise, be it in managing problems specific to different regions of the country or as specialists in such fields as energy, finance, trade, and taxation, in order to deal with the increasingly complex environment that the country faces. Despite their different perspectives, the officials would be united around their common goals of furthering economic development, ensuring stability, and safeguarding the country's sovereignty.

However, others point to what they believe was a lost decade under the Hu-Wang administration, where a popular saying was that "decisions made in Zhongnanhai [the leadership compound in Beijing] never come out." They are concerned that, without a strong leader to force through the painful structural reforms that would see China on the way to healthier economic growth, the country will continue on a path that is ultimately unsustainable. A collective leadership, they argue, is inherently ineffective, and leads to political infighting, bureaucratic deadlock, and strategic drift. While some resent Xi's personalism, others believe that China needs a strong leader, to take pride in a China that has asserted what they see as its rightful role in the international order and are pleased with his accomplishments. However, although a leader who has centralized power under himself may be better positioned to overcome resistance to necessary structural reforms, should those fail the responsibility for that failure will be his as well.

Suggestions for Further Reading

Kevin Carrico, "Putinism with Chinese Characteristics: The Foreign Origins of Xi Jinping's Cult of Personality," *China Brief*, Vol. 17, No. 17 (December 22, 2017).

Cheng Li, *Chinese Politics in the Xi Jinping Era* (Washington, DC: Brookings Institution Press, 2016).

Barry Naughton, "The General Secretary's Extended Reach: Xi Jinping Combines Economics and Politics," *China Leadership Monitor*, No. 54 (September 2017). Stanford, CA: The Hoover Institution.

Anthony Saich "What Does General Secretary Xi Jinping Dream About?" Cambridge, MA: Harvard University Kennedy School, Ash Center Occasional Papers, August 2017.

Jinping Xi, *The Governance of China*, Vol. I (Beijing: Foreign Languages Press, 2014); Vol. II (Beijing: Foreign Languages Press, 2018).

CHAPTER 7

The Politics of the Economy

Introduction

Economics was the touchstone of the Chinese revolution: the substructure that, according to Karl Marx, determines not only the government but all else as well. Industrialization was a major priority for the new government in order to bring the People's Republic of China (PRC) into the ranks of the world's most advanced nations and to provide better living standards for the people of the country. However, party and government also wished to avoid many of the problems that have been associated with industrialization. In other countries, this process had frequently exacerbated the differences between rich and poor. In the Western world, it was only after the industrial revolution had taken place that serious efforts were made to correct extreme inequities. Moreover, progress toward industrialization is rarely smooth: historical experience indicates that the more rapid the progress, the greater the tensions that are generated within a society. The Chinese Communist Party's (CCPs) desire for social stability, albeit with certain salient exceptions such as the Cultural Revolution, was thus also a constraint on rapid industrialization.

In formulating its economic policies, the CCP had two goals: equality and prosperity. The first of these is idealistic; the second, materialistic. In practice, it has proved difficult to pursue both simultaneously. In general, economic policy since 1949 has tended to emphasize either one or the other. The first tendency was more pronounced during Mao Zedong's leadership; the second under the leadership of his successors. However, economic policy both during the Maoist era and thereafter has also been characterized by fluctuations between emphasis on one goal or the other. Under Mao, rigid commitment to equality typically resulted in dampening incentives to produce, leading to economic downturn and scarcities. Party and government then relaxed the commitment to equal distribution of resources, leading to an upturn in production statistics but at the cost of increasing income differentials. This interplay of ideology and scarcity under Mao's rule was unfortunately reminiscent of the swings of the business cycle that early communists like Marx and Engels believed their approach would eliminate. Although ideology is no longer an important factor in decision making, structural problems in the economy have continued. Jiang Zemin and his successors essentially carried forward and extended Deng Xiaoping's reforms, which favored prosperity at the expense of equality, even as they sought to correct the imbalances engendered by the reforms. There have been successes—for example, inflation was greatly reduced. But income gaps widened, and corruption became endemic.

The Early Years: 1949–1950

Initially, the party's chief economic tasks were to bring the ruinous inflation of the late 1940s under control and to rebuild the country's war-torn infrastructure and production facilities. Inflation was dealt with through a series of measures, beginning with revaluing the nation's currency to a more realistic rate in order to reduce the lure of black market currency transactions. It was further announced that anyone indulging in currency speculation would be punished. Several well-publicized executions convinced doubters that the new leadership meant what it said. Regional and other variant currencies were abolished; henceforth, everyone was to use the *yuan*, also known as the *renminbi* (RMB), or people's currency. The party nationalized the banking system, placed it firmly under CCP control, and established a centralized state economic planning system based on the Soviet model.

Prices were fixed at what party and government considered a fair level, with stiff penalties for those who violated the rules. Trading cooperatives were established to bring food into the cities. To curb panic buying and encourage people to save, the newly founded People's Bank established unit prices based on a market basket of commodities. Someone depositing a sum of money equal to one unit in a bank account was guaranteed that sum, plus however much the unit had gone up to at the time of withdrawal and a small interest rate. In the unlikely event that deflation had occurred, investors were guaranteed the return of the amount they had deposited. People gradually gained confidence in the currency, and inflationary pressures subsided. Interestingly, this plan had originally been proposed by Kuomintang (KMT) economists, but their party had been too weak and corrupt to carry it out.

With internal peace achieved at last, railroads and irrigation works could be rebuilt. The cooperation of patriotic bourgeoisie, with their technical and managerial skills, proved invaluable, as did the labor contributed by young soldiers. State farms were established and factories rebuilt. By 1952, a semblance of normalcy had returned. Hence, this is the year commonly used as the baseline from which to calculate production statistics.

The Socialist Transformation of Agriculture: 1949–1978

The Chinese communist revolution was, in essence, an agrarian revolution. The communists had spent more than 20 years working in rural areas, and with over 80 percent of the population engaged in agriculture at the time, Mao

Zedong understandably viewed the peasant question as the central problem of the Chinese revolution.

To attract peasant support during the civil war, the CCP called for land redistribution. After coming to power, the party proceeded to make good on this promise. Since another important goal of land reform was to overthrow the old ruling class in rural areas, class struggle was used as a tool in redistribution. This meant that precise criteria for the distinctions between one class and another were needed. By 1950, the rural population had been classified into six classes: landlords, semi-landlords, rich peasants, middle peasants, poor peasants, and laborers. Each class was in turn subdivided into several other categories. The government devised standards for determining these, but in practical terms lines were difficult to draw and rural cadres often made arbitrary judgments. Hence, individuals who possessed the same amount of land might be classified quite differently in different localities.

Those designated as landlords had their houses, furniture, and even personal possessions confiscated in a movement characterized by emotionally charged mass trials and immediate executions. While ending the influence of the landlords and forging a bond between the party and the poor peasants, land reform actually resulted in relatively limited gains for the rural economy, neither increasing per capita landholding nor raising the rate of capital formation in agriculture. It also created three new problems.

First, more than 50 million new landowners were created because of the leadership's decision to grant equal shares of land to the family members of party workers, the armed forces, and the mass organizations, such as peasants' and women's associations. This reduced the size of the average farm and hence the ability of the peasant to accumulate capital.

Second, land reform resulted in new frictions while not ending rural class stratification. Disputes arose, for example, over how to allocate responsibility for the draft animals that had been confiscated from landlords. Since many were assigned to groups of peasants rather than to specific households, it was in the individual family's short-term interest to work the beasts as hard as possible and feed them as little as possible. Hence, a large number of animals died from lack of proper care. Also, a new rich peasant class began to arise. Not surprisingly, most of them were party members.

Third, land reform led to severe food shortages in the cities. This occurred because whereas landlords had typically shipped their grain to be sold in urban markets, newly landed peasants preferred to eat more themselves.

To deal with these problems and prevent the resurgence of what it saw as capitalist tendencies in the rural economy, the leadership began to push the peasants toward collective arrangements. The first stage in this, mutual aid teams (MATs), began to be set up around 1951. Groups of peasant households were to help each other by exchanging tools, draft animals, and labor power. These first teams usually consisted of three to five households and were temporary; after the busy period for farming they disbanded. Indeed, peasants in some areas had engaged in similarly informal practices for centuries. Later, the

MATs were formalized, contained five to ten households, and became permanent, year-round arrangements.

Next came the formation of lower level agricultural producers' cooperatives (APCs). Under this arrangement, land, farm animals, and farm implements were pooled, and a larger number of households, perhaps 35, participated in each pool. Members retained the title to their land, which was entered into the account books of the APCs as a share of the household's capital contribution to the cooperative. Other capital assets like farm implements, transport vehicles, and draft animals were treated in the same way, remaining privately owned but under unified control. A certain amount of land, not to exceed 5 percent of the average household's total, could be retained for private use. Referred to as private plots, this land was worked by individual families who, within certain limits, could decide how to use it and how to dispose of what they produced on it.

The APCs' aggregate amount of agricultural and sideline production, the latter coming from such activities as handicrafts like weaving straw hats and baskets, would have a portion deducted to meet depreciation costs. The remainder comprised the cooperative's total income for the year. Part of this was paid to the state as taxes, and part went into reserve and welfare funds for the cooperative. The rest was distributed to the members as payment for their work and for the use of their land, animals, and tools. Payments for work were tallied in units called work points that were calculated according to the difficulty of the task and the number of days spent on it. An extremely physically demanding job might command ten work points a day; jobs that were considered easier received smaller amounts.

At least in theory, the cooperatives had two major advantages over MATs. First, pooling land would eliminate the chief structural weakness of Chinese agriculture: small, uneconomic, and dispersed holdings. Simply removing the boundary lines between private holdings would create extra acreage for cultivation. Second, reducing the number of production units would enable the government to exercise closer control over planning, investment, and consumption.

There were many negative aspects to the cooperatives as well. Management was foremost among them. Supervising 30 to 40 households took a great deal of planning, administration, and bookkeeping. Evaluating job performance in terms of work points could be subjective and was always difficult. In addition, a large number of tasks were involved, with legitimate differences of opinion existing on the matter of comparable worth. Whether a job was classified at eight or at seven work points per day, for example, could make a substantial difference to one's yearly income. In addition, the great majority of peasants were illiterate and therefore unable to cope with even the simplest bookkeeping tasks.

Although aware of strong resistance to joining the lower level APCs, the leadership, after some wavering, decided in 1956 to forge on to higher level APCs. When peasants joined these, their land and other principal means of production were transferred from private to collective ownership, and payments for land shares and other means of production were abolished. One's income thus depended wholly on accumulated work points. Members could, however, retain their small, private plots and keep whatever they raised on them. Averaging 158 households each, the new units were also 4 to 5 times as large as lower level APCs.

By the end of 1956, almost 90 percent of the PRC's cooperatives were of the advanced type. Their proponents noted three major advantages to the new arrangement. First, the larger units facilitated land consolidation and the rational use of land better than lower level APCs. Second, since land rent had constituted a significant part of rich peasants' income, the abolition of rent payments would increase the wages of poor peasants while lowering those of the rich, producing greater equality. Third, a higher level of collectivization was needed to carry out the massive water conservation campaign that party and government had scheduled for the winter of 1957/1958.

However, peasants were even more unhappy with the higher level APC than they had been with its lower level version. Many who had only recently realized their dream of becoming landowners reacted badly to seeing their property and animals snatched away. The higher level cooperatives also further separated individuals' level of productivity from the rewards they received, thus further dampening peasants' incentive to work hard. Peasant income declined, and there was a drastic drop in pig production. Serious shortages of pork, the staple meat in the Chinese diet, were reported in many urban areas. From the time the collectives were first initiated, most peasants had harbored doubts about their ability to raise their incomes and improve living conditions. As time went on, more and more of them became convinced that their doubts were justified.

The leadership, faced with yet another decision to either retreat from collectivization or push forward, chose the latter. The result, touted by official propaganda as "fresh as the morning sun" and "the ladder to communist paradise," was the rural commune. As with other aspects of the Great Leap Forward, of which the commune was such an important part, the process of communization was characterized by extreme haste. An experimental model commune was organized in April 1958 in Henan province. In the closing days of August, the party directed that its example be generalized throughout China, and by the end of September, more than 98 percent of peasant households had been included in the communes.

The huge size of the communes—averaging 5,000 households, or about 32 times as large as higher level APCs—would allow them to command the resources of vastly greater amounts of land and labor. The commune was more than this, however, being described as "the basic unit of the social structure [of China], combining industry, agriculture, trade, education, and the military [.] [I]t is the basic unit of social power." Whereas the original APCs had been organized purely for agricultural production, the communes merged peasants, workers, tradesmen, students, and militia members into a single unit to engage in afforestation, animal husbandry, and subsidiary occupations, as well as agriculture. The communes also ran factories, banks, and commercial enterprises; handled credit and commodity distribution; did cultural and educational work; and controlled their own militia and political organizations. In terms of administrative functions, communes replaced townships, which had been of comparable size.

Under the commune system, private plots were abolished. In their zeal to eliminate private property, some cadres even took away peasants' wristwatches, alarm clocks, and cookware. Confiscating pots and pans meant that their former owners had to eat in communal dining halls. Metal cookware was then melted down and contributed to the backyard blast furnaces the peasants were directed to set up. The shortage of bookkeepers was solved by abolishing work points; henceforth, one was to contribute work to the commune to the best of one's ability and receive from it food and the other necessities of life. Under true communism, no work points would be needed; ergo, no one was needed to tally them.

As noted in Chapter 4, the result was disaster. Crops died through neglect, owners slaughtered their animals in preference to turning them over to the communes, cadres were attacked, and public property sabotaged. Basic-level cadres, hard-pressed by unrealistically high production quotas, resorted to reporting inflated crop production statistics, which were then passed along to higher levels that had a tendency to inflate them still further. A party central committee plenum in August 1959 officially admitted that no one knew what production actually was. After bitter arguments among top leaders, the plenum agreed to rescind some of the more objectionable aspects of the Great Leap Forward. For example, brigades rather than communes were given the responsibility for managing the reintroduced accounting system and also for setting production targets. Since the brigade was comparable in size to the former higher level APC, this was a distinct step backward for the party. Egalitarianism in income distribution was also abandoned, as was the slogan "from each according to his ability, to each according to his need." Private plots were reinstated. But these measures were not taken quickly enough to save the situation.

As the agricultural crisis worsened in 1960, production teams, which occupied the level below brigades in the administrative hierarchy, were made the basic decision-making units determining output quotas and the distribution of resources. Teams were approximately equal to lower level APCs in size. Communes themselves were reduced to about the size of the average marketing community in traditional China. Advocates of the China-is-China-is-China school of political analysis interpreted this as confirmation of their views.

To stimulate peasant initiative, a system called "three guarantees and one reward" was instituted. Recipients were provided with guaranteed output, time, and cost levels, and a bonus (reward) from the team if their output exceeded the agreed amounts. In 1961, when the agricultural situation had become even more serious, a still more liberal policy, called the "three selfs and one guarantee," was instituted. It went further than its predecessor by directing that all communal land be distributed among individual households as "responsibility land," with each household agreeing to produce a certain amount.

The more idealistic members of the party elite bitterly resented this backsliding. Particularly after the economy began to improve in 1962, there were arguments about whether—and, if so, when—to abandon these concessions to capitalism and forge forward toward communism again. During the early stages of the Cultural Revolution, with ideologues dominating the party elite, many of the concessions were abolished. Mergers increased the size of communes. Poor and lower middle peasants were told to assume power. In many areas, private plots were again confiscated, sideline occupations banned, and rural markets closed. Radicals called them "tails of capitalism."

Some communes moved from a three-level to a two-level system of management by making brigades rather than production teams the basic unit of accounting. A major mass campaign was launched to publicize the achievements of Dazhai, a model production brigade that had adopted the two-level system. Dazhai was also lauded for having allegedly overcome all sorts of hardships, including poor land, drought, and invasions by predatory insects, to achieve impressive increases in production. The proper ideological outlook, one's "redness," was believed to be the key to success. In keeping with this notion, political attitude was added to hard physical labor as a criterion for allocating one's share of the collective income.

The result of these changes was rural unrest and agricultural stagnation. Hoping to avoid the errors of the Great Leap Forward, the PRC's draft constitution of 1970 affirmed the three-level system of ownership, stating that the production team would be the basic unit of management. A 1971 Central Committee directive stressed the need to avoid "absolute egalitarianism," and emphasized that one's income would be based on one's work. The agricultural system which emerged from the Cultural Revolution thus closely resembled that which prevailed from 1962 to 1965. The agricultural distribution system was restored, though peasants, mindful of the disruptions of the past, remained apprehensive. Agricultural growth was disappointing, barely keeping up with the increase in population. In fact, per capita output of foodstuffs fell below the levels of the early 1930s.

Industrial Policy in the Maoist Era

In contrast to the hesitations and retreats which characterized the collectivization of agriculture, the industrial structure was brought under state control more quickly, and with remarkably little resistance. As the KMT's successor, the CCP took over its predecessor's enterprises. Certain other enterprises were taken over on the grounds that they had been owned by war criminals or collaborators, whether or not convincing evidence existed to substantiate these charges. Although direct expropriation could have been easily accomplished, it was not widely used. The party's tactics generally consisted of squeezing out private enterprise through tax pressures, credit rationing, capital levies, state competition, and union demands.

By the beginning of 1952, the "five-anti" campaign (see Chapter 4) had been launched against the capitalist class. Employees were encouraged to report their bosses to the authorities if they had been involved in any of the "antis," and mass denunciation meetings often turned violent. The aim seems to have been to humiliate and demoralize businesspeople in order to reduce their resistance to absorption by the state. Massive fines were extracted from merchants and industrialists, some of whom committed suicide. For others, the fines depleted working capital to levels that made doing business virtually impossible. At this point, having their companies taken over by the state may actually have been a relief. The fines were also a convenient method for capturing the savings of the capitalist class, which the government used to finance its construction plans.

Also at the time of the Cultural Revolution, several other changes were made in industry in general. Their net effect was to further depress work enthusiasm. Unlike certain other Cultural Revolution practices that were quickly discontinued, these changes remained in effect until after Mao's death. Perhaps the most important change was the discontinuation of bonuses that had been awarded to those whose work group had been designated superior. Extra pay for overtime work was abolished as well. A temporary phenomenon of the Cultural Revolution, but one with lasting effects, was that workers were encouraged to struggle against their bosses. These measures, decided upon in order to further egalitarian goals, had devastating effects on productivity. Workers had no incentive to produce, and managers, fearing that their workers would denounce them, had no incentive to make them produce. They also had no rewards to offer employees to inspire them to work hard.

Because little was produced under these circumstances, goods were in short supply. Here, too, the factory facilities might come in handy. Machine-shop workers had access to tools and metal, and could make cookware using whatever materials were available. Sometimes this meant using expensive metals that could have been more productively employed—for example, in the manufacture of precision machinery. People who worked in plywood manufacturing factories brought home sheets of it for desks and tabletops. A widespread and pervasive underground trading system grew up: the plywood factory worker's tabletop for the metal worker's cook pot, and so forth. Although illegal, such practices filled important needs for people; once started, the system was difficult to stop. Corruption was fostered in hundreds of ways. For example, workers who wanted to stay away from work might present the factory doctor with gifts of useful items that the doctor could not easily obtain by other means. In return, the doctor would certify that they were too sick to work. Both parties gained from this transaction, although society as a whole suffered.

Maoist Economic Policies Assessed

Mao's economic policies achieved certain important goals. The Chinese economy was unequivocally freed from foreign domination, and the postwar inflation was quickly brought under control. In addition, the nationalization of the private banking system and unification of the monetary system enabled the government to suppress speculative activities and prevent the recurrence of inflation. Centralizing and unifying the currency had other benefits as well. It provided the basis for a national market in which the supply of money could be planned and its value stabilized. The state banking system enabled the central government to exercise a greater degree of control over the economy than had ever been the case before. This control enabled party and state to invest in the development of hitherto backward areas, generally in the country's hinterlands, which had not enjoyed the benefits of infusions of foreign capital prior to 1949. Shanghai's and Wuhan's surpluses could be used to develop Qinghai and Anhui.

By contrast, the socialist transformation of the economy had mixed results. It enabled the further development of a centrally planned economy, and the government's large-scale purchases of food, textiles, and other basic necessities made possible effective rationing and distribution during times of crop failure. The socialist transformation also helped increase government revenue and accumulation. By buying out the capitalist sector, party and government could channel 95 percent of the after-tax earnings of private firms into the state treasury, part of which went into investment. Massive disruptions and unemployment were averted.

On the debit side, the fact that entrepreneurship was held in low regard could only inhibit the process of industrialization, as indeed it had when Confucianism held sway. Having so few incentives to produce more, people worked as little as they could. Although *un*employment was not a major problem, *under*employment definitely was. In practice, it was virtually impossible to fire a worker. Overstaffed and under-motivated, Chinese enterprises generally produced the quantities assigned to them under the state plan's quota system but were relatively unconcerned with the quality or marketability of those items. Investing money in backward hinterlands may have been good in terms of promoting equality, but it did not always make economic sense: Better returns might have been realized by reinvesting coastal Shanghai's profits in Shanghai than in cold, arid, and remote Qinghai.

Moreover, the numerous rapid shifts in the party's concept of what was or was not ideologically acceptable had caused the average Chinese to become profoundly distrustful of the system and its leaders. Experience had taught that it was better to avoid responding to new signals, or at least to lag behind as far as possible. While perfectly rational in terms of individual experience, this attitude was nevertheless detrimental to economic development.

Although Maoist policies were undertaken in support of egalitarian goals, in reality they had an effect that was just the opposite: To get along reasonably well, one was forced to develop personal ties that were quite outside the system and, by most definitions of the word, corrupt. Those who succeeded best in this underground system were, not surprisingly, greatly resented. Their existence also led to widespread cynicism about the value of collectivism and egalitarianism, thus undermining popular support for those goals.

Economic Policy under Deng Xiaoping

When Deng Xiaoping returned to power, he was highly critical of the country's economic situation, saying that it had stagnated under the Gang of Four—and, unmentioned but quite clearly implied, under Mao. The ambitious Four Modernizations program associated with his name was actually introduced by Deng's mentor, Zhou Enlai, at his last public speech in January 1975, though it was not widely publicized, much less acted upon. Hua Guofeng had also mentioned it in February 1978. In December, at the widely publicized Third Plenum of the CCP's Eleventh Central Committee, Deng reintroduced the Four Modernizations with much fanfare, and added to them a sweeping reform of the planning and management systems in industry and agriculture. Although these changes were momentous and would eventually result in dismantling much of the socialist economy, this process would take place gradually: Deng described it as "crossing the river by feeling the stones." Following the disintegration of the Soviet empire a decade later, Western economists advocated that the socialist economies of those countries be dismantled rapidly—the so-called "big-bang theory." The sudden change caused the economies of several of these countries to contract, with detrimental effects on the standard of living for many groups within them. Chinese leaders believed that this vindicated the wisdom of their gradual approach in moving toward a market economy.

The original order of the modernizations put industry first, with heavy industry receiving priority over light industry. Second was agriculture; third, science and technology; and fourth, national defense. By March 1979, the order had been changed to put agriculture first, followed by light and then heavy industry. The priorities of science and technology and of defense remained third and fourth, respectively.

The reform program had four major objectives:

- instituting a contract responsibility system in agricultural areas;
- reviving individual businesses in urban areas;
- decentralizing a substantial amount of authority to state enterprises;
- reforming the irrational price system.

Agricultural Reforms

Deng, who had been criticized during the Cultural Revolution for condoning "capitalist" practices, now publicly championed the concept of material incentives. Henceforth, he announced, people would have to sell to the state only a certain specified amount at state-set prices. Anything they raised or produced beyond these quotas was theirs to keep or to sell on the free market. Local fairs and markets, once forbidden, were now actively encouraged. Specialized production—for example, planting tomatoes rather than grain, since tomatoes fetched a higher price—was acceptable, provided that it suited local conditions.

Dazhai, the production brigade that had been the model for all to emulate since 1964, was criticized, with its leaders held responsible for low labor productivity and accused of falsifying production records. Dazhai and other widely publicized models were reported to have had huge amounts of state funds funneled into them to create the impression that their accomplishments were the result of applying left-wing egalitarian policies.

To bolster agriculture, more credit was made available to it. The share allocated to agriculture by state capital investment rose from 10.7 percent in 1978 to 14 percent in 1979. Even so, there were problems at the start. Peasants, whose past bitter experiences with their leaders' mercurial changes had made them extremely cautious, were concerned that the new policies might be aimed at ferreting out hidden rightists, which they would immediately be classified as if they tried the policies. Even if there were no ulterior motives, they reasoned, the policies might be changed in a year or two, and a campaign would be launched to cut off the "tails of capitalism;" that is, themselves.

Cadres might be resistant even when peasants were not. In one infamous incident that received extensive publicity, a cadre who was either ideologically opposed to heeding Deng's call for specialized production or fearful of its consequences for him personally ordered an entire field of watermelons to be dug up and destroyed. The media seized this opportunity to point out what it portrayed as a basic fallacy of leftism: not only was the peasants' cash crop gone but it was too late in the season for them to plant another, more ideologically acceptable crop in its place.

For a time, the government tried to hold the unit of accounting at the team level, but by 1979 had acquiesced to peasants' strong preference for using the household instead. In that same year, it also agreed to a substantial increase in agricultural procurement prices that made production more profitable. The 1980 harvest, however, was blighted by poor weather.

By 1981, a combination of government reassurance and better weather ushered in a period of rapid growth. Grain production rose rapidly, by more than 5 percent per year. Several excellent harvests culminated in a record crop in 1984, and in 1985, China was actually a net exporter of grain. However, other problems came to the fore. Certain functions that had been performed by the communes before they had been dismantled were now simply not being performed at all. Disputes broke out over issues like water use. The problems of dividing up a collective's property among the households that had been its component parts replicated almost precisely those that had characterized the parceling out of landlords' possessions three decades before. Once again, draft animals were assigned to several families, who overworked and underfed them. As before, many of the animals died.

Other problems concerned who received which items and at what price. Who would get the contracts for running such potentially profitable entities as orchards and fishponds? Who would get which pieces of land? The main issue here was not *how much* land, since equality of size could be easily measured. Rather, it was *which* land. Plots with good soil that were close to water supplies, homes, and roads were obviously preferable to plots that did not possess these attributes. What was not clear was the best method to parcel out plots of land, most of which had some but not all of the desired characteristics, among the large number of claimants. Cadres used different methods but found that whatever scheme they chose, some peasants would accuse them of favoritism. Even where they opted to draw lots, someone would accuse them of manipulating the process.

Cadres understandably felt resentful of Deng's reforms for putting them in this situation, which amounted to presiding over the dismantling of their own power and privileges. The team leader became the village leader, and peasants became more outspoken. However, many of the village leaders quickly perceived that there were advantages for them too. For example, under the new system, the village would retain ownership of collective property and businesses. This gave the village cadres the right to dictate the terms of land contracts and choose the people who would run the village enterprises. In essence, cadres might make themselves into socialist landlords. They could arrange for themselves, their friends, and their relatives to get the best land and contracts at the lowest prices. Cadres could also impose arbitrary taxes and manipulate the distribution of fertilizer or other commodities that the peasants needed.

Special relationships often grew up between the newly wealthy "10,000-yuan" households—meaning those favored few whose yearly income equaled or exceeded 10,000 yuan—and the cadres. Cadres might receive expensive gifts from the affluent households, or even shares in their businesses. Punning on Karl Marx's theory of primitive capitalist accumulation, dissident economist He Qinglian refers to this process as "primitive socialist accumulation." Watching those who were advantaged under the Maoist system become those who were advantaged under the market system, less privileged individuals began to refer to them as the "never-left-out class."

If wealthy households were uncooperative, irregularities could be "discovered" in their accounting procedures or in the treatment of those whom they hired. A time-consuming investigation would follow, accompanied by much bad publicity. Some wealthy households were "persuaded" to donate one of their businesses to the town out of gratitude for all that the party and government had done for them. The newly wealthy household's neighbors who had not become wealthy typically had little sympathy for them and were unlikely to defend them against such treatment. Often, in fact, jealousy led such people to indulge in economically counterproductive activities. Prosperous families found themselves the targets of sabotage: Their warehouses could be burned, their animals maimed, and their vehicles immobilized.

Not all cadres were corrupt, and jealousy toward one's more affluent neighbors did not usually take such vicious forms. But the sum total of the several different types of behavior described here very definitely deprived some peasants of many of the benefits of Deng's new policies. For others, knowledge of what might happen discouraged them from trying too hard to become wealthy.

After a few years of increased investment in agriculture in the late 1970s, state investments in the sector began to decline. Neither local government agencies nor peasants took up the slack. Rural officials typically preferred to develop profitable industries on farmland rather than invest in agricultural infrastructure. Peasants continued to fear that changes in the central government's agricultural policies might deprive them of any benefits that might come from investments in the infrastructure. They therefore preferred to put their money into better housing and consumer goods. Rural industry boomed as a result of these decisions, taking a substantial amount of land away from agricultural production. As noted in Chapter 5, the controversy within the leadership over how to deal with agricultural difficulties became public with the September 1985 exchange between Deng Xiaoping and leftist economist Chen Yun. It was to be an ongoing problem.

The Private Sector

In urban areas, Deng's reforms called for a rapid revival of the private sector. Under Mao, it had been despised as a remnant of capitalism, and even after the official rehabilitation of the private sector, many workers were reluctant to join it. Changing the mindset that state sector jobs were preferable to all others took time. Initially, a substantial proportion of those entering the private sector were ex-convicts, youth who had been in reform school, retirees, and others who had few alternatives for employment. Some feared a change in the party line; others did not wish to leave the security of factory jobs: Even though one earned very little, the demands and risks were few. In essence, these workers had a guaranteed livelihood or, in popular speech, an "iron rice bowl." Others, some because they were unemployed and some because they had entrepreneurial personalities, decided to try their hand at such endeavors as running restaurants, beauty parlors, taxicab fleets, and bicycle repair shops.

By 2008, the private sector employed over 200 million people and generated two-thirds of the PRC's industrial output. Most private sector jobs were in the service industry, often referred to as the tertiary sector of the economy, after agriculture and mining (primary sector) and manufacturing (secondary sector). Although typically charging higher prices than the state, their services were actually available when those that, in theory, should have been provided by the state were not. Typically as well, the quality of service was superior. As state-run enterprises declined in importance, the economic contributions of individual and collectively owned businesses burgeoned. In 1998, in a startling departure from Maoist ideals, an individual who owned a private company received the official designation of "model worker."

More Responsibility for State Enterprises

The linchpin of economic reform, however, lay elsewhere: in the delegation of greater authority to individual enterprises in order to transform them into more independent units that would be responsible for their own successes and failures. With the iron rice bowl broken, the state would no longer subsidize factories or other enterprises that were unprofitable. After a relatively short transition period, those that could not adapt to the new realities would have to go out of business.

Beginning in 1979, the government issued a number of directives and regulations designed to implement decentralization and the fiscal responsibility of enterprises. Administrative organization was to be simplified, with more decision-making power devolving to lower levels on the assumption that they were better positioned than Beijing bureaucrats to judge what was best. Many state-imposed mandatory quotas were lowered as well. Taxes were levied in lieu of requiring factories to turn over their profits to the state. After-tax profits were to be retained by the factory for investment, expansion, and distribution as bonuses to deserving employees. To the carrot of returning profits to the factories that produced them, a stick was added in the form of a bankruptcy law enabling enterprises that persisted in running at a loss to be dismantled.

These reforms had a number of positive effects. Factories did, in general, try harder to produce goods that people found attractive and wished to buy. Many workers put more effort into their jobs and found themselves rewarded with more money and more consumer goods in the stores to spend it on. Clothes became more varied, stylish, and better fitting. Families acquired refrigerators, washing machines, and televisions. Some were even able to buy cars.

There were problems as well, however. It was difficult to make the bankruptcy law work: A very large number of factories operated at a loss, and forcing them out of business would turn a lot of unhappy workers out on the streets, with potential for major social unrest. Having to pay unemployment benefits to the workers would erase much of what might have been gained by ending the state subsidies that had kept the factory in business. Despite the wide publicity given to a few plant closings, most factories continued operating. In 1991, Chinese economists reported that almost two-thirds of their country's 102,000 state-owned industrial enterprises were losing money. At the same time, the PRC's finance minister stated that losses by state enterprises exceeded profits by a ratio of nearly eight to one. Subsidies to such factories absorbed nearly one-third of government revenue in 1990. Rather than using bonuses to reward outstanding workers, factories tended to divide the money equally among all workers, regardless of how hard they had worked. This reduced the efficacy of the bonus as an incentive. Economists complained that not only had the reforms failed to smash the iron rice bowl, but everyone continued to "eat from the same big pot."

Reforming the Price System

The fourth of Deng's reforms, reforming the price system to reflect supply and demand rather than having prices artificially set by central government planners, was enormously difficult. To remove controls on prices overnight would have caused chaos, as low, state-set prices fluctuated wildly in search of market prices that were as yet unknown. Hence, it was reasonable for the government to opt for a phased changeover instead. In 1983, a transitional, two-tier price system was adopted: a government-set price for materials covered by the state plan and a negotiated price which was normally well above that of the government-set price. For most agricultural products, there was a third, or market, price, which was determined by supply and demand and was usually even higher. Unfortunately, the tiered price system had the unintended result of encouraging hoarding and speculation. Individuals who were able to gain access to goods at the low, state-set price bought up as much as they could and then held the commodities off the market until they could sell at high negotiated prices. Officials fulminated against such behavior, warning that economic crimes would be severely prosecuted. Some people were indeed given stiff sentences, including execution, but hoarding and profiteering continued. These practices bid up the price of needed commodities and caused serious economic inefficiencies.

Scarcities in basic raw materials caused other problems because, while government-controlled prices for coal, oil, iron ore, and many other mineral products continued to be far below their actual production costs, the products made from them could be sold at negotiated prices, which were significantly higher. Hence, producers of these commodities could make huge profits—provided that they could obtain the necessary raw materials. The situation was particularly serious with regard to coal, which supplied more than 70 percent of China's energy needs at that time. Would-be purchasers went to enormous lengths to gain access. Bribes, though strictly illegal, became common.

Guandao, or official corruption, was indulged in not only by high-ranking cadres but also by their princeling children. Deng's open-door policy toward trading with foreign countries encouraged many non-Chinese companies to seek contracts and joint ventures with the PRC. The government set up four special economic zones (SEZs), all of them on the PRC's southeastern coast, to facilitate attracting foreign investment. Later on, Hainan province was also made a SEZ, and a number of cities were accorded certain special provisions with regard to doing business with foreigners. Many overseas investors were attracted by the lure of the Chinese market but found that cutting through the tangle of the PRC's overlapping bureaucracies, with their respective rivalries, seemingly inexhaustible supplies of red tape, and unpublished regulations, was a nightmare. They discovered that access to the right top official, often through gifts to one of his or her children, could be the key to getting the right stamp, or "chop," of legitimization. Children of high-ranking officials were also prominent members of state-trading corporations that supervised trade transactions with foreign countries. They were pleased to take advantage of offers to inspect the home offices of the foreign corporation with which they might want to do business. Gourmet dining and sightseeing expeditions could be charged to the corporation's expense account. Some took jobs at these corporations. For these princelings, dealing with foreigners was the key to the good life.

Although industry boomed, these practices led to shortages of energy and raw materials: factories might be able to work only two to three days a week because they lacked such basics as power and water. Imports surged in the second half of 1988 as China turned to foreign suppliers for many of the items it could not supply domestically. These included sugar, cotton, and grain. The country's trade balance deteriorated. The government therefore decided to grant incentives to state-trading companies to help increase exports. These measures succeeded in bringing about a rapid increase in exports but caused other problems. Because an irrational domestic price structure severely underpriced raw materials and energy, trading companies rushed to export these commodities and sell them at international prices, which were much higher. Thus, the companies made large profits by selling such items as coal, cotton, and silk at the very same time that domestic factories reported shortages of the same goods.

Rapid growth in exports also widened regional income disparities, which were already a source of debate within the leadership. In the name of economic efficiency, the government had for the past decade invested its money where it thought it could get the best returns, as opposed to the Maoist preference for redistributing funds away from more profitable coastal enterprises in order to bring about the economic development of the country's backward hinterland. Deng's policies meant that the coastal provinces forged ahead economically, while the hinterland fell further behind. By encouraging rapid export growth in 1988, the government exacerbated this trend. With their more modern factories, better-skilled workforce, and access to the ports and rail lines that link China with the outside world, coastal provinces could more easily take advantage of central government incentives to export than could provinces of the hinterland. This, in turn, gave coastal areas better access to credit and foreign exchange, more rapid gains in income, and greater independence from Beijing.

The interior provinces grew increasingly unhappy with this situation and retaliated by erecting trade barriers to protect themselves, aiming to prevent the more affluent, coastal provinces from bidding up the prices for their coal, grain, and other products. In some areas, local authorities set up checkpoints at roads, railway stations, ports, or provincial borders to block the shipment of goods they had not specifically authorized. Local area banks limited their loans to, or raised interest rates for, enterprises that purchased goods from other regions. Local courts favored local interests in handing down their rulings. Worried about the potential destruction of the national market that the communist party had worked so hard to establish, the central government issued directives prohibiting various regionalist practices. Arguments that regionalism was bad for the country, and, in the long run, even bad for the regions, yielded no noticeable improvement in the phenomenon.

Meanwhile, inflation was a far more serious concern. The official inflation rate for 1988 was 18.5 percent, which is generally believed to understate the problem. Food prices rose more than 50 percent, causing serious difficulties for many: in China, unlike more developed countries, consumers spent more than 60 percent of their income on food. Panic buying and runs on banks occurred in many areas during the summer of 1988. Since consumer bank accounts amounted to 27 percent of the PRC's gross national product, the government was concerned to stop the runs on banks as quickly as possible.

Reforming the Reforms

In September 1988, stringent measures were announced to slow down capital construction, restrict spending, and control inflation. The intent was to discourage bank-financed investment outside the state plan. Control over the production and marketing of certain steel products and nonferrous metals was recentralized.

In addition, the central government re-established its monopoly over the distribution of fertilizer, pesticides, and plastic sheeting to control speculation in farm inputs.

Control over foreign trade was also reasserted. For example, the number of corporations authorized to import certain products was restricted, while the number of products subject to export licenses, quotas, and outright bans was expanded. The government also reduced the shares of foreign exchange that the PRC's five special economic zones were permitted to retain from their exports. The results of this retrenchment program were not what the government hoped for. Growth in capital construction spending did fall sharply but had a major impact on state enterprises: Rural enterprises grew three times as fast as state-dominated enterprises. Many factories were able to circumvent the government's credit controls by drawing on the resources of widespread nongovernment financial institutions. This was particularly easy for those located on the PRC's southern coast, which had access to capital from Hong Kong and abroad. Inflation continued to increase, by more than 25 percent in the first half of 1989. The 1988 retrenchment was a vivid lesson in how difficult it would be for party and government to reclaim the economic levers of power once they had been surrendered.

The rapidly rising inflation rate, the growth of inequalities in the distribution of income, and the pervasive nature of official corruption were major grievances expressed by antigovernment demonstrators at Tiananmen Square and elsewhere in the spring of 1989. While rejecting calls for abstract rights such as freedom and democracy, the government made serious efforts to address the economic issues they raised, resulting in greater central government control over the economy. A 39-point plan adopted in November 1989 ordered joint ventures that already had local or provincial control to apply to the central government for import–export licenses for previously uncontrolled items. The central bank withdrew large amounts of money from circulation. Officials accused private businesses of evading taxes, engaging in illicit activities, and causing income disparities. Some businesspeople were prosecuted for such activities and given stiff sentences; some corrupt officials were treated in the same fashion. Export industries received heavy subsidies at the same time that imports were severely restricted.

The collective effect of these measures, plus the economic sanctions imposed by some foreign countries on China after the government's bloody suppression of the demonstrations, was to plunge the PRC's economy into a steep downturn. On the positive side, inflation declined to 4 percent. Export subsidies and import restrictions resulted in a doubling of the country's foreign exchange reserves, to over $23 billion, and there was now a trade surplus. However, the costs were high. Real gross domestic product (GDP) grew at only 1.8 percent in the first half of 1990, losses in state enterprises were twice those of 1989, and unemployment soared. Large supplies of consumer durables piled up in warehouses as potential buyers reacted to economic uncertainties by postponing purchases. The state taxation bureau was able to collect only half of what it had expected, partly because the economy had contracted and partly because widespread tax evasion continued.

The government subsequently rescinded certain measures, which seemed to ease unemployment and encourage consumer purchasing a little. GDP grew by 5.2 percent in 1990 and by 7 percent in 1991; the inflation rate in 1991 was a modest 2.9 percent. Party and government pronouncements continued to affirm the need for both structural reforms and economic retrenchment, thus reflecting their uncertainty about how to proceed. Pressures and counter-pressures from leftists, who preferred more central planning, and reformers, who preferred greater reliance on the market, resulted in vacillating policies, as did central government pressures for greater central control and provincial counter-pressures for more leeway in economic decision making. Analysts described the Chinese economy as suspended in a state of disequilibrium.

In early 1992, Deng Xiaoping made a heavily publicized visit to several of the SEZs, praising their achievements and thereby signaling that a new period of reforms was about to begin. Annual growth rates surged into the 12 to 13 percent range. However, inflation again became a problem. In addition, the economic restructuring that was part of the reforms meant that a number of workers were dismissed. Worker unrest became a serious problem: In Tianjin, employees in a state-owned watch factory smashed equipment and fought with police after hearing that mass layoffs were imminent. In another city, a bank director's house was firebombed by a recently dismissed staff member.

In an effort to streamline the bloated and inefficient bureaucracy, officials were urged to "jump into the sea," meaning to go into business for themselves as opposed to working for party or government. A number of them did, often succeeding by using connections they had made in their previous jobs. This gave such individuals an advantage over those without connections in the bureaucracy, and led to complaints of unfair competition. Many other officials, not wishing to lose the subsidized housing that came with their jobs, took on new positions without quitting. Knowing they would be difficult to dismiss, they put in the absolute minimum amount of time on their official duties, thereby rendering party and government still less efficient.

Agriculture, too, had problems. According to government figures, the income gap between rural and urban dwellers widened from 1:1.7 in 1985 to 1:1.24 in 1991, and continued to increase rapidly. Peasants were also being squeezed off their land. Between 1949 and 1991, China's total acreage under cultivation was reduced from 1.468 billion *mu* (one mu equals approximately 0.16 acre) to 1.435 billion *mu*, while the number of rural laborers during the same period rose from 173 million to 428 million. Although the town and township enterprises that were first set up in the 1980s absorbed nearly 100 million rural laborers, this left over 150 million surplus laborers in the countryside, many of whom jammed trains and roads in search of work elsewhere. Efforts to stop what were called blind population shifts failed, and emphasis shifted to trying to better channel the "floating population" toward the jobs that could best help the country's economic development.

To make matters worse, governments that were eager to devote resources to large-scale investment often found they had no money left and opted to issue IOUs. Other investment-hungry officials who wanted agricultural land for construction projects either tried to confiscate it or offered peasants less than they thought their land was worth. New kinds of taxes proliferated as well. A widespread lament was that "the KMT had too many taxes and the CCP had too many meetings, but now the CCP has even more taxes than it has meetings."

Despite these frictions, economic reforms continued. In October 1992, the Fourteenth Party Congress declared its intention to establish a "socialist market economic system." Commentaries explained this apparent contradiction in terms of using the advantages of capitalist market economies in order to develop socialized, large-scale production "while maintaining a balance . . . between the two." Guided by this market Leninism, growth rates forged ahead.

By mid-1993, the problem was no longer an economy that had stalled but rather one that appeared to be locked on overdrive. Prices soared, and people rushed to buy gold to preserve their savings or to invest them in something that would outpace inflation. Investment fever threatened to get out of hand. More than 100,000 people lost money when the bonds they had been told would yield 24 percent interest turned out to be worthless. The head of the issuing company was apprehended, tried, and executed, but just as unsettling as the scheme itself was the revelation that the company had not acted in isolation: more than 100 party and government officials were implicated, and journalists for official newspapers had been bribed to write articles that described the bonds favorably. It was also alleged that high-ranking party and government officials were guilty of insider trading on the Hong Kong stock market. Since they had advance knowledge of announcements from Beijing that could be expected to affect share prices in Hong Kong, such individuals were in a position to amass a fortune quickly. Ordinary people found ways to evade tax assessments, which were officially estimated to cost the government over $15 billion each year.

A new fiscal system was introduced in 1994 which was designed to raise the central government's share of revenue, but provinces resisted implementing it. In the same year, the government, reacting to peasants' anger at the many taxes that they were burdened with, ordered that levies on peasants should not exceed 5 percent of their incomes. Inflation again became a problem. Official figures, which are widely believed to underestimate actual inflation, placed the 1994 rate at a post-1949 high of 21.8 percent. Financial analysts were skeptical that the economy could achieve a "soft landing;" that is, that inflation could be lowered without provoking a severe economic downturn.

To their surprise, the government's plans were successful. Not only did the economy achieve a soft landing, but tax revenues began to increase as well. Although in 1996 central-government tax revenues had fallen to 10.3 percent of GDP, they rebounded to 16.6 percent in 2001 and had regained their pre-reform rate of over 20 percent by 2012. Inflation was modest, while GDP grew at satisfactory rates.

New Problems for Deng's Successors

At the time of Deng Xiaoping's death in February 1997, China's economic prospects looked bright. Foreign observers extrapolated healthy growth rates into the twenty-first century and issued glowing predictions for prosperity. All, however, was not well. Economic growth rates were sluggish. Initially, this did not appear to be a problem: Even the lower rates were impressive, and the trade-off in lower inflation was welcome. Later, however, concerns grew about how long the downward trajectory would continue. GDP grew by only 8.8 percent in 1997 *vis-à-vis* an expected 10 percent, and the inflation rate, a modest 2 percent, had slipped into deflation by the end of the year. A World Bank report warned that if reforms were not implemented soon, the result might be "sinosclerosis."

The leadership promised a major restructuring effort and an 8 percent growth in GDP for 1998. It argued that this was the minimum figure necessary to create jobs for new entrants to the labor market and to re-employ those who would lose their existing jobs in the restructuring that leaders believed was necessary to keep the economy healthy. However, provincial officials, told that they must achieve an 8 percent growth rate, responded by reporting figures that were even higher. In a process known as "wringing the water" from statistics, the central government declared the growth rate for 1998 to be 7.8 percent. It also introduced a massive fiscal stimulus package that included large public works projects as a way to keep the economy growing. This it did, although incurring large budget deficits as a result. Growth rates rebounded impressively, albeit amid complaints that artificially stimulated growth was, ultimately, unhealthy growth. Ideally, growth should come from increased productivity rather than infusions of capital from the government. By 2002, the government had decided that 7 percent was the minimum necessary for job creation and to avoid widespread labor unrest.

As indicated above, there are problems with inaccurate statistics. Not all are caused by lower level officials inflating growth rates: prosperous areas may deliberately underreport figures to reduce the amount of taxes they have to pay. There is also a massive underground economy, estimated to be several billion dollars; if reported, it would raise GDP by several percentage points. Some argue that debates about numbers are irrelevant, since the quality of economic growth is more important than the quantity thereof. For example, although building up inventories of unsaleable goods counts as economic growth, it does not represent an improvement in people's lives or in the prosperity of the state. In early 2006, the government revised the GDP figures for the period 1993 to 2004 upward by an aggregate of 17 percent. At the same time, it revised the GDPs of 12 provinces downward. Debates over precise numbers aside, growth rates were impressive, exceeding 10 percent a year from 2002 through 2008 (Figure 7.1). In 2005, the PRC passed Great Britain to become the world's fourth largest economy,

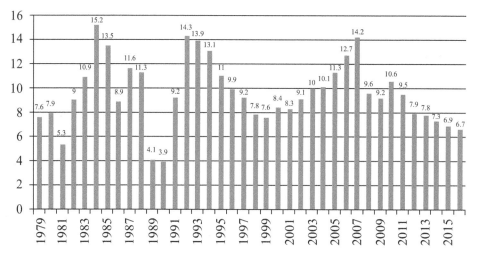

FIGURE 7.1 Growth of China's Gross Domestic Product (GDP)

Source: State Statistical Bureau (2017).

surpassing Germany in 2008; and, despite somewhat slower growth due to the global economic downturn, it edged past Japan in 2011. It should be noted, however, that the per capita income of these countries, and many others, is much higher than that of the PRC.

In 2006 and for most of the period since then, the PRC has had the world's largest foreign exchange reserves. In 2006 as well, China's trade surplus with the rest of the world rose by an astonishing 74 percent, to $177.5 billion; by the end of 2008, it rose to $297 billion before dropping a little due to a combination of foreign pressure and the effects of the global financial crisis.

These impressive gains were accompanied by familiar problems. Growth continued to be highly unequal, resulting in stunning prosperity in some areas and abject poverty in others. Increasing labor unrest was also evident, as an estimated 60 million people who were displaced from their jobs as a result of restructuring looked for new positions. The government set up retraining centers to help, with indifferent results. A few people managed to get better positions than before, but most had to settle for lower paying jobs or even no jobs at all. In recent years, new entrants to the workforce have exceeded the number of new jobs by about 20 percent.

Pension funds proved inadequate. When factories defaulted on commitments to displaced workers—sometimes unavoidably because funds did not exist, at other times because corrupt managers had embezzled the money—tens of thousands of workers took to the streets in protest. These protests typically concerned a single factory and were suppressed, generally within a few days. In an effort to limit the possibility that demonstrations will spread to other cities, the media are forbidden to report on labor unrest, though text messaging has undermined the usefulness of this technique. One measure that the government has found successful involves undermining support for protest leaders by making minimal concessions, such as small cash payments to the rank and file. At the same time, officials attempt to divide the leaders of the demonstrations by buying some off and intimidating or incarcerating others. Demonstrators who tried to organize a union independent of the government-controlled All China Federation of Trade Unions, for example, were arrested. Reflecting on Karl Marx's call to the workers of the world to unite, since they had nothing to lose but their chains, a Westerner commented that China's workers were trying to unite at the risk of being put *in* chains.

Peasants fared still worse than workers. Their incomes, typically much less than those of city dwellers, declined still more as a result of cheaper imports entering China following the PRC's admission to the World Trade Organization in 2002. Official statistics indicate that at the end of 2012, the income of rural citizens was less than one-third of that of city dwellers. According to the Chinese Academy of Social Sciences, when one adjusts for the 40 percent of farmers' incomes needed to purchase such items as chemical fertilizer, pesticides, and seeds, the ratio is 5.2 to 1 in favor of city dwellers. Moreover, since urbanites have access to goods and services that are simply unavailable in the countryside, the discrepancy is even greater. Planners worried about millions of impoverished peasants flocking to the cities and thereby worsening unemployment problems there.

The 1994 fiscal reform, while increasing the share of revenue to the central government, threw rural finance into a deep structural crisis that was transferred downward and ultimately fell on villages and townships. In the 2002–2006 period, many peasant burdens were alleviated by the tax-for-fee reform of 2002–2004 and the abolition of the agricultural tax, but at the cost of worsening local finances. Farmers nonetheless remain liable for income taxes, local taxes, and a number of other levies. Land seizures also became a new source of tension, leading to an upsurge in peasant protests.

Despite different calculations of China's Gini coefficient, an internationally recognized measure of income disparity in which "0" represents perfect equality and "1" perfect inequality, estimates agree that it has risen steadily. Although the official figure is 0.47, a study done by researchers at a university in Chengdu reports that it is 0.61, higher than Mexico's 0.48, America's 0.38, and Poland's 0.3. By contrast, the PRC's Gini coefficient was 0.36 in 1990 and, in 1978, 0.18. Since 0.4 is considered to be the danger level, this was alarming. Some Latin American and sub-Saharan African states have scores at or above 0.6, but, since the founding principles of its revolution included both egalitarianism and a commitment to the welfare of the workers and peasants, the inequity appears to be felt more keenly in the PRC. Because people seem to be less bothered by inequality per se than by the perception of inequity, a crucial factor may be the government's ability to maintain the public's confidence that hard work will bring increased prosperity. Planners hope that such large income disparities will not be permanent. Eminent economist Simon Kuznets observed that inequality tends to increase during the early stages of development but decrease in later stages. Initially, pockets of modern economic growth generate high incomes in a few limited areas, while income remains low in most of the traditional economy. Later, however, growth disperses into those areas.

An attempt to reduce disparities between coastal and inland areas of the PRC, the "invest in the west" campaign, was begun in 2000. It received much favorable publicity but produced few substantive results. Foreign investors brought to the area were not impressed with the prospects for return on their capital. Domestically, a great deal of privately expressed cynicism existed as well. Members of the Chinese People's Political Consultative Conference and National People's Congress worried about "empty words and wasteful duplication," as well as about corruption reducing the effect of the money invested. Disparities continued to grow: a study by Xi'an's Northwest University revealed that the east–west wealth gap actually widened in the first five years of the program.

Poverty-alleviation efforts have shown declining results and even, in some cases, reversed. As always, caution should be exercised in accepting these figures, since poor counties may want to remain under the poverty line, or be reclassified beneath it, in order to be eligible for national and international subsidies. Official statistics indicate that the percentage of the population living below the poverty line has declined to 2.8, but a Beijing-based team calculates it at 10 percent. There are disputes over where the poverty line should be drawn. In 2012, the PRC raised its figure by 80 percent, though that is still below the U.N.'s standard of $1.25 a day at 2005 prices.

Future Concerns

While much of the world marveled at China's impressive growth statistics and worried about the ability of their own economies to compete, others pointed out structural problems that did not bode well for the country's future. Economists have suggested that China's incremental approach to reform has reached the limits of its effectiveness, and that rather than continue Deng Xiaoping's formula of crossing the river by feeling the stones, the country needs to be comprehensively restructured. Central to this restructuring is the conviction that the economy must be moved away from its heavy reliance on investment and export for growth and toward expanded domestic consumption.

Unfortunately, solving one problem seems inexorably to create others. For example, one way to encourage workers to spend more would be to give them greater confidence in their future earning power. A labor contract law that came into effect in 2008 is considered a milestone in legislation designed to protect workers' rights. However, it also encouraged a number of factories to relocate elsewhere. As labor rights activists point out, the interests of workers remain precarious in practical terms: management has routinely ignored or violated other laws, often in collusion with local authorities. Activists argue that not until the government gives workers the right of collective bargaining will these rights be meaningful. Party and government leaders, however, worry that granting these rights would increase upward pressure on wages, thereby reducing profitability, economic growth, and ultimately, social stability.

Increasing rural prosperity would also encourage household consumption as well as defuse rising social unrest in agricultural areas. Rural areas comprise nearly half of China, but account for only one-third of retail sales for consumer products. The income gap between urban and rural residents has continued to widen, thereby reducing the purchasing power of that sector. Since the advent of the capitalist economy, many farmers have been swindled out of their land by a combination of corrupt local officials and urban developers. Theoretically, all land is owned by the state, but farmers may hold leases on it, often based on murky contract language which is difficult to decipher, particularly by those with marginal education. Peasant dissatisfaction with confiscated land has been a major cause of rural unrest.

One solution would be to allow outright ownership, which would make confiscation more difficult as well as providing incentives to invest labor and other resources that would make land use more efficient, raising yields and incomes. Opposition took many forms, from ideological—all land should be owned by the state—to instrumental—local authorities want to keep the right to requisition land in order to raise money—to the practical—farmers who are forced to borrow as a result of poor harvests or personal problems like medical bills would quickly lose their land, resulting in wide-scale pauperization that would increase, rather than decrease, social tension and income gaps. In 2009, a compromise extended the length of leaseholds from 30 to 60 years.

The dysfunctional financial system is also difficult to reform. Under a 1997 policy of seizing the larger state-owned enterprises (SOEs) and letting go of the small ones, the government transformed many SOEs into shareholding enterprises by issuing minority shares to investors. However, in 2003, wishing to forestall in China what had happened in Russia—oligarchs taking over state assets as private individuals—the PRC leadership set up the State-owned Assets Supervision and Administration Commission (SASAC) to re-establish central control. To recapitalize ailing banks, the People's Bank injected $60 billion into the four major state-owned commercial banks between 2003 and 2005. It has been pointed out that if the Chinese government were to cede control over its banks, the banks would curtail their nonmarket lending and strengthen their balance sheets. Market lending would use Chinese savings more efficiently: long-term, real GDP growth would be higher, and individual households would earn a better return on their savings. A frustrated economist observed that without reform of the SOEs there can be no banking reform, but without banking reform there can be no reform of the SOEs. Although the gradualist banking reforms have resulted in some improvements, banks continue to be asked to satisfy contradictory objectives: financing employment and social stability while, at the same time, transforming themselves into commercially viable corporate entities. In essence, this is the problem facing the central government as a whole.

In 2006, 24 key industrial and technology sectors were made wholly or majority state controlled in a policy known as *guojin, mintui*: state advances, private sector retreats. The mainstays of *guojin, mintui* are more than 100 huge SOEs, many of them monopolies in 11 sectors that have been deemed crucial to the country's economy. Specialized in operations such as energy, water and mineral resources, the environment, manufacturing, and transportation, they are deemed "national champion" industries, and receive special subsidies that give them advantages over private industry. While some SOEs are profitable, others are "zombie corporations" who must borrow to pay the interest due on their loans, but cannot pay off the principal, thereby resorting to even more borrowing. As is common in such situations, they have a tendency to use money unwisely, and must continue to receive state subsidies that are ultimately funded by Chinese taxpayers. These industries are also closely controlled by the CCP, whose organization department appoints their top officers. Known as the "black class" because of the color of the state-owned cars they are issued, SOE managers enjoy high salaries and other benefits.

When the Chinese economy began to feel the effects of the worldwide economic crisis of 2008, there were abrupt declines in nearly every sector, leading to a sharp loss of consumer confidence. The government responded with a massive economic stimulus package which envisioned spending about 7 percent of the country's GDP on infrastructure projects such as railroads, subways, and airports as well as rebuilding areas that had been devastated by the May 2008 earthquake. This intensified the *guojin, mintui* process at the expense of the economically more profitable private sector. Critics argue that this is sapping the entrepreneurial vitality that has been responsible for the PRC's spectacular economic growth since 1978; proponents counter that close control is necessary to provide a stabilizing influence in a chaotic marketplace. Initial results seemed to confirm supporters of closer state control: As most of the rest of the world struggled to emerge from the financial crisis in 2009, the Chinese economy grew by 8.7 percent, and by 11.2 percent in 2010. Admirers described this as proof that the "China model" of state-led economic growth worked, as opposed to what they viewed as the failure of free market Western capitalism and liberal democracy.

Others argued that the stimulus may simply have worsened an inevitable day of reckoning, since it allowed needed structural reforms to be postponed rather than dealt with immediately. Stories of bridges to nowhere and dangerously shoddy construction abound. High rates of industrial expansion that are artificially stimulated by cheap government loans raised fears that a crash is inevitable. Corruption is estimated to siphon off an estimated 15 percent of annual GDP.

In another response to the global economic crisis, regulators adopted a more permissive attitude toward the financial system, which led to various kinds of off-balance sheet lending. Funds escaped from the state banking system's rigidly controlled interest rates into more lucrative market-driven areas. The shadow banking system grew, abetted by the explosive growth of internet finance. However, debts and debt chains grew rapidly: the potential for profit increased, but so did risk factors. In March 2017, a major effort began to tighten control over the financial sector and end the shady practices that had evolved. While a positive step, economists pointed out that previous efforts to clamp down on excess liquidity have been short-lived, since as soon as they begin to curtail growth they are abandoned. An additional difficulty is that almost every high-ranking leader is believed to have at least one relative in the financial sector and hence is involved in the practices being scrutinized.

Mindful that the economy was overly dependent on investments and exports, and insufficiently driven by growth in domestic consumption, the government was able to achieve good results, moving consumption from 35 percent of GDP in 2012 to 51.6 percent in 2016. This is comparable to India's rate but a full ten points below that of Brazil, and 71 percent in the U.S. The percentage increase of China's GPD from consumption now exceeds that of either primary or tertiary industry (Figure 7.2).

Another initiative involves investing financial reserves abroad. China has fostered the founding of three banks for the BRICS (Brazil, Russia, India, and South Africa), Central Asia, and most prominently, the Asia Infrastructure Investment Bank (AIIB), with the PRC as major stockholder in each. The AIIB, initiated by Xi Jinping in 2013, will finance an innovative reworking of the land and sea silk roads. If successful, it could alleviate the critical shortage of infrastructure that inhibits economic development in numerous Asian states, while spurring demand for Chinese construction and export industries as the PRC's domestic economic growth slows.

There are also concerns that a shrinking labor force may cause problems for economic competitiveness in the future. While the problem of creating jobs for

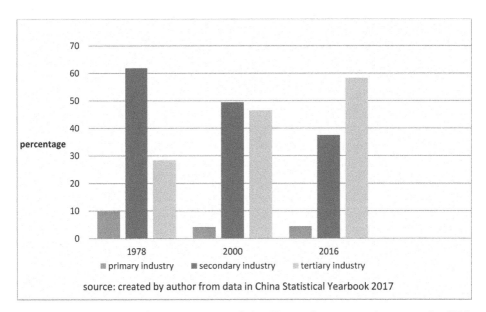

source: created by author from data in China Statistical Yearbook 2017

FIGURE 7.2 Share of Contributions of the Three Sectors to Increase in GDP, 1978–2016

the millions of new entrants to the job market each year persists, and could be exacerbated by the increasing use of automation, the working-age population peaked in 2015 and has since begun to shrink. In several major cities, shortages of highly skilled workers in some sectors have raised their compensation levels. This in turn has incentivized corporations to shift their operations to countries where wages are lower.

Other worrisome signs include a large buildup of unsold inventories in many state-owned factories; a glut of low interest loans and credits that were extended to state administrative agencies and their influential clients while neglecting the needs of those individuals, small businesses, and families who were the intended recipients of the loans; and massive embezzlement of stimulus funds by officials. Local government debts are another source of concern. According to official statistics, widely believed to be underestimates, they had risen to an alarming 31 percent of GDP by the end of 2013. Should the central government allow local governments to default, there could be serious consequences for social stability. Alternatively, bailing them out would be expensive and a disincentive to curbing unwise spending in the future.

Government officials also worry about the lack of indigenous innovation, meaning that the country's manufacturers must copy from other countries or produce goods for them rather than develop new products themselves. Inflation remains a problem even as economic growth appears to be slowing. There are concerns about a property bubble fueled by speculators.

Faced with a fragile economic recovery on the one hand and rising inflationary pressures on the other, decision makers find it difficult to implement the far-reaching restructuring that a 2012 World Bank report indicates will be necessary if the PRC is to continue growing, or, as the report warned, become stuck in a middle-income trap. Some economists believe that implicit in the World Bank's report is the more ominous warning that the alternative to restructuring may be an economic downturn, which could in turn intensify social unrest. Chinese analyst Pei Minxin estimates that privatizing the SOEs would jeopardize ten million jobs: five million of them in the party and another five million in the government agencies that profit from strong state control of the economy. Reducing the SOEs' power would make the Chinese economy far more efficient, but, Pei points out, it is highly unlikely that a one-party government would risk destroying its own political base.

The government's supporters point out that the impressive economic growth rates of past years could not possibly be sustained indefinitely, and that China can continue to develop at rates that would be the envy of most other economies, in the range of 6 to 7 percent a year,: what Xi Jinping has referred to as "the new normal" for the foreseeable future.

Others argue that with growth being artificially stimulated, a moment of reckoning may be imminent. As the CCP's Nineteenth Party Congress was taking place, the governor of China's central bank warned that excessive optimism could lead to a "Minsky moment," meaning the sudden collapse of asset prices following long periods of economic prosperity and growth.

Conclusions

The Chinese economy has turned in an impressive performance in the years after Deng Xiaoping assumed a leadership rule. However, systemic flaws engendered by the reforms became prominent and seemed destined to end the upswing in prosperity. Among these serious structural defects are disparities of income:

- *among regions.* Despite some easing as higher wages on China's eastern coast give some industries the incentive to move inland, income levels in inland and western provinces continue to lag behind. Average incomes in Shanghai are more than five times as large as those in Gansu province.
- *between urban and rural areas.* Farmers earn less than one-third of city dwellers' income: though slightly less than half the population of the PRC, rural residents own less than one-fifth of the country's savings.
- *among different industries, enterprises, and units.* Wages have risen the fastest in finance, power production, and real estate, but relatively slowly in agriculture, forestry, and fishing.
- *among social strata.* The self-employed and owners of private enterprise receive higher wages than do workers in state enterprises.
- *among urban residents.* Citizens of Shanghai and Guangzhou earn far more than residents of "rust belt" cities, such as those in Liaoning and Heilongjiang provinces.
- *within communities.* "Poverty belts" have grown up around cities like Beijing and Tianjin; a Chinese economist has described Beijing as a European city surrounded by an African countryside.

Financial markets are described as chaotic, distorted, and corrupted. The regulatory environment is weak, with laws and regulations often unenforced or ignored by local government officials. This adversely affects the quality of the goods which companies produce as companies seek to cut costs by skirting the rules. Often, connections with party and government officials rather than market forces determine financial success for companies. These inhibit competition and undermine the efficient allocation of goods and services.

The social costs of reform are huge, with postponement a tempting option. Yet, as economists warn, delaying will increase the disruptions of the reform that must inevitably take place. Thus far, ameliorative steps have had only modest success. It is not clear whether recent modest declines in growth rates represent the inevitable cooling down of a maturing economy or a prolonged slide with potentially severe repercussions; nor is it clear how successful Xi Jinping's administration will be in dealing with the economic reform that all agree is necessary.

The transition from a centrally planned economy to a market economy is exceedingly difficult, with differences of opinion continuing on the proper balance between central government guidance and market regulation. Although a broad consensus exists within the current elite regarding the need to press on, and soon, there are disagreements concerning the pace and timing of reform. While marketization has had a mainly positive effect on Chinese development, left-leaning analysts point out that planning remains essential to the economy in a number of ways, including the overall balancing of supply and demand, economic restructuring, maintaining fair competition, environmental protection, and social equity.

It is possible that the PRC can muddle through the current situation, as it has surmounted comparable difficulties in the past, but neither can the possibility for significant instability be ignored.

Suggestions for Further Reading

Roselyn Hsueh, "Chinese-Style: Strategic Value of Sectors, Sectoral Characteristics, and Globalization," *Governance: An International Journal of Policy, Administration, and Institutions*," Vol. 29, No. 1 January 2016, pp. 85–102.

Xiaoshuo Hou, *Community Capitalism in China: The State, the Market, and Collectivism* (Cambridge: Cambridge University Press, 2013).

Chen Li, "Holding 'China Inc.' Together: The CCP and the Rise of China's *Yangqi*," *China Quarterly*, No. 228, December 2016, pp. 227–249.

Wayne Morrison, *China's Economic Rise: History, Trends, Challenges, and Implications for the United States* (Washington, DC: U.S. Library of Congress Congressional Research Service, August 31, 2017).

Barry Naughton, "Economic Policy in the Aftermath of the 19th Party Congress," *China Leadership Monitor*, No. 55, January 2018.

CHAPTER 8

Crime and Punishment
The Legal System of the PRC

All societies attempt to regulate the conduct of their members, though they may differ widely in the sorts of behavior they condemn and sanction, the mechanisms through which judgments are made, and the punishments that are meted out. For example, one society may choose to encourage large families by providing incentives for childbearing and prison terms for the use or sale of contraceptives; another society, believing that it is important to limit population growth, may employ a completely opposite incentive/punishment scheme. Some societies prefer informal rules enforced by family and group sanctions; others rely on detailed written codes enforced by an elaborate hierarchy of courts and prisons. The types of punishment a society deems to be appropriate may vary as widely as ostracizing the offender at the one extreme, to painful forms of execution at the other.

The Chinese communist leadership group in 1949 was the survivor of several decades of violent struggle against the Kuomintang (KMT), warlords, the Japanese, and a number of internal rivals. None of these struggles was characterized by respect for legalities. These were not life experiences that predisposed the Chinese Communist Party (CCP) leaders to believe in the sanctity of a court system, or in the notion that society could be bettered by reasoned appeals to the consciences of its rulers. Communist ideology, moreover, rejected the entire concept of the impartiality and inherent fairness of the legal system. To the contrary, the legal system was regarded as a tool in the hands of the ruling class—in China's case, feudal and bourgeois powers—to oppress and exploit the workers and peasants and to inhibit the forces of progress.

Another factor predisposing the leadership against a formal legal system may not have been consciously intended: the traditional Chinese preference for informality in settling disputes and imposing sanctions. Also, like communism, the traditional Chinese legal system saw law as subordinate to a dominant political philosophy—in its case, Confucianism.

Mao Zedong was a fervent believer in the concept of permanent revolution. He was convinced that progress toward communism could be achieved only by the continuous disruption of settled routines, lest the momentum of the revolution be lost and the evils of the old society re-emerge. Violence was the order of the day, with Mao stating bluntly that the old society could not be transformed by genteel means. This attitude also militated against the development of a formal legal system, with its implications of predictability. Initially, therefore, the emphasis was on destroying the old legal system, with some rather violent alternatives imposed in order to cleanse its evils.

The People's Republic of China's (PRCs) legal system since 1949 may be analyzed in terms of the interplay between two models of law: the jural and the societal. The jural model focuses on formal, elaborate, and codified rules enforced by a regular judicial hierarchy, whereas the societal model emphasizes socially approved norms and values. Both jural and societal influences were evident in the legal procedures of the communist-controlled base areas prior to 1949. On the one hand, there was extensive use of the mass line in creating and enforcing consensus on ideological matters, and the techniques of mediation were employed in settling civil disputes. On the other hand, people's governments enacted a number of basic laws, and they established a formal judicial system that included courts, the right to defense, and public trials.

Less-than-peaceful Coexistence of the Societal and Jural Models: 1949–1953

During the early years of the PRC, societal and jural models existed, as they had in Yan'an and the other base areas, in a complementary, if sometimes competitive, manner. The government abolished all KMT laws and judicial organs and, under the aegis of the Common Program passed by the Chinese People's Political Consultative Conference (CPPCC) in 1949, gradually set up a formal system of its own. As in the Soviet Union, a state organ called the *procuracy* (sometimes referred to as the *procuratorate*) was founded to investigate and supervise the judicial system. The procuracy is intended to oversee the actions of the public security (police) force that lead to arrests and prosecution and to ensure that public security investigations follow correct legal procedures. Assuming that public security personnel have observed correct procedures, the procuracy collects information on those to be tried and acts as prosecutor in criminal trials.

One important feature of the post-1949 system that, at least until fairly recently, aided public security and procuracy in collecting information is the *dang'an*, or dossier, that is kept on every urbanite from the time she or he enters elementary school. There are generally two sets of identical dossiers: one at the workplace and another at the public security bureau. Entered in it are one's photograph, a list of family members and relatives, school records and grade transcripts, date of entry into the Communist Youth League and CCP (if one chose to opt for membership therein), promotions and level of work performance, and political evaluations. Any single piece of information, or combination thereof, could be vitally important to one's career prospects and to any investigation begun on an individual by the authorities. Depending on the party line at a given time, having a relative from a bad class background, for example, could have severe consequences in terms of job assignment. Since China has no freedom of information act, there is no guarantee that one can examine this dossier in order to point out a false entry or protest an unfair political evaluation. Residence registration, which required an individual to remain in a given area unless given specific permission to move or travel, was also a valuable tool in keeping track of people. In addition to the procuracy and public security organs, the new government established a three-tier judicial system—basic, intermediate, and supreme court levels—with one right of appeal. An estimated 148 laws and regulations were adopted from 1949 through 1953, of which the most important were the Marriage Law (1950), the Land Reform Law (1950), the Trade Union Law (1950), the Act for the Punishment of Counterrevolutionaries (1951), and the Act for Punishment of Corruption (1952).

At the same time, however, public security organs dispensed justice without reference to the procuracy, the court system, or the law. Arbitrary arrest and detention, forced confessions, and ad hoc punishments were regularly reported during this period. They were even celebrated in the literature and drama of the time (see, for example, the plot of *The White-haired Girl*, discussed in Chapter 12).

During the countrywide mass campaigns, such as the "three anti" and the "five anti," land reform, and anti-counterrevolutionary movements, hastily convened people's tribunals meted out revolutionary justice at mass trials. Mao Zedong stated that 800,000 people deemed to be reactionaries and bad elements received death sentences at such trials; other estimates run into the millions. Many more people were sentenced to long terms of reform through labor under conditions so poor that only the exceptionally strong and fortunate survived. These methods were defended as absolutely necessary. Reactionary forces from the old society were considered to be very strong and simply biding their time before regrouping to attempt to strangle the infant new society. Only by completely destroying them could this comeback be prevented.

The Jural Model in Ascendance: 1954–1957

The promulgation of China's first state constitution in 1954 seemed to indicate the party's commitment to the institutionalization of its rule. The constitution established the National People's Congress (NPC) as the highest organ of state authority. The NPC, along with its standing committee, was vested with broad powers of legislation, amendment, and appointment. The constitution also established the State Council as China's chief administrative organ, and designated the State Council, the Supreme People's Court, and the Supreme People's Procuracy as comprising the central government structure. All three were made accountable to the NPC and its standing committee, which had the power to appoint or remove its officials. The NPC deputies were protected against arrest and detention except by consent of the parent body or, when the NPC was not in session, its standing committee.

Organic laws for the people's courts and people's procuracies established separate hierarchies for each under the NPC and its standing committee. The people's courts, divided into basic, intermediate, and higher levels and headed by the Supreme People's Court, were given sole authority to administer justice. Similar tiers were created for the people's procuracies. Headed by the Supreme People's Procuracy, the various levels were collectively vested with supervisory power over the execution of the law. For the first time, albeit in limited form, the PRC seemed to accept the concept of judicial independence, with the constitution declaring: "in administering justice, the people's courts are independent, subject only to the law." In fact, however, courts were made responsible to people's congresses at corresponding levels. Since earlier laws had subordinated courts to the leadership of the people's governments—that is, to the executive rather than the legislative authority—this represented a significant step toward the jural model.

Other articles of the constitution guaranteed equality before the law: freedom of speech, of the press, of association, of demonstration, and of religion, as well as the right to work, to leisure, to education, and to social assistance. Explicit protection against arbitrary arrest was provided by an article declaring that "freedom of the person of citizens of the PRC is inviolable. No citizen may be arrested except by decision of a people's court or a people's procuratorate." An Arrest and Detention Act, also promulgated in 1954, added detailed procedures to the guarantee. A large number of substantive and procedural laws and regulations were drawn up, often using Soviet codes as models.

Supplementing the work of courts and procuracies, a system of lawyers began to take shape. Colleges and universities established legal training programs to teach the new socialist legal philosophy and laws. By mid-1957, China had over 800 legal advisory offices, employing more than 2,500 full-time lawyers nationwide.

Although the legal situation during this period was a definite improvement over immediate postrevolutionary practices, both people's rights and judicial independence remained qualified. In keeping with the communist belief that law was a tool of the ruling class, those who had been designated as reactionaries or class enemies had no constitutional rights whatsoever. The constitution's guarantee of equality before the law did not mean that legislation would be equally applied to all, regardless of class. The idea of different rights for different classes resonates with the *li* and *fa* distinction in traditional China, as does the coexistence of societal and jural models. However, it is unlikely that the PRC leaders made any conscious connection between their concept of the law and that of traditional China.

As the post-1949 system took shape, it became apparent that there was no presumption of innocence on behalf of the defendant: The accused was assumed to be guilty unless he or she could amass strong evidence to the contrary. Moreover, a gap remained between written guarantees and actual practice. Even those fortunate few with impeccable class backgrounds might find redress difficult to obtain. Nonetheless, there could be no doubt that the mid-1950s showed a noticeable trend toward the regularization and institutionalization of the judicial system.

In 1956, at the Eighth National Congress of the CCP, Central Committee Vice-Chair Liu Shaoqi defended these changes. With the passing of the period of "revolutionary storm and stress," new relations of production had been established, which called for a corresponding change in methods. The existence of a complete legal system had become an absolute necessity in order to foster production. Individuals should understand that as long as they did not violate the laws, their civil rights would be guaranteed. Interestingly, in light of future developments, Mao Zedong's speech at the same party congress warned of the evils of bureaucracy and the dangers of becoming isolated from the masses.

Resurgence of the Societal Model: 1957–1965

During the Hundred Flowers movement of 1957, lawyers and others involved in the judicial system spoke out against its defects. Their criticisms included gaps in laws and legislation, lack of any benefit of the doubt for the accused, and aberrations in the administration of justice. One critic reportedly described his country as being without either laws or justice. The ensuing backlash of the anti-rightist campaign and frenzy of the Great Leap Forward effectively ended China's evolution toward a formal, Soviet-style judicial system and substituted a highly arbitrary, societal model.

Legal specialists, like all others who possessed professional expertise of any sort, were excellent targets for attacks on "so-called bourgeois scientific objectivism." They were accused of disregarding the class character of the law and of prattling about ridiculous concepts like equality for all—even for counterrevolutionaries. The principles of relying on facts as the basis for trials and law as the criterion for making decisions were regarded as an abandonment of party policy. They were also seen as attempting to apply abstract legal concepts in isolation from the reality of the political context as a whole. The pre-1957 defense system, with its use of lawyers to represent the accused, was criticized as "protecting bad elements" and obscuring the distinctions between class elements and the people.

Judicial training programs at colleges and universities were curtailed. Codification programs were suspended, and legal research ceased. The legal profession itself was phased out. Teachers and students of law, as well as lawyers themselves, were sent to the countryside to engage in productive labor. Many prominent jurists, including four supreme court judges, were purged as rightists. Although the constitution itself remained in place, the court no longer functioned according to its constitutional mandate. If this caused any concern, it was never publicly stated.

Similarly, with its personnel under attack, the procuracy could no longer effectively question the legality of arrests and prosecutions by public security organs. Public security personnel gained much power as a result. So did party secretaries, who were empowered to decide cases and determine punishments without reference to relevant legal statutes. In effect, the judicial process became totally controlled by party committees and administered by public security organs.

Another feature of this period was its renewed attention to the mass line in judicial work. Court trials continued to take place. However, they incorporated efforts to demystify the legal process through such methods as adding mass debates, bringing the courts directly to the people, using new rules and procedures designed to be more easily understandable, and carrying out justice on the spot. The retrenchment years that followed the failure of the Great Leap Forward saw a partial if less than energetic return to some aspects of the jural model. For example, several codification projects were revived. But, in general, informal revolutionary norms prevailed.

The Societal Model Rampant: 1966–1976

Even this relatively strong representation of the societal model was not pure enough for Cultural Revolution ideologues. Their reasoning was that, since the CCP was the ruling party, its policy was ipso facto the law. Hence all formal laws should be eliminated and replaced with party policy. A *People's Daily* article that appeared on January 31, 1967 was actually entitled "In Praise of Lawlessness." Although specifically advocating the destruction of *bourgeois* law, it indicated that this meant the entire legal and constitutional structure of the party and the government. This structure had, radicals believed, kept the country's "bourgeois-capitalist," and therefore merely pseudo-communist, leadership in power. Many high-ranking leaders, and hundreds of thousands of lesser beings, were removed with complete disregard for constitutional procedures. Often, it was alleged that they had "wormed their way" into the party during the 1920s and had been serving as minions of the KMT or the Soviet revisionists ever since.

Mao Zedong instructed his Red Guard followers to "smash the *gongjianfa*"— an abbreviation for the public security, procuracy, and courts, collectively, that in essence encompassed the entire judicial system. Bands of young guards responded enthusiastically, descending on *gongjianfa* offices, attacking their personnel, and destroying records. Not coincidentally, some of these records contained their own dossiers as well as those of friends and family members. The first vice-minister of public security, the chief procurator, and the president of the supreme court were all removed from office. Mass justice was the order of the day. It was sometimes dispensed at denunciation meetings so huge that they were held in sports stadia. The prosecutors included self-appointed individuals, revolutionary committees, and military control groups. At least in some instances and in some places during the Cultural Revolution, the army was empowered to perform *gongjianfa* functions. Presumably, the military was called in to re-impose order on what had become a level of chaos that was unacceptable even to most radical leaders.

By late 1968, the violent phase of the Cultural Revolution had abated to the extent that a new party constitution could be drawn up. It was adopted in April 1969. Foreign observers, noting that a new state constitution did not follow along, surmised—correctly, as it turned out—that high-level policy disagreements were taking place. After 1970, the army's control over law enforcement gradually receded, and in January 1975 a new state constitution was finally promulgated.

Reflecting radical influences, the 1975 constitution abolished the procuracy and deleted the 1954 constitution's protection of NPC deputies against arrest or trial without the consent of the NPC or its standing committee. Provisions concerning citizens' rights were drastically reduced: from 19 articles to 4. Among those rights conspicuously absent from the new document were freedom of residence, freedom to do scientific research, and freedom to create literary and artistic works. Since none of these had actually been truly free in the past, their deletions had few immediate consequences.

Surprisingly, in view of the attacks on religion during the Cultural Revolution, the 1975 document continued to guarantee the freedom to believe. However, it added the right *not* to believe and the right to propagate atheism. Certain other new rights were added as well, including the right to strike and what came to be known as the "four bigs," short for the four big freedoms: freedom to "speak out freely, air views fully, hold debates, and write big-character posters."

The procuracy, which had not functioned since the earliest days of the Cultural Revolution, was formally abolished by the 1975 constitution and its functions transferred to the ministry of public security. In view of the harsh criticisms leveled at public security organs during the Cultural Revolution, one must assume that by 1975 the ministry had been thoroughly reorganized and revolutionized. The 1954 constitution's provision for judicial independence was dropped, and the courts were made subordinate to the control of the political leadership, as opposed to people's congresses, at corresponding levels. The 1975 document formalized the position of the mass line in judicial work and allowed for mass trials in major counterrevolutionary cases.

As of the time of Mao Zedong's death in 1976, most offenses and disputes were handled by extrajudicial institutions, such as party committees and public security organs. In urban areas, many of the latter had come under the influence of radical elements who were positioning themselves for the post-Mao power struggle. They had been absorbing militia and even firefighting functions. The potential for abuse was clear, and official sources from this period record a number of instances of individuals receiving harsh sentences for real or imagined insults to pictures of Mao, and of public security units forcibly imposing their own notions of proper revolutionary clothing and hairstyles on ordinary citizens. Since urban public security units were also the foot soldiers in a high-level ideological power struggle, punishments were often meted out to those whose political views were regarded as insufficiently orthodox. The verdict against Deng Xiaoping after the Tiananmen incident of April 1976 is merely the most spectacular of these.

Interestingly, foreign visitors to the PRC, perhaps reflecting a weariness with time-consuming attention to the fine points of law, its arcane jargon, and the too-frequent resort to the court system that characterize many Western societies, were generally favorably impressed with the Chinese system of justice. It soon became apparent, however, that large numbers of Chinese did not share their views.

Law and Justice in the Post-Mao Era: Return to the Jural Model

With Deng Xiaoping's return to power, the PRC's legal system abruptly changed its emphasis again, this time toward the jural model. Deng's reasons were partly economic and partly personal. From an economic point of view, Deng realized that Chinese entrepreneurs needed protection for both their individual rights and those of their businesses if they were to risk breaking so sharply from past practices. In addition, foreign companies required codes and other guarantees before they would feel comfortable investing in the PRC or trading with it on any significant scale. From a personal point of view, Deng wished to overturn the legal system that had punished him so harshly twice in one decade: One of the earlier verdicts to be reversed was that on the Tiananmen incident of April 1976. Henceforth, stated the official directive, demonstrators were to be referred to as revolutionary heroes rather than counterrevolutionaries.

The rapid nature of the party's reversal of legal policy, though receiving overwhelming popular support, needed to be explained to the masses, who had for so long been indoctrinated with principles that were exactly the opposite of those that now prevailed. Awkward explanations attempted to convince people of "the erroneous nature of the long-held viewpoint that party policy itself is law." This unconvincing rationalization notwithstanding, China, in the period from 1978 to 1982, successively adopted two new state constitutions, codified a number of important laws, restructured its judicial system, reinstituted the legal profession, and revived legal research and legal education.

The New Legal System

In March 1978, a new state constitution was adopted, replacing that of 1975. More akin to the 1954 constitution than to its immediate predecessor, the 1978 document restored the procuracy and required public security personnel to obtain the approval of the judiciary or the procuracy before making an arrest. Local procuracies and courts were made responsible only to people's congresses at corresponding levels, not to their executive organs as well, as had been the case in the 1975 constitution. The accused regained the rights to defense and to open trials. Many of the freedoms promised by the 1954 constitution were also revived, though the freedom to change residence was not. The leadership did not want to encourage the several million people who had been sent out to rural areas over the past two decades to return to their original homes. Many were desperate to do so. Later in 1978, a party plenary meeting reaffirmed the independence of the judiciary and the equality of all people before the law, regardless of class background.

The demands placed on the new legal system by millions of people who felt wronged under the old system threatened to overwhelm it. In the 18 months between January 1978 and June 1979, people's courts examined 708,000 cases and found that more than 166,000 of them had involved false accusations. These

708,000 were the fortunate ones: court dockets became so crowded, and trained legal personnel were so few, that most plaintiffs faced long delays. Fears grew that many cases might never be heard at all. Some of those affected believed it was because the authorities simply did not care about them; others suspected, often correctly, that their cases were so potentially disruptive to the social structure of the area that officials did not want to deal with them. Those whose cases were heard but not decided in their favor became disgruntled, because they felt they had been denied justice yet again.

Both those who were annoyed at not having their cases heard and those who believed their cases had not been heard properly began to exercise their constitutional rights to strike and demonstrate. Seeking redress, hundreds of thousands of people flooded into Beijing and other major cities. Their plight was documented by the foreign media rather too often for the taste of the leadership. During the following year, the government responded by removing from the constitution the "four bigs" and the right to strike. Officials explained that these rights were created by the hated Gang of Four and hence, by implication, were irredeemably tainted. Moreover, since people's rights were now adequately protected in other ways, to have these rights in the constitution was as unnecessary as "adding legs to the picture of a snake."

Others, however, argued that the leadership's actions showed they regarded human rights not as a birthright but as merely *instrumental* or *bureaucratic*. As such, rights can be dispensed with if they do not seem to serve the needs of public policy. In fact, if one accepts the concept of human rights as instrumental, the public interest may *require* their suspension. In this case, and in those of subsequent mass demonstrations, it could be—and was—argued that China's major goal is economic development and the creation of national prosperity. Since demonstrations disrupt social stability and normal economic activities, they are inimical to the national interest and subversive in nature. Those who back such subversive activities are therefore counterrevolutionaries.

This retreat notwithstanding, the leadership continued its commitment to the institutionalization of a formal system of justice. The constitution adopted in 1982, and still in force, describes China as a "people's democratic dictatorship" rather than as a "dictatorship of the proletariat." It not only reinstated the 1954 constitution's provision that no deputy to the NPC might be arrested or tried without the consent of the NPC or its standing committee but also added a clause exempting deputies from prosecution for speeches or votes at NPC meetings. People's courts and procuracies were not to be subject to interference by administrative organs, public organizations, or individuals, though it should be noted that because the CCP is not one of these, it is not restricted by the provision. Party leaders have consistently described the concept of the separation of powers as being bourgeois in origin and unsuitable for China. They have also pointed out that to have each branch of the government go its own way is conducive to inconsistent and confusing policies, with the potential for creating chaos.

The 1982 constitution also puts more emphasis on individual rights than its 1978 counterpart. Major new additions were the imposition of a two-term limit on the president of China (removed in 2018), the inviolability of the personal dignity of PRC citizens, and the prohibition against insult, libel, false charges, and slander. Also prohibited are unlawful deprivation or restriction of citizens' freedom of person by detention or other means, and unlawful searches. Trials are to be public, except under special circumstances. However, the 1982 constitution also added new duties for citizens: They must safeguard state secrets and refrain from infringing upon the interests "of the state, of society, and of the collective, or upon the lawful freedoms and rights of other citizens." All of these have been used to restrict individual freedoms.

Conspicuous among the freedoms of the 1954 constitution that have not been reinstated is the right to change residence. The leadership, understandably concerned about the possibility of massive population movements disrupting the PRC's economic and social systems, presumably does not wish to give those who may be contemplating such moves a legal right to call upon. However, as will be seen in Chapter 11, over the past two decades almost 250 million people have been able to change where they live even without the legal right to do so.

The 1982 constitution has been amended several times. Broadly speaking, the additions have been motivated by the evolution of the economic system begun by Deng Xiaoping. The 1988 revisions enhanced the legal status of those who engaged in private business and sanctioned the transfer of land-use rights. The additions made in 1993 also related to economic reform and opening up. Proposed immediately after Deng's tour of the Shenzhen Special Economic Zone (see Chapter 5), they made more explicit the commitment to reform and opening up. Amendments gave legal protection to private enterprise, recognized the validity of multiple forms of ownership, and declared that the government must use laws to rule the country. The amendments of 2004 provided for protection of private property and human rights.

Legal Developments

Within the framework provided by Deng Xiaoping's instructions and the successive new constitutions, a large number of changes were made in the judicial system within a very short time. In addition to the supreme court and higher-, intermediate-, and basic-level people's courts, specialized courts were established to handle military, maritime, and railway matters, respectively (Figure 8.1). The functions of the first two are obvious; the last has jurisdiction over criminal cases that occur along rail lines and aboard trains as well as cases of economic disputes related to rail transportation.

The main responsibility of the supreme court is to supervise the administration of justice by lower courts at various levels and by the special courts. Since its establishment, the supreme court has considered only a handful of cases that are considered especially important, such as the cases of Japanese war criminals and that of the Gang of Four. China's supreme court is not empowered to determine the constitutionality of legislation or of government policies: the constitution reserves that right to the Standing Committee of the National People's Congress.

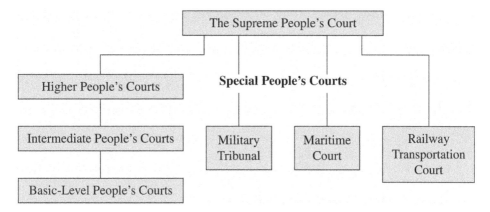

FIGURE 8.1 Organizational System of the People's Courts of the People's Republic of China (PRC)

Source: Adapted from Zhang Min and Shan Changzong, "Inside China's Court System," *Beijing Review,* November 5–11, 1990, p. 16.

However, a 1981 decision by the Standing Committee gave the court the authority to interpret law relating to questions involving the specific application of laws and decrees in court trials. There is no requirement that these interpretations be made public, which means that parties to a case, whether domestic, foreign, corporate, or individual, have no assurance that the rules on which the court is relying will be made known to them. This is not an issue in all cases, but it is more likely to occur in new or sensitive areas.

The Trial Process

People's courts at each level are composed of a president, vice-presidents, presiding judges, deputy presiding judges, and a number of ordinary judges. Decisions may be made by judges or by a collegiate bench formed jointly by judges and a people's jury. Judges receive no special training, nor is there an examination for them to take. On-the-job experience is considered important. Educational standards, though low, are improving. In 1995, only 5 percent of the PRC's judges had a four-year college degree of any sort; by 2002, nearly 10 percent had law degrees and the number continues to rise. Non-legally trained judges include demobilized soldiers, former clerks, and vehicle drivers. Whatever their backgrounds, Chinese sources describe judges' salaries and social status as low.

Jurors, sometimes called people's assessors, enjoy equal rights with judges and can examine the files of a case, verify facts and evidence, and interrogate the parties to the case and all witnesses. They have the right to decide on a case, together with the judges, and to sign the court decision. Any citizen who has reached the age of 23 and is eligible to vote and stand for election may serve as a people's assessor. Jurors are selected by their people's congress, judges, their work units, or other groups. A reform implemented in 2005 requires a minimum of two years' college education, but this can be waived for well-respected older people. In addition, whereas assessors had often been appointed by judges and behaved like what critics described as ornaments, the new law specified that they were to be appointed only by local people's congress standing committees. Assessors found guilty of malpractice or making wrong judgments could be punished. While the new standards aimed at elevating sentencing standards and reducing corruption, they raised troubling questions. First, would the representatives of the local people's congress choose objective, unbiased individuals? Second, would punishment for so-called wrong judgments be meted out fairly?

The accused has the right to a lawyer and also the right to defend himself or to ask one of his relatives to do so. Until the late 1990s, a lawyer's loyalty was expected to be with the collective interests of the people rather than with his or her client. Since leniency is frequently accorded to those who confess and show remorse, continued insistence on one's innocence is likely to produce a more severe sentence than would admitting guilt. The purpose of the courts has thus not been to determine guilt or innocence but to decide on punishment. Very few cases result in acquittal. It is possible to appeal one's sentence by having it referred to a higher level court, though in practice this is rarely done. If the procuracy finds errors in the judgment made by the lower courts, it can counterplea. The court of second instance will then re-examine the case; its judgment is final. In stark contrast to many foreign legal systems, justice is swift: Executions have been carried out within an hour of sentencing. Even when the sentence is appealed (in the case of the death penalty, an appeal is supposed to be automatic), the final disposition of the case may be accomplished within one week.

Although the constitution provides for public trial except under special circumstances, there are varying interpretations of what constitutes an open trial. Tickets are issued in accordance with the number of seats in the courtroom but may mysteriously have all been given out some time before the proceedings begin. Foreigners, including journalists, are not normally able to attend trials. In June 1998, courts were ordered open to the non-foreign public; presenting an identity card was henceforth to be the sole prerequisite for admission. However, few people have thus far actually exercised their right to attend trials, and judges seem uncomfortable with the presence of those who do.

Other departures from constitutional and criminal code guarantees also occur. Although the government apparently intended its trial of the Gang of Four in 1980 to demonstrate to the world China's commitment to a just legal system, most international observers regarded the proceedings as carefully stage-managed to achieve maximum publicity for verdicts that had been predetermined. The trial of democracy wall dissident Wei Jingsheng had the same effect.

Several people who were arrested after the quelling of the spring 1989 demonstrations in Tiananmen Square appeared to have been beaten, and the trial of one dissident was accompanied by charges of blatant evidence tampering. His lawyers complained that they had not been allowed to interview the witnesses for the prosecution. None of the witnesses appeared in court and therefore could not be cross-examined. Several of them had been told to leave Beijing before the trial began. The witnesses' statements were contained on tape-recordings believed to have been surreptitiously made by public security personnel and then edited. Even granting their admissibility as evidence, none of the statements on the tapes constituted counterrevolutionary or seditious behavior. The accused was nonetheless convicted and sentenced to concurrent jail terms of 13 years for attempting to overthrow the government and two years for creating counter-revolutionary propaganda and instigation.

Mediation

The great majority of cases—on the order of 90 percent or more—are not handled by courts at all but through the mediation process. There is widespread distrust of the court system, which is also perceived as being unnecessarily bureaucratic and slow moving, despite the speed with which it moves once a case is actually brought to trial. Many people also believe that resorting to the court system involves loss of face: individuals should be able to resolve their problems among themselves, and an inability to do so may be perceived as a failing on their part. There is also the belief that more serious cases, including physical violence and major theft, often arise out of less serious disputes that might have been resolved through mediation before tempers grew too short. These might include disputes within families or among neighbors over the division of labor or property rights. In urban areas, three-generation families may occupy a one-bedroom apartment and share kitchen and toilet facilities with a number of other families. The frictions that may arise in such situations are easily imaginable.

Yet another reason for reluctance to resort to the court system is the attention it may call to oneself. Reporting the theft of an expensive object, such as costly jewelry or an imported wristwatch, may lead public security personnel, who are not necessarily honest themselves, to focus on how the owner obtained the item in the first place.

Mediation can be conducted by a variety of different groups. It is even applied during court proceedings, where it can be used as early in the process as immediately after the facts are investigated or as late as the court of second instance in handling appeals. Most mediation, however, is conducted outside the court system. People's mediation committees, street committees in one's neighborhood, or one's work unit may take on the task. Street committees were typically composed of retired men and women—energetic busybodies who poked into all kinds of family disputes and quarrels among neighbors—who volunteered for the task. Although some people appear to genuinely appreciate their services, others regard street committees as an unwanted intrusion. They are colloquially referred to by various names, including "small feet inspection teams"—because when they were founded in the early 1950s, many of the elderly women who formed the majority of their membership had had their feet bound as children—or "eight grannies with seven teeth."

Given the crowded living conditions in China, it is difficult to keep secrets. When neighbors fight, street committee members will hear about it and step in to try to resolve differences. They record serious disputes and those likely to have larger implications in a logbook that is kept in the street committee office. Members also keep watch for robbers, prevent children from misbehaving, conduct political study sessions to keep people abreast of new party policies, and try to mediate family quarrels. One street committee member described her organization's goal as "educating people to live harmoniously and act peacefully."

Neighborhood teams have mediated in divorce cases and lectured gangs of rowdy teens. One observer, having watched an elderly lady face down a group of sullen boys a quarter of her age, attributed a great deal of the teams' success to the enforced immobility of urban life in China. In a number of urban areas, the greater freedom of movement engendered by Deng Xiaoping's economic reforms led to loosened social controls. Some welcomed the greater degree of privacy, while others became uneasy because they felt less safe.

In addition to their mediation function, street committees serve as adjuncts to public security work. Naturally, serving as an informant can make one unpopular. Not only committee members but even public security personnel have suffered the wrath of their victims and those who sympathize with the victims. In some cases, those informed upon hire assassins to wreak vengeance. Other informants find life made difficult for them in various ways, referred to as "being given tight shoes to wear." This may take forms that cannot be directly linked to retaliatory behavior. There are, after all, many reasons besides a desire for revenge why a person might be demoted in rank or transferred to a less desirable area. Here as well, mediation may be applied.

Neighborhood committees have been folded into so-called communities, *shequ*, in some areas, staffed with younger, better-educated, salaried professionals rather than elderly retirees. Their activities may even include finding day care for the retirees. Several motives are involved. First, with the old work unit system and the social services it used to perform in decay, it is hoped that the communities can take over the tasks the work unit used to perform. A second reason is to put the communist party back in touch with people at the most basic level of society. The old functions have not disappeared: committees remain powerful in the issuance of such important documents as driver's licenses, permissions to marry, have children, determine eligibility for minimum subsistence allowances, and in admonitions to parents to have their children vaccinated against disease. Authorities want staff members to report on the activities of the country's increasingly outspoken and mobile population—informing them, for example, of the presence of illegal migrants, members of unregistered organizations, or unusual occurrences of any sort.

Petitions

Those who believe that justice has been denied can file petitions with higher authorities. Their numbers rose rapidly, from 4.8 million in 1995 to upward of 10 million a decade later—from two to three times the civil cases filed with the courts each year. Theoretically, petitions serve as an extrajudicial channel through which citizens who feel wronged by official decisions can find redress. Petitions allow higher level authorities a means through which they can gauge the effectiveness of lower level governance. They may intervene if they perceive a threat to social stability. The assignment of guilt or innocence seems to be secondary to avoiding what are called mass incidents.

Since officials whose areas have a high incidence of disgruntled citizens face disciplinary measures from above, they react by concealing petitions rather than investigating and dealing with them. Those disgruntled petitioners who take their grievances to higher levels, including Beijing, may be restrained by other means. Local authorities hire gangs of thugs who listen carefully for the accents of their areas, retrieve the petitioners, and send them back, sometimes after beating and torturing them. If petitioners come to the attention of capital police, they may offer to "sell" the petitioners back to local authorities. If the local authorities do not agree to pay, the petitioners' grievances will be processed. Hence, most local governments are willing to buy, reasoning that they can find a way to recoup their expenses from the unlucky victims or their families.

Those apprehended may be sentenced to reform through labor, prison, psychiatric facilities, or consigned to what are known as black jails—private prisons where conditions are so bad that they are colloquially referred to as "palaces of hell." Not a few have died in these jails. Chinese legal analysts complain that a practice originally established to resolve political problems has evolved into one that is replacing the judicial system. In a mid-2013 reform that could lessen such abuses, the State Bureau of Lessons and Calls was ordered to stop compiling a monthly ranking of the number of "illegal petitioners." The expectation is that officials who need not fear that large numbers of petitioners will hurt their careers will have less incentive to retaliate against them. Surprisingly, Chinese data indicate that although petitioning resolves only 0.2 percent of the grievances brought through this channel, 30 percent of petitioners consider the practice easier and more convenient than court proceedings.

Another institution that has perverted its original purpose is the Urban Management Enforcement Bureau, or chengguan. Introduced in the late 1990s to deal with a broad range of street-level issues such as illegal vendors, unlicensed cabs, and unscrupulous tour guides, it quickly evolved into an entity whose personnel apprehend people in order to extract fines, regardless of whether they have committed the offenses of which they are accused. In 2013, a massive public outcry after four chengguan members beat an unlicensed watermelon seller to death resulted in the chengguan being sentenced to prison.

Reform Through Labor (RTL)

Originally created in the early 1950s to suppress those deemed counter-revolutionaries, the focus of RTL or *laojiao* has shifted toward the maintenance of social stability. Not a formal part of the penal system, those sentenced to it typically perform hard labor under conditions that are said to be just as bad as faced by those who are formally sentenced. RTL allows police to incarcerate people without trial from one to three years, with the possibility of a fourth, for offenses in any of six vaguely defined categories such as speaking in opposition to the CCP or socialism, instigating low-level turmoil, drug use, vagrancy, behavior that disrupts workplace or school order, and even chronic complaining. Misuse of RTL has been the subject of much criticism: public opinion became incensed when a woman who complained about police failure to deal with the rape of her young daughter was sentenced to 18 months. In another case, a man received two years for tweeting other people's opinions on political reform. How many people are held under RTL is difficult to determine: official sources reported 170,000 in 2009, but just over 60,000 in 2012. Human rights organizations speculate that the sharp reduction may have resulted from people being transferred from RTL to black jails or other types of correction facilities. After much criticism, the system was abolished in 2013, although abuses continue in other forms.

The Penal System

For those who are convicted, a number of different sentences may be applied. There has been a progressive decrease in the number of crimes punishable by death; the most recent revision, in 2015, brought the number down to 46, down from nearly 80 in the early Deng era. Many are for nonviolent acts that include luring women into prostitution, embezzlement, and damaging state property. Political offenders are not normally executed, although at least one person is known to have received the death penalty for attacking a military vehicle during the PLA's suppression of the demonstrations during the spring of 1989. The usual method of execution was by a bullet to the back of the head, with the family of the offender billed for the cost of the bullet. In the late 1990s, the option of lethal injection began and has become widespread. In addition, criminals are no longer paraded through the streets on their way to execution.

Although objection to the death penalty has grown in much of the rest of the world, most Chinese believe that it is necessary as a deterrent against serious crimes, and are surprised to hear that in some other countries execution is considered to be a cruel and unusual punishment. Many people do object to the fact that penalties are not applied consistently and that, in the midst of anti-crime campaigns, prisoners can be sentenced to death for offenses that were not capital crimes when they were committed. According to human rights groups, China carries out almost 90 percent of the world's executions, though it must be remembered that the PRC has the world's largest population, and also that many countries do not have the death penalty for any crime.

Restrictions on media reporting notwithstanding, there have been several embarrassing revelations regarding death penalties wrongly meted out. Many of the confessions appear to have been extracted through torture. In one well-publicized case, a man who had allegedly murdered his wife was vindicated when the woman reappeared, explaining that she had simply run away. In 2006, the supreme court was given power to review death penalty cases, with the government announcing that it planned to execute fewer people, and to execute more cautiously. According to official statistics, the high court overturned 15 percent of the death sentences appealed to it during the first half of 2008. Although the number of executions was not revealed, human rights organizations believe that the numbers went down in 2007, but rose again thereafter.

Western experts estimate that about 700,000 people are convicted of crimes each year. In addition, a huge number, perhaps as many as 5 million, of minor offenders who are not categorized as criminals receive 15 to 20 days of security administration police detention. Although the government portrays its prisons as humane institutions aiming at rehabilitation while providing good nutrition, medical care, exercise, and job training, former prisoners describe a completely different situation. Conditions are believed to be worst for major political prisoners. Many are held in solitary confinement for long periods in tiny, poorly heated, and dimly lit cells on near-starvation rations and without access to medical care. They may be denied the use of an exercise yard. Cubicles may be as small as 12 square feet, with only a bed, a cold-water tap, an open sewer for a toilet, and mealy food. Reading matter may be limited to titles produced by state-run publishing houses. Conditions in black jails are even worse.

If official statistics are to be believed, the PRC's prison population is not exceptionally large by international standards when considered on a per capita basis. In the past, the population of prisons and camps rose rapidly during periods of mass campaigns for political orthodoxy, and still does following party and government decisions to crack down on crime. Reform is to be accomplished through two means: first, study of political materials approved by the CCP, followed by oral and written self-criticisms; and second, by performing hard labor. The government claims that recidivism rates are very low, about 6 percent or 7 percent; foreign studies, citing detailed mainland sources, put the actual figure at over 83 percent.

The basic form of the prison system is based on Soviet legal codes dating from 1933, but in China, prisons are economic enterprises as well. Each facility is expected not only to be self-supporting but also to produce a profit for the state. Because of their dual functions of rehabilitation and production, they are under dual administration. The ministry of justice has responsibility for prisoners in their role as prisoners, and the relevant economic industry has responsibility for whatever commodities the institution produces: coal, textiles, tea, and the like. In keeping with this production function, each prison has its own production plan, accounting and purchasing departments, and so on. There are even two names: for example, the Xi'an Municipal Number 1 Prison is also known as the Chang'an (Long Peace) Chemical Company.

Since prisons are expected to be economically profitable, their profit-and-loss statements are an important criterion determining the success of their administrators' careers. Prisoners who do not meet work quotas may be denied permission to write to their families or receive visits from them. In more extreme cases they may have their food rations reduced, be placed in solitary confinement, or beaten. Even illness may not be an acceptable reason for low production, since one's supervisor may take the position of "no work, no food."

Because prisoners can be made to work for little more than basic subsistence and cannot leave to take other work or threaten to go on strike, the products of their labor can be sold for very low prices. Several Western nations have laws against importing the products of what they term slave labor. The Chinese government has vehemently denied that it exports items produced by prisoners, though this can be disputed by reference to official PRC publications.

There have also been persistent reports of organ harvesting—that is, prisons selling the organs of recently executed inmates to wealthy individuals who need transplants. Prison officials state that the inmate has freely consented to become a donor; family members and human rights groups question whether the individual's permission was actually obtained and, if it were, whether it was truly voluntary. Adherents to the Falun Gong religious group have claimed that their members are singled out for organ harvesting, in some cases before the individual is actually dead.

Although the harsh punishments described here would certainly seem sufficient to deter most people from committing any proscribed acts, such has not been the case. During the era of Maoist austerity, possessing items of conspicuous consumption—even as modest as hair ribbons or bottles of foreign liquor—could mark their owners as bourgeois and, therefore, the objects of struggle sessions. Hence, money and material goods were dangerous. When Deng Xiaoping declared that it was acceptable for some people to become rich before others and that it was no crime to live well, many people were tempted to take chances. For example, responding to the government's encouragement for the formation of group cooperatives in the service industries, small hotels proliferated. Some came to be used for gambling, prostitution, smuggling, or other illegal activities. Smuggling was likewise facilitated by the increased exchange of goods between China and other countries and by the larger number of tourists and businesspeople entering and leaving China.

As mentioned previously, Deng's economic reforms caused dossiers to lose some of their effectiveness as a method of social surveillance. Entrepreneurial companies tend to care more for a job applicant's saleable skills than prior peccadilloes and may not bother to check their files. For the wealthy, bribing the right official to change their dossiers is another possibility. Not everyone is able to exercise these options, however, and maintaining an impeccable or at least an innocuous dossier is still a desideratum.

In 1994, the government loosened several of the restrictions in its residence registration system, with another change introduced in 2010. These tacitly accepted the reality that Deng's economic reforms had enabled large numbers of people to circumvent the restrictions (see Chapter 11) but simultaneously weakened yet another of the government's control mechanisms. What to do about the migrant or floating population, officially reported as 245 million as of 2017, has become a major issue for the government. The migrants are economically useful, since they perform the "three-d" jobs—dirty, difficult, and dangerous—that many urban residents find distasteful. However, their technically illegal presence means that the migrants are ineligible for most social services, major contributors to the crime rate, a health hazard, a threat to family planning policies (see Chapter 11), and easy prey for corrupt police.

The 2010 proposal envisioned a nationwide residence permit system to reform the household registration system, but with many caveats. A point system advanced by Guangdong, for example, was limited to migrants from rural areas within the province only, with criteria that included age, education, adherence to family planning policies, a clean criminal record, participation in community service, social security status, and several other determinants. Municipal authorities felt that they could not afford to grant residence permits to all migrants owing to the huge cost entailed in providing social welfare benefits, such as education, housing, and health care, for which the migrants would become eligible. Skeptics scoffed that the new proposals amounted to talking about change while enforcing the previous policy; others saw them as a transitional step toward abolishing the household registration system and therefore representing progress.

With party and government controls attenuated, other organizations became more important. Secret societies, which had scarcely been mentioned since the early days of the communist government, reappeared and began to play a prominent role in criminal activities. Because many of these societies had branches in different parts of China as well as in foreign countries, they were able to coordinate the movement of large sums of money and large quantities of goods around the country and beyond its borders. Some of the money and goods were used to bribe officials at various levels to ignore the societies' activities. Party–gangster ("red–black") collusion extends to the highest levels of party and government. In 1993, the PRC's minister of public security created a furor when he admitted that the police maintained links with the notorious Triad society and had once even enlisted its aid in protecting a Chinese leader traveling abroad. In major cities, gang syndicates practice tax farming: They take charge of tax collection, agreeing to pay the authorities a previously agreed-upon sum while retaining for themselves anything beyond that sum. Gangs have laundered money in the form of foreign investment and cooperated with the Russian mafia to prey on merchants in the Russian Far East.

The rising crime rate, which included a marked increase in violent crime, became a major issue, both for the leadership and for the ordinary person. It is difficult to compare crime statistics in the PRC with those of other countries, since many acts that are classified as offenses in China are not legally actionable elsewhere. What concerns most Chinese, however, is not the crime rate in other countries but what they perceive as a deterioration in their own situation. Several crackdowns notwithstanding, the incidence of crime continues to be worrisome. One reason is that criminals are often able to bribe the police and other authorities, including those at high levels of party and government. Sometimes, corrupt officials receive a percentage of the profits, becoming rent seekers on criminal activities. Several of the bribers have argued, convincingly, that, given the irrational nature of the economic system and the attitude of the authorities they must deal with, it is impossible for a business to prosper unless its owner pays off the authorities.

The legal developments of the 1990s and early twenty-first century reflect cross-cutting pressures on decision makers. One goal is to placate the complaints of human rights advocates, both foreign and domestic; a second, often in conflict with the first, is to respond to public demands to deal with the rising crime rate. Finally, but not least in importance, policy makers want to ensure that reforms do not result in weakening party control over the judicial process. In 1991, a civil procedure law was passed that, among other provisions, allows class action lawsuits. These have been used with some success by, for example, persons who have suffered deteriorating health and loss of income from factories that pollute the environment. While the ability to bring class action suits is clearly advantageous for would-be plaintiffs, suits are most likely to be successful when they simultaneously benefit the central government. Beijing has found it difficult to control local officials and factory managers, and is pleased to throw its influence behind such class actions. By contrast, a class action suit by aggrieved democracy activists or relatives of those killed by the military in the Tiananmen Square demonstrations of 1989 is not possible, at least under current conditions.

A law on lawyers promulgated in 1996 established the basis for attorneys to move from being state-subsidized legal workers to independent professionals responsible to their clients and to the law. As part of this responsibility, clients who were harmed by their lawyers' incompetence could claim compensation. The law also stipulated that lawyers must set aside an unspecified portion of their time to provide legal aid services to the poor. Although the accused has the right to hire an attorney, the government is not obliged to provide defendants with a lawyer unless they are blind, deaf, or mute, or, as of 2013, indigent. Lawyers may be reluctant to take on the cases of political dissidents or those with a grievance against the powerful, since they may be severely beaten or even murdered if they do so. Because their licenses, which are issued by the state rather than by bar associations, must be renewed annually, lawyers who take on unpopular cases can be dealt with quickly. Attorneys who offered to defend Tibetans charged with instigating riots and who advised earthquake victims of their rights under the law were warned of exactly this consequence. In mid-2013, lawyers attempting to investigate a black jail were badly beaten.

In a seemingly important advance, a criminal procedure law that went into effect in 1996 proclaimed that the accused were not to be considered guilty until convicted by a court. The law also gave defendants greater access to lawyers and abolished the procedure of *shoushen*, or "sheltering for examination," under which police had been able to detain people for three months and even, in practice, much longer without charging them with any crime. Originally devised to prevent transient suspected criminals whose status and residence were not known from leaving, shoushen was frequently misused, and was criticized by both Chinese and foreigners concerned with human rights.

The reform was not quite all that it appeared to be, however, since the new law gave police the right to hold suspects without charge for up to seven months or, in "complicated" cases, indefinitely. Moreover, there is no requirement that defendants be told that they have a right to counsel: most people do not know and are not told. Police also retain the right to attend lawyer–client meetings "as necessary." And despite the rule that no one is to be considered guilty until convicted, the conviction rate remains above 99 percent.

The crime of counter-revolution was abolished, although this also proved more cosmetic than real. One can still be charged with "endangering state security" or "disturbing public order." Both terms are so vague as to leave their application open to abuse. People have been charged with endangering state security for insisting on their right to run for public office, for publishing lists of telephone numbers, and for spreading rumors, regardless of the truth or falsehood thereof. After official figures showed the number of reported popular protests rising from 74,000 in 2004 to 87,000 in 2005, the government ceased releasing statistics on them.

Critics point out that changes in laws mean little so long as the elite can continue to exercise control through a comprehensive, non-transparent system of state secrets. Classified information includes data such as the number of laid-off workers in state enterprises; unusual deaths in prisons, juvenile detention facilities, and education through labor; rules for contact with overseas religious organizations; and pollution levels. In 2008, a human rights activist who visited earthquake-hit areas to deliver food and medicine to survivors was arrested for possession of state secrets: he was found to be counseling grieving parents on how to pursue a legal campaign on behalf of children who had died in shoddily constructed schools.

Although the PRC promised, as part of its bid for the 2008 Olympics, to establish an impartial legal system, human rights advocates charged in early 2007 that conditions had worsened rather than improved. As a case in point, new supreme court regulations issued in 2006 allowed court officials to deny the release of information which they did not want released. Although the likely motivation for this change was to avoid improper disclosure, critics pointed out that the preferences of court officials cannot represent the law and that the new rules would allow them to cover up corruption. Parodying Lenin's "two steps forward, one step backward," they described the PRC's legal reforms as one step forward, two steps backward.

In 2008, new regulations enhanced the party's control over the judiciary in an apparent attempt to maintain stability and suppress expressions of dissent. The CCP's Legal Affairs Commission, which has control over the police, the procuracy, and the courts, received expanded powers over those organizations. Hu Jintao was quoted as saying that the foremost task of these organs is to "steadfastly safeguard the CCP's ruling party status as well as the nation's security and the interests of the people." Critics interpreted this as an effort to further politicize the legal system by enhancing party control in the name of maintaining social stability. Another practice strongly objected to by human rights activists, *shuanggui*, so-called dual detention, applies to party members.

There are problems in making even good laws work properly. Major concerns include:

- *local governments control the establishment, funding, and personnel of judicial organs, allowing them to interfere with judicial procedures.* Because of this local protectionism, litigants from other areas find that their cases are postponed indefinitely, so that they disappear "like rocks dropped into the sea." Law enforcement personnel from other areas have been attacked, beaten, and/or detained when they have tried to investigate irregularities.
- *party and government officials treat the judiciary as an administrative body.* For example, they obstruct investigations into construction irregularities for fear that they will affect approval of future projects and, therefore, harm economic development in their jurisdictions.
- *low professional standards.* Proper legal procedures are either ignored or circumvented. In some cases, personnel have divulged confidential information to units or individuals which law enforcement departments are investigating.

Given these circumstances, it is not surprising that the new laws do not function as human rights advocates would wish. For example, the 1996 Criminal Procedures Law adopted the presumption of innocence, expanded the right to counsel, increased the role of the courts so as to eliminate the prior practice of pretrial determination of guilt, and limited public security organs to 30 days' detention of persons "strongly suspected of wandering around committing crimes, committing multiple crimes, or forming gangs to commit crimes." But the requirement for public security organs to inform detainees' families of the reasons for detention and of the place of custody within 24 hours after the individual is detained may be waived if police believe it could hinder the investigation or if they have no way of notifying the families. Police may also deny that suspects are actually being detained, saying that they are being "accommodated" (forcibly) in a guest house run by the police, for which the individuals are required to pay room and board. Persons thus accommodated are warned that, should they wish to protest, they risk being actually charged.

In addition, even though lawyers are now able to call witnesses, they have no way of making them appear in court, or even to be interviewed. In these situations, cross-examination becomes impossible, and the entire investigative process may become a sham. Although the law stipulates that clients be able to meet with their lawyers within 48 hours of their arrest, the authorities may, through various tactics, prevent such meetings for months. Police sometimes sit in on these meetings or even stop them. Lawyers who become too insistent, or too successful in unpopular cases, may themselves be jailed on trumped-up charges that are difficult to disprove, have their license to practice revoked, or be indicted for perjury if a witness recants. Lawyers are especially vulnerable to such treatment in cases with high political salience, whether at the central government or local level. Bar associations exist, but they are weak and have thus far been ineffective in protecting the professional rights of their members.

Under provisions that came into effect in 2013, lawyers must pledge to "fulfill the sacred mission of socialism with Chinese characteristics and uphold the leadership of the CCP," with legal experts protesting that lawyers should only pay attention to the law itself and be faithful to their clients. Another new ruling allows judges to prohibit legal representatives from participating in litigation for six months to a year if they "disrupt the order" of hearings, which seems to include emailing or microblogging about hearings.

Although it is not legal, torture is used to extract confessions from recalcitrant suspects, some of whom are not guilty. It is impossible to tell how widespread this practice is. A number of factors are involved. Given popular concern with crime, police are more concerned with cracking cases than they are about abusing suspects. Second, given their meager training in investigative techniques and forensic science, the police have few other ways to get a suspect to confess. As long as confessions extracted through torture remain admissible in court proceedings, laws forbidding torture will exist in name only.

The "strike-hard" campaigns introduced in 1996 put police under pressure to produce results, and civil liberties inevitably suffered. More than 2,000 executions were reported in the course of a few months. Human rights activists pointed out that this was yet another example of the subordination of law to politics: a crime is a crime whenever it is committed and should carry the same sentence. The implication of the "strike-hard" campaign is that criminals might be prosecuted leniently the year before the campaign and again the year after. The campaign also seems to have been used as a convenient tool to arrest and incarcerate those suspected of ethnic separatism, political activism, and practicing religion in non-state-sanctioned settings.

Black marketeering continues to be a problem, as does the kidnapping of women and children. The women are forced into prostitution or sold to desperate farmers who are unable to find wives in the more normal fashion, while the children are sold to childless couples or set to work in factories as virtual slaves. Thieves on motorbikes ride up behind well-dressed pedestrians, snatch their purses or briefcases, and speed away. Organized gangs have proliferated. Rather than fight each other, some gangs reportedly divide cities into "turf" for each gang. In some areas, villagers turn to local strongmen to deal with their problems and disputes, completely circumventing the party apparatus. Secret societies also provide an alternate channel of authority and decision making, as do powerful clans. Clan heads and religious leaders may serve as arbiters in disputes, sometimes even at the request of the party organization itself.

Not least among the justice ministry's problems is corruption between the police force and judicial system. High-ranking Bank of China officials have laundered more than $485 million through Las Vegas casinos; the deputy chief of the supreme court was found to be involved with organized corruption in Guangdong; and the chief of the Beijing cyber police was convicted of fabricating evidence to convict a company because its business rival paid him a large sum of money to do so. In 2017, the country's long-serving justice minister, a member of the party's Central Committee, was removed from her job and charged with accepting bribes. How to deal with corrupt officials has been an ongoing problem that successive leaders have repeatedly vowed to address, but with no tangible results. Xi Jinping's forceful campaign against it has been tainted by charges of politicization, since it has targeted his enemies disproportionately. A prominent Chinese lawyer observed that, although his country has many beautiful laws, enforcing them is quite another issue.

Nonetheless, the fact that more people have been using the courts to settle certain types of grievances indicates that there is a degree of public confidence in the system. Some homeowners, for example, have managed to successfully resist developers, although this is not the norm.

Conclusions

In the post-Mao era, the goals of the legal system may be summarized as follows:

- providing the framework for a market-oriented, internationally open system;
- controlling corrupt behavior that subverts economic development, much of which is connected to party or government officials;
- muting pressures for major political change.

On the positive side, the educational level of court personnel has improved, and serious legal scholarship has developed. However, party control over the judicial system, which during the Deng era appeared to be weakening, has been reasserted. Hu Jintao seemed to have concluded that law had failed to further the interests of party and government, and to prefer mediation to resolve disputes. Xi Jinping appears to view law as instrumentalist: supporting economic development while serving to consolidate his personal power. He has been explicit about the need for strong party control of the legal system. Under his administration, the system has become less liberal and more centralized, There is no effective way to enforce constitutional rights, since the courts are not empowered to do so, and the standing committee of the National People's Congress, which is empowered to do so, has thus far not chosen to exercise its authority. In sum, there is little evidence that a rule of law which includes liberal democracy and gives priority to civil and political rights is evolving. The Chinese legal system would appear to be moving toward the institutionalization of a statist, quasi-socialist, neo-authoritarian system. At least at present, China's legal system appears to more closely resemble the expectations of the communist neo-traditionalist model than those of pluralistic liberalism. One scholar sees the evolution of a different kind of pluralism quite outside the rule of law, characterizing it as a hybrid of authoritarian politics, mass line justice, and bureaucratic law institutionalized through the courts.

Although post-Mao legal reforms represent a significant improvement over the legal nihilist views of the Cultural Revolution, the instrumental bureaucratic view of law runs counter to the legal relationship of state and society that a market-oriented economy and civil society would seem to require. In several important respects, the PRC's legal system is not like that prevalent in the West.

For example, the judiciary is not independent, the presumption of innocence for the accused is not well established, decisions are made much more quickly and with fewer opportunities for review, and mediation plays a much greater role than in the West.

Generally speaking, law is viewed as an instrument of government, with citizens as the objects of legal regulation. Courts often try to discourage litigation. The Chinese legal system is willing to forgo the enforcement of rights when other pressing values seem to be at stake, to the point where, as one expert has observed, the system recognizes interests more than rights. In the late 1990s, it seemed that the Chinese legal system, though continuing to restrain human rights at its highest levels, might nonetheless be moving in the direction of producing an effective system of control over abuses of human rights by lower level officials. By the latter part of the following decade, assessments became more pessimistic. Reform-minded Chinese jurists have complained that the rule of law is in full retreat. Referring to the revised criminal procedure law, one expert described the progressive parts as like a woman with bound feet, while the regressive parts are like an adulterer on the run. The ambiguous language of the law has been likened to a gunnysack into which the police can fit any excuse they want. Human rights lawyer Teng Biao characterizes the system as "Lenin plus Emperor Qin Shi Huang—modern totalitarianism combined with pre-modern Chinese legalist philosophy, and nothing more than a tool to further control society."

How important it is to have a universal legal system is a controversial matter among scholars. Some take a relativist position, claiming that while the PRC's legal system would not be suitable for much of the rest of the world, it is nonetheless, if fairly administered, admirably suited to China. Others argue that human rights are mankind's birthright, and not subject to restriction on the basis of alleged cultural differences. What is clear, however, is that in many important ways the current Chinese legal system does not live up to its own standards as defined by its constitution and judicial codes, and that there is widespread dissatisfaction with its current condition.

Suggestions for Further Reading

Jacques deLisle, "Chinese Model 2.0: Legality, Developmentalism, and Leninism Under Xi Jinping," *Journal of Contemporary China*, December 2016, pp. 68–84.

"Development of the Rule of Law," Congressional-Executive Commission on China, *Annual Report 2017* (Washington, DC: Government Printing Office, October 5, 2017) pp. 223–281.

William Hurst, "Chinese Law and Governance: Moving Beyond Responsive Authoritarianism and the Rule of Law," *Journal of Chinese Governance*, Vol. 1, No. 3, 2016, pp. 457–469.

Pitman Potter, *China's Legal System* (Cambridge: Polity Press, 2013).

Yuhua Wang, "Court Funding and Judicial Corruption in China," *The China Journal*, January 2013, pp. 43–63.

CHAPTER 9

The Role of the Military

Party and Army

Mao Zedong's statement that "political power grows out of the barrel of a gun" illustrates the value he placed on the military as a means for bringing about the revolution. However, Mao also indicated that he considered the military to be a means to victory rather than an entity to be valued in itself: He immediately qualified the statement quoted above by adding: "the party must always control the gun, the gun must never control the party."

This statement implies a clear-cut distinction between the party and the military that strongly overstates the cleavage between the two. Particularly in the decades before it came to power, the Chinese Communist Party (CCP) was beset by powerful enemies, and sheer survival necessitated that the leadership be well versed in military strategy and tactics. Mao and most other high-ranking party leaders also held high military positions. Although some officers of the Red Army, as it was then called, had received formal military training, many had not. Of those with military training, a few had attended provincial military academies or been sent abroad to study, usually in Japan or the Soviet Union. Most of the rest had received short courses at the Whampoa Military Academy (see Chapter 3) or at Yan'an's Kangda military school. Typically, these were short courses of perhaps six months' duration, and the curriculum was heavy on political indoctrination.

Basically, the Red Army was commanded by amateurs, a situation not unlike that of the Confucian state held in such contempt by party leaders. What the proper sphere of the military should be after the party had come to power proved a troublesome question. The desire to have China assume a respected position in the ranks of world powers was, as proponents of the strategic interaction school (discussed in Chapter 1) argue, an important factor in the communist leadership's calculations. Realization of this desire demanded a carefully trained and well-equipped, professional army. Differences of opinion over the emphasis to be placed on training ideologically correct amateurs *vis-à-vis* technologically competent, professional military members has been an ongoing theme of defense politics in the People's Republic of China (PRC) and a variant of the red-versus-expert debate introduced in Chapter 1.

Initially, the infant Chinese communist movement was uncomfortable with the whole concept of an organized professional military, since they associated it with the warlords whose regimes they so vehemently opposed. Those CCP members who had read Marx knew that the revolt of the proletariat was supposed to come about spontaneously, but bitter experience soon taught the party that this was unlikely to happen. As noted in Chapter 3, CCP attempts at putsches were put down relatively easily, with surviving party members fleeing to rural areas to avoid extermination. It was at this point that the party reluctantly accepted the need for a regular military organization.

When the Red Army was founded on August 1, 1927, and for several years thereafter, it was a ragtag group that included idealistic but untrained communists, deserters from warlord armies, veterans of peasant militias, and bandits. Mao Zedong believed that the last category was the most numerous. His complaints about officers mistreating their troops, lack of discipline, and "the roving insurgent mentality" (banditry) indicate the difficulties of welding this disparate mass into a fighting force in support of communist goals. Communist leaders were concerned that the Red Army would degenerate into the warlord bandit force that formed a significant part of its origins.

Despite this inauspicious start, the party was able to wrest power from its Kuomintang (KMT) rivals in 1949. During the intervening two decades, the Red Army, renamed the People's Liberation Army (PLA) after 1949, had evolved into a well-disciplined force that provided effective support for the party's expansion on, and eventual control of, the Chinese mainland. In the process, it developed certain characteristics that are collectively referred to as the Maoist model. However, one should be aware that, first, the model evolved gradually in response to circumstances, and second, leaders other than Mao played important roles in its development. Major elements of this model include:

- *the military as an instrument for the achievement of political goals.* As such, the military must be unequivocally subordinate to the CCP. This is indicated by the statement that, although political power grows out of a gun, the party must always control the gun. After the founding of the PRC, soldiers were expected to assume responsibilities for organizing the masses and helping them to establish political power. Within the army, party control was exercised through a hierarchy of party committees headed by commissars and paralleling the military chain of command at all levels.
- *the relative importance of acquiring correct political views over the acquisition of advanced technology as a technique of army building.* A corollary of the primacy of political over military goals, it criticized the prioritization of military training and weapons acquisition as a purely military viewpoint.
- *close relations between the army and the people.* Mao maintained that without the support of the masses, the successful pursuit of war, like any other political action, is impossible. Comparing the masses to water and the army to fish, he noted that an army which fails to maintain rapport with the people will be opposed by the people.
- *the strategy of People's War.* The army, supported by paramilitary forces and a sympathetic populace, would lure the enemy deep into its territory until the invading force was overextended and dispersed. Communist troops

would avoid the defense of fixed points, preferring highly mobile, guerrilla-type tactics to isolate enemy units from one another. The element of surprise was considered crucial. When superior forces could be concentrated against dispersed units, communist troops were to surround and destroy them. When this could not be done, they were to withdraw and practice harassment tactics. Following a protracted period during which opposition forces became progressively more exhausted and demoralized, the enemy would surrender.

- *a high degree of democracy within the military.* From the earliest days of the Red Army, Mao insisted that officers must not mistreat soldiers, and should eat, sleep, work, and study alongside their men, "sharing weal and woe" with them. Nonetheless, Mao drew a distinction between democracy, of which he approved, and absolute egalitarianism, which he emphatically opposed. Although distinctions were made between officers and men in terms of certain privileges, they were relatively minor by comparison with those of other military organizations.

- *economic functions of the military.* To minimize the costs of the military to society, the army was to strive for maximum self-sufficiency. Insofar as possible, units were to raise their own food, mend their clothing, knit their socks, and build and service their barracks. Further, the army was to help build and maintain the civilian economy.

- *the army as a model for society.* In addition to being of the people and for the people, the army was to serve as a model for mass behavior. Mass media described efforts to solve the country's economic and social problems as a battle, and enjoined citizens to emulate the army's energy, organization, discipline, and devotion to duty while launching a concerted attack on the evils of the old society. The slogan "everyone a soldier" referred to civilian personnel engaged in economic and social reforms.

- *lack of clear distinctions between the military and civilian leaderships.* As mentioned previously, a high percentage of the early PLA leaders had little or no formal military education. In addition, political and military powers were tightly intertwined during the period of the civil war. This close connection between military and civilian administration continued for several years after the CCP came to power. The six Military and Administrative Regions into which China was divided after 1949 exercised both civil and military functions. When they were abolished a few years later, many military leaders assumed administrative duties. Subsequently, some who had received formal military training, and others who had not, assumed positions in the PLA or in the party and government organizations supervising it.

While such career patterns of exit from and re-entry into the military are far from the norm, they occurred often enough, and at a high enough level, to blur the distinctions between the military and civilian elites. For example, Wei Guoqing, a military academy graduate, held several important military positions during the revolutionary war and for several years after. In 1958, he became first party secretary of the newly founded Guangxi Zhuang Autonomous Region, and was one of a handful of first party secretaries to survive the Cultural Revolution. In 1977, he returned to the PLA as head of its general political department. Wei served in this capacity until 1982, when he was fired after differing with Deng Xiaoping about loosening restrictions on art and literature. During the Cultural Revolution, a majority of the members of the politburo and the party's Central Committee were military officers. For a time in the late 1980s, China's president served simultaneously as general secretary of the Central Military Commission (CMC); the country's vice-president was another veteran soldier.

Assessing the Maoist Model

Mao's followers claimed that his concept of the military and its relationship to society was revolutionary and represented a startling break with the past. These claims were often premised on a fallacious comparison: contrasting Mao's ideals with the reality of the badly deteriorated civil–military relationships that characterized early twentieth-century China. A more valid comparison would be between Maoist ideals and the ideals of the classical Chinese tradition. Here, one finds striking similarities between the Maoist model and concepts prevalent in China for millennia. For example, "The army is the fish and the people are the water" is first found in the works of Mencius, a disciple of Confucius who wrote in the third century B.C. Other "revolutionary" concepts derive from Sun Zi, the great military theorist who pre-dated Mencius by several centuries. The principle of isolating and surrounding an enemy to destroy him is basic to the ancient Chinese game of *weiqi*, better known in the West by its Japanese name, *go*.

Civilian control of the military was also a firmly held value in traditional Chinese society. Much of the credit for putting down the rebellions that plagued nineteenth-century China belongs to scholar-statesmen who assumed command of armies despite their lack of formal military training. They, too, believed that correct ideology—in their case, Confucianism—was more important than advanced technology. Chinese tradition also favored the idea that an army should be self-sufficient as far as possible. The notion that Chinese armies in outlying areas should grow their own food and provide for most of their other needs can be traced as far back as the first century A.D.

The Maoist military model is not simply a restatement of traditional Chinese attitudes toward the military; it also represents the selective choice of certain elements from the past and the disavowal of others. One traditional attitude that was unequivocally rejected was the position of the soldier at the bottom of the social hierarchy, in which scholars occupied the top position, followed by peasants and merchants. The elements of classical Chinese military tradition that Mao borrowed were combined in a blend that, although falling short of ingenious creativity, was innovative and well suited to the situation the party found itself in prior to 1949.

The Influence of the Korean War on the PLA

Although the CCP now portrays its military activities during the pre-1949 period as a series of heroic encounters against numerically and technologically superior Japanese and KMT forces, the Red Army actually devoted relatively little effort to fighting the Japanese. Moreover, KMT mismanagement, and the subsequent demoralization of its forces, contributed at least as much to the communist military victory as the heroism of the Red Army's soldiers. The chief formative influence on the military had been internal to the CCP. To borrow a phrase from eminent social scientist Samuel Huntington, the *societal imperative*, which arises from the pre-eminent social forces, ideologies, and institutions of the community, had been the dominant force shaping the formation of the Red Army.

Following the founding of the PRC, the military, now renamed the People's Liberation Army, played an even more important domestic role. Soldiers contributed to the rehabilitation of China's battle-scarred economy. They also assisted in the land redistribution process, set up state farms, and supported the collectivization of industry and agriculture. In addition to its economic functions, the army played an active political role. PLA work teams brought the party's message to areas that had had little prior exposure to communism and helped establish communist organs of political power. The army also guarded against the sabotage activities of anticommunist remnant groups, thus helping the party to consolidate power.

China's entry into the Korean War in late 1950 gave increased emphasis to external determinants in shaping the country's military. Although external military threats to the newly founded socialist regime had always concerned the party's leadership, these became increasingly salient when Chinese communist "volunteers," fighting beyond their country's borders for the first time, confronted United Nations forces.

Committing some of their best units to battle, the Chinese leadership apparently anticipated a relatively quick and easy victory, believing that their superior military doctrine could defeat the better-equipped enemy. However, after two months of initial successes, PLA weaknesses in firepower, air support, logistics, and communications became painfully evident. Chinese communist weapons and tactics were ineffective against the enemy's superior technology and mechanization, and the Chinese forces suffered heavy casualties. Morale plummeted. A new commander, Marshal Peng Dehuai, was named, and the Chinese forces fell back to defensive positions. Additional troops were sent to reinforce them, and the Soviet Union increased its military aid and assistance. Eventually, the Korean War reached a stalemate.

This experience convinced many Chinese leaders, both within and outside the military, that a reassessment of the PLA's organization, strategy, tactics, and weapons was needed. In Huntington's terminology, the *functional imperative*, which stems from threats to a society's security, gained importance relative to the societal imperative. Significant changes in the direction of specialization and professionalization took place within the Chinese military during the mid-1950s.

When the PRC adopted its first constitution in 1954, Peng Dehuai was named the new government's first minister of defense. It was under his aegis that many of these changes occurred. They included:

- *the modernization of weaponry.* The Soviet Union sent substantial quantities of tanks, planes, artillery, and ordnance to China to aid the PRC during the final phase of the Korean War and for several years thereafter. Although obsolescent and supplied in smaller quantities than the Chinese leadership wanted, these weapons significantly upgraded the PLA's arsenal. With them came several thousand Soviet military advisers to instruct the PLA in their use and to help China establish its own defense industry. The net effect was a strong Soviet influence over the development of the PLA.
- *training and discipline.* The introduction of more advanced weaponry required higher education for soldiers for longer periods, and more specialized kinds of training. Military personnel spent more time in these pursuits and less on economic development projects, whether on behalf of the society as a whole or for the benefit of the PLA itself. Increasing specialization also created a need for careful coordination of the many different specialties, which in turn required more elaborate procedures and tighter discipline. Training methods reflected the experience of Soviet advisers, focusing greater attention on concepts that had not been a part of the Chinese experience and which, at times, were even antithetical to Chinese concepts. For example, the Soviets emphasized highly mechanized and positional warfare. In addition, their officers had the habit of treating enlisted men quite badly.
- *rank system.* In early 1955, a rank system established 14 categories, ranging from second lieutenant to supreme marshal. Officers were also classified into categories based on fields of specialization. Educational qualifications were established for entry into the various ranks, and a more formal system for entry into military schools was set up. Officers were to wear the epaulettes and insignia of their rank, and a system of military honors was introduced. The method of remuneration changed, from providing military personnel with food and a small allowance to cover incidental expenses, to one of cash payments based on rank. In 1960, the ratio between the pay of a marshal and that of a private was 160:1. This was far greater than the differences between the highest and lowest paid members of Western capitalist armies, and especially striking in a military that was proud of its egalitarian tradition.
- *conscription.* A law passed in mid-1955 regularized the recruitment of military personnel, enabling whatever number of recruits had been decided upon to be selected from a pool of those who had been declared eligible. This superseded the previous practice of relying on volunteers.

These reforms improved the efficiency of operation and overall combat capabilities of the PLA. However, increasingly audible voices within the leadership, and from the population at large, complained that these advances in the PLA's ability to cope with external threat had come at the expense of ideological principles and were therefore detrimental to domestic social progress. External and internal imperatives, or red and expert points of view, were in conflict over the correct course of development for the PLA.

The Revolt against Professionalism

Critics charged that the cherished socialist values of democracy and egalitarianism were being destroyed. Conscription had sharpened the distinctions between amateur and professional soldiers, and the rank system had encouraged status distinctions and arrogant behavior among the officers. Establishing educational qualifications for officers meant that an increasing number were drawn from the bourgeois classes, to whom education had been more readily available and whose families tended to value it more. Not having risen through the ranks, it was claimed, diminished their ability to understand the problems of the rank and file.

Officers who no longer ate with their troops were less motivated to deal with complaints of poor-quality food, and, while stricter discipline might increase efficiency in a battlefield situation, it also made officers less likely to ask for the opinions of their subordinates. In blatant violation of PLA tradition, some officers used physical force to discipline their troops. As officers gave less attention to their subordinates, they gave more to weapons procurement and maintenance, thus contradicting the principle of the primacy of people over weapons.

Relationships between the military and the civilian population had also become strained. Civilian homes and land had been requisitioned by the PLA for barracks and training grounds, and peasants' crops were sometimes ruined by army maneuvers. Civilians resented displays of conspicuous consumption by more affluent military families, and noticed that some PLA members supplemented their incomes through black market activities. Civilians were also angered by an increase in incidents involving soldiers' behavior toward local women.

Greater specialization of functions led to a sharper distinction between military and political work within the PLA. Commissars complained that commanders made decisions without consulting them; officers retorted that since commissars did not trouble themselves with military matters, their opinions were of little value. The number of party members in the armed forces declined during the late 1950s, and some units did away with commissars completely. Critics argued that this undermined the principle of party control over the military. Many also felt that the Soviet model was inappropriate for China, and blamed it for distorting the PLA's principles.

During the anti-rightist campaign of 1957, certain efforts were made to rectify these perceived distortions. These escalated massively during the following year as part of the Great Leap Forward. Officers were required to attend lengthy political study sessions, and an "officers to the ranks" program called for commanders to spend one month each year eating, sleeping, working, and passing their leisure time with ordinary soldiers. They were also assigned tasks, such as cleaning spittoons and latrines, caring for animals, and weeding crops, in order to lessen their arrogance and give them an understanding of their subordinates' point of view.

PLA members were reminded of the importance of good relations with civilians, and the army worked on behalf of economic development on an unprecedented scale. The media reported that the PLA contributed 59 million days to economic development in 1958 alone. Although this figure, like all other statistics from the period of the Great Leap Forward, was apt to be grossly exaggerated, there is no doubt that the PLA was heavily involved in nonmilitary activities, leaving little time for training. Simultaneously, the militia was raised to virtual parity with the PLA. The "everyone a soldier" movement of 1958 claimed to have enrolled over 200 million ordinary citizens in the militia. Maoist "reds" believed that allocating an important role to the militia would make the country better able to fight a true People's War while simultaneously undercutting the PLA's claims to a superior position because of its vaunted expertise in defense matters. The disparity between military and civilian living standards was redressed through such measures as lowering officers' pay and reducing the quality of the army's food and uniforms.

In 1959, Defense Minister Peng Dehuai, widely regarded as supportive of "expert" professionalist views, was dismissed after he criticized Mao for championing the Great Leap Forward. Peng was replaced by Lin Biao, who might then be considered to espouse "red" amateur positions. What actually happened is a great deal more complicated. Although Peng almost certainly resisted radical policies that he felt weakened PLA morale and combat capabilities, the proximate cause for his dismissal was his criticism of the economic and social policies of the Leap—something on which a purely professional soldier would normally avoid commenting. It fell to Lin to regularize and reorganize the PLA into a force capable of ensuring the country's defense—a task that required substantial attention to professional criteria.

Secret Chinese military documents published in the PRC in 1961 and later made public by the U.S. Central Intelligence Agency reveal the devastating effect that the Great Leap Forward had on the PLA. Widespread malnutrition and poor sanitary conditions caused debilitating diseases among young men who had been selected from the country's most physically fit. Weapons maintenance had deteriorated, leading to a rise in accidents caused by malfunctioning equipment. This was particularly noticeable in the air force, where equipment was expensive and hard to replace. Repudiation of the Soviet model had exacerbated strains in Sino–Soviet relations to the point where the USSR ceased giving military aid and withdrew its advisers to the Chinese military. This further compounded the problems of equipment replacement. PLA morale was dangerously low.

By October 1962, the PLA had improved to the extent that it gained a decisive victory over Indian forces during a confrontation in the Himalayas. The Chinese triumph was made easier by India's poor planning and mismanagement. Nonetheless, the PLA coped successfully with long supply lines through difficult terrain inhabited by a hostile Tibetan population: there had been a major rebellion against Chinese rule in Tibet in 1959. India's shortcomings notwithstanding, China's performance was impressive. Lin had refurbished the PLA through a variety of measures, some consonant with concepts of redness and the societal imperative, and some with those of expertise and the external imperative.

Reds, or amateurs, were pleased with Lin's vigorous efforts to reassert the party's control over the military, including strengthening the supervisory role of the party's CMC. Commission directives revitalized the system of party committees within the military and restored commissars to a position of parity with commanders. The CMC also initiated an intensive campaign to instill a sense of political loyalty in the rank-and-file soldier. A "five good" movement admonished soldiers to excel in political thinking, military training, work style, fulfillment of tasks, and physical education; prizes were awarded to outstanding units and individuals. This was followed by a campaign to learn from Lei Feng, a young soldier who was martyred in the line of duty—if that is a proper description of someone who expired after a truckload of telephone poles backed into him. Excerpts from what was alleged to be Lei's diary were published to inspire soldiers to emulate his many noble virtues.

Experts, or professionals, were pleased when the number of days that the PLA was to devote to economic development was drastically reduced, leaving more time for training. The "officers to the ranks" program continued, but on a smaller scale and with a different purpose. Rather than lessening the distinctions between officers and common soldiers, the program now facilitated the transmission of directives from the top echelons to the bottom, and enabled officers to exercise better control. The militia was also reorganized so as to appeal to advocates of military professionalism: it was reduced in size and salience, directed more toward economic development than military activities, and subordinated to joint party–PLA control as opposed to its position of virtual parity with the PLA during the Great Leap Forward.

Both amateurs and professionals could take comfort from Lin's pronouncements on the issues of people versus weapons and of democracy within the military. On the former, Lin declared that one should give unqualified preference to people, while adding that cadres "should on the one hand oppose the purely technical viewpoint which departs from reality and on the other oppose the empty-minded politician who disregards techniques and professional operations." Lin applied the same sort of subtle modification to the concept of military democracy. Although Mao himself had carefully qualified the limits of democracy, persons acting in his name during the Great Leap Forward had not been equally fastidious. Lin, while strongly supporting the concept of military democracy, defined it so as to include the need for discipline and exclude egalitarianism and anarchism, thus encompassing both radical and professional views.

In 1964, the Chinese leadership indicated its approval of the military by launching a mass campaign to "learn from the PLA." Citizens were enjoined to apply the army's skill at being both ideologically correct and technically proficient ("both red and expert" was the slogan used) to their daily lives and to the work of party and government organizations. Lin Biao had, it appeared, achieved a successful synthesis of the PLA's different roles.

The synthesis proved short-lived when Mao decided that the "learn from the PLA" campaign had not been a success and that, in any case, the army was insufficiently radical. In May 1965, in a move that was unequivocally pro-amateur and anti-professional, the PLA's rank system was abolished. During the same year, the military's official newspaper began an attack on "bourgeois" intellectuals that proved to be the opening round of the Cultural Revolution. Significantly, it began with an attack on a play set in the Ming dynasty whose hero bore a striking resemblance to Peng Dehuai, Lin Biao's predecessor as minister of defense (see Chapter 12). All expertise, including military expertise, came under attack as bourgeois and anti-Maoist. The slogans being chanted left no doubt that the correct ideological line no longer sought a blend of politically reliable people with superb training and advanced weapons: people counted; weapons and training did not.

Many PLA leaders came under attack, and the command structure was severely affected. Still, the military suffered less than most other institutions due to concern about external attack. At this time, China was surrounded by hostile powers: the Soviet Union, India, and Taiwan all seemed menacing. Moreover, the United States maintained a large and growing military presence in Vietnam, just a few hundred miles from the Chinese border. Internal factors also tended to bolster the army's position. The chaos of the Cultural Revolution was sometimes so extreme that the leadership felt it best to call in the army to restore domestic order. Although the PLA was regularly enjoined to "support the left," its peacekeeping mission frequently put it on the side of the moderates. Radical ideologues were critical of the PLA's conduct at such times.

Lin Biao, whether because he had shrewdly calculated which way the political wind was blowing or from a sincere conviction that this was the proper course of action at this particular point in time, strongly espoused leftist/radical causes in general and amateur views with regard to the military. He and many of his fellow Fourth Field Army members profited handsomely in terms of promotions. Nonetheless, the PLA's interventions on behalf of domestic order convinced other radicals that the army as a whole could not be counted on to support them. They began to organize the militia as a counterweight to the PLA. This effort was, however, scarcely noticeable at the time.

The army emerged from the Cultural Revolution with greatly increased powers. Mao had ordered it to back worker-peasant teams when they entered the universities during the summer of 1968 and to quell student violence. The PLA ran study classes to "re-educate" Red Guards, and became a fixture on university campuses and in industrial enterprises. There was heavy military representation in the party and government organizations that emerged from the Cultural Revolution, and frequently a PLA officer held, concurrently, the top party, government, and military positions in a province. The PLA's societal role had reached its zenith. In April 1969, the CCP's Ninth Party Congress adopted a new constitution that designated Lin Biao as Mao's successor.

Although Lin was an avowed radical and apparently had an even more radical constituency, any further moves away from military professionalism were inhibited by deteriorating Sino–Soviet relations. Localized but potentially serious armed clashes on the eastern border began in March 1969 and spread to the western border during the summer. The PLA's military training increased, as did emphasis on the care and maintenance of weapons. Military budgets rose. In a number of cases, major defense plants were either relocated to or established in remote parts of China, making it more difficult for the USSR to destroy them. This "third-line" strategy was, however, exceedingly costly, and in light of the deficiencies of the transportation network in the country's outlying areas, made it much harder to get the products of third-line industries into the hands of the troops.

Lin Biao's death under mysterious circumstances in the fall of 1971 (see Chapter 4) was followed by a purge of officers loyal to him, many of them from his Fourth Field Army and presumably also radical in their views. This meant a concomitant increase in the power of moderates and professionals in the PLA. Such an explanation is consonant with an intensification of Shanghai radicals' renewed efforts, beginning in 1973, to build up the militia as a counterweight to the regular army. In December of the same year, Mao Zedong rotated eight of the eleven military region commanders. Although the commanders assumed leading military positions in different regions, they lost the positions they had held in provincial party and government and were not given new ones. The transfers thus reasserted the party's control over the gun and, specifically, over the moderates and professionals in the PLA who constituted most of the gun after the demise of Lin and his faction.

The radical-inspired reorganization of the militia had the same aim: Many of the People's Armed Forces Departments, through which the PLA exercised control of the militia, were abolished. Militia units were put under a new organization, the militia headquarters, which was subordinate to the party. The reorganized militia incorporated public security and firefighting functions. It was further strengthened through receiving substantial quantities of weapons, many of them produced in factories in Shanghai, the radicals' power base. The new militia was urban based, to take advantage of radical elements within the cities. Rural areas, which had typically been the mainstay of militia recruitment, tended to be less activist. In 1975, a new Chinese constitution gave the militia equal status with the PLA.

These moves did not go unnoticed by professionals. Deng Xiaoping, purged from his post as party secretary general during the Cultural Revolution and rehabilitated only in 1973, became the symbol of resistance to radicals and the champion of military professionalism. In January 1975, Deng was named PLA chief of staff and appointed to the CMC as well. He bluntly characterized the army as a "mess" created by its "support the left" work during the Cultural Revolution, and pledged to prepare the PLA to fight future wars in terms of "iron and steel"—that is, weapons. Deng also opposed the new-style urban militia, even sending the PLA to disband unruly militia elements in the city of Hangzhou during the summer of 1975.

Radicals interpreted these actions as negating the primacy of politics over the gun and of people over weapons. By this time, both Mao Zedong and Zhou Enlai were elderly and ailing, and the radicals' opposition to Deng and his policies was intensified by fears that he and his supporters might assume their positions. They were able to oust Deng from power in the Tiananmen incident in April 1976, in which the militia played a highly publicized role. But when Mao died a few months later, radicals' attempts to stage a militia-led uprising to put themselves in power failed dismally. Only in Shanghai did the militia's effort assume major proportions. The PLA aborted the uprising with ease, simultaneously destroying the power of radical leaders. Although the militia continued to exist in a reorganized form, it would never regain its previous level of prominence. Deng, backed by professionals in the military, was rehabilitated during the summer of 1977, almost immediately assuming his old position of head of the PLA's General Staff Department and vice-chair of the CMC. Shortly thereafter, he became head of the CMC and relinquished his general staff position to a long-time protégé, Yang Dezhi.

Professionalism Returns

The pendulum again swung in the direction of professionalism. Deng, his views clearly unchanged despite his past disgrace, instituted sweeping changes within the military. These included:

- *a reworking of strategic doctrine,* called "People's War under Modern Conditions." Described as an adaptation of Mao's principles to modern times, the doctrine was characterized by greater attention to positional warfare, modern weaponry, and combined arms. The concept of luring an enemy deeply into China and then surrounding and attacking him was amended to include the possibility of forward defense: many Chinese military strategists believed that by the time an enemy had been lured deeply enough into the PRC for this to work, the enemy would have destroyed much of the country's vital industries and transportation nodes. China's "defensive counterattack" against Vietnam in early 1979 showed awareness that the enemy might have to be engaged in his own territory. The strategy was sufficiently different from the People's War that, in the opinion of many analysts, it should be considered wholly separate. They believe that the original name was retained to preserve a façade of continuity with the past, when in reality the doctrine represented a sharp break with it. In 1978/1979, when relations with the Soviet Union were strained, the PLA was told to prepare for an "early, major, and nuclear war" with the USSR. In 1985, by which time Sino–Soviet relations had improved, there was yet another change in strategy. The military was to expect and train for local, limited wars on the PRC's periphery. After the Gulf War of 1991 showed the technological superiority of the of U.S. military, doctrine emphasized the need to conduct information warfare under high-tech conditions.

- *more attention to training.* Troop training programs were ordered to be reorganized. Less time was to be given to political study sessions and more to the study of strategy and tactics. Training exercises were to be adapted to the sort of real-life situations that combat troops might actually be expected to face and to reflect the weather and terrain conditions of particular geographical areas.
- *efforts to acquire advanced weaponry.* Both foreign and indigenous sources were to be utilized. The National Defense Science, Technology, and Industry Commission was charged with supervising research and manufacturing for the PRC's seven ministries that dealt with defense production. In addition, a number of military procurement missions were sent abroad to examine a wide variety of foreign weaponry and related items, including tanks, trucks, helicopters, warplanes, missiles, lasers, and computers.
- *reorganization of the PLA into a smaller, younger, and more responsive force.* Plans were announced to cut the size of the military by a quarter, meaning one million people. The number of military regions was reduced from eleven to seven, thereby cutting down on the number of headquarters and their personnel. The new military regions were authorized to command tank and artillery divisions as well as other specialized service branches; in the past, these branches had been directly under the armed forces' supreme command. New regulations provided for the reinstitution of a rank system and set limits for time in grade. Older officers, many of whom were in their seventies, with some in their eighties and nineties, were encouraged, and in some cases forced, to retire. This made it possible to promote younger, more vigorous people to command positions.
- *more stringent educational qualifications for the military.* Units at and above the corps level were ordered to sponsor classes to bring PLA cadres up to the level of senior middle school or technical middle school. Self-study was also encouraged: those willing to enroll in night school, or in television or correspondence courses, were to be given assistance in doing so. Tests of general and specialized knowledge were to be administered. Those who could not, or would not, meet the required standards would either be denied promotion or be demoted. The Communist Youth League was told to persuade outstanding college graduates to join the PLA.

A three-tier system was created to train junior, mid-level, and senior officers, with more than 100 military academies participating. The apex of the system is the National Defense University, which was founded in December 1985 by merging three PLA academies—military, political, and logistical. Each had previously been operated by the relevant general department of the PLA. Consolidating the resources and expertise of the formerly separate institutes was aimed at producing a more efficient instructional system. Another, though unstated, reason behind the decision to integrate the three academies may have been to reduce the departmental compartmentalization and attendant factionalism that the separate institutions tended to reinforce.

• *reasserof party and government control over the military, with the PLA more clearly separated from party and government.* There was a marked decrease in the number of individuals holding positions in either two or all three of the party, government, and military hierarchies. By 1990, there were no individuals with a primarily military background in the standing committee of the politburo, and very few in the politburo itself. A 1987 change in the party constitution dropped the requirement that the chair of the CMC must be a member of the standing committee.

The railway corps, heretofore under PLA control, was transferred to the railway ministry, and the capital construction corps was also civilianized. The People's Armed Police was created from the PLA and charged with internal security functions that had heretofore been carried out by the army. The increased functional specialization made possible by these more clearly differentiated military and nonmilitary roles constituted a major step away from the amateur, "red" position and toward expertise.

Although abrupt, these changes did not represent a total break with the past. The military retained an important role in China's industrial enterprises. Indeed, the army's continued participation was considered vital to the success of the country's economic modernization. Encouraged by explicit party/government directives, the PLA actually went into business for itself, in the form of large marketing enterprises for both civilian and military items. Many of its products were sold to other countries. There was no noticeable diminution of the PLA's charge to provide for its own food and other items. Military units also participated regularly in mass tree-planting campaigns and other activities designed to help civilians and blunt the edge of civil–military tensions.

Not surprisingly, the magnitude and abruptness of Deng's innovations caused a number of problems. Advocates of the old-style People's War pointed out that, given the weaknesses of the PLA's weaponry, a forward defense would expose the Chinese side to being outflanked and overrun. In addition, they contended, the disadvantages of positional warfare had been shown by the Red Army's ability to capture cities from the countryside during the war against Chiang Kai-shek.

Advocates believed that the Maoist concept of People's War retained its basic validity in the capital-poor, labor-intensive Chinese context; they also saw a none-too-veiled attack on Mao as implicit in the revision of his military doctrine. More attention to troop training and the acquisition of weaponry raised fears that troops were receiving less instruction in proper political attitudes. It was, moreover, expensive to develop and purchase technologically sophisticated weapons. China faced no imminent external threat, whereas its internal needs were many and urgent. The societal imperative, they believed, far outweighed the external imperative.

Military modernization was ranked lowest among Deng Xiaoping's Four Modernizations, and the amount of money that could be devoted to technological improvements fell far short of perceived needs. There was also the question of how much to procure indigenously and how much to acquire from foreign sources. Local design bureaus and those that feared dependence on external sup-pliers strongly favored the indigenous route; others pointed out that in the past, this path had proved slow and inadequate. Arguments also existed over which kinds of weapons should receive priority.

Reorganization met massive resistance. Reducing the army by one million meant turning a large number of people out into a civilian job market that could ill afford to absorb them. Officers had joined the military with the expectation of a lifetime career: To be demobilized unexpectedly caused anger and hurt as well as financial difficulties. There was also the matter of who got demobilized and who was allowed to stay. Personal connections, the ever-present *guanxi*, played an important role. Streamlining also involved merging certain units, causing other problems. Typically, members served their entire career in the same unit, and strong loyalty networks developed. Those who were transferred into new units found that they were regarded with suspicion and treated as outsiders. In a few cases, soldiers who managed to retain their weapons after discharge formed bandit groups and preyed upon local populations. Officers who were told to retire because, at age 50, they were considered to be too old noted that both the head of the CMC, Deng, and the CMC general secretary, Yang Shangkun, were in their eighties.

At the lower end of the military hierarchy, there were very different prob-lems: while older officers did not wish to leave the PLA, younger people did not wish to join. Deng's agricultural reforms had a strong disincentive effect on mil-itary service, since it was now more profitable to stay in the countryside. More-over, draft-age youth were also marriage-age youth, and finding a suitable bride while serving in the 90 percent male PLA was exceedingly difficult. The plight of bachelor soldiers was made more difficult since, at this time, peasant men earned higher incomes. Hence young women and their families tended to consider them more desirable matches than poorly paid PLA members. For the first time in the history of the PRC, large numbers of peasant youth, heretofore the mainstay of the military, began to avoid the draft.

Commanders were not pleased at the thought of compensating for the drop in numbers of peasant youth by enrolling urban young people in their place. First, since peasants constituted more than 70 percent of the PRC's population, the pool of urban youth was much smaller. Second, though recognizing that city youth were generally better educated than their rural peers, commanders felt that they were also too soft for the rigors of military life, and too infected with bourgeois ideology to make good soldiers. Rural young people were inured to hardship and far less likely to pose discipline problems.

Urban youth were as unwilling to join the army as their commanders were to have them. Prior to Deng's reforms, joining the PLA had been an important ave-nue of upward mobility for peasant youth, and often the only realistic way that a young man could escape the tedium of his village. However, joining the mili-tary gave fewer advantages to urbanites. Even city youth who were unemployed tended to regard waiting for a job as preferable to committing themselves to military service. Work units tried in various ways, including bribery, to keep their best workers while persuading PLA recruiters to accept social misfits, those with criminal records, physical weaklings, and illiterates. Individuals tried to bargain with recruiters: they would join if the military could provide them with something they desired. One might want to be taught a specific trade; another might demand a driver's license that he had otherwise been unable to obtain.

Some individuals and units solved their quality-of-life difficulties by illegal means. The military's greater access to foreign exchange, vehicles, and storehouses facilitated such activities as smuggling. In one spectacular case, the participation by most members of a division-level unit in Guangdong resulted in a large number of convictions, including that of both its commander and its commissar. The unit had been engaged in an illegal vehicle purchase-and-resale scheme that was discovered only when one of its members was robbed and murdered by the owner of a vehicle that the officer was attempting to purchase. The scheme came to light almost accidentally, since the officers were able to conceal their comrade's death for several weeks. Variations on this theme abound.

Problems also appeared in the effort to upgrade the educational qualifications of the PLA in order to prepare its members to take part in more complex training exercises and in the use of more sophisticated weapons. An article in the official military newspaper complained that "cadres are tired of studying and students are dropping out," thus having a bad effect on the already low scientific and cultural level of the PLA. Since educated people were leaving the PLA in greater numbers than they were entering, the educational situation was growing worse. In 1988, the PLA set examinations for some of its officers, with alarming results. The commander of one regiment proved unable to read a map and, when asked to mark a specific location, was seven miles off target. When asked what sorts of arms the parachute troops of a certain country were likely to be equipped with, one colonel thought long and hard, eventually replying that he did not know.

The existence of major problems should not obscure the fact that there were gains as well as losses. Training exercises did become more sophisticated. Some weapons were upgraded, and China became one of the world's largest arms exporters. Although the PRC's weapons were generally not state of the art, they were reasonably priced and hence attractive to many Third World countries. Training programs were instituted to provide soldiers with skills that they could use in the civilian job market after demobilization, and the resettlement of veterans began to receive more systematic attention. Although the debate between amateurs and professionals continued, the PLA was moving in the direction of greater professionalism and increased capabilities.

The Effect of the June Fourth Incident on the PLA

The declaration of martial law in May 1989 (see Chapter 5) brought the PLA directly into an internal political dispute. The leadership apparently judged the People's Armed Police incapable of handling the massive demonstrations of that time, and returned the military to internal security duties. In essence, the PLA was also being called upon to resolve a leadership struggle at the highest levels of party and government. This ran directly counter to the trend of separating and differentiating military from civilian administrative functions that Deng had been fostering during the previous decade.

While Deng backed this reversal of his own policies, several commanders, including individuals whom Deng himself had appointed, were reluctant to do so. A number of soldiers said openly, in front of television cameras, that the people's army must not be used against the people. Deng spent several days lining up support from the various military regions, and even then there were reports of skirmishes between different divisions. After the demonstrations were crushed and the leadership crisis resolved, the newly reconstituted elite tried in a number of ways to ensure that this situation would not recur. Collectively, these policies represented a step away from professionalism and toward the amateur model.

Awards were issued to servicemen who had acted strongly against the alleged handful of counterrevolutionaries who had instigated the subversive demonstrations, and the campaign to learn from Lei Feng was revived. Army newspapers also reiterated, time and again, the impossibility of separating the army from politics: the PLA was the party's own army and must take its direction from the party. Yet another technique to ensure loyalty was to encourage research on the Chinese communist military's glorious past when, at least as seen through the haze of nostalgia, right and wrong were easily distinguishable.

The results of these efforts were mixed. For example, the campaign to learn from Lei Feng met considerable cynicism. It was rumored to have been designed by president and, concurrently, CMC general secretary Yang Shangkun to enhance the power of his faction. This included his younger half-brother, Yang Baibing, who was head of the PLA's general political department. Moreover, some of the research published on the PLA's glorious history came to less-than-idealized judgments about past campaigns.

Following the PLA's suppression of the 1989 demonstrations, foreign analysts predicted, first, that the military would play a much more important role in high-level decision making and, second, that the "Yang family village" would play a major role in that decision making. The first prediction was quickly disproved: military leaders were not promoted to leading positions within party and government in any greater numbers than before; nor was there any indication that the military was exercising increased influence on policy in other ways.

The second prediction, on the power of the Yangs, proved erroneous as well. Immediately before the CCP's Fourteenth Party Congress in the fall of 1992, rumors began to circulate that high-level changes were to be made in the military, with the aim of destroying the Yangs' power. Yang Baibing was accused of a variety of unacceptable actions, including having held a private meeting at a Beijing hotel to plan security arrangements for after Deng's death. Although the charges were never confirmed, the Yangs' fortunes definitely took a turn for the worse. Yang Shangkun resigned as president of China and from his CMC position, while Yang Baibing was replaced as head of the general political department and on the military commission.

Although Yang Baibing received a seat on the politburo, the Yangs' ties with their power base, the PLA, had been severed. A number of officers believed to be part of their "village" were also removed from their positions. Since there had been no hint of disloyalty to Deng Xiaoping himself, the most likely explanation for the purge is that the paramount leader wished to ensure that the PLA would remain loyal to his chosen successor, Jiang Zemin, after Deng's death. This hypothesis was confirmed when two elderly generals with no known factional bases of their own, Liu Huaqing and Zhang Zhen, replaced the Yangs on the CMC. Liu was appointed to the standing committee of the politburo as well, in what seemed to be a setback for Deng's plans to separate the military from the party. That it was felt necessary to reassign officers in order to deal with military factionalism bearing on the selection of the next civilian leader of China would also seem to indicate the persistence of a strong societal role for the PLA.

Pressures for increasing the PLA's functional role existed as well. The impressive performance of the American military in the UN–Iraq war of 1991 and the disintegration of the Soviet Union during the same year helped focus the Chinese leadership's attention on the combat capabilities of the PLA. PLA officers, shocked at the sophistication of U.S. weapons, told Western military attachés that they did not see how the PRC could ever catch up. The 1991 Iraq war seemed to have dealt a final blow to the Chinese communist strategy of overwhelming an enemy with sheer numbers of troops. A strategic reassessment shifted emphasis from limited regional conflict to limited high-technology war. There was intense interest in the American military's Revolution in Military Affairs, in which networked computers combine with precision-guided weapons to destroy the enemy's war-fighting capabilities. The PLA began to purchase arms from Russia and continued to work with Israeli arms dealers.

The Military in the Post-Deng Era

With the Yangs' power diminished, Jiang Zemin worked to establish his control over the military. He created new billets for three-star generals (the PLA's highest rank) for commanders and commissars of the seven military regions and personally conferred the awards. Jiang also made well-publicized visits to military units throughout the country: the media described these as showing his love for the troops and appreciation of the important work they were doing. Legislation on retirement ages passed under Deng Xiaoping's direction was scrupulously observed. In addition to creating a younger and, presumably, more vigorous and better-educated PLA, this also meant that within a short period of time, all top military officers had been chosen by Jiang and could be presumed loyal to him. Jiang also maintained the practice begun by Deng of transferring commanders and commissars among the military regions. This reduced the ability of the incumbents to become entrenched with local power holders in ways that could reinforce regional ability to modify or evade central government policies. Hu Jintao and Xi Jinping have continued these practices.

One very important societal function remained: the PLA's business empire. As mentioned above, Deng Xiaoping had encouraged the PLA to help in China's modernization effort through producing and marketing both civilian products and weapons. It did so enthusiastically, though the motive appeared to be profit rather than modernization. By the mid-1990s, products such as washing machines, refrigerators, and socks accounted for nearly 70 percent of defense-sector production. The military ran at least 10,000 businesses, with profits of $5 billion to $10 billion a year. The growth of these businesses was accompanied by massive corruption. Many of the profits were not declared; therefore, no taxes were paid on them. In 1993, China's defense minister warned that if such practices continued, the country's "'Great Steel Wall' [a common metaphor for the PLA] will self-destruct." A Chinese Academy of Social Sciences report issued shortly thereafter argued that the PLA should be removed from business and returned to its proper role of defending the country. Aware of the high cost of this switch from the PLA's societal role to its functional role, the author of the report suggested that military industries be purchased for a fair price so that soldiers could concentrate on training.

In July 1998, as part of an anti-corruption drive, Jiang Zemin actually took this action. However, the divestment may have taken place more in form than in reality: less profitable enterprises were sold off, but more successful ones simply changed ownership while remaining at least partially under PLA control. From 8,000 to 10,000 enterprises, including some of the most lucrative ones, were retained. Still, the fact that the order to divest could have been given indicates that the PLA had advanced another step toward functionalism.

The military is nonetheless regarded as the *party's* army rather than as belonging to the state, and political qualifications, though far less stringent than in Mao Zedong's era, remain important. As faith in Marxism receded, patriotic considerations came to the fore as a focus of devotion. So, as well, did material factors: to keep pace with the private sector, the PLA raised starting salaries for new officers and noncommissioned officers by 80 percent to 100 percent in 2006 and began offering an attractive package of additional tax-free subsidies and allowances.

Military budget increases that had begun in 1989 continued at an impressive rate. Considered in current dollars, defense expenditures multiplied over 40 times between 1988 and 2017 (see Figure 9.1).

Most of this happened during a period in which, owing to the disintegration of the Soviet Union, the defense budgets of the major powers were sharply reduced. Since the PRC faces no external threat and has many pressing domestic concerns that could be addressed with the money being spent on the PLA, China's neighbors have expressed concern that Beijing is bent on aggressive behavior. The leadership has sought to calm these fears by explaining that increments in defense expenditure have reflected the need to compensate for inflation and provide soldiers with a better living standard. However, one cannot be certain of this, for several reasons.

First, official figures are generally believed to underestimate actual inflation rates, although it is difficult to say by exactly how much. Second, even if inflation

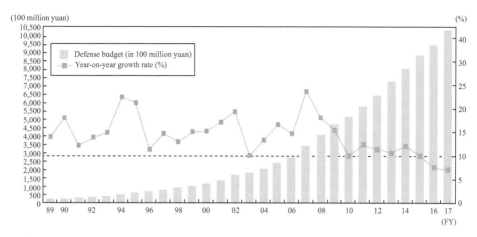

FIGURE 9.1 Military Budget Increases

Source: Japanese Ministry of Defense White Paper (2017).

rates were known to be accurate, they would not tell us how inflation impacted the defense sector. Third, the PLA received double-digit budget increments in 1997/1998 and again in 2009: years when the inflation rate ranged from 2 percent to below zero. The 7.5 percent increase announced for 2010, the lowest since 1988, was not considered to reflect curtailed interest in building up defense but as part of an attempt to wean the economy away from the huge fiscal stimulus injected into the economy in 2009 to avert financial disaster (see Chapter 7). Moreover, comparing defense allocations with other projected expenditures in the 2010 budget shows that the military was in fact one of the least disadvantaged sectors. Defense expenditures again reached double-digit levels in the next several years.

The argument that the PLA was being compensated for divesting its commercial empire is also less than convincing, since the double-digit increases reported for 1997 and 1998 occurred before the order to divest was given in July 1998. Finally, the actual defense budget is much larger than the reported defense budget. For example, weapons purchases from the former Soviet Union were made from a separate budget under the State Council. The costs for other large expenditures, such as nuclear research and development, are hidden or otherwise unavailable. Estimates of true defense spending have typically fallen into the two- to three-times range, though the most recently released official figures seem to be more in line with actual expenditures. Defense is believed to represent 1 to 2 percent of GDP and 7 to 10 percent of central government expenditures. By any calculations, these represent substantial amounts, albeit telling us nothing about how well the money has been spent: in the PLA as in other sectors of the economy, waste and corruption abound.

There is no question that important advances are being made, with foreign purchases being replaced with domestically developed weapons. The PLA's journals contain many articles stressing the need to develop both "information-ized warfare" and "asymmetric warfare." The former involves creating a structure that coordinates command, control, communications, computers, information/intelligence, surveillance, targeting, acquisition, and reconnaissance to attack enemy targets. These identify an enemy's weak points and, using an "assassin's mace" weapon, deliver a killing blow through attacking these vulnerabilities. In the case of the United States, these weak points are judged to be its military's heavy reliance on high-technology weapons and the American public's aversion to casualties. PLA analysts discussed the ability to seize control of a battlefield from a much more powerful enemy (unnamed, but presumably the United States) by inserting computer viruses into the opponent's communication systems. In a book entitled *Unlimited Warfare*, two senior colonels opined that since the PRC was a poor country, it had to use whatever means it could. International military codes of conduct could be ignored since, they argued, incorrectly, Western powers had devised the codes in order to advantage themselves. Among the techniques the colonels suggested were chemical and biological warfare, terrorism, and altering environmental conditions in order to produce changes in the climate of the enemy's territory.

Chinese military doctrine also encompasses nonlethal aspects, chief among which are the so-called Three Warfares: psychological, public opinion, and legal. These should begin before the onset of combat operations, with the PRC seeking to undermine enemy morale. It must use its mass media to promote Chinese views while blocking and refuting the adversary's media in order to persuade international public opinion of the validity of China's claims.

Despite the attention given to state-of-the-art weaponry and asymmetric warfare, People's War remains enshrined in military doctrine. However, a reworking has defined it as "a form of organization of war that has nothing to do with the level of military technology." People's War now encompasses the mass mobilization of civilian resources in support of conflict, as exemplified by the passage in 2010 of a national defense mobilization law. The law, which is explicitly linked to the concept of People's War, provides the statutory basis for the mobilization of civilian resources for military purposes. But it appears to be less about People's War per se than an effort to solve long-standing central–local government tensions over the latter's obligations to military units billeted in their areas. The law provides compensation for requisitioned assets and mandates that items taken be either returned or fair value remitted for their loss. That the law could be passed only after a decade of debate indicates the intensity of the disagreements that must have taken place over it.

Xi Jinping instituted far-reaching changes in the PLA designed to make it both a more capable and a more politically reliable fighting force—both red and expert. Explicitly linking political loyalty to his anti-corruption campaign put officers on notice that any manifestations of lack of allegiance to himself would be followed by close scrutiny of their and their families' finances. Motivated by a conviction that institutional barriers were creating ineffective joint command systems, the country's seven military regions were replaced by five theater commands, sometimes referred to as combat zones: one each for east, west, north, south, and central China. He also replaced the previously existing four military departments with 15, with the aim of dispersing their functions and placing the successor group directly under the control of the Central Military Commission which he heads. New services were also created: the PLA Rocket Force, which took over the Second Artillery Force, was charged with responsibility for China's increasingly powerful nuclear arsenal. The Strategic Support Force would deal with cyber war and high-tech warfare in space (Figure 9.2).

At the Nineteenth Party Congress, the CMC was downsized from 11 to 7, all of whom, with the exception of Xi, are generals or admirals. The paramilitary People's Armed Police (PAP), which serves as backup for the military in times of war while serving domestically in putting down protests and counterterrorism, was placed under the direct supervision of the CMC. Previously, the PAP was under a dual command structure of the CMC and Ministry of State Security.

A further demobilization of troops is to fall disproportionately on the ground forces. Consonant with China's more assertive maritime and aerial activities, the strategy of anti-access/anti-area denial, or A2/AD, aims at enforcing China's expansive claims to a self-designated nine-dash line that the United Nations Permanent Court of Arbitration has ruled has no basis in international law and is opposed by states that fear it impinges on freedom of navigation on the high seas.

New weapons have also favored the navy and air force. In 2013, China launched its first aircraft carrier, the *Liaoning*, with two more soon to join it. A new anti-ship ballistic missile (ASBM) has the ability to destroy aircraft carriers: the United States and Russia agreed several years ago not to build them, and there are no ship-board defenses against ASBMs. China's submarine force has been augmented in numbers and quality: the navy now has a long-range sea-based nuclear capability and can engage adversary surface ships up to 1,000 nautical miles from the Chinese coast.

The PRC has the world's largest inventory of extended-range ground-launched ballistic missiles; its air force is rapidly improving its ability to conduct interdiction missions at extended ranges beyond China's periphery; and there is an active drone program. Both Japan and the U.S. territory of Guam are within range of PRC missiles. Hypersonic missiles, whose high speeds and maneuverability are beyond their adversaries' ability to defend against, have been tested.

Exercises are becoming truly joint, as opposed to earlier ones where each service participated without actually interacting. Sustained attention is being devoted to cyber warfare, with the majority of incidents of hacking into the computer networks of foreign governments and businesses being traced to PLA-affiliated sites. While some foreign observers see these developments as threatening, others point out that, as an expanding global trading power, the PRC has legitimate concerns with protecting the security of its commercial interests.

Still, foreign observers who wonder what the PRC's end goal is continue to press for more transparency on this issue. In response, the government began issuing defense White Papers approximately every two years beginning in 1998,

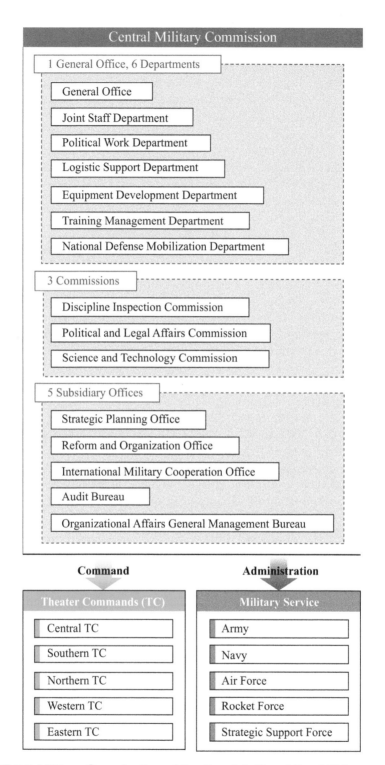

FIGURE 9.2 Military Organization of the People's Republic of China

Source: Japan National Institute of Defense White Paper (2017).

but foreign analysts found that the papers did not address major concerns. Nor has the inauguration of a ministry of defense website in 2009. Although White Papers are written in bland form, careful readers can discern important clues, particularly by comparing the texts with those of previous iterations. Analysts noticed, for example, that the 2006 document omitted previous versions' call for a ban on space-based weapons. The reason soon became apparent: in January 2007, the PLA conducted a successful anti-satellite missile test against an obsolescent weather satellite. Heightening concerns about transparency, the government did not confirm that the test, first revealed by the Western press, had taken place until five days later, in the wake of rumors that the PLA had not kept Hu Jintao informed of its plans.

The most recent White Paper indicated concern over rising terrorism, separatism, and extremism, all of which have negative impacts on the security of China's periphery. This, the paper argued, justified the creation and weaponization of artificial islands in the South China Sea as well as other measures designed to protect the PRC's maritime interests. Like its predecessor, this iteration omitted previous versions' pledge that the PRC would never be the first country to use nuclear weapons.

Conclusions

The PLA has been transformed from a mass army designed for protracted wars of attrition on its territory to a thoroughly modern force capable of fighting high-intensity conflicts beyond China's borders against adversaries equipped with state-of-the-art technology. Post-Mao military reforms have produced a younger, better-educated, and better-trained PLA with greater technical capabilities and improved weaponry. Rising military budgets, purchases of advanced weapons and military systems from abroad, and the development of an increasingly sophisticated indigenous defense technology industry have raised questions among many of China's neighbors as to the PRC's military intentions. However, the PLA has not fought in many years and hence is an untested force. The effect of the anti-corruption campaign is also believed to have adversely affected military morale.

In the post-Mao era, the functional role of the PLA greatly increased as its societal role diminished. Although the PLA still performs a societal role in times of crisis—for example, helping out the population in the aftermath of floods and earthquakes—it is now firmly focused on its functional responsibilities. Since the Fifteenth Party Congress in 1997, no member of the military has been named to the standing committee of the politburo. Although the PLA has other ways to express its views to party and government leaders, the fact that the standing committee has no serving military officer carries important symbolism.

The greater separation of the military from party and government hierarchies may portend the evolution of a sharper sense of PLA interests as separate from those of party and government, which might then insist that its corporate voice be heard and accommodated by the system.

Soon after assuming office, Xi aligned himself with "the China dream" of a militarily strong and economically prosperous PRC, the title of a book written by a senior military academician three years before – and which is now required reading in China's military academies.

Chinese observers have, however, noted an apparent paradox of the PLA's increasing professionalization alongside the increase of cronyism. Charges brought against top military leaders during Xi Jinping's anti-corruption campaign revealed that promotions to higher rank were often bought rather than awarded on the basis of merit, and that personal connections were more important to success than military skills. Xi, warning that military corruption meant defeat in war, has vowed to wipe it out through stricter party control. Yet there is skepticism that, given the absence of checks and balances within the system, this will be possible. Even so, there can be little doubt that Xi is in control of an increasingly powerful gun.

Suggestions for Further Reading

James Char and Richard A. Bitzinger, "A new Direction in the People's Liberation Army's Emergent Strategic Thinking, Roles, and Missions," *China Quarterly*, Vol. 232, December 2017, pp. 841–865.

June Teufel Dreyer, "China's Military Reorganization." Philadelphia, PA: Foreign Policy Research Institute e-Note, March 2016.

International Institute for Strategic Studies, *The Military Balance 2018* (London: IISS, 2018).

Xiaoting Li, "Cronyism and Military Corruption in the Post-Deng Xiaoping Era: Rethinking the Party-commands-the-gun Model," *Journal of Contemporary China*, Vol. 26, No. 107 (September 2017), pp. 696–710.

U.S. Department of Defense, *Military and Security Developments Involving the People's Republic of China, 2017*. Available at www.defense.gov/Portals/1/Documents/pubs/2017_China_Military_Power_Report.PDF.

CHAPTER 10

Education

Education, broadly defined both as the transmission of cultural norms and expectations, and as training in specific job-related skills, presents every society with difficult choices. In less developed countries like China, limited financial resources and a lack of trained teachers placed further constraints on the educational system. As a newly founded revolutionary state, the People's Republic of China (PRC) had an additional difficulty: that of transforming many existing beliefs and practices.

Devising a System

The Chinese communist party faced decisions on whom to educate, on what topics, and in what numbers. At one extreme it could opt for providing large numbers of people with a relatively low standard of education; at the other, it could train a much smaller number of people in areas that would enhance the nation's prestige. For example, a few superbly trained medical scientists equipped with state-of-the-art laboratories and equipment could be expected to achieve major breakthroughs in disease prevention, thus adding to their country's prestige. Similarly, a substantial amount of money devoted to educating and equipping nuclear physicists would allow the PRC to join the nuclear club, whose members had heretofore been a small number of Western powers. The former goal appealed to the egalitarian strain of Chinese communist ideology; the latter to adherents of the strategic interaction theory.

There were also questions about how much time in the curriculum should be devoted to the study of politics and ideology and how much to more substantive material like mathematics and foreign languages. How to treat China's past was a difficult question: Despite diatribes about the dead weight of tradition inhibiting the country's modernization and industrialization, to negate that tradition completely would leave the PRC without a national identity. The leadership was concerned with matters such as what aspects of tradition to preserve and how to blend those with a still largely formless concept called socialist culture. Also at issue was whether to give preferential treatment—and, if so, how much—to the children of workers, peasants, and party members as opposed to those of the bourgeoisie and nonparty members. Every decision involved a trade-off that would benefit one or another social group. As in so many other aspects of policy making in the PRC, arguments took the form of red-versus-expert polemics.

Initially, the party's task involved expanding and revising the educational system which it had inherited from the republican government. Textbooks were rewritten to praise communism, the communist party, and the Soviet Union. The value of socialist thought, the evils of capitalism, and the wisdom of Mao Zedong's views were taught in various degrees of sophistication, depending on the level of the educational institution involved. The importance of collective behavior was inculcated, starting from the earliest years. Textbooks stressed the value of the masses in making history rather than, as heretofore, giving credit to emperors and high-ranking ministers.

As in other areas of PRC policy making, there was a heavy Soviet influence on the educational system. This included emphasis on mathematics, science, and technology, noticeable not only at the theoretical level but also in the founding of a network of vocational schools to train technicians. Many textbooks were simply translated from Russian into Chinese, some of them generating numerous complaints because the examples they gave were so inappropriate to the Chinese context, and at least some children of landlords were discriminated against by the educational system. However, in general, academic criteria were applied impartially during this early period, with relatively little emphasis on class background.

At the same time, the educational system was greatly expanded, with the goal being to provide schooling for all, including the children of the poorest peasants and factory workers. For adults, spare-time literacy classes were established. In factories, these might be held after the work shift ended; in farming communities, during the slack season. Normal schools were set up in areas that had not previously had them in order to train more teachers.

The government tried in various ways to make it easier for people to become literate. For example, it propounded the use of *baihua* in writing Chinese, which was closer to the way people actually spoke the language than the terse and more elegant *wenyan* previously favored by scholars. It also popularized the use of a phonetic system known as *pinyin* so as to standardize the pronunciation of the Chinese characters across the country. The PRC's vast expanse includes a number of linguistic dialect groups and subgroups, several of which are mutually unintelligible. The new regime propounded the use of what is known in the West as mandarin. Since the communists had a very negative opinion of the old official class, they referred to the language as *guoyu*, the national language, or *putonghua*, meaning ordinary speech.

Basic lists of the most frequently used characters were drawn up, with books, newspapers, and magazines to use only those. Eliminating a large number of complicated and seldom-used characters would make it easier to learn how to read. The forms of some complicated characters were simplified: For example, a character written with 11 strokes of the pen might be reduced to 4 (Figure 10.1). The standard for literacy was later established as the ability to recognize 1,500 characters (for peasants) or 2,000 characters (for workers and urbanites). The intent was to enable people to read popular newspapers and periodicals, keep basic accounts, and write simple statements. It would appear that in earlier periods, the ability to recognize 1,000 or 1,200 characters sufficed as the standard for literacy.

Original Character	Simplified Character	*Pinyin* Pronunciation	Meaning
寶	宝	bao	treasure
叢	丛	cong	crowd together
歸	归	gui	return
國	国	guo	country
蘭	兰	lan	orchid
龍	龙	long	dragon
慶	庆	qing	celebrate
勸	劝	quan	advise
無	无	wu	without
壓	压	ya	oppress

FIGURE 10.1 Selected Characters, Simplified Forms, and *Pinyin* Pronunciations

Source: Created by the author.

In 1949, the literacy rate was estimated at about 25 percent—not especially low for a developing country. By 1955, it had more than doubled. That many of these people had not reached a very high level of literacy should not detract from the achievements of the government's efforts. Most of what the Chinese communist government did was not its own invention: the use of baihua in preference to the literary language had been one of the demands of the May Fourth marchers in 1919. The pinyin system of transliteration had been devised under the Kuomintang government, and simplified characters had been used by writers in a hurry for at least a millennium. What was new and impressive was the energy and organization involved in putting these techniques together and in popularizing them so widely.

A formal educational system evolved that was not very different from the one prevalent in the West. Six years of primary school were followed by three years of junior high school, three years of senior high school, and six years of university. This was supplemented by a variety of vocational and technical schools, with the whole fairly tightly controlled by the ministry of education in Beijing. Chinese culture had always emphasized hard work and placed great value on education, so student motivation was not a problem. The main concern during this period was to prevent young people from ruining their health because they studied too hard.

Although the system was impressive in many ways, there were complaints that it was elitist. Frequently, the most successful students turned out to be the progeny of the bourgeoisie who, being better-educated themselves, could more easily help their children to learn. Mao Zedong occasionally voiced strong anti-intellectual feelings, perhaps derived from the days when he was looked down upon by Moscow-educated party bureaucrats who referred to him as a "dirt" (rural) communist. The Hundred Flowers campaign of 1957 had the effect of reinforcing these anti-intellectual tendencies, since many of the most articulate criticisms of communist rule came from the more educated segment of society.

The Drive for Egalitarianism and Return to Expertise

The ensuing anti-rightist campaign and Great Leap Forward aimed at broadening and flattening the educational system. In 1958 alone, the number of children in kindergarten reportedly increased from 1 million to 30 million; those in primary school from 64 million to 86 million; and enrollment in secondary schools from 7 million to 10 million. Although all statistics from this period should be regarded with skepticism, the almost explosive expansion of the system cannot be doubted. Since it was impossible for resources and trained personnel to expand at the same rate, a decline in standards was inevitable.

At the same time, elitist education was sharply attacked, as was so-called bourgeois scientific objectivism. A number of research projects were canceled in midcourse, since their aims were deemed too far from the country's primary goal: increasing production levels. Intellectuals were sent to the countryside to labor alongside peasants, both to reduce their arrogance and to narrow the cultural gap between city and countryside. Greater emphasis was placed on spare-time schools. Schools were even closed for a time so that faculty and students could participate in making steel in backyard blast furnaces.

Young people with peasant or proletarian backgrounds were given preferential admission to institutes of higher learning, and the ideological component of school curricula was increased. Teaching methods were changed to emphasize the dictum that education must serve the interests of the working class and that it must be integrated with productive labor. Politics was to take command.

Although the slogan of the time called for every student to be both red and expert, redness received far more attention than expertise. Academic standards declined markedly.

The failure of the Great Leap Forward was accompanied by a return to pre-1957 teaching standards. Academic achievement was again valued. Certain institutions, usually in major urban centers, were designated key schools and provided with exceptional resources, better-trained teachers, and the most promising young students. However, the same criticisms of this educational system emerged as during the anti-rightist campaign, adding fuel to the ensuing fury of the Cultural Revolution.

Redness Revisited: The Cultural Revolution

The theoretical debate on education during the Cultural Revolution centered on the need to suppress bourgeois and feudal attitudes in the pedagogical system so that "the revolutionary successor generation" could be properly prepared to assume its role in the march toward communism. However, most of the specific criticisms of the system as it existed in 1965 turned on less lofty issues. One was that children of poor and lower middle-class peasant families found it very difficult to attend school, or, if they did manage to enter, to stay in. Tuition fees, though minuscule by Western standards, were simply beyond the capacity of many poor peasant families. Often, the school was so far away that a child could not come home at night, so boarding fees had to be paid as well. Examinations determined promotion; those who did not pass would have to repeat a grade, thus prolonging the time they spent away from productive labor and raising the cost for their parents. Age limits for each grade excluded those who might have to start late, or expelled those who could not pass a certain subject within a given period of time.

In cities, where parents had less need for their children's labor and schools tended to be within easy walking distance, the entrance exam for high school was more likely to be the focus of discontent: workers felt that the children of the bourgeoisie and intellectuals were advantaged by virtue of their superior cultural levels. At the same time, the children of bourgeoisie and intellectuals resented the preferential treatment given to children of well-connected cadres. Ideologues argued that examinations were inherently improper: By placing individual self-interest above anything else, exams undermined the collectivist values on which socialism was based. They also fostered the creation of a promotion-conscious elite, reminding a number of people uncomfortably of the mandarins of yore.

Another prominent criticism was that course material was excessively abstract, with very long assignments and heavy emphasis on cramming and memorizing. Students were not taught to analyze. In addition—and an irrefutable argument in the climate of the Cultural Revolution—they had little time to study the really important topic: the thought of Mao Zedong.

A third criticism was that owing to the tight control exercised by the ministry of education in Beijing, local needs were not taken into consideration. For example, school vacations in tea-growing areas of Zhejiang were set according to a schedule devised to be in harmony with the very different needs of rice-growing areas elsewhere. Finally, villagers who had been assigned a bad teacher could do nothing to dismiss her or him, since the individual was considered a state cadre.

An entire folklore grew up around the theme of the thin, pale-faced, near-sighted intellectual who really knew nothing about survival or productive labor. This image was invariably contrasted with the quick-minded and open-hearted "local expert" who, keen-eyed, fit, and tan from hard physical labor, knew how to grow rice and wheat from extensive practical experience without regard to tedious scholarly discourses on hybrid seed strains.

For a time, no one could be sure of what was acceptable in teaching methods or content. Since students were encouraged to smash the old society and to exchange revolutionary experiences, most schools simply closed down. A number of students chose to denounce their teachers and school administrators as exemplars of the evils of the old society. Teachers and school administrators were "struggled against" and humiliated in various ways. Some were tortured to death; others committed suicide to escape further torment. All learned people, not only teachers, were targets of derision; Mao castigated them as the "stinking ninth category," the eight others of which included such obvious villains as capitalists. Bonfires were made of books deemed to be tainted with bourgeois thought, which nearly everything except the works of Mao was suspected of being. The educational system ceased to function. Despite general agreement that schools should be reopened, widely divergent opinions on what should be taught and how prevented the resumption of a normal academic schedule for several years.

When schools began to function again in 1968, a number of changes were evident. Instead of an entrance examination, students were selected on the basis of recommendations. Political criteria became important, as did one's willingness to engage in productive labor for several years before applying to a university. Outstanding workers and peasants who were political activists would receive preferential admission to universities even if they had received only a junior high school education, provided that they had been endorsed by their work units and party authorities. Although many such individuals were able to attend university under this new system, its aims were perverted in various ways. First, children of cadres found it easier to obtain the necessary official endorsements. Second, those sent down to the countryside could have their class labels changed to "peasant" at the end of two years. Hence, those university students who were classified as peasants were often not really peasants. Third, it was easier for the well-connected to get their class designations changed.

The age limits for admission to various levels of the educational system were widened, and the curriculum was shortened. Six years of elementary school were to be compressed into five, and the three years each of junior and senior high school combined into a single, four-year segment. University took just three years.

The curriculum was simplified, with new teaching materials introduced. There was a noticeable bias against "bourgeois expertise": one group of students was reportedly writing its own textbook on organic chemistry. Other students were described as trying to discover the principles involved in inventing a radio. Illiterate but wise local peasants were brought in to assist in writing textbooks as well as lecture on such topics as growing crops.

Decentralization was another feature of the educational system to emerge from the Cultural Revolution. In rural areas, it became common for production brigades to run primary schools and communes to assume responsibility for secondary education. In urban areas, primary schools might be run by street committees and secondary schools by factories. Teachers would be members of these units rather than employees of the state, and local people would be able to ensure that the curriculum was linked with reality. In rural brigades, which were habitually short of people able to keep accounts, teachers' arithmetic skills could be put to immediate practical use. By managing their own school finances, local areas would be free to abolish tuition fees and to support schools in whatever ways they found most convenient—for example, payments in kind. Hence, it was hoped, more children would be able to receive an education.

A great deal of emphasis was placed on integrating study with productive labor, albeit with varying ideas on how this should be done. For example, if schools were combined with factories, should the school have a separate administration or be run by the factory administration? Having students actually participate in productive labor proved a somewhat easier problem to deal with. The visiting chancellor of a major U.S. university system observed a group of high school students making electrical turn signals for automobiles. They soldered wires, put on metal tapes, finished off the unit, and took the completed sets to an automobile factory. The chancellor was most impressed, though he mentioned no precautions with regard to quality control.

With the examination system discredited as a means of evaluating student performance, a combination of other criteria took its place. Test results, homework, and a child's attitude toward study and labor were all taken into consideration. It became harder to have a student repeat a grade, though it could be done if the child performed poorly in two of the three major subjects (political study, Chinese language, and arithmetic), if the parents agreed, and if the poor performance had been due to laziness. If a child failed because of ill health, the parents might be reimbursed for additional tuition costs.

For graduates of junior or senior high school—in certain areas, even the former were considered intellectuals in the PRC's categorization at this time—the *xiaxiang*, or down-to-the-countryside, movement was intensified. Young people were urged to volunteer, with sanctions available for use against those who did not. The party's admonition to integrate themselves with the peasants was not popular with most students, who felt that they had not spent so many years in school in order to waste what they had learned. They found life in rural areas very harsh, with few diversions. Routes out of the countryside were also very few: One could find a job at an urban factory, join the military, or enter a university. None was easy or simple. Here again, however, the children of cadres had connections that eased the process.

Egalitarians versus Experts: The Search for a Synthesis

Mao had decreed in July 1968 that college students be selected from the ranks of workers, peasants, and soldiers. Universities did not really begin reopening until 1970, and many not until 1971 or 1972. Almost immediately, there was a great deal of concern with the poor quality of the applicants. This and perhaps the demise of the radical Lin Biao led to certain modifications in the Cultural Revolution educational system. Toward the end of 1972, an examination system began to be reinstated. Radically different from the rigorous *gaokao*, or university entrance exam, of pre-Cultural Revolution days, the new system called for papers to be jointly assessed by teachers, pupils, and members of the local Workers Propaganda Team, followed by a discussion with the examinee. Open-book examinations were also reported. As one indication of how far standards had fallen, a 1973 directive ordered that a student's academic accomplishments had to be at least at the level of junior high school before he or she could be considered for university entrance. That the document was issued indicated that a sufficient number of applicants had fallen below even this modest standard.

Even these limited moves toward tightening academic standards caused controversy. People who favored more stringent educational requirements were pitted against those who felt that any reversal of the policies adopted during the Cultural Revolution amounted to a sellout of its principles, as well as those of the workers and poor and lower middle-class peasants. When examinations were reintroduced, there was an instant adverse reaction.

During the summer of 1973, the provincial newspaper *Liaoning Daily* published a letter from a young man named Zhang Tiesheng. A high school graduate who had been sent to the countryside, he found himself unable to answer the exam questions, explaining on the back cover of the booklet, and in a subsequent letter to the provincial authorities, that because of his duties as leader of a production brigade he had had no time to prepare for the examination. This note soon reverberated throughout the country, its main point being the converse of what Zhang stated: the implication that people who *had* done well in their university entrance examinations had probably been neglecting their obligations to productive labor. After a time, indicating that there were differences of opinion within the leadership on the examination issue, Zhang's letter was reprinted in *People's Daily*. Responding to this unmistakable signal that the sentiments expressed in Zhang's letter had high-level backing, provincial radio stations took up the questions raised in it as well. Not surprisingly, they agreed enthusiastically with Zhang.

Nor was this the only example of opposition to examinations. In January 1974, *People's Daily* published a letter from a high school student in Guangzhou (Canton), who complained that when he could not understand two problems on a mathematics exam and had asked the student next to him for help, the teacher had failed him for cheating. The young man asserted:

> [t]eachers are wrong when they say that one should not consult other people during an exam. The main task of the student is learning. Suppose a student does not understand a subject. With the help of another student, he now understands the subject. Is this not itself a kind of achievement?

Other students, even including some at primary school, took up the call, denouncing their teachers in the pages of major newspapers for discouraging group learning in tests. This tug-of-war between reds and experts on educational matters continued for several years.

The era of the Cultural Revolution was not without its research accomplishments. During this period, Chinese scientists announced a major medical breakthrough in the laboratory synthesis of insulin. The country's nuclear program, which had first detonated a bomb in 1964, continued to make progress, and a satellite was launched in 1970, making China the third country in the world, after the Soviet Union and the United States, to have done so. However, these advances occurred in small, well-protected areas. In general, educational levels fell sharply during the period from 1966 through 1978. An entire generation that could have been of immense value to the country's modernization was lost.

The Search for Academic Excellence

Deng Xiaoping's return to power and the priority he placed on economic modernization led to an abrupt reversal of educational policies. Rather than serving ideological goals, the pedagogical system was to support economic ends. A reinstated *gaokao* given to would-be college entrants in 1978 revealed appallingly low levels of knowledge. Deng and his faction were openly derisive of the old system. The requirement that all students spend periods of time at productive labor, they argued, distracted the most able ones from their main job of learning, and lengthened the period of time before they accumulated sufficient skills to be truly productive into society. Mental labor was deemed to be as legitimate as physical labor. Moreover, allowing students to write their own textbooks produced little of value, since the students did not know enough about the topics. Puzzling how to build a radio was a waste of time: one should be taught how to construct such a device with the idea of being able to add to and improve upon what was already known, not repeat it.

Henceforth, emphasis was to be placed on mathematics, science, and foreign languages; political study courses were downplayed and the requirement for productive labor at all levels modified. The new system was unabashedly elitist. Ninety-eight of China's then 715 tertiary-level educational institutions were designated as key schools, giving them priority both in the allocation of resources and in the choice of students who had scored highest in examinations. In order to provide higher education with well-qualified candidates, key schools were also established at primary and secondary levels beginning in 1978. Entrance to these schools was also determined by intellectual ability, as tested by examination. They received more funds, more equipment, and better-trained teachers. Universities established special ties with some of the best high schools, with the aim of improving teaching at the secondary level, and also of attracting that school's brightest students to attend their university. Technical high schools, which had almost completely disappeared during the Cultural Revolution, were reinstated in order to provide qualified candidates for colleges of engineering and mid-level technicians.

Expertise was again honored, and redness downplayed. Zhang Tiesheng, the student who had so strenuously objected to university entrance examinations, was arrested on charges of hooliganism and sentenced to reform through labor. The designation "stinking ninth category" was removed from intellectuals, whose talents were now deemed absolutely necessary for their country's rapid modernization.

The new system also revived the track structure of the early 1960s that had been so heavily criticized during the Cultural Revolution. Its new incarnation was far more differentiated than the original. From kindergarten on, children were tested and channeled to ordinary or key schools, and, within those schools, to fast, average, or slow classes. Key schools at primary and secondary levels were six years each while ordinary schools were five years each, and the type of instruction at the former was more detailed than at the latter. Hence, a pupil from an ordinary school had almost no chance of being admitted to a key school at a later stage.

In addition, nearly all key schools were located in cities at county-seat level or higher. They accepted only pupils who were registered residents thereof, thereby excluding the rural and ex-urban children who amounted to nearly 80 percent of the PRC's then school-age population. The assumption was that rural children would remain in the countryside and participate in production there. Ordinary high schools would be turned into vocational schools, perhaps with a half-work, half-study system, and rural youth would be discouraged from seeking admission to senior high schools and universities. This amounted to a deliberately discriminatory policy of cultivating an intellectual elite among urban youth while excluding rural children from the competition.

In urban areas, parents put tremendous pressure on their children to do well in examinations so that they could attend college. The odds were heavily against succeeding. One study showed that only 4.7 percent of those senior high school students who took the college entrance examinations passed and that just 0.5 percent of the PRC's college-age students actually attended institutions of higher learning. By contrast, the figure for many developed countries is in the range of 20 to 30 percent. Postgraduate study was even more exclusionary, and the opportunity to study in foreign countries was still more difficult to obtain. With so much competition for so few places, and so much perceived as depending on success, there was a tremendous sense of disappointment among those who failed. Newspaper articles in the early 1980s advised such students not to feel bitter, and to try to help their country's modernization effort by working hard at whatever job the state deemed appropriate for them.

Other problems emerged. The party answered charges of elitism by pointing out that the previous non-examination system had provided numerous opportunities for favoritism and back-door cronyism: The examination at least provided an objective measure of success. With four-fifths of the population effectively excluded from this allegedly objective competition, it is unlikely that this argument convinced too many critics. Moreover, the back door continued to operate: a disproportionate number of those selected to study abroad were children of high-ranking officials. A surprisingly large number of Chinese students were able to point out that one of Deng Xiaoping's sons was studying at America's University of Rochester. When the young man's wife had a child in the United States, the couple was widely suspected of having done so in order to receive preference in procuring American citizenship.

Some of these elitist policies were revised or phased out. For example, almost all high schools are now six years, although there are experiments with four-year junior high schools in some areas to help train students for agriculture, plus a two-year senior high school for those who wish to go on. In many cities, key schools at junior high level were closed. One is expected to attend the nearest junior high school, although there are ways around this, including paying bribes and using connections. Linking admissions to payment is forbidden but widely practiced. The sums of money involved can be very large. Schools may also issue "educational stocks" that parents must purchase before their child is admitted. Some institutions allow grades to be purchased. In Beijing, as many as 50 percent of junior high school students in some key schools were admitted through methods that were not based on merit. By the late 1990s, 36 percent of those sitting for college entrance exams passed, though the process had not actually become easier: a number of applicants were weeded out by a preliminary exam for graduation from high school. Parents often regard a child's failure as their fault, and educational schools for parents proliferated in order to teach parents how to better prepare their offspring for the exams.

Despite the government's concerns, elitism and the role of money remained important, as did hard work. The 12 hours or more each day that these highly motivated students spend in the elite schools' well-equipped classrooms and laboratories typically result in outstanding test scores. Teachers describe many of the students as only children whose parents and grandparents are focused on their success. Some parents even move to the area where their children attend school to make sure they study.

Another form of elitism emerged for the children of the newly rich: private schools. Some kindergartens charge higher tuition fees than universities, sometimes even amounting to the life wages of an ordinary worker. In addition to receiving superior instruction, students at a number of these schools wear designer uniforms and enjoy the finest sports facilities, with their teachers housed in attractive on-campus buildings.

Responding to resentment over the growing inequality of educational opportunities, officials tended to agree, while pointing out that this is an unavoidable consequence of the development of the commodity economy. By the early years of the twenty-first century, there were over 60,000 elite private schools. Efforts to impose rules on how much tuition these schools can charge have been resisted by those who argue that restraining private institutions' ability to offer the highest quality educational experience will simply incentivize parents to send their children abroad to study. According to the Institute of International Education, the number of Chinese students in the U.S.A. alone more than tripled between 2008 and 2015, and they are coming at increasingly younger ages.

In rural areas, the decollectivization of agriculture removed an important underpinning of the collective management of education. When the household became the unit of production, peasants found their children's presence at home more valuable, and many ceased to send them to school. The number of illiterates in China actually increased during the early 1980s. The government became concerned, and, among other responses, it promulgated a nine-year compulsory education decree in 1985. However, as in other areas of policy making, what is ordered from Beijing is not necessarily implemented at local levels. The number of students who actually receive nine years of education is considerably lower than government statistics suggest. Local officials exaggerate enrollment figures; in some schools children whose names appear on class lists are not actually attending the school. Schools have sold diplomas to children who never studied there, and can borrow students from elsewhere to fill classrooms when inspectors come.

Dropout rates reach as high as 10 percent in some areas. Even so, the studies have found that many rural county governments have fallen heavily into debt in order to pay for the compulsory education plan. Lack of funds has led to a serious shortage of teachers, with many schools using unqualified substitutes to reduce costs. The government spends an average of 40 percent less per year on rural students than on urban students. Several reasons are involved in the high rural dropout rate. One is the perception—correct in many cases—that brainwork earns less than physical labor. Therefore, any effort spent studying is wasted. A second factor contributing to high dropout rates is that many businesses have taken to hiring children at very low wages, even by Chinese standards. This practice has been repeatedly condemned by the State Education Commission, but it continues. A third reason is the rising cost of tuition, books, and other school expenses. Some of these increases are understandable. The high inflation of the mid- to late 1980s meant higher prices for books, electric power, food, and other school needs. When the central government basically ceased to subsidize primary education in the early 1990s, the situation grew worse. Since education budgets did not keep pace with the rate of inflation, many schools began increasing their fees to make up the shortfall.

In some instances, however, the increases in fees were so exorbitant that parents and government bodies began to suspect malfeasance; occasionally, they were able to prove it. In urban areas, a parent's work unit might agree to pay the child's education fees, but in rural areas, where the entire burden fell on individual households, the impact was much greater. Moreover, peasants saw little benefit in terms of a better future for their children. Hence, the number of rural dropouts began to rise. Parents who wanted to keep their children in school grew increasingly unhappy. Fees were assessed creatively, for items such as fresh flowers, watching students' bicycles, and being assigned a seat near the stove in winter. In one Shaanxi village whose education budget had fallen short, thousands of children were barred from classes when their parents could not pay an additional 50 yuan ($6) levy on top of the usual fees. In Guangdong, 1,000 people participated in a two-day protest against high tuition fees. Five people received jail sentences of up to ten years for incitement to riot.

Straitened educational budgets could be met by means other than raising fees, sometimes with disastrous consequences. In Jiangxi, more than 40 children died when the fireworks they were assembling to earn money for their elementary school exploded. In Gansu, education officials discovered that primary and high school children were traveling two hours each way to work in cotton fields for below-market wages that were paid to their school; in Anhui, students were required to pick tea; and a Guizhou school forced girls into prostitution.

Other problems contribute to the difficulties of remaining in school. Dilapidated buildings pose dangers to children, especially during the rainy season. While many of these structures are old, some are simply poorly constructed. Periodic earthquakes have destroyed many schools, killing hundreds of children, while surrounding buildings remained standing. Rebuilt, they fared no better in subsequent quakes. Bereaved parents demanded an investigation, staging angry protests when local authorities tried to cover up malfeasance rather than remove its causes.

Failure to meet safety standards has been alleged as the reason for closing a number of urban schools that serve the children of migrant workers. The children's parents suspect the real reason is that permanent residents of the neighborhoods in which the schools are located object to their presence. They argue that although the makeshift schools may be substandard, their children are not wanted in regular schools, and that an inferior education is preferable to no education at all.

Regional differences are important, with resources favoring eastern China over the country's western areas. There is also an economic divide. Academic pressures can be intense in more affluent urban areas, but in poor areas even key schools may not be popular. In some areas, the number of available places in senior high school is less than 40 percent of the number of students who enter junior high school. Since many of them see no realistic chance of continuing their education, dropout rates are high. Those who complete the program often prefer to apply to technical or specialist schools or teacher-training institutions, because the state will give them jobs after graduation.

When economic reforms made salaries in other professions more lucrative, teachers dropped out as well. Financial problems and poor working conditions were the primary reasons. The difficulties are most acute in schools run by rural communities. Wages are low, health allowances are inadequate, and teachers receive no bonuses or other subsidies. The Chinese press has lamented that it is therefore impossible for teachers to maintain normal living standards.

In addition to the disincentives of low pay, teachers have sometimes become the victims of vindictive parents. In Anhui, a student whose parents had been summoned to school because he was frequently late for class assaulted his teacher with a machete, inflicting serious injuries. In another area, a teacher who was accused of not having intervened quickly enough to stop a fight between two students received a large fine when one of them died. The teacher was forced to go into hiding after the parents threatened to kill him.

In 2006, a new policy allowed more than 50 million students in rural western areas of China to be exempt from paying tuition fees and incidental school fees. In the following year, the program was extended to 100 million more pupils, with the cost to be split between central and local governments according to the financial capacity of each. Given the parlous financial capacity of many local governments, the program has proved difficult to implement. A 2008 report found that over 85 percent of the counties it investigated had misappropriated funds, so that the added spending had not benefited students. Many schools were forced to operate on only 55 percent of their budgets, running up large debts. Back pay owed to teachers accounted for a significant proportion of these debts. Central government officials complained that lower levels had shown little commitment to the country's nine-year compulsory education law.

A final factor contributing to the high dropout rate stems from teachers concentrating their attention on those students deemed most likely to pass the entrance exams at the expense of those who are less academically promising. Believing that they are regarded as backward, these students may lose their self-esteem, begin to cut classes, and eventually cease to attend altogether. The children of migrant laborers are particularly discriminated against. Again, the State Education Commission recognizes the problem and has urged schools to pay attention to the needs of all students rather than just those of a select few. The results have been indifferent: there are more immediate pressures on urban schools to have their best and brightest students pass the university entrance exams.

Sometimes, these pressures take the form of teacher-assisted cheating. The incentive for teachers and officials may be financial—they are paid for their services. Money is not always the issue, however: the percentage of exam-passers is one criterion in the evaluation of teachers' job performance, and they want to look better in the eyes of their superiors. A series of scandals showed a variety of methods, ranging from the obvious—teachers selling answers or agreeing to change already posted grades for a fee—to the high-technology ingenious. In Beijing, invigilators had the areas around test-taking centers checked for abnormal radio waves, and the central China city of Luoyang hired a drone to detect radios that were broadcasting answers. The authorities announced that those caught up in such schemes would be charged with theft of state secrets and sentenced to seven years in jail. Opinion polls reveal that clever cheats often receive the respect of their peers, with students commenting that such cheating is a kind of ability. In Hubei, educators who imposed strict measures to prevent cheating were attacked by students and their parents, who argued that since the practice was so widespread, not being allowed to do it constituted an unfair penalty against them.

Some cities have instituted fingerprint scanners to detect those who hire others to take exams for them, paying several thousands of dollars to the substitute. Similar amounts have been quoted for purchasing admission slips to university, with the higher end price being required for the more selective institutions. Parents can, and occasionally have, protested against these illegal practices, but most do not, since they fear retaliation against their child. In some cases, connections rather than money appear to be decisive. In one widely publicized instance, the website of Shanghai's prestigious Jiaotong University accidentally posted the names of high-ranking officials who had supported the applications of students who had been accepted.

Geography also plays a role in admissions: A 2012 study revealed that top-ranked Beijing University has 100 times more students from the capital than from Guangdong and Anhui provinces. Shanghai's most prestigious university, Fudan, enrolls 274 more students from that city than from Shandong province, even though Shandong's population is four times that of Shanghai. Efforts to change this have been strongly resisted by people in areas that were advantaged by the previous admissions policy,

Study abroad is popular, although only one-third of those who choose to do so return. Those who do not are criticized for depriving the country's modernization effort of their skills—in effect, biting the hand that fed them. China's brain drain has been called the worst in the world, although it may be only temporary. As wages and working conditions in China rise, returning home may become a more attractive option. The government has established science parks in selected areas, offering seed money and tax incentives for start-up ventures to encourage the return of talented nationals. The establishment of such centers has, however, exacerbated another problem: the brain drain out of Chinese provinces where such incentives do not exist and toward cities, such as Beijing and Shanghai, where they do.

In the past, the matter of state-assigned jobs for university graduates caused considerable friction between students and state authorities. In 1987, more than 5,000 of 360,000 graduates were rejected by their designated employers, and the government abolished the system of guaranteed job assignments for new graduates. From the students' point of view, there were advantages and disadvantages to this: one might be assigned to a remote area and/or be given responsibilities different from those one had trained for, but one was at least guaranteed a job. Officials defended the change, saying it would ensure that supply met demand. Under the previous system, too few students had elected specializations, such as English, computer software, accounting, and civil engineering, for which there was a need. And too many had opted for history and basic science, fields in which there were many more qualified people than openings.

Two years later, the government reversed itself, saying that completely free competition for jobs was "still not a suitable option for China." Students had spent so much time during their senior year looking for jobs that their academic performance suffered. Moreover, if the state assigned graduates to jobs, it could be more confident that they went where the demand was greatest. During the period when the self-found job system was in force, increasingly larger numbers of students, even those who had rural origins themselves, had chosen to stay in urban areas. The education minister also candidly admitted that allowing students to find their own jobs had caused a marked increase in corruption and favoritism. Although the minister did not say so, transferring the responsibility for job assignments back to the state would have the effect of transferring the focus of corruption back to the state as well. Another, likewise unspoken, reason that the state took over the job-assignment system again was to control student behavior.

A few years later, the state returned the responsibility for finding work to the students themselves, reviving familiar problems. The need to locate one's own employment reintroduced problems of favoritism in awarding jobs and reluctance to go to where one's talents were most needed. The feeling among students and intellectuals that the government was unresponsive to their difficulties was an important factor in the demonstrations at Tiananmen Square and elsewhere in China during the spring of 1989. Indeed, the immediate precipitant of the protests was the rumor that former first party secretary Hu Yaobang had died after suffering a heart attack in an argument with a leading leftist over the education budget. The demonstrators' agenda included the establishment of a student union that would allow them influence over an educational establishment which they perceived as being badly in need of change.

The government's suppression of the protests was followed by restrictive measures to ensure that the educational system produced "trustworthy Marxists" loyal to party and government. Student activists were apprehended and given lengthy prison terms. The internal management system of the entire educational system, from primary schools through university-level institutions in major cities, was reformed to give greater influence to party committees. Mandatory military training was instituted, as it had been, for a brief period, following the student demonstrations of 1986/1987. In the case of Beijing and Fudan universities, this training, which included political study sessions in addition to marching and drills, took the entire freshman year. Applications to these institutions dropped so precipitously that in 1993 the military training requirement was dropped.

At the same time, professors' pay was raised. When privatization of housing was instituted a few years later, professors were given the opportunity to buy their living quarters, most of them conveniently located on campus, at a fraction of their market value. Improved social status assuaged many of the grievances the professors had protested against. Gradually, the mood of distrust between students and their professors with party and government leaders abated.

In 1994, the government began a plan to have university students finance their own education. By 2000, all students had to pay tuition fees, and they would also be able to find their own jobs. The expected problems arose. Although the fees were initially quite modest—under $1,000 dollars a year—they were beyond the means of about 10 percent of students. Universities and colleges were told to allocate 10 percent of tuition fees to provide scholarships for poor students, but this provision fell short of what was needed. Numerous sad stories concerning lack of money for these fees appeared: A desperate father who could not pay his son's tuition fees committed suicide, as did an ill mother, knowing that the family could not afford to pay for both her medical bills and her child's education. These fees impact students differently, since the highest ranked universities receive state funding that allows them to charge lower tuition fees.

For those who wanted a college degree but were unwilling, or unable, to spend the time or money to attend an institution of higher learning, forged degrees could be purchased. In one widely publicized instance, the education documents submitted by *all* the applicants for a local government vacancy were found to be forged. Those involved took considerable risks: Forgery is punishable by up to ten years in prison; sellers are treated as accomplices. In order to raise money, some universities, or individual departments thereof, spun off subsidiary institutions, promising that graduates would receive the same degrees as regular students even though admission standards were not as high. In 2006, there were protests, some of them quite unruly, when students discovered that their diplomas were not what they had been promised. These protests were eventually defused through such methods as offering to refund tuition fees or to accommodate the students in other programs.

It is difficult to tell how widespread these practices are, and one should be wary of generalizing on the basis of a few highly publicized examples. Most Chinese schools, though extremely spartan in terms of equipment and creature comforts, are not hazardous to their inhabitants' lives. Most teachers do not assist their students to cheat, and neither they nor their students must fear for their lives. Despite the obstacles to academic success, some motivated rural children manage to enter even the most prestigious universities and distinguish themselves in professional careers, and most students probably resist the temptation to cheat. But there is a consensus that the system is not functioning properly.

Plans for improvement continue, although progress has been slow. In 1993, the head of China's State Education Commission described the four major problems in basic-level education as insufficient funding, arrears in teachers' wages, dropouts, and the illegal charging of school fees; 25 years later, the same issues remain priorities. Some ameliorative work has been undertaken. Guangzhou has given favorable development opportunities to privately run locally organized and legally registered schools. Shanghai's migrant children's schools are fully supported by the city's education commission. Private or semi-private funds, such as Project Hope, to which Chinese and foreigners are invited to contribute, have enabled a number of dropouts to return to school, though corruption has short-changed those poor students who so badly need help.

Because of the demand for low-wage labor, rural dropouts can leave for factory jobs in the cities, thus relieving pressure from farmers for better educational opportunities. At the same time however, critics claim, China is being deprived of an important reservoir of potential talent that could help the country reach its goal of becoming the world's leading information technology center by the mid-twenty-first century. They are also concerned that, as China moves up the value-added chain of production, it will need better educated workers, who are not being trained in sufficient numbers under the current system.

Expanding vocational training seemed to hold promise: In 1996, then-premier Li Peng expressed the hope that such training would help stem the falling literacy rate in certain rural areas. However, the plan proved unpopular with students despite employment rates exceeding 90 percent for graduates due to the widespread attitudes that those with blue-collar jobs are of lower *suzhi*, or quality. Given a choice between attending a third-tier university and vocational training, the great majority chose the former; as of 2013, only 4 percent of post-high school students were in vocational institutions.

Several major revisions in the basic educational system have been attempted, with less than satisfactory results. A two-stage program to improve rural education began in 2000. Schools were to be repaired or rebuilt, classes set up to upgrade teachers' skills, and books were to be supplied free of charge. School fees were waived for children from poor families. In 2002, the State Council ordered county governments to take over from township and village governments the responsibility of providing nine years of compulsory education. Observers pointed out that corruption could siphon off funds meant for these improvements and that the success of the reform was dependent on the uncertain goodwill and diligence of county governments. Distance learning was also proposed, though skeptics observed that neither students nor teachers in the rural areas that were most in need of help had ever touched a computer. Even were they able to, electricity costs, which can be three times those of urban areas, would make the cost of using the computers prohibitive. The large number of shoddily built schools that have collapsed in earthquakes indicated the deficiencies of the school repair program; several of the rebuilt schools were no safer, collapsing again in later earthquakes.

A plan approved by the State Council in 2010 aimed to solve many of the same issues which the 2000 plan should have resolved. By 2020, the urban–rural gap in education is to be narrowed, teachers' skills upgraded, sturdier schools constructed, and corruption eliminated. At least 90 percent of middle school graduates will attend high school, and the average citizen will receive 11.2 years of education. There was considerable public skepticism about whether these goals would be achieved. The government claimed to have admitted 21.3 percent more students from poor rural areas to universities in 2016, but it will be several years before the efficacy of the reform can be assessed.

At the second-city level, Chinese data show a widening urban–rural education gap. Whereas Beijing's labor force has an upper secondary school attainment rate of 71 percent, and Shanghai's is 58 percent, Guangxi's and Guizhou's are only 19 and 15 percent, respectively.

In response to complaints about the corruption involved in getting children accepted into prestige schools, the government in 2006 required schools to post their fees on government websites and ordered an end to the distinction between key schools and ordinary schools. An educational expert commented that since everyone knows the many ways around publicly posted fee schedules as well as which schools have the highest rates of admission to higher level institutions, he expected both directives to be ignored. A recent study found that schools operated beyond the control of the central government, quoting one headmaster as saying, "Policy is one thing and implementation is quite another."

Another major innovation aims at encouraging creativity and teaching children to think for themselves. This is to include livelier textbooks and new teaching methods designed to encourage dialogue between pupils and instructors. Implementation will entail changes in the entire educational culture. Both teachers and parents have expressed strong preferences for strict classroom discipline, with rigorous homework assignments. Critics also worry that teaching children to challenge authority in the classroom will encourage a dangerous culture of dissent in society at large. Those who are being taught to challenge their teachers while children may, as adults, feel free to challenge the party, government, police, and judges.

Teachers who ask how to reconcile the conflicting pressures of teaching children to think creatively at the same time that they are urging respect for authority are advised to use "one soft hand, one hard." Although catchy, the slogan is difficult to put into practice. Moreover, as long as college entrance exams emphasize rote learning, teachers will continue to prepare their students by emphasizing rote learning. Allowing the examination system to be supplemented by letters of recommendation, so that one's future does not depend on rote memory answers on a single test, has been proposed. However, opponents argue that this would simply compound existing problems of corruption and favoritism to the children of the wealthy and well connected.

Provincial educational authorities restricted the plan's provision for more freedom of choice in textbooks in order to protect provincial publishing houses. Educational reform also included consolidation of universities, since the previous system had encouraged a plethora of low-level facilities with overlapping departments and too many narrow disciplines. Between 1992 and 2000, 490 universities and colleges were merged into 204. While redundancy may have been reduced, other problems were created. An analysis conducted by the Chinese Academy of Social Sciences revealed that the newly consolidated universities launched a number of large building projects, on the grounds that they would have to accommodate more students. Some of the projects, however, involved construction of less necessary facilities like golf courses and guest houses. Many universities ran up huge debts, with most of their income then being spent on paying the interest thereon rather than on improving the quality of education. In China's western and central regions, local governments are legally required to reserve limited education funds for primary and secondary schools, compounding the debt problems of universities located in those areas.

General agreement exists that the PRC's universities are still far from the world-class institutions they aspire to be. Still, some progress has been made. The 2018 Times Higher Education World University Ranking list included 7 Chinese universities among its top 200, up from just two in past years. Even so, only two were in the top 50: Beida (Beijing University) at 27th and Tsinghua at 30th. Rating agencies typically put heavy weight on research output in assigning scores, leading critics to charge that the government is gaming the system in a way that alters the mission of the university from an educational institution to a factory producing what the rankings reward, with quantity of publications prized over quality.

Pressure to produce scientific breakthroughs may be a factor in the sharp increase in fraud and plagiarism cases in the academic community. A number of researchers and administrators were found to have falsified their academic backgrounds. Experts estimated that about 90 percent of research papers and scientific projects were flawed, for reasons ranging from plagiarism to overstatement of the significance of the research. In one case, a dean at one of China's most eminent universities was discovered to have falsely claimed that he invented a computer chip; in another, university administrators were found to be covering up a case of blatant plagiarism lest the reputation of the institution be adversely affected.

With quantity seemingly taking precedence over quality, there were concerns that the goal of the PRC becoming a world leader in scientific innovation might be sacrificed. China's most renowned scientist, Qian Xuesen, complained to then-premier Wen Jiabao that not a single university had come up with an innovative mechanism to nurture inventions in science and technology. Lacking an innovative way of teaching, he continued, it was not surprising that they had not produced world-class talent. Several programs are attempting to address these issues. The 863 program, named for its establishment in March 1986, allocated several hundred billion dollars to nine key technological fields that include bio-, laser, and marine technology. Project 211 aims at raising the research standards of 117 Chinese universities in the twenty-first century, and Project 985 provided funding to an elite group of nine universities to build research centers, upgrade facilities, hire world-class faculty, and send Chinese scholars abroad. Thirty more universities, funded somewhat less generously, were later added.

In terms of university entrance, there is much criticism of the gaokao. Although it continues to emphasize rote learning rather than analytical skills, a number of changes have been instituted. Under a pilot program introduced in 2017, students will no longer be required to choose either liberal arts or science subjects. They will continue to be tested in Chinese, math and English, but can choose the topics of the other three subjects from among six electives, such as chemistry, history, and politics.

With the expansion of universities that began in 1999, about 22 percent of the PRC's college-age population now attends universities; the government hopes to increase this to 40 percent by 2020. The question remains whether the economy will be able to absorb the larger number of degree holders. When they began graduating in 2003, the larger number of college graduates had more trouble finding suitable jobs, and salaries were lower for many of those who did. Approximately one-third remain unemployed, while others toil at low-wage jobs where their skills are unused. According to data collected by the Chinese Academy of Social Sciences, the earnings of college graduates are now on a par with or even lower than those of migrant workers. Universities appear to have resorted to ruses to disguise the high unemployment rate of their students by, for example, requiring that they present proof that they have obtained a job before their graduation certificate can be issued.

Employers have complained that many do not have the skills they should have: the rapid expansion of the system meant that less academically qualified students appeared on campuses where the facilities were inadequate for their needs and well-qualified professors were not available to teach them. Students began to joke about being cabbages, vegetables known for their low price. A few committed suicide; others, referred to as the ant tribe, clustered together in low-rent fringe districts of major cities, causing government officials to worry about social instability in those areas.

The image of universities as venues for the free exchange of ideas has also been inhibited by Xi Jinping's concern with conformity to his interpretation of socialist ideology. While the motivation is clearly to avoid the social instability that might accompany the clash of ideas, the imposition of ideological rigidity would seem directly counter to the desire to teach students to think creatively. In 2017, university leaders were told that they must become "socialist states-men" who persevere in building their institutions into bastions of socialism and against the spread of Western values. Those universities who are perceived as insufficiently ideologically rigorous are to be shamed, with observers being sent to nearly 2,600 universities to monitor their mandatory ideology classes. Those who speak out have had their classes canceled and are liable to lose their jobs. At the same time, the government's National Social Science Fund has underwritten increasing numbers of projects on Marxism and party history (see Figure 10.2).

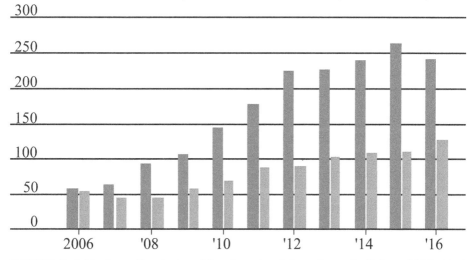

FIGURE 10.2 Projects Funded on Marxism–Leninism, Party-building, 2006–2016

Following the conclusion of the CCP's Nineteenth Party Congress, universities in many parts of China founded centers for the study of Xi Jinping thought, as educators quietly raised concerns about the chilling effect on academic discourse.

Conclusions

The twists and turns of China's educational policies over the past five decades have been costly. Arguments between those who favor emphasis on political studies and a broadly egalitarian system vis-à-vis those who would prefer to emphasize technical specialization and are comfortable with a more elitist system have consumed precious time and creative energies, and caused much bitterness. Rampant plagiarism, corruption, and exorbitant schools fees and surcharges continue to exist despite efforts to curb them.

Nonetheless, the PRC's educational system has succeeded in changing a literacy rate of 25 percent to one that exceeds 90 percent, a significant achievement. Some skepticism is in order, since counties told to reduce illiteracy by a certain date may simply report that they have done so, whether or not residents have actually learned to read. Moreover, standards for literacy can vary widely, with the lower end, in rural villages, reportedly being as little as the ability to recognize the characters for the numbers from one to ten. Some of those who pass more stringent character identification tests become illiterate again because they do not read for long periods of time. To its dismay, the government also discovered a resurgence in the use of local dialects. A national survey revealed that 47 percent of the population could not communicate in the national language. Moreover, the average educational level is 5.6 years nationwide, indicating that even though most people have learned to read, they do not possess a very high level of literacy. Only two-thirds of students complete primary school.

Although local governments spend as much as half of their budgets on education, they still impose tuition fees that are high enough for 4 million children to drop out each year because their families cannot afford to pay. A study by the Chinese Academy of Social Sciences found that spending on education ranked sixth on a list of serious public concerns and that school bills consumed over 10 percent of the average household budget.

Progress is unevenly distributed. Urban students are more than twice as likely to attend secondary school, and richer provinces spend 50 percent more per student than poorer ones. The gap between the western part of the country and other areas is even greater. Especially in rural areas, males are more likely to be literate than females, and Han Chinese are more likely to be educated compared to ethnic minorities. Ninety-two percent of China's illiterates live in rural areas, 70 percent of them women. The illiteracy rate in Tibet is nearly 50 percent.

Academics blame the deficiencies of the PRC's educational system for China's poor showing in international competitiveness. The World Economic Forum's Global Competitiveness Report for 2016/2017 ranked China's education and training at 74th of the 135 countries it reported on, citing the educational level of the population as one of the major problematic factors of doing business there.

The red-versus-expert debate in education has been resolved in the sense that the value of expertise is now acknowledged, but it continues in the sense of post-Mao reforms having produced a markedly pro-urban and elitist system that many Chinese find disturbing, and that has the potential for creating social unrest. Social stratification, they fear, is becoming solidified and may trigger class conflict, just as Marx predicted. The leveling effect of education is being lost: rural children, or those whose parents lack the requisite money and connections to enter them in prestigious elementary education facilities, are immediately disadvantaged. With poor teachers and inadequate resources, they cannot study well; thus, they lose interest and drop out. Having little or no education, they cannot escape poverty, and the PRC is deprived of some of its potentially brightest minds. At the same time, officials continue to be concerned that the educational system lacks the ability to attract the best and brightest intellects and provide them with an atmosphere in which their talents can be nurtured.

In 2016 China spent a little over 4 percent of GDP on education, somewhat more than in previous years yet significantly below the 6 percent of GDP that the 34 countries comprising the Organization for Economic Cooperation and Development (OECD) spend.

The leadership is aware that an inadequate educational system will hinder the country's economic development. It continues to try to create the kind of widely available and academically excellent system that will support continued economic development while simultaneously instilling loyalty to party and government, and maintaining social stability.

Suggestions for Further Reading

David Goodman, "China's Universities and Social Change: Expectations, Aspirations, and Consequences," *Mexico y La Cuenta del Pacifica*, September–December 2015, pp. 19–38.

David Moser, *A Billion Voices: Language Reform in China* (London: Penguin, 2016).

Dennis Normile, "One in Three Chinese Children Faces an Education Apocalypse," *Science*, vol. 357, no. 6357 (September 2017), pp. 1226–1230.

Terry Woronov, *Class Work: Vocational Schools and Chinese Urban Youth* (Stanford, CA: Stanford University Press 2016).

Linxiu Zhang et al., "The Human Capital Costs of the Middle Income Trap: The Case of China," *International Association of Agricultural Economics*, Vol. 44, supplement 2012, pp. 151–162.

CHAPTER 11

Quality-of-life Issues
Health, Demography, and the Environment

The health of China's population is important not only in terms of the government's commitment to its people's well-being but also to the ability of the people to enhance economic development. Good health is a factor in good productivity and, conversely, poor health contributes to poor productivity. Reducing infant mortality and lowering death rates may, however, cause problems of overpopulation: There are simply too many people among whom to divide the fruits of economic development. Moreover, a large population uses more resources and also creates more waste, leading to pollution and environmental degradation. Hence, the issues of health, demography, and the environment are closely intertwined not only with each other but also with economic prosperity. With varying degrees of intensity over time, all have been of considerable concern to party and government.

Health

China's medical system was in very bad condition when the communist party took power in 1949. It was not unusual for hundreds of thousands to die in widespread natural disasters, such as floods, droughts, and earthquakes, which were then followed by epidemics and famines. Most people had little understanding of the value of sanitation procedures. Infant mortality was very high, as was the incidence of infectious, parasitic, and hereditary diseases.

There were a few bright spots in this dismal picture. The Kuomintang government founded a national health administration in the late 1920s, and health programs were an important part of the government's plans for rural reconstruction. China also had a number of missionary hospitals, jointly staffed by foreign and foreign-trained Chinese personnel. A few medical schools were set up in China as well. A grant from the Rockefeller Foundation made possible the establishment of Peking Union Medical College, which, among other activities, did research on the causes of China's most devastating diseases. The reports left by health care workers during the republican era provide vivid insights into the frustrations experienced by this relatively small group of medically trained personnel trying to function in a vast countryside of ignorance and superstition.

Commendable as these efforts were, they were mere drops in an ocean of need, and had, in any case, been adversely affected by the decades of fighting the Sino–Japanese War and Chinese civil wars. Most Chinese did not have access to modern medical facilities even where they did exist. Traditional Chinese medicine should be credited with impressive achievements. Acupuncture has many admirers in developed countries, and some herbal medicines have proved to be astonishingly effective. Many others, however, have at best a placebo effect. Diseases scarcely known in more developed countries ravaged millions of people. One example is schistosomiasis, a disease caused by the liver fluke. Using the snails that inhabit waterways and rice paddies as its intermediary, the parasite slowly devours the internal organs of its victims and, if not properly treated, causes a prolonged and extremely painful death. It impacted one in ten persons south of the Yangtze River in the first half of the twentieth century. Kala-azar disease, which attacks the liver and spleen, affected more than half a million persons, most of them in north China. It is spread by sandflies and reaches humans through the dogs on which the flies live.

The communist government, though determined to improve this situation, had limited resources to draw on and many other pressing problems. During 1949/1950, only 1 percent of total government expenditure was allocated to health care; during the subsequent five years, it never exceeded 2.6 percent. A three-pronged strategy was adopted. First, the emphasis was to be on preventive rather than curative medicine. Second, traditional Chinese medicine was to be employed where it was deemed useful. And third, medical education was to be established at different academic levels and supplemented by large numbers of paramedics. These approaches reflected practical considerations that were well suited to the People's Republic of China's (PRCs) resources. Teams were sent out to investigate the country's health problems and, where possible, administer treatment. Certain diseases were targeted for special attention. Venereal disease, bubonic (black) plague, and malaria were treated for free. Other treatments were not free, but efforts were made to set the costs at affordable levels.

The techniques of mass mobilization were employed in health care as in other areas. In 1952, the first "patriotic public health campaign" began, with the goal of teaching tens of millions of people the link between sanitation and good health. Lantern slides, posters, and theatrical performances spread the word. Mass movements were organized to clear away huge quantities of garbage, often the accumulation of many years. People were instructed to kill mosquitoes and rats, with quotas established for the number to be killed and turned in. This campaign had its frustrations, as when cadres discovered that some people were raising rats and nurturing insects in order to more easily meet their quotas. But positive results outweighed such disappointing episodes, and genuine progress was made. Patriotic public health campaigns became collective clean-up efforts for a week each spring and fall.

Prior to 1949, peasant families often lived together with, or in very close proximity to, their cattle, pigs, and chickens. Dilapidated animal shelters and manure pits were common sights in rural villages. Government teams ordered or cajoled villagers to set up public latrines. Since manure was valued as a fertilizer, more people were resistant to this form of communism than one might think. Peasants were taught to put stone walls beneath the latrines, so that excrement would not pollute the drinking water supply through seepage into underground streams. They were also told how long waste matter should stay in the latrines before it could be used as fertilizer in the fields.

The mass-campaign technique was also employed against specific diseases. For example, people were first informed about how schistosomiasis spread and then mobilized to drain the water of affected ponds and ditches and turn over the earth. They were advised to kill the snails by burning them with matches or pouring boiling water over them rather than touching the creatures. Drugs were supplied to those already infected with schistosomiasis. Although harsh, they succeeded in reducing the number of sufferers.

Considerable effort was devoted to draining swamps where malaria-carrying mosquitoes bred. This, too, met with resistance: peasants in some areas were reluctant to disturb the local deities whom they believed to reside in the marshes. As for kala-azar disease, the government ordered dogs to be removed from urban areas and their numbers were greatly reduced in the countryside. Insecticides were employed against the sandflies that had lived on the dogs, and drugs were provided for those who had kala-azar.

Another major focus of post-1949 health programs was infant mortality. Maternal and child health stations were established, and midwives were instructed to boil their instruments before using them. Traditionally, the midwife would either bite off the umbilical cord or sever it with an unclean knife, placing a piece of dung or unsterile cloth over the cut. Hence, the relatively simple and inexpensive techniques of sterilization introduced by party health workers greatly reduced the number of deaths from tetanus and childbirth fever.

Initial efforts produced impressive results, though the cyclical nature of mass campaigns did not provide the kind of sustained effort needed for effective disease control. In addition, despite the Chinese Communist Party (CCP)'s commitment to ameliorate peasants' lives, the majority of China's health care facilities were located in urban areas. Even the more modern urban hospitals were dirty by Western standards. Another problem was that medicine was in short supply. During the first decade of the PRC, the government's emphasis was on Western medicine, though traditional remedies continued to be used. For many people, traditional medicines were the drug of choice; others opted to use both types of remedy at once.

As part of its commitment to "walking on two legs," meaning the traditional and the modern, the Great Leap Forward attempted to raise Chinese medicine to equal status with that of the West. Although tremendous successes were claimed for the large-scale reintroduction of old remedies, they must be evaluated in the general context of the hyperbolic rhetoric of the Great Leap period. The Leap's slogan "More, better, faster, and cheaper" did little to improve the quality of medical care, and the famines that followed the collapse of its policies caused untold numbers of deaths as millions starved or succumbed to diseases from which better-nourished people normally recover.

When economic conditions began to improve in 1962, health care improved as well, at least in the cities. In 1965, as the country was approaching the Cultural Revolution, Mao Zedong issued a scathing denunciation of the system: China's 500 million peasants were suffering while medical "gentlemen" lived in comfort in the cities. The focus of health care must shift to rural areas. Those who worked there need not have studied medicine for many years, nor could villages afford such people. Even junior high school students could be trained in basic procedures, and learn while on the job. The system hastened to comply with the chairman's strongly populist message. Nonetheless, in most ways, the Cultural Revolution was not good for health care. One consequence of the chaos in party and government institutions was that little attention was paid to patriotic sanitation campaigns, regular inoculations, and the extermination of mosquitoes. Disruptions to rail services meant that medical supplies might not reach their intended destinations. A major cholera epidemic broke out in 1967, the first in many years. The Cultural Revolution's virulently anti-specialist attitudes also resulted in health care experts being forced to spend many hours doing manual labor, reducing the time they could spend on patient care. Some elitist research projects continued: During the height of the revolution's frenzy, Chinese doctors announced that they had successfully synthesized insulin, a first in world medical history. Many doctors were, however, sent to the countryside for varying periods of time. This might have improved the quality of rural medical care, as Mao had wanted. Unfortunately, the doctors sent out to the countryside were frequently not allowed to practice medicine but were ordered to perform tasks designed to teach humility, such as slopping pigs or cleaning out latrines.

By far the best-known contribution of the Cultural Revolution to health care was the institution of "barefoot doctors." Neither barefoot nor physicians, they were actually a corps of paramedics with perhaps three to six months' training in relatively simple but commonly needed medical techniques. Following their training, the new barefoot doctors were expected to improve their qualifications with on-the-job experience supplemented by such additional training courses as might be made available. Certain barefoot doctors attained skill levels far beyond those generally associated with paramedics and were able to perform operations that included appendectomies and caesarean sections.

The barefoot doctors generally worked as part of a cooperative medical system set up by the production brigade to serve its members. Because the central and provincial governments gave very little financial support to rural medical care, most medical costs were paid by individuals, families, or the collective. Members of a production brigade could choose whether or not to have a cooperative medical plan. If the answer were yes, each brigade member paid a small fee of a few yuan a year, and the brigade welfare fund subsidized the rest. Cooperative health plans differed widely in what they covered; generally speaking, prosperous brigades paid a higher percentage of the costs for a wider variety of illnesses. When brigades decided not to have a cooperative medical plan—nearly always because they were too poor to do so—the patient had to pay the entire cost of visits to the barefoot doctor, drugs, and hospital costs. Serious imbalances therefore occurred in the medical insurance system, since the best coverage generally belonged to those who least needed it.

Particularly in rural areas, this system changed markedly with the dissolution of the commune system in the early 1980s. Collective medical insurance plans disappeared along with the collectives, and the number of barefoot doctors declined sharply. The emphasis of the health care system shifted from preventing illness toward treatment after the patient became ill. Many barefoot doctors were required to contract for farmland along with anyone else who was classified as a rural resident. Some became the equivalent of private practitioners, charging a fee for their services and taking a profit on the medicines they dispensed. The official media began to complain that unqualified people in rural and urban areas alike were pretending to be doctors and charging exorbitant fees for bogus treatments and fake medicines. The fake medicines were sometimes not mere placebos but actually dangerous to the user.

The government's attempts to clamp down had marginal results. For example, in 2001, after nearly 200,000 Chinese died from bogus or tainted medications, it closed down half of the country's pharmaceutical factories for turning out substandard products. But the problems continued unabated. Concerns spread beyond the PRC when exported foods, drugs, and even toys began killing citizens abroad. Milk powder containing melamine, which mimics protein in quality testing, caused kidney failure in the children who ingested it. Although those found guilty were executed, the problem returned two years later: The milk powder had been taken off the market but not destroyed. Repackaged, it reappeared on store shelves and, in a 2016 case, a student died after being treated with a bogus cancer treatment advertised on Baidu, China's largest search engine.

Another distinctly negative effect of the reforms was the return of diseases scarcely heard of in the PRC for decades. Hepatitis, plague, and schistosomiasis reappeared, as did syphilis. When owning pet dogs became a symbol of prosperity, rabies returned as well. Other diseases recurred because children were no longer being regularly immunized. Separate polls revealed that a leading concern of both workers and peasants was getting sick.

The previous state medical care system, modest as it was, had cost the state excessive amounts of money. Government efforts to make hospitals more self-reliant caused health care costs to rise by 20 percent and more each year from the 1990s onward, far in excess of the increase in gross domestic product (GDP). Because hospitals were forbidden to raise fees for services, they covered the shortfalls in their budgets by overprescribing medicines and tests to patients who were covered by their enterprises. Since the enterprises were also now expected to be self-reliant, some ran out of money to even pay their workers, much less cover their medical costs. Cash-strapped hospitals turned away patients who could not pay deposit fees, sometimes with fatal results. Riots have broken out when news spreads that a person has died after being refused treatment.

Patients, too, can be motivated by materialistic motives. If the sick person cannot be completely cured or dies, she or her survivors may insist on financial compensation, even when there has been no apparent malpractice. They may threaten the staff with bodily harm and sometimes carry out such threats. Several thousand personal are injured each year, with millions of yuan of medical facilities destroyed. The government acknowledges the gravity of the medical situation. Nearly half of the millions of Chinese who live below the poverty line were put there by catastrophic medical expenses. The average age of the population is rising, and older people typically have greater health needs than the young. Hence, greater demands for medical services are expected at the same time that fewer working people are available to pay the costs.

During the 1990s, there was a precipitous rise in the use of narcotics—again, something that had been essentially eradicated in the 1950s. The mass media reminded people of the events surrounding the Opium War of 1840 and pointed out the deleterious effects that drug use had, not only for individuals and their families but also for the strength of the country internationally. Despite stiff new penalties, drug use continued to spread. Starting from Yunnan province, which borders Southeast Asia's Golden Triangle, drugs were brought into China by local ethnic minorities whose communications networks spread the drugs throughout the provinces. Secret societies (see Chapter 2), which, like narcotics, were believed to have been eradicated after 1949, reappeared as well and became heavily involved in the drug trade. An internal ministry of public security document noted that among the numerous gangs involved, the Triad society had been particularly successful in bribing officials to ignore their activities.

The same gangs who control narcotics are involved in prostitution, another revival from the ill-remembered days before 1949, and one that also facilitates the transmission of AIDS. Although prostitution is a crime according to the central government, some local governments view it as a source of revenue: bar girls pay taxes on their supposedly illegal activities. According to one survey, less than 6 percent use condoms. Drug use and unprotected sex account for only part of the spread of AIDS. Unsanitary methods of blood donation are a major contributing factor: so-called bloodheads pay desperately poor people to donate blood, centrifuge the pooled blood of many people to separate the components they want, and then return the leftover pooled portion to donors. Thus, the AIDS virus, as well as hepatitis and other diseases, quickly spread. In one of the most heavily impacted areas, Wanshou village in rural Henan, the infection rate exceeded 65 percent. County officials, behaving much like bureaucrats in traditional China, tried to conceal the epidemic. In this case, they were abetted by the central government, which arrested several individuals who were trying to educate the population on how the disease is contracted and what measures they can take to protect themselves. Officially, 700,000 Chinese are HIV infected, although there is massive underreporting from local areas, and World Health Organization experts believe the number may be ten times as high.

Similar attempts to conceal the outbreak of severe acute respiratory syndrome (SARS) in 2003 allowed the virulent disease to spread both within China and to foreign countries, causing hundreds of deaths. In addition, lack of attention to developing safety standards for the workplace has resulted in a high incidence of occupation-related accidents. The burgeoning "floating population," now officially said to be 280 million persons, presents another challenge to health care. The spread of disease among migrants is facilitated by limited incomes that force many of them to live in crowded, unsanitary accommodations and perform dirty jobs. As noted above, problems with drugs and AIDS are growing, as are environmentally related diseases. The incidence of traffic accidents has increased with the number of cars: More than 600 people die each day on the PRC's roads.

Chinese sources complain that the newly prosperous are increasingly consuming rich foods, exercising less, and smoking and drinking more. The leading causes of death have indeed shifted away from infectious diseases such as dysentery and cholera and toward a pattern more like those of developed countries. By the late 1990s, cancer claimed more lives than any other disease, with China accounting for a quarter of the world's total. Lung cancer is the most common sort—pollution is one important factor, although smoking is the major cause. The government estimates that it kills over a million Chinese a year, either directly or indirectly: nearly two-thirds of adult males are regular smokers. Health authorities understand the risk, but efforts to discourage smoking are inhibited by the fact that revenue from cigarette sales is important, and provides jobs for large numbers of people. Bans on smoking in public places in a few large cities are widely ignored. Government-owned tobacco companies support scores of elementary schools, even advertising their products therein. According to one message, tobacco helps one to become successful, presumably by enabling better concentration when studying.

Despite increased central government expenditures on health, totaling 5.5 percent of GDP, people complain that coverage remains woefully inadequate. Hospitals have resisted implementing new regulations and, despite the zero-profit policy on drugs, corruption, overprescribing for kickbacks remain.

City dwellers, particularly those who work for state-owned enterprises, are more likely to have adequate, as opposed to basic, coverage. Wealthier areas have introduced "smart cards," allowing users to simply swipe them for immediate insurance payment, being responsible for any remaining costs themselves. The more prosperous increasingly seek medical care in foreign countries.

In many rural areas, however, health care remains rudimentary: the urban bias in health care which Mao Zedong railed against continues to exist. The World Health Organization rates Chinese health care 126th out of the 191 nations it evaluates, but as 188th in fairness of distribution. As announced in 2009, the aim is to provide affordable and equitable basic health care for all by 2020. By 2017, the basic health insurance systems for rural and non-working urban residents had been merged, though government sources admitted that subsidies for basic public health services remain inadequate, that too many people in rural areas lack convenient access to medical facilities, and that more work must be done on disease prevention programs. Medical practitioners must be motivated, and improvements in doctor–patient interactions are needed.

Improvements continue: "one-stop" health care settlements are being established for impoverished households, and in 2015 a serious disease insurance scheme was introduced. According to Xi Jinping, basic medical insurance was available to over 95 percent of the population by the end of 2016.

Problems notwithstanding, as of 2016, the average life expectancy at birth in China is 76.5, on a par with most developed countries, markedly above the mid-fifties life spans in many sub-Saharan African states, although several years below that of the world's longest-lived people, the Japanese, at 83.

Demography

Confucius considered a large population a sign of prosperity and contentment: an indication that the mandate of heaven lay securely on the dynasty. In addition, the Confucian family system encouraged the idea of large families. Imperial bureaucrats were also in favor of large populations, since more people would mean increased tax revenues. Thus, the government considered it important to keep an accurate population count. China conducted its first census in 2 A.D.; other censuses took place at irregular intervals thereafter. The population remained remarkably stable for over 1,000 years, fluctuating between 37 million and 60 million in response to the presence or absence of natural disasters.

Starting from the early years of the Ming dynasty in the fourteenth century, China began a period of six centuries of population growth. Originally encouraged by the development of faster growing varieties of rice, it was later also helped by the introduction of new types of food from the Americas and by technological innovations. New areas were opened to cultivation, and irrigation works were extended. Some Chinese began to worry about the Malthusian dilemma of land expanding arithmetically whereas population increased geometrically— much faster than new land could be put under cultivation, even where such land was available.

The century preceding the communist takeover was, as has been seen, characterized by dynastic decline, societal disintegration, civil war, and foreign invasion. With their attention absorbed by a struggle for control, Chinese communist leaders were not so much concerned with the absolute size of the population as with the percentage of it that was under their jurisdiction. Karl Marx had, moreover, taken issue with Malthus, declaring that poverty was not caused by too large a population but by an unfair distribution of economic resources. Under socialism, these resources would be distributed equally, and all would prosper.

Despite the benign attitudes of Confucius and Marx toward a large population, the results of the PRC's first census, in 1953, shocked the leadership. On hearing that China had 582.6 million people, Mao is reported to have wondered how there could possibly be that many. The country had been at peace since 1950, and this, together with the aforementioned better health care measures, led to a rise in the number of births while the mortality rate dropped sharply. A few voices, hesitant at first, began to question Marx's theory of population and to advocate family planning. Accused by their critics of bourgeois Malthusianism, they denied that birth control had anything to do with Malthus. Rather, it was needed in order to protect the health of the mother, ensure that parents could give the best of care to each child they brought into the world, and allow them sufficient time to study and work hard in order to build socialism in China.

Beginning in 1955, China began to manufacture large quantities of contraceptives. However, even these quantities could meet the needs of only 2.2 percent of the couples of childbearing age, and the quality of what was available was often poor. Condoms were unlubricated, intrauterine devices uncomfortable, and contraceptive foams and jellies unreliable. Those who wanted to practice family planning—and the overwhelming majority of people apparently did not—often had to resort to folk remedies. One of these involved the consumption of large numbers of live, whole tadpoles; this was supposed to prevent conception for five years. Advocates pointed out that their formula had the advantages of being safe, effective (?), and inexpensive. Unfortunately, they admitted, it had the disadvantage of being feasible only in the spring—since the tadpoles would turn into frogs thereafter.

It is unlikely that this first effort to reduce births succeeded in significantly reducing fertility rates, with the possible exception of a few large cities. It did, however, show the government how difficult population stabilization would be. Research began on better methods of contraception. China's doctors devised the vacuum aspiration method of abortion, which is both much simpler and safer than the previously used dilation-and-curettage technique. It was quickly adopted worldwide.

Led by eminent economist Ma Yinchu, who was also president of Beijing University, the movement for a family planning program gained momentum. As the Hundred Flowers campaign unfolded, Ma decided that it was time to speak out. Delegates to the fourth session of the First National People's Congress heard Ma contend that it was absolutely necessary for China to control its population in order to decrease consumption and, thereby, increase the accumulation of capital. Because, said Ma, the PRC's large population was basically unskilled, it would also be inappropriate to rush into mechanization and industrialization; this would result in reducing the number of jobs and cause greater unemployment. He advocated shifting China's emphasis to light industry, which could absorb a larger labor force.

Unfortunately for Ma, the Hundred Flowers began to wilt shortly after his speech. Among the many indictments issued against him, Ma was vilified for being a Malthusian, an anti-Marxist, and a poor economist. He was forced to relinquish his position at Beijing University. Undaunted, Ma continued to write papers but was forbidden to publish them. The leadership, reasoning that everyone comes into the world with two hands but only one mouth, decided that a large population was actually good for production. A massive application of labor power would unleash the forces of production; the resulting huge expansion of agriculture and industry would refute conclusively the bourgeois notion that the growth of population would outstrip the growth of production. The media stopped encouraging birth control and began talking about the need for more people.

Some analysts believe that the birth control effort begun in 1955 was not actually abandoned but simply went underground. However, the starvation and malnutrition that followed the collapse of the Great Leap Forward did more to curb population growth than any family planning information. They also definitively discredited the notion that the larger the population, the better for production. By early 1962, there was renewed pressure for family planning. The Great Leap's "more, better, faster, and cheaper" slogan was replaced by "later [marriage], longer [intervals between births], and fewer [children]." Young people were urged to postpone marriage until their mid- to late twenties and to have only two children, preferably spaced three to five years apart. Greater efforts were made to provide inexpensive and convenient contraceptives. The government also encouraged research, leading to the development of a birth control pill.

In 1964, a family planning office was established under the supervision of the State Council. Provinces and large cities set up guidance committees to coordinate propaganda work and the distribution of contraceptives. Their efforts were heavily focused on urban areas. Partly, this was because urban areas were more likely to have modern medical systems and be able to supply contraceptives and perform abortions. Partly, it was because the party's control system was better in urban areas: Residents could be threatened with loss of jobs or withdrawal of other privileges more easily than in the countryside.

Various techniques were used. Some areas would issue ration coupons for up to three children; parents who insisted on having more would have to feed everyone on proportionately less food. Neighborhood health stations kept track of menstrual cycles, methods of contraception, and previous births. Typically, this information was posted on wall charts for all to see. Factories and work units were assigned quotas for the maximum number of births allowed; couples wishing to have a baby had to apply for permission. Should one couple conceive out of turn, another couple would have to postpone childbearing. This created tremendous pressure, from both one's superiors and one's peer group, to conform to the plan. The shortage of housing in major cities undoubtedly also discouraged the creation of large families. Fertility seems to have declined rapidly in many cities from 1962 to 1966. However, the overwhelming majority of the PRC's citizens lived in the countryside.

The family planning program, like most other officially sponsored plans, disintegrated during the Cultural Revolution. Still, since the period of time involved was fairly short, no large number of births resulted. By 1970, official pressure for family planning was back again, but new problems awaited. The large number of babies born in the early 1950s, before population-planning measures became effective, had reached childbearing age themselves, threatening an all-time high in births even if every couple were to agree to only two children. Agricultural production had been essentially stagnant, and Malthus's theory began to seem like an imminent reality.

In December 1978, delegates to the Eleventh National Party Congress's Third Plenum were informed that only drastic curbs in population growth would enable the PRC to achieve the ambitious economic goals of Deng Xiaoping's

Four Modernizations plan. A month later, a policy of encouraging all couples to limit themselves to one child was announced. The hope was to keep the population level below 1.1 billion by the end of the twentieth century and, eventually, to stabilize it at below 700 million. Ma Yinchu, aged 98, was rehabilitated and made honorary president of Beijing University.

A combination of incentives and penalties was introduced to ensure compliance. Families who pledged to limit their children to one were promised free education and medical care for the child up to age 18, and preferential admission to kindergarten and other child care facilities. The child would be exempt from being sent to rural areas to work and from military service. Mothers would receive extended maternity leave; the family would get priority in obtaining housing. One-child families would even be eligible for larger living quarters. A small cash subsidy and extra food rations were also to be provided.

Those who did not agree to have only one child would be immediately disadvantaged, since they would be pushed further down the list for housing, kindergarten admission, and the like. In addition, their child would be more likely to be sent to the countryside or selected for military service. For those who insisted on having three or more children, sanctions were imposed. Fines were levied, ranging anywhere from 5 to 15 percent of parental income until the children reached the age of 14 or 15. The rationale was that this sum was needed to compensate the state for the costs it incurred in educating and otherwise caring for the extra children. If the offending parents were cadres, they could be fired or expelled from the party. Billboards all over China featured attractive parents admiring their adorable toddler (always a girl, in view of strong popular preferences for male children) with captions like "Daddy, Mommy, and me" or "one child is best." This symbolized the image of the ideal family the government wanted its citizens to internalize.

The one-child policy worked quite well in China's large cities, where couples had already decided that one child was all they wanted or were sufficiently indifferent to the idea of a second child that they found the government's incentives attractive. However, the great majority of China's people did not live in large cities, the trend toward urbanization notwithstanding. The one-child policy was highly unpopular from the beginning. People were legitimately troubled by a number of questions that the architects of the new policy had left unanswered. Since the care of the elderly has traditionally fallen to their children, how could a married couple composed of two persons, each of whom is an only child, bear the burden of responsibility for four infirm parents? In terms of the country as a whole, how could a small group of younger people support a huge elderly population and still achieve high economic growth rates? What about the psychological health of the child? With all the hopes of the family centered on the success of one offspring, the burden might be too much to bear and adversely affect the child's mental health. Alternatively it was argued that only children are apt to be spoiled brats. The image of a pampered "little emperor" being fussed over by hordes of worshipful relatives quickly became prevalent. Military officers worried about the sort of recruit pool that would result from the new policies.

While many families were willing to stop at one child if that child were a son, nature did not grant that wish in slightly less than 50 percent of first births. The incentive was to try again and, if the second child were a girl as well, as many additional times as it took to produce a boy. There are sound economic reasons for preferring sons to daughters in China. Traditionally, when a woman marries, she goes to live with her husband's family, which then gains the use of her labor while her own family loses it. Since most men are physically stronger than most women, their labor is more highly valued. Also, despite the PRC's professions on equality of the sexes—Mao Zedong's "Women hold up half of the sky" is dutifully repeated every March in honor of Women's Day—females are frequently paid less than men for the same tasks. Although the law provides for equal pay for equal worth, the government's own surveys find that women receive about 70 percent of what men earn for the same work. Moreover, most women work in lower skilled and lower paid jobs than men.

Horrifying stories followed attempts to impose the one-child policy strictly. Many baby girls were drowned, suffocated, or strangled. Other unwanted girls, and boys with birth defects, were abandoned, filling orphanages that had neither the money nor the staff to properly care for them. In the mid-1990s, a BBC television crew filmed the conditions under which these infants lived; it reported that certain children were consigned to "dying rooms," where they slowly starved to death.

Disappointed fathers of daughters, or their families, beat the mother, often to death, or insisted on a divorce. When it was announced that parents could have a second child if the first were non-hereditarily handicapped, there were reports of parents maiming helpless children. Cadres under pressure to impose the one-child limit forced abortions on women who were late in pregnancy. The cadres, in turn, risked retaliation from relatives and friends of the women. Some couples did not register the birth of girls; others decided not to register their marriages. When wives got pregnant with an additional child, the couple would often simply leave their area until the child was born. Alternatively, they could join the floating population. With the introduction of Deng's economic incentive system, people were no longer so tied to their work units. In 1991, the State Family Planning Commission began issuing a series of increasingly stringent regulations to crack down on migrants' childbearing. An unintended result of the confusing mass of rules and certificates that the new regulations called for was to deprive many migrant women of health care; migrant women comprise a disproportionate number of maternal deaths.

Nor did these techniques exhaust the tactics used by those who wished to evade the one-child policy. Women who had been fitted with intrauterine devices against their will paid physicians, and even witch doctors, to remove them. Those who had had sterilization operations arranged to have them reversed. These illegal acts were facilitated by the fact that there were now many private medical practitioners. In the countryside, where Deng's agricultural reforms had made the household the unit of production, peasants reasoned that it made sense to have more children to provide the family with more labor power. They regarded the fine for excess births as just another annoying tax and either paid it or bribed officials to ignore the births. Since peasants built and owned their own homes, giving preference in housing to one-child families was no incentive. Nor was preference in school entrance, since many peasants did not aspire to long periods of education for their children.

The threat to remove cadres from their jobs or expel them from the party if they failed to set a good example for the masses was also less than completely effective. In the PRC's new incentive-based economy, being a cadre was no longer as desirable as it had once been; nor was party membership so esteemed. Even in the cities, results were less than hoped for. There was a tendency for the promised incentives to disappear. For example, inflation wiped out the value of promised cash bonuses, even where they were paid. Where there was an acute lack of housing and nearly everyone held a one-child certificate, being given priority for housing meant little.

In short, the government had lost many of the economic levers over public behavior that it had once had. Faced with widespread passive resistance to the one-child policy, the leadership had to come to terms with the limitations on its ability to control population growth. The idea of *reducing* the population to 700 million—or at all—dropped quietly from the press. Instead, the media began to speak, none too confidently, of holding the population to 1.2 billion, and later 1.3 billion, by the year 2000 rather than 1.1 billion—that is, 200 million more people than originally anticipated.

Since Deng introduced these measures, policies have alternated between tougher measures to ensure compliance and softer measures that permit second births under certain specified conditions. Shifting emphases put the cadres responsible for enforcing them in a difficult position. In 1991, faced with widespread flouting of regulations, the government instituted draconian enforcement measures. Pregnant women were forced to undergo induced labor, which generally killed the fetus, and then were sterilized. Huge fines were levied for out-of-plan children; sometimes, the family's possessions were confiscated and its home destroyed. Hospital officials who supplied falsified sterilization papers faced the possibility of prison or even execution.

The introduction of ultrasound scanning machines, which allow prospective parents to know the sex of the fetus, helped the government's goal of reducing the birth rate while thwarting its desire to achieve a more balanced male/female ratio. Word about the new machines spread rapidly to even remote parts of the countryside, and in Deng Xiaoping's money-conscious society it made excellent economic sense for hospitals and even private practitioners to purchase them. Although the going rate for the brief procedure is more than many farmers make in a month, couples are nonetheless willing to pay. The government tried banning the use of scanners for sex determination, but since the machines are simultaneously used to discover birth defects, this is hard to enforce. Many women who are told that the fetus is female immediately schedule an abortion. When asked how they feel this skewed sex ratio will impact their chances of having grandsons, people tend to reply that having grandsons depends on having sons first. In 2006, a bill to criminalize sex-selective abortion was brought before the

National People's Congress, eliciting so much controversy that it was withdrawn. Recently, there have been signs that the more extreme gender imbalance is abating somewhat.

The gender imbalance has ominous consequences, since millions of young men will find fewer and fewer women to marry. In a society where Confucian beliefs about the importance of producing a male heir remain deeply rooted, this could result in significant social tension. Sometimes, measures taken to reduce births proved counterproductive: The fines levied for over-plan births became an important source of income for local governments, who therefore had no incentive to discourage them. A very different problem is the graying of society. Sociologists consider a society aging if more than 10 percent of its population is over 60; according to 2016 statistics, China's was 16.7 percent, with demographers predicting that it would be about one-third by 2050. Given the deficiencies in medical care delivery systems (see the previous section on health) and social security, this could place an intolerable burden on society. There will also be fewer younger people to care for them. Other countries, such as Japan and several European nations, are aging, but China may be the first society to age before it becomes affluent (see Figure 11.1).

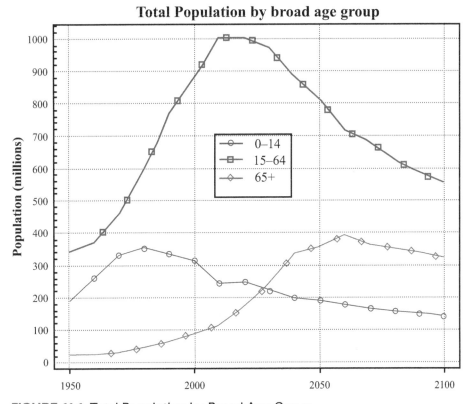

FIGURE 11.1 Total Population by Broad Age Group

Source: United Nations, Department of Economic and Social Affairs, Population Division (2017). *World Population Prospects: The 2017 Revision,* Volume II: *Demographic Profiles.* ST/ESA/SER.A/400.

By 2017, the population was 1.38 billion, and predicted to peak at 1.6 billion in 2030. However, Chinese demographers privately estimate that 25 to 35 percent of births are simply not reported, and that the true population is about a 100 million larger (see Figure 11.1).

Even accepting the higher figure, it is a remarkable achievement for a developing country to have reduced its population growth rate this far and so quickly. However, since births are lowest among educated professionals and highest among the poor and marginally literate, there are concerns that the quality of the population may decline.

In 2016, a more lenient policy allowing married couples to have two children went into effect. In the first year, the number of total births was said to be between 1.3 and 1.9 million more than the previous year, well below the 3 million births originally predicted. However, this could be temporary, since a lunar calendar year believed to be more auspicious for childbirth was soon to arrive. This, too, is not certain, since more and more couples seem to have decided that,

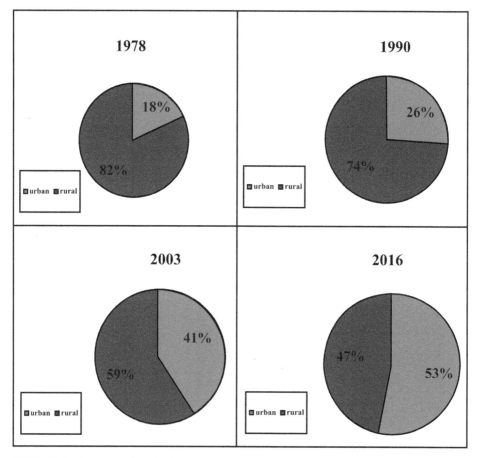

FIGURE 11.2 Increasing Urbanization, 1978–2016

Source: Compiled by the author from State Statistical Bureau (1978–2016).

given the high cost of education and the disruption to their careers, a single child is enough. Officials hope that allowing couples to have more children will decrease the preference for boys, and that the sex ratio will even out by 2030.

While increasing the population means more people available to support each retiree, they will need food, housing, and jobs; and the additional waste matter they create will have to be dealt with. Increasing the rate of urbanization, now over 50 percent (see Figure 11.2), is one suggestion, though there are huge challenges in terms of taking agricultural land out of use to build new satellite cities, constructing transportation to and from hubs, founding schools and hospitals in the new areas, ensuring adequate supplies of water, and devising drainage and sewage systems. The most ambitious of these plans, the Xiong'an New Area, was introduced in 2017. Located south of Beijing and aimed at reducing congestion and pollution in the capital, it is to house 4.5 million people in an area three times the size of New York City.

The Environment

China has traditionally been a country in which the population pressed hard against existing land and resources, resulting in a substantial amount of environmental degradation. The loess plateau described in Chapter 3 is believed to be the largest and most seriously eroded area in the world. Even had they understood the causes of degradation better, people whose immediate survival was at stake had little reason to be concerned about the penalty it would impose on future generations.

The Chinese communist party came to power dedicated to the goal of rapid industrialization and showed little concern for environmental problems. For decades, party and government officials would not acknowledge that such problems even existed, much less try to deal with them. As late as 1972, a Western reporter who commented on the soot pouring from dozens of factory smokestacks was told that pollution was a product of rapacious capitalists who did not care what they did to the environment. Since China no longer had rapacious capitalists, the Chinese people did not need to be afraid of pollution.

In fact, concern *did* exist. For example, many people were acutely aware that the Great Leap Forward had caused tremendous environmental problems. In 1958, large quantities of the country's coal were wasted in trying to make steel using backyard blast furnaces, forcing peasants in some areas to denude the countryside of trees and bushes in order to get enough fuel to survive the winter. In Tibet during the 1970s, an ill-conceived plan to substitute wheat for barley had exhausted the soil and caused famine. People who lived near belching smokestacks complained about the soot. Responding to these and other concerns, in August 1973 the State Council convened a national conference on environmental protection work.

In 1974, the Office of Environmental Protection was established under the State Council, and similar units were set up at the provincial level in many parts of the country. However, establishing the national unit as an office meant that it did not have authority over subordinate levels in the same way as might a ministry or commission. The office could coordinate and plan, but it could not order compliance. The National People's Congress passed the PRC's first environmental protection law in 1979, though deficiencies in financing, personnel, and organization made its provisions difficult to enforce.

Environmental degradation became a matter of public concern by the end of the 1980s, and continues to be so. By 2008, more than 400 of the mainland's 669 largest cities had water shortages, and nearly every year brings news of a new low in river levels. North China has suffered from chronic drought since the 1980s, while flooding has become more serious in the south. By 2030, when the population is predicted to be 1.6 billion, per capita water resources will be 1,760 cubic meters, barely above what experts believe is the critical limit of 1,700. Current levels of 2,200 cubic meters per person are only a quarter of the world's average. Water shortages are common in major cities at certain times of year, and factories have had to close production lines for lack of water.

Serious pollution means that very little of the water that remains is drinkable. The economic boom has resulted in geometric increases of environmental contaminants. Rural areas also suffer from agricultural runoff tainted with chemical fertilizers and toxic pesticides. In some areas, high levels of metal and organic pollutants cause cancer and deformities in humans and marine life. In a number of areas, drinking wells that have been used for centuries have had to be abandoned, and it has become impossible for fish to live in some rivers and lakes. Periodic "red tides," which result in toxic seafood, threaten coastal cities. Polluted drinking water has also been linked to a rise in hepatitis and stomach, liver, and intestinal cancers. Chinese experts complain that such water as exists is inefficiently used, and suggest that if households and businesses were charged a per-unit fee for water, the situation would improve noticeably. Desalinization has also been suggested, though it is currently very expensive.

Another very expensive project is the South–North water diversion project initiated in 2002. In addition to misgivings about the wisdom of such a large-scale and expensive undertaking, there has been fierce opposition from officials in the areas where the water is to be diverted, resistance from those who must be relocated, and unforeseen technical difficulties relating to geographical hazards and pollution control.

The huge increase in the population of coastal China has resulted in shortages of surface water. Groundwater has been used to make up the difference, meaning that the land level drops. In addition to causing structural damage to buildings and highways, this means that coastal cities are more prone to flooding, particularly if the rise in sea levels that has been predicted actually occurs. Urban planners have been warned to take this into account when formulating development schemes. Suzhou, whose beauty gave it the nickname Venice of the East, has sunk by 1.5 meters since the 1950s, compared with only 24 centimeters in the last century for its Italian counterpart. Ningbo, a major port city, may sink below sea level by 2030. Incursions of salt water inland lead to salinization of the soil, reduced crop yields, and further erosion. Development in the Pearl River

Delta area has brought unprecedented prosperity to many of its residents, but the construction of large numbers of bridges, harbor terminals, and container berths over the past 30 years is destroying the ecosystem.

In Yunnan, sharp rises in the price of rubber led the government to encourage the expansion of rubber tree plantations with grievous damage to the environment of one of the PRC's most scenic areas. A World Bank study placed the PRC's environmental sustainability index near the bottom of the countries of the world, warning that the ecological underpinning of Chinese society is fraying. It estimates that air and water pollution cost the PRC $100 billion a year, equal to about 5.8 percent of GDP, mostly in increased health costs. Air pollution is a growing concern. In 2008, the PRC achieved the dubious distinction of becoming the world's leading emitter of greenhouse gases. According to World Health Organization data, 16 of the 20 cities in the world that suffer from the worst air pollution are in China. Most of China's energy needs are met by coal, which is typically of low quality, untreated, and burned from relatively low smokestacks, thus adding to the amount of pollutants released into the air. Particularly in winter, a large proportion of urban residents suffer from bronchitis. Those who can afford it invest several thousand dollars in air filtration equipment for their apartments.

As more people own cars, smog grows worse: China buys cheap "sour crude" oil on world markets. It is lower in price, but contains far more sulfur, a major cause of air pollution. Fearful that choking smog would obstruct the long-coveted 2008 Olympic games, Beijing officials ordered every-other-day driving for cars based on whether the last digit on their license plates ended in an odd or even number, and shut down several factories temporarily. Although some managed to evade the restrictions through such ruses as purchasing additional license plates with different endings, the measures helped. However, matters deteriorated again soon thereafter: worse smog enveloped Beijing, which is not even China's most polluted city. A 2017 survey by the University of Chicago's Energy Policy Institute found that poor air quality was shaving an average of three-and-half years off the lives of the PRC's citizens, and, among the 338 cities surveyed by the country's Ministry of Environmental Protection, only 84 met national guidelines.

Soil erosion and desertification are problems as well, leading to reductions in soil fertility and agricultural production. The mass of sediment eroded from upstream erosion is eventually deposited in downstream rivers and lakes, increasing the risks of flooding. One important contributing cause is deforestation. Depending on one's source, only 12 to 19 percent of the PRC's land area still has forest cover, compared with 33 percent in the United States, 35 percent in the former USSR, and 26 percent in India.

China had 21,000 more square miles of desert in 2016 than in 1975: with so many trees being cut for firewood and so many factories and farms drawing on groundwater, more land continues to dry up. The government's efforts to create a "great green wall" to stem the advance of the deserts have been less successful than hoped for: many trees, planted where they do not grow naturally, die. The others soak up groundwater that normally nourishes native grasses and shrubs, thus actually expanding desertification. Farmers and herders resent being forced off their land to make way for the trees.

Another highly touted initiative, but one which may prove to be a far larger problem, is the controversial Three Gorges project. A massive dam was constructed across the most scenic stretch of the Yangtze River in order to produce clean electricity, enhance river transport capacity, and help channel water to drought-prone north China. Critics charged that the huge cost (up to $1 trillion) of the project could have been better spent on other endeavors, and predicted that, although the dam may alleviate flooding in one part of the Yangtze, it will increase flooding in other parts. Construction work meant razing entire cities, thousands of villages, and large swathes of farmland whose inhabitants were not properly compensated for their relocation expenses; rare flora and fauna were destroyed as well.

Landslides also became an issue, since the area surrounding the large reservoir that is part of the dam complex is characterized by loose-textured soil, and by frequent floods and rainstorms. As subterranean water levels rise, so do the incidence and size of landslides. As has happened elsewhere, the creation of such a large reservoir may induce earthquakes, but even if not, the ecological consequences will be catastrophic. Some Chinese scientists posited a connection between a recent series of earthquakes in southwestern China and the construction of dams in the area, while local officials claimed that the Three Gorges Dam worsened the severe drought of 2010. Central authorities denied any causality with the events.

Silt causes a rise in riverbed levels and a reduction in lake water volume. Sandstorms have become larger and more prevalent. When riverbeds rise, floods become more likely. The siltation of the Yellow River, "China's Sorrow," is an ongoing phenomenon. But changes in the course of the Yellow River, which historically occurred every few hundred years, became more frequent in recent centuries. By the late 1990s, however, the Yellow River was running dry: water was being pumped out at double the recharge rate to serve industrial and human needs. Vows to ameliorate the situation did not prevent its worsening: Whereas 40 percent of the Yellow River's water was drinkable in the 1990s, this figure had shrunk to one-third by 2007. And impossible as it must have appeared to those fleeing the periodic Yangtze floods, that body of water was expected to dry up as well. As floods become more likely in some areas, desertification increases in others.

Reflecting a growing feeling that environmental deterioration was proceeding unchecked, the State Council raised the status of the Office of Environmental Protection to commission level in 1984; made it an agency, the State Environmental Protection Agency (SEPA), in 1988; and raised it to ministry status (MEP) in 2008. Officials have repeatedly been warned that their annual performance evaluations would take their efforts on behalf of the environment into account. In practice, it has proved easier to falsify results: A SEPA report released at the end of 2006 revealed that although regional data indicated that emissions had been reduced by 2 percent, they had actually *increased* by 2 percent. Official data tend to be suspect, and recently there have been charges that those of international organizations may be as well. In responding to critics' charges that major environmental protection groups have not protested against China's destruction of coral reefs in order to reinforce its claim to areas of the South China Sea, organization officials respond that they are able to operate in China only with the permission of the Chinese government. Compounding their difficulties, many of the organizations' most generous donors operate businesses in China.

Due to conflict between a vertical chain of command from the MEP and a horizontal one from authorities at provincial, county, and township levels, jurisdictional issues have so far defied attempts to expand the scope of environmental bureaus and to clarify the division of responsibilities among the ministries and levels of government involved. Local environmental bureaus responsible for enforcing central government regulations are understaffed and often tied to the industries they are supposed to regulate. The majority of the biggest polluters are state-run industries and factories that cannot realistically be shut down or severely punished. Local officials often protect pollution-causing industries, since they contribute to tax revenues as well as provide employment.

A number of factories have included fines in their production costs rather than improve their ability to control pollution. Others simply ignore the regulations, reasoning that they cost too much to comply with and that there is small risk of being caught. At present, interest in short-term profits and material benefits far exceeds concern for the environment. When regulations are enforced, tragic consequences have ensued. After years of complaining about a factory that was spewing hydrogen sulfide gas, residents finally succeeded in getting it closed down. Angry at being unemployed, factory workers turned on area residents at random, murdering two people in an exceptionally grisly fashion and injuring many more. In another area, police arrested farmers who protested that pollution from a paper mill was poisoning their crop, charging them with obstructing public duties. In Sichuan, a man who took part in an environmental protest in which a policeman was killed was executed after a closed-door trial without his lawyers being informed. Frustrated environmental officials have closed down factories, only to see them reopen a few days later. Shockingly, China is now importing a substantial proportion of the garbage of the rest of the world: Millions of tons of "e-waste"—discarded computers, television sets, and mobile phones—are shipped to the PRC for recycling, adding to the huge amounts of domestically produced toxic by-products. In 2017, the import of 24 kinds of waste material was banned, though there are doubts on how effective the ban will be.

Since China occupies a large proportion of the world's land area and has so many people, the PRC's environmental situation is also important to the stabilization of the global environment. Given the PRC's growing demand for energy to fuel its economic expansion, and the fact that China uses energy far less efficiently than developed countries, emissions are expected to be double those of the United States by 2050 if left unchecked. Should China remain an environmental spoiler, the effects on the rest of the planet could be severe. For this reason, leaders of the international ecology movement have made efforts to persuade China to sign multilateral environmental agreements. In 2002, Beijing ratified the Kyoto Protocol on regulating greenhouse gas emissions, passed a new domestic law aiming at water conservation, and issued new regulations on pollution, energy use, and recycling. How much good this will do remains to be seen. A few years later, the PRC became the world's largest source of greenhouse gas emissions. Although the leadership is aware of a looming ecological catastrophe, it worries that strenuous efforts to control emissions would adversely affect the PRC's economic growth rate. It has argued that, since developed countries became interested in environmental protection only after they had industrialized, having generated much pollution in the process, developing states have a right to do so as well. Others counter that China is fast approaching an environmental tipping point, after which a cascading series of catastrophic events will cause the collapse of the ecosystem, and that because the PRC is so large, the consequences will be global rather than confined to China alone.

In 2017, the government announced that it planned to spend at least $360 billion on renewable energy over the next three years. Still, this impressive sum may fall well below what is needed, even assuming that the funds are well spent. Sometimes even well-intentioned initiatives have unexpectedly bad consequences, as when hydroelectric turbines kill fish who swim into them, or birds fly into wind turbines

Corruption is serious; for example, "beancurd" dikes built with watered-down concrete crumble, causing floods. In addition, poor coordination between central and provincial authorities makes water control much more difficult. Failure to coordinate efforts has been held responsible for exacerbating situations in which high waters turn into disastrous floods. Officials also complain that many enterprise managers engage in "guerrilla warfare" with regulating agencies and then go to great lengths to cover up what they have done so that they need not clean it up. Local officials still answer to local authorities, who place economic growth above all.

Thanks in part to government publicity, there is greater public concern with environmental issues. An innovative and daring project for flushing the silt from the Yellow River received an international prize named for the former prime minister of Singapore. Several cities have taken steps to curb pollution, sometimes seeking out foreign assistance, Japan, the United States, and Singapore having been particularly active in this area. Shanghai's leaders, who are keenly aware that a clean environment is important to their plans to continue to attract foreign investment, have made real efforts to implement improvements. Guangzhou has also made impressive progress. Other cities exhibit varying degrees of concern. Since most are far less prosperous than Shanghai and Guangzhou, they have fewer resources to devote to the environment.

The PRC's "green" movement has burgeoned, despite the leadership's concern that environmental concerns may provide the impetus for a potential pro-democracy crusade. Misgivings about dams provide a further boost to environmental activism. Chinese experts have described a number of the dams as shoddily constructed and likely to fail in times of natural disaster. Also, since they are aware that those who have been forced to relocate often fail to receive promised new housing and other compensation, people have become more militant.

Conclusions

Better health care and a long period of peace led to a sharp increase in China's already large population. Efforts to convince the PRC's citizenry of the need for family planning have had impressive results, but have neither reduced nor stabilized the size of the population. Efforts to improve the living standards of this much larger number of people led to intensive exploitation of existing resources and a worrisome deterioration of the environment. These have taken a toll on economic growth, as well as on the general health of the population. Party and government leaders are cognizant of the intricately intertwined issues of health, demography, the environment, and economic growth. The trade-offs among these issues are difficult to make and, in terms of public opinion, have potentially explosive consequences. The enormous nature of the task involved and the decreasing ability of the central government to exact compliance from its subordinate units and from the citizenry at large make it doubtful that these quality-of-life problems can be solved easily or soon.

Suggestions for Further Reading

Vince Beiser, "The Great Green Wall," *Mother Jones*, September 2017.

David Blumenthal and William Hsiao, "Lessons from the East—China's Rapidly Evolving Health Care System," *New England Journal of Medicine*, April 2, 2015.

Judith Shapiro, *China's Environmental Challenges* (Cambridge: Polity Press, 2012).

Elanah Urestsky, *Occupational Hazards: Sex, Business, and HIV in Post-Mao China* (Stanford, CA: Stanford University Press, 2016).

Winnie Chi-Man Yip et al., "Early Appraisal of China's Huge and Complex Health Reforms," *Lancet*, March 3, 2012: 833–842.

CHAPTER 12

Conformity and Dissent

The Arts, the Media, and Social Control

Artist and Society in China

The relationship of the artist to society has been a thorny problem in modern China. As in most other civilizations, tensions exist between those who advocate the philosophy of art for the sake of art and those who believe in art as social criticism. There have also been familiar conflicts between art as entertainment and art aimed at bettering the minds and souls of its audience. An issue of particular salience in China has been how to treat past literary and artistic works, both those that are foreign and those of traditional China.

"Serious" writers and artists tended to be quite critical of works done primarily for entertainment. For example, they referred contemptuously to the popular fiction that flourished in the first several decades of the twentieth century as "the Mandarin Duck and Butterfly School." Particularly after the May Fourth movement, artists and writers attempted to grapple with the problems of what had caused China's abject weakness with regard to the West and how to remedy the situation. Typically, they found the roots of decay in Chinese civilization itself.

This is a recurrent theme in the works of Lu Xun, who is considered China's greatest modern writer. Lu's short stories directly criticized contemporary society and challenged his readers to struggle for a better China. In *The Diary of a Madman* written in 1919, Lu Xun implies that despite its professions of benevolence and righteousness, Chinese culture is cannibalistic. At the end of the story, the madman asks if perhaps there are still some children who have not yet become cannibals. He pleads that if they exist, they must be saved. The protagonist of Lu's most famous work, *The True Story of Ah Q*, reacts to repeated bullying and humiliation by pretending that he has achieved spiritual victories. When people who are physically weaker cross Ah Q's path, he bullies them. However, since most of the people around him are stronger, Ah Q lives in a world of self-deception. He cheers himself up no matter how perilous the circumstances, assuming an air of superiority despite the obvious defeats he is suffering. Ah Q, of course, represents Lu Xun's view of China.

Another well-known writer chose his pen-name, Ba Jin, from the Chinese transliteration of the first syllable of the Russian anarchist Bakunin and the last

272

syllable of another Russian anarchist, Kropotkin. His novel *Family* is a scathing indictment of the Confucian kinship system and its harmful effects on both individuals and the larger society. A number of other intellectuals added their voices as well. Although highly critical of the lingering vestiges of Confucian orthodoxy—the formal structure thereof having largely collapsed by the 1930s—there was little consensus on what should take its place. The communist party, believing that Marxist orthodoxy could succeed in strengthening China where Confucianism had failed, courted these writers and artists.

The Party, Art, and Social Protest

The party sponsored a number of artistic endeavors to help bring its message to the masses. Jiang Qing, who would later marry Mao Zedong, acted in guerrilla theater performances and films with left-leaning messages. Many writers and artists, some of them communists and others not, lent their talents to these endeavors. In 1930, the League of Left-Wing Writers was founded, its name purposely chosen to soften the appearance of communist control. Little effort was expended in trying to impose rigid ideological criteria on the works of its members: To do so might well have alienated many of them. Lu Xun explicitly rejected the idea that works of propaganda could have any literary value. Lu never joined the party and, since he died in 1936, never lived under communist rule. His writings indicate that despite the posthumous honors the Chinese Communist Party (CCP) bestowed on him, Lu would have been very uncomfortable in post-1949 China.

After the Xi'an incident in December 1936, many left-leaning writers and artists made their way to Yan'an, where the party was pleased to make use of their talents in revolutionizing and propagandizing the masses. In May 1938, the Lu Xun Academy of the Arts was founded to train and nurture these talents. It was at Yan'an that the *Yellow River Cantata* was composed: The river is considered symbolic of China itself. The future People's Republic of China (PRC) also acquired a national anthem at this time, "The March of the Volunteers," as well as many revolutionary songs designed to uplift the spirits and encourage on behalf of the socialist cause. The stirring anthem "The East Is Red" was another product of Yan'an. In this early manifestation of the cult of Mao, the chairman is compared to the sun in heaven. Literature, art, and music for the masses were also encouraged.

The first of the revolutionary operas, *The White-Haired Girl*, was composed at Yan'an. More like Russian ballet than Chinese opera, it tells the story of a young woman whose hair turns white after she is raped by a landlord. She flees to the hills after this sordid experience. The Red Army later liberates the area and puts the landlord on trial. The climax of the opera is the young woman's denunciation of the criminal, followed by the masses taking vengeance on him.

Despite the production of many politically correct works, tensions between art and politics arose when artists began to criticize the shortcomings of the

Yan'an government. One example involves a short story, "In the Hospital," published in 1941 by feminist writer Ding Ling. The protagonist, a young woman from Shanghai, describes an administration composed of incompetent old cadres who do not know how to run the hospital and are indifferent to the needs of its patients and staff. Her attempts to correct the problems she sees result in her being slandered and censured. Finally, in frustration, the heroine leaves the hospital. Most readers understood that Ding Ling meant the hospital to symbolize the Yan'an government; what happens to the heroine represents the inability of well-meaning individuals to correct its problems.

Artists saw their criticism as constructive, since they were trying to correct defects in the system. However, party leaders were convinced that critical works were destructive, since they might undermine the masses' faith in the party and its infallibility. Ding Ling and others like her were forced to make self-criticisms during the *zhengfeng*, or rectification campaign. In May 1942, Mao Zedong delivered a speech at the Yan'an Forum on Art and Literature that laid down guidelines—albeit guidelines that could be interpreted either strictly or loosely— for literature, art, and journalism that endured for a half-century thereafter. Mao stated explicitly that there is no such thing as art for art's sake. It exists primarily for politics, and not for amusement or entertainment. Moreover, he maintained, all of the arts have a class character.

Post-1949 Control Mechanisms

Although relatively few artists were likely to be comfortable with these guidelines, the day-to-day tasks of survival in Yan'an, with its harsh climate and wartime conditions, mitigated the tensions between the party and its literary and artistic workers. After 1949, this was no longer the case. While many intellectuals sincerely felt that they were serving the party loyally, they wanted to follow their own ideals rather than party guidelines when choosing themes for their work. As a result, intellectuals were attacked by the leadership and its career bureaucrats, who slowly pushed them aside.

The party moved quickly to assert its control over the arts. During the summer of 1949, the All-China Federation of Literature and Art Circles (ACFLAC) was founded. One of the largest of the mass organizations, it was essentially an umbrella structure that supervised nine national organizations representing major branches of the arts. These included the Chinese Writers' Association, the Chinese Artists' Association, the Chinese Musicians' Association, the Chinese Filmmakers' Association, the Chinese Dancers' Association, the Chinese Dramatists' Association, the Chinese Balladeers' Association, the Chinese Folk Literature and Art Association, and the Chinese Acrobats' Association.

The organizations held periodic meetings at which their leaders conveyed party and government documents to the membership. Discussions were held on the documents and other matters relevant to members' professional concerns. The associations also published magazines that, at least prior to 1979, were considered the most prestigious in their respective fields. Those who did not conform to the party line found it very difficult to have their work published by such journals. The associations also controlled the prizes that were so important to the prestige of writers and artists.

A small number of established, older artists and writers drew their salaries directly from these professional organizations. The great majority, however, had as their work unit the troupe, film company, or magazine to which they belonged. The units issued salaries, assigned housing, controlled transfers, held political study meetings, and so on, functioning very much as those of other work units. The troupes, companies, and magazines were subordinate to their relevant professional associations and, ultimately, to the ACFLAC. Those who refused to conform to the party line could be expelled from their units, meaning loss of salary, housing, and the opportunity to practice their profession. These were powerful incentives to produce politically correct works.

Other, less drastic means were at the government's disposal. For example, funding had to be obtained before work could proceed on a film. The script had to undergo several levels of approval, from that of party leaders at the studio to the provincial department of culture to the propaganda department of the provincial party committee, or to the ministry of culture and the ministry of propaganda directly if the script were from a central-level company. The movie was scrutinized again after filming was completed. At that point, it could be rejected outright or held indefinitely in a kind of limbo, with no decision being rendered. Or it could, and still can, be withdrawn after it has been released to theaters.

Given the risks of deviating from established orthodoxy, one may well ask why anyone dares to do so. First, many writers and artists consider that it is their responsibility as intellectuals to protest against social injustice. Second, it is not always clear where the limits of the permissible lie, and many writers and artists find it tempting to test the boundaries. Third, the party line has changed frequently, ranging from relative tolerance of a variety of viewpoints to rigid ideological orthodoxy. One can always hope that a work that is criticized at one point will later be tolerated. Perhaps its creator will even be praised for her or his courage.

Party leaders favored socialist realism in literature and art; they explicitly rejected what they referred to as "the doctrine of the wavering middle." This meant that heroes had to be completely heroic. They must be in no doubt that the course of action they had chosen was the correct one, no matter how adverse the consequences to themselves and to their families. Conversely, villains had to be completely reprehensible. Writers who portrayed Japanese soldiers or Kuomintang (KMT) officials as worrying about the fate of the peasants or of their own families were harshly criticized.

Artists were to portray the workers and peasants as happy under all circumstances. Among the absurdities produced was a painting depicting several female electrical repair workers atop a pole swaying precariously in an ice storm. In drawing their facial expressions, the artist chose neither intense concentration nor anxiety over the dangerous position they were in but broad, apple-cheeked smiles. The message, no matter how unrealistic, was that the women were pleased to be doing their bit for the masses and the state by repairing the downed lines. A short story had a herdsman singing to his sheep, telling them how lucky they were to live under communist rule, since now they were owned by the people instead of by a landlord. No great amount of sophistication was needed to figure out that it was of little consequence to the sheep whether they were eaten by the people or by a landlord.

In general, these works were not well received by audiences; nor did writers and artists wish to produce them. One writer, Hu Feng, became the target of a mass campaign in 1954/1955 for protesting what he referred to as "mechanicalism" in literature and predicting that if Marxism were used as a substitute for realism, artistic endeavors would be blocked and art itself destroyed. He and writers associated with him disparaged Mao's Yan'an talks as discouraging creativity. Hu was also unwilling to use native folk styles in literature. He was criticized for insulting Chinese culture, for worshiping Western bourgeois ideology, and for misrepresenting Marxism–Leninism.

Repression and Reaction

Some writers responded by producing works that scrupulously conformed to the party line; others simply ceased to write. Party leaders were aware of, and unhappy about, this drop in the quality and quantity of literature. During the Hundred Flowers campaign that began in 1956, writers and artists were encouraged to voice their grievances and, after an initial period of hesitation, began to do so. Predictably, they denounced the philistine attitudes of petty bureaucrats and demanded to paint and write in styles other than socialist realism. Writers asked for independent publishing houses. Musicians expressed their desire to play more Western music and to compose in more experimental styles. There were also demands for better pay and working conditions.

Whereas writers and artists regarded party supervision as interference by petty bureaucratic mentalities, party and government officials regarded literary and art workers as spoiled, arrogant people who worshiped creativity to the point of mysticism. Many bureaucrats found it difficult to see value in the products of the literary and art workers' output: their usefulness could not be measured in the same way as a bushel of rice or a new tractor. In the anti-rightist campaign and the Great Leap Forward that followed the wilting of the Hundred Flowers, they wreaked vengeance. Artists, writers, and musicians had their fees reduced drastically, sometimes by as much as 50 percent. The intent was to make them, and other intellectuals, comparable to ordinary workers in income level. Thousands were sent to the countryside to learn about the lives of the peasants firsthand, so that they could portray rural life more realistically in their future compositions. This was not to be done through mere observation but through actual labor. Intellectuals were assigned to feed pigs, shovel manure, and clean privies. While it is possible that this experience might have enabled musicians to better understand peasant folk tunes, artists to depict rural scenes more accurately, and writers to capture the flavor of peasant dialect, most of them believed that the real reason they had been sent to the countryside was to punish them for having spoken out.

The glorification of the amateur and denigration of expertise were important facets of the Great Leap Forward. At the same time that writers, musicians, and artists were ordered to learn from the peasants, peasants were urged to write, paint, and compose. Just as with industry and agriculture during the Leap, quotas were set for the production of songs, stories, and artwork. And just as in industry and agriculture, the quotas were raised again and again. Press releases spoke only of over-fulfillment. Thousands of songs were produced, often with such catchy titles as "Carrying Manure up the Hill" or "Dance of the Mongolian Sheepherders." The government put its favorites on records and cassettes and made them available for export. Short stories, generally extolling the joys of hard labor or the valiant fight against Japanese and KMT aggressors, were not only made available domestically but were also translated and sent abroad. Art became rigidly socialist realist, with a heavy emphasis on folk forms, such as paper cuts.

Despite the Great Leap Forward's emphasis on folk forms, proletarianization of the arts, and the spirit of Yan'an, it was far less hostile to so-called bourgeois culture and to China's so-called decadent feudal past than the Cultural Revolution that was to come. During the Leap, which also placed great value on doing things in large collectives, huge singing groups performed Western choral music, and enormous orchestras performed Beethoven's Ninth Symphony. In addition, there were concerts featuring ancient Chinese instruments.

The abject failure of the Great Leap Forward provided socially responsible intellectuals with an excellent issue to criticize. Since speaking out openly continued to be dangerous, oblique criticisms and metaphors were the weapons of choice. Veiling one's charges in the form of a short story or journal article that ostensibly dealt with the past became popular. Several examples of using the past to ridicule the present appear in Chapter 4. One of the most controversial plays of the period, *Hai Jui Dismissed*, is a perfect example of the genre. The real Hai Jui was simultaneously a censor and a governor during the Ming dynasty. A zealous official, he informed the emperor that tax evasion by landlords in the Suzhou area was ravaging the lives of the peasants there. The Suzhou landowners, who had their own faction at court, began to conspire against Hai Jui. As a result of their machinations, the emperor dismissed him.

In *Hai Jui Dismissed*, the protagonist is depicted as having brought the exploiters of the people to justice, returning to the peasants land that had been stolen by government officials, and then being dismissed from office by the emperor. Some of his language sounds curiously modern. For example, Hai Jui frequently refers to local officials appropriating people's land by force and making it difficult to farm. He also mentions large numbers of "wrongful judgments" that need to be straightened out and warns the emperor that only when these problems have been solved can there be a return to peace and prosperity.

Since the play's author, Wu Han, was a historian who specialized in the Ming dynasty, it is unlikely that the discrepancies between the real Hai Jui and the Hai Jui of the play were accidental mistakes. Careful readers understood that the author was criticizing defense minister Peng Dehuai's dismissal in 1959, after Peng protested to Mao about the effects of the Great Leap Forward's communization—that is, expropriation of peasants' land by the party. Although people like Wu Han may have sincerely believed that they were helping the party by pointing out its mistakes, many party leaders did not appreciate their efforts.

Another subtle way to criticize was by using metaphor. For example, since party hagiography compared Mao Zedong to the sun, one could compose poetry ostensibly about the sun and its role in growing crops while adding that even the sun has spots. Art, too, could be used as a weapon. In December 1964, the back cover of the official journal of the Communist Youth League contained a picture that, at first glance, was a typical exercise in socialist realism: a team of peasants harvesting grain. Closer scrutiny revealed Chinese characters formed by the way stubble in the painting's foreground had been cut. They read "Kill Mao Zedong" and "Long Live Chiang Kai-shek." In the background, one of a group of three red flags, symbolizing the then-current "three red banners" slogan, had fallen to the ground. The peasants were happily striding forward but not actually following a shadowy and unhappy-looking figure at the head of the line. Embarrassed authorities quickly tried to recall all of the journal's issues, but were only partially successful.

Culture and the Cultural Revolution

While protest of this sort was widespread, it was scarcely the norm. In fact, protest was barely noticeable in the rising tide of the cult of Chairman Mao that began in 1962. In all but name, "The East Is Red" replaced "March of the Volunteers" as China's national anthem. It was also the title of a lavishly costumed and choreographed revolutionary opera composed in honor of the fifteenth anniversary of the founding of the PRC on October 1, 1964. The Cultural Revolution took this cult to an extreme: Almost nothing but the works of Mao was considered safe reading. Classical Chinese literature was castigated for advocating the viewpoint of the ruling class and depicting "ghosts and beauties." Artists who painted traditional landscapes were condemned for not portraying the revolution.

Foreign works were no better regarded: Shakespeare's works were vilified for representing the ideology of the ruling class. Ideologues maintained that therefore they must not be allowed to spread their insidious poison. Tolstoy's *Anna Karenina* had a "revisionist outlook," while Balzac's ideas were "ridiculous and false." Classical music "paralyzed revolutionary resolution." The authors of protest literature and art were persecuted, often to death. Red Guards threatened to break the fingers of musicians. Both Western and pre-modern Chinese books, art, and music were attacked.

Sometimes, this posed dilemmas. For example, if both Western musical instruments and ancient Chinese musical instruments were proscribed, how could the new revolutionary operas be performed? Radicals who condemned the piano as a "coffin in which notes rattled about like the bones of the bourgeoisie" did not realize that Madame Mao, a driving force in the Cultural Revolution and the impetus behind the revolutionary operas, was fond of the instrument. When questioned about this apparent inconsistency, she reportedly replied, "We have liberated the piano." While it is easy to ridicule this statement, there is a serious point behind it. In effect, the Cultural Revolution's answer to the century-old problem of how to import Western technical knowledge without eroding Chinese values in the process was to detach European musical instruments and their techniques from the context in which they had been created.

Despite the reprieve of the piano, cultural life during the Cultural Revolution was relatively limited. Troupes performed the same eight revolutionary operas over and over again. Mao was the sole approved author of books. Stirring choruses of "The East Is Red" introduced each new segment of Radio Beijing approximately every 15 minutes, followed by an inspirational quotation from the chairman. Artists, working in materials as diverse as oils, plaster, jade, and rose quartz, produced images of Mao greeting the worshipful masses of the world, Mao meeting ethnic minority children, and just plain Mao. Hit songs had titles like "Chairman Mao Is the Red, Red Sun in All Our Hearts" and "Chairman Mao Visits Our Village."

For some people, danger was preferable to boredom. The maker of a classical bamboo flute adorned his instrument with a protest poem written in Tang dynasty style; the flute had been exported to the West before the counterrevolutionary act was discovered. Amateur authors produced their own works by hand. After appropriating paper from their own or someone else's work unit, they would secretly write their stories, perhaps by flashlight, huddled under a blanket. This method somewhat limited the length of the work. Sometimes, eight or more people would share copying duties. The finished manuscripts could then be quietly passed around among friends. Participants risked severe punishment for either creating or reading works outside the officially approved topics, but they were not typical dissidents. Surviving copies of these manuscripts indicate that favorite topics were love stories, detective and spy thrillers, knight-errant fiction, and pornography. The values found therein are remarkably similar to those of popular fiction in the Qing and early republican periods.

When the furor of the Cultural Revolution had died down, cultural life became slightly more relaxed. Within the Chinese population itself, there were stirrings of dissent. Protest wall posters began to appear, calling for implementation of the rights and freedoms guaranteed by the constitution and obliquely criticizing the party and Mao. Typically, they were tacked up mysteriously in the dark of night, and signed with pseudonyms such as Golden Monkey and Li Yizhe. Golden Monkey was apparently never caught, but Li Yizhe, actually an acronym for parts of the names of each of three students, received long prison sentences for attempting to exercise their rights.

Certain periodicals served to transmit the viewpoint of specific factions. For example, the journal *Study and Criticism* represented the Shanghai-based radical faction. Literature and journalism now served as vehicles for a power struggle within the leadership. During the early 1970s, a campaign against Confucianism assumed several confusing forms. Shanghai radicals led by Madame Mao intended the campaign to be directed against Zhou Enlai, with his plausibly Confucian attributes of pragmatism and desire to bring harmony to a China that the Cultural Revolution had nearly torn apart. Zhou and his group fought back with long articles and essays denouncing very different aspects of Confucius in order to attack Lin Biao's followers and the Gang of Four. As a case in point, they praised Confucius's enemies, the Legalists, for having introduced universal law and unification—both antithetical to the radical agenda of arbitrary sentencing and class struggle.

A little later, in 1975, another denunciation campaign began. This one was directed against *The Water Margin*, one of Mao's favorite childhood novels. Like the campaign against Confucianism, it had Zhou Enlai as its target. By changing certain details of *The Water Margin*'s Robin Hood-like plot, the Gang of Four was pleading that unless the king (Mao) took drastic action immediately, a reactionary and his followers (Zhou Enlai and Deng Xiaoping) would suppress his revolutionary generals (the Gang of Four) after the king's death. Ironically, with a few small modifications, the Gang accurately foretold its own defeat.

The Arts under Deng Xiaoping
Restrained Dissent

The arts and journalism participated in the general loosening of social controls that accompanied Deng Xiaoping's rise to power. The eight revolutionary operas were withdrawn "for a time," with the explanation that they had been performed so often that people were bored with them. The official media urged artists and writers to portray life realistically, seeing not only "success, brightness, festive flowers, and children's laughing faces, but also the dregs of the past, the dark clouds, and the tears and sorrows of the ordinary people." Within the strictures of the criteria proclaimed by Mao in his 1957 Hundred Flowers speech "On the Correct Handling of Contradictions among the People," artists were to be free to create. These criteria included standards like being beneficial rather than harmful to socialist construction and strengthening rather than weakening the leadership of the CCP. In other words, they were sufficiently ambiguous that different people could interpret them in different ways.

Here were new boundaries whose limits would have to be tested. First to respond were cartoonists, who produced scathing and sometimes lurid satires of Jiang Qing and her supporters. Cross-talk comedians poked earthy fun at the Gang of Four, drawing on humor that had flourished *sotto voce* for many years. These were soon joined by a form of writing that came to be known as scar literature, after the title of a short story that appeared in 1978. The protagonist of "Scar" is forced to repudiate her parents during the Cultural Revolution, when they are falsely accused of being counterrevolutionaries. Later, the young man she loves is forced to break off his relationship with her when he finds out about her parents' label. In short, her life has been ruined by political and ideological power struggles.

The publication of this story encouraged many others to write about their own family tragedies. Scar literature was acceptable to the new leadership, most of whom had themselves suffered terribly during the Cultural Revolution. It was also useful to their desire to repudiate Maoist radicalism. Although scar literature was well received by the populace, it is unremittingly gloomy and is not considered very interesting artistically.

Protest Gains Momentum

Some artists became more adventurous in ways that the leadership found more difficult to accept. In 1980, a play entitled *Unrequited Love* appeared and was later made into a movie entitled *Sun and Man*. Its plot concerns a Chinese artist who, although well established in the West, returns to China after the revolution to help build his country. At first, things go relatively well. Then, owing to his "bourgeois" background and the taint of his stay in the West, the artist is persecuted. During the Cultural Revolution, he loses his job and his family, eventually escaping to a cold, arid plain where he must steal food to stay alive. The film poses the question "You love your country. But does your country love you?" As the plot unfolds, the central character is stumbling, seemingly at random, through the snow. When the camera pans upward, the audience sees that rather than stumbling randomly, his path has traced a question mark. He freezes to death as the sun, a symbol of Mao, shines on his body. In the final scene, a flock of birds flies overhead in an inverted V formation, which is also the shape of the Chinese character for mankind.

Sun and Man went far beyond a criticism of the Cultural Revolution, daring to question the basic relationship between the party and the people, even those who had given their utmost in support of their country. As such, it typifies a second stage in the evolution of the arts under Deng. By suggesting that the evils and aberrations of society predate the Cultural Revolution, it implied that the flaws lay in the basic nature of the socialist system itself. The movie was strongly criticized by the official media in 1981 and its author forced to make a self-criticism. But this suppression did not occur until the film had been widely circulated.

A play with a similar theme, *Bus Stop*, concerns a group of people who wait ten years for a bus that never arrives. Again, the plot is metaphorical: the people represent China, and the bus the social transformation that they have been promised will solve their problems. *Bus Stop* had a brief run in Beijing, after which it was closed and severely criticized. To official chagrin, its author, Gao Xingjian, was awarded the Nobel Prize for literature in 2000—the first Chinese ever to receive the honor.

The leadership also had its problems with the plastic arts. In 1979, a group of 30 avant-garde artists who called themselves the Stars organized a modern art exhibition in a Beijing park. As non-members of the official Beijing Artists' Association, they had a difficult time securing permission to hold the exhibition.

It included paintings in a variety of modern Western styles that had earlier been proscribed: French impressionism, abstractionism, and the nude. The fact that the exhibition could be held at all attests to the loosening of controls over art at this time.

Among the show's offerings were wood sculptures done by a young former Red Guard named Wang Keping. The most attention-getting was carved in the fashion of a Buddha wearing a cap with a red star in place of the usual headdress. Whereas the traditional Buddha has both eyes closed, Wang's rendition, whose features bear a remarkable resemblance to Mao Zedong's, has one eye slightly open. This is, the sculptor explained, so that he can see who is worshiping him. The consistent theme of Wang's work is of arbitrary, unfeeling repression by a bureaucracy that has lost touch with the people.

In sharp contrast to the tight control of literature and journalism during the Mao years, small journals and newspapers proliferated. Their contributors seemed to delight in provoking the leadership. For example, one of the ways the leadership sought to enhance the PRC's foreign exchange reserves was to set up "friendship stores," which sold certain goods only to foreigners, for hard currency. Ordinary citizens who attempted to enter such stores were turned away by guards, often very rudely. How, one journal asked, did this differ from the sign "no dogs or Chinese allowed" that was allegedly posted at the entrance to a park in the foreign concession of Shanghai before the revolution?

The journal was ordered to cease publication, and its editor was sent to jail. This temporarily reduced, but did not halt, the production of objectionable material from unauthorized sources. Particularly worrisome to the leadership was the degree of sympathy which dissidents seemed to enjoy within the party. At a major speech delivered to 10,000 party cadres at the Great Hall of the People in January 1980, Deng Xiaoping asked rhetorically why it was that "certain secret publications" were printed so beautifully. Observing that their authors could not possibly possess printing plants, Deng concluded that the publications could only have appeared with the support of party members, many of whom must be cadres.

Another worrisome development from the leadership's point of view was the "unhealthy" intrusion of romance into the new music, films, plays, and novels. Such stories might or might not be accompanied by overtones of political protest. Regardless, they proved very popular with the average citizen, whose chief emotional role model for years had been Lei Feng, the young soldier whose only love was for Chairman Mao (see Chapter 9). The government worried that too much attention was being paid to romance, and that this misdirection of energies would distract people from the much more important goal of building China's economy. Little could be done to stop this development. Efforts at repression of domestic production simply enhanced the value of videocassettes—often pornographic—smuggled in from Hong Kong, or of tapes of love songs from various countries. The music of a young woman from Taiwan, surnamed Teng (Deng in *pinyin*), was so sought after in the PRC that it gave rise to a popular saying: "The day belongs to Deng Xiaoping, but the night belongs to Teng Li-chun."

Another genre of dubious value from the leadership's point of view was science fiction. In the abstract, this form of literature was valuable, since it promoted science and technology, which were collectively one of the Four Modernizations. However, as science fiction was actually written, the implications were frequently quite different. The description of life on other planets was often consciously intended to contrast with conditions in China: officials discovered, for example, a less than subtle story in which a group of aliens emerge from their spaceship and immediately begin to denounce socialism.

Experimenting with Capitalism in the Arts

In the early phase of Deng's reforms, the party tried to apply capitalist principles to literature and art. However, the need to attract paying customers led to behavior that displeased party and government officials. Performers quickly learned that audiences liked plays or musical performances with "unhealthy" romantic themes and in which the actors wore provocative (from the government's point of view) clothing while moving sinuously across the stage. Similarly, writers discovered that detective stories, spy novels, and steamy romances sold better than works on politically correct topics.

The Campaign against Spiritual Pollution

Individuals and their objectionable works were sporadically suppressed almost from the beginning of the post-Mao liberalization. Typically, this was more likely to have reflected differences among party members over what was acceptable than anger over the actual works and their creators. Within the leadership, ideological hard-liners jousted with reformers, creating dangers for writers and artists, who were reminded of the traditional Chinese saying "when elephants fight, the grass will be trampled." As early as 1980, China's most famous movie actor, aware that he was dying of an incurable form of cancer, decided to speak openly. Lashing out against "meddling by nonprofessionals," the film star urged Chinese artists and writers to exercise control over the political system instead of being controlled by it. Interestingly, the article appeared not on a wall poster or in an unofficial journal but in *People's Daily*, the official newspaper of the party central committee.

By the end of 1983, ideological hard-liners had gained the upper hand, initiating a full-scale campaign against "spiritual pollution" that had an adverse effect on writers and artists. Several editors of *People's Daily* were dismissed on grounds that the newspaper was taking too independent a stance and "dwelling too much on leftist mistakes." The avant-garde artists' group the Stars voluntarily disbanded, with many of its members eventually leaving the country. Separated from the emotional world that had inspired their work, the artists lost a great deal of their effectiveness. The campaign against spiritual pollution was, however, short-lived, and the arts again flourished. Some things that had earlier been regarded as objectionable were now tolerated, albeit grudgingly and only if discreetly rendered—for example, the right of artists to use nude models.

Literature continued to tweak the leadership and to incur its periodic ire. During the height of Deng Xiaoping's campaign to rejuvenate the leadership by forcing elderly party and government officials to resign, a youth newspaper in Shenzhen was shut down for suggesting that the octogenarian Deng set an example by doing so himself.

Looming Confrontation

Other authors concentrated on the question of why, more than a century after beginning efforts to make China the equal of the West, their country was still internationally weak and economically poor. Their answer was similar to that of Lu Xun: The defects were to be found in the Chinese character itself. One writer, advocating that China correct what he believed to be an excess of national pride, likened the Yellow River—a symbol of China—to a stream of urine. Another, based in Taiwan but well known in the PRC, wrote a book entitled *The Ugly Chinaman*. It complained that, among other things, the Chinese are too conformist, too loud, too cruel, too crass, and above all, too willing to tolerate injustice. Implicitly or explicitly, these critics argued for a greater degree of Westernization. Their solutions bear a close resemblance to the science and democracy solutions proposed by their counterparts a century earlier.

The student demonstrations of December 1986 and early 1987 set off just such a chain reaction for what the government regarded as Western values. A number of journalists were dismissed, and Liu Binyan, one of the most famous, was expelled from the CCP along with the outspoken astrophysicist dissident Fang Lizhi. A Shanghai newspaper, the *World Economic Herald*, which had been sympathetic to the students, was nearly shut down. There was another effort to eradicate illegal publications. Only temporarily daunted, China's writers and artists soon returned to heterodox themes. In 1988, a television drama caused considerable anxiety in official circles. Known abroad as *River Elegy*, the literal translation of the Chinese title is "Premature Death of a River." The river is the Yellow River, representing Chinese civilization, and the implication is that it died at an early age. The message of *River Elegy* is the necessity of the Yellow River merging with the blue Pacific Ocean, symbolic of the West, and into which the Yellow River actually does flow. The *World Economic Herald* continued to be obliquely critical of officialdom. In January 1989, the paper's editor compared his philosophy of journalism to playing ping pong: "If you hit the ball and miss the end of the table, you lose. If you hit the near end of the table, it's too easy. So you want to aim to just nick the end of the table. That's our policy."

The Tiananmen Demonstrations and Their Aftermath

In April 1989, the party decided that the *Herald* had missed the end of the table, banning it for supporting the student demonstrations that were taking place in many Chinese cities that spring. After the demonstrations had been put down, the expected repression began. In contrast to the spirited denunciations of artists and writers during prior periods of repression, the period that followed the quelling of the 1989 demonstrations was more akin to slow asphyxiation. The number of newspapers was reduced, and it was announced that no additional licenses would be granted. New guidelines were issued for art exhibitions. Film studios experienced sharp budget cuts. *Sister Jiang*, a politically correct opera first produced in the early 1960s but not seen in many years, reopened. The diary of selfless hero Lei Feng was republished. Stage and screen productions renewed their attention to Mao Zedong as a subject, and the People's Liberation Army prepared to spend $21.3 million—far in excess of the cost of all 150 films made in China during 1989—to produce a three-part epic, *Great Strategic Battles*. At the same time, the latest works of several of the PRC's most acclaimed directors were quietly banned.

Party leaders urged everyone to study the lessons of Yan'an, when men were men and art was politics. A newly appointed leader of the Chinese Writers' Association compared literature to groceries: In both cases, the government should encourage what is nutritious and ban what is poisonous. As one cynic observed, this is precisely the reason why, under socialism, both the best groceries and the best literature are found in the black market.

There was considerable resistance to the party's new policies. For example, the first part of *Great Strategic Battles* contains a scene in which it looks as though the valiant communist troops may be annihilated by KMT forces. Audiences cheered. On June 4, the first anniversary of the Tiananmen incident, public security forces were deployed on university campuses to guard against demonstrations. The students threw small bottles, *xiaoping*, out of windows to symbolize their attitudes toward Deng Xiaoping, whose name is written with a different Chinese character and actually means "small peace." They also broadcast a Western rock hit containing the lyrics "every move you make, every breath you take, I'll be watching you." As the students knew, but the security force apparently did not, the group that recorded it was called The Police.

Cui Jian, an ethnic Korean and former trumpeter in the Beijing Philharmonic, emerged as the nation's rock superstar. His lyrics are profoundly subversive. For example, the "Official Banquet Song" expresses Cui's view of the bureaucracy. In it, a high-ranking cadre describes the different restaurants he frequents, closing with the lines "anyway, it's not my money—so eat, drink, and be merry." Another number involved Cui tying a red bandanna over his eyes to symbolize a population that communist propaganda has blinded from reality. Whether Cui was allowed to continue to perform because he was too famous to arrest or because the leadership simply paid no attention to his lyrics is a matter of speculation.

As before, periods of relative freedom alternated with periods of restrictive policy. However, repression was never as severe as it had been in the Maoist period. As mentioned previously, the attempt to achieve politically correct art and journalism which followed the suppression of the Tiananmen demonstrations met with considerable resistance. When Deng Xiaoping criticized the left during his 1992 visit to the Shenzhen Special Economic Zone, intellectuals were emboldened. For example, a fall 1992 adaptation of theater-of-the-absurd playwright Friedrich Dürrenmatt's *Romulus the Great* satirized Deng and the effect of his reforms. Set in ancient Rome at the time when the barbarians (the West) were storming the gates of the capital (Beijing), emperor Romulus (Deng) announces that he intends to save the empire (communism) by destroying it. The only hope, he says, is to go into a business partnership with the barbarian tycoons, since the hard choice is between a catastrophic capitalism and a capital catastrophe. A theater-goer commented ruefully that her country had reached the point where the theater of the absurd seemed a straightforward description of the PRC's reality. The play closed briefly, but not because of censorship: The leadership had requested that a special performance be given for them in the Zhongnanhai compound where most of them lived.

Expression, Repression, and Social Control

In the mid-1990s, there was a new period of repression. In fall 1995, a neo-leftist "10,000 Character Memorial" appeared which called for the recentralization of a state-owned economy. Neo-leftists cited Marxism–Leninism to justify their calls for the reassertion of central party and government power; the director of the propaganda department called for the arts to serve socialism. A number of new books were banned by the party's propaganda department because of "serious problems in political and ideological inclination." Computer networks were required to register with the government; those with political and pornographic content were made illegal. A few months later, the authorities blocked access to hundreds of websites.

Also noticeable during this period was another ideological camp, the neo-conservatives. Like neo-leftists, they argued for strong state power though, unlike the neo-leftists, they did so for practical rather than ideological reasons: a strong state, neo-conservatives believed, was needed to ensure stability. The alternative would be chaos. A third strain, neo-traditionalism or neo-Confucianism, argued that modernization was not the same as Westernization: the Chinese tradition, including the works of Confucius, provided the underpinnings of a uniquely Chinese form of modernization. Neo-traditionalists had much in common with the proponents of "Asian values" elsewhere in Asia. Nationalism was popular with all of these groups. To some extent, this stemmed from a disillusion with the promise of the West: a number of its proponents had studied abroad and did not like some, or many, things they had seen there. Nationalism, as manifested in such works as *China Can Say No*, fitted in with the wishes of party and government until it threatened to disrupt relations with Japan and the United States. At this point, the authorities moved to rein in the nationalists.

Fear of the consequences of globalization may also have been a factor influencing several of these groups. The neo-traditionalists, like their forebears a century earlier, were particularly concerned with the effect of the outside world on what they considered the core values of Chinese tradition. Others were concerned that foreign ideas would erode socialist values. Liberals, whose voices continued to be heard, countered that neo-traditionalists really knew nothing about the Chinese tradition or Confucius: they had been educated under a Marxist system and were simply inventing a past that was useful for their purposes. Liberals also attempted to refute the neo-leftists: A book called *Crossing Swords* strongly asserted the need for continued reforms and criticized the "10,000 Character Memorial" for opposing the PRC's interactions with Western capitalist states. Neo-leftists responded in a manner that would have been highly unlikely during the Mao era: by suing the authors of *Crossing Swords* for quoting the memorial without permission and for allegedly misrepresenting its contents. In short, by the late 1990s, many different schools of thought contended and were fairly well tolerated by the leadership.

Although Jiang Zemin's time in office saw tighter restrictions than under Deng Xiaoping, people were able to criticize leaders and their policies in private with little fear of retribution, unlike the Mao years. Academic journals could also print critical articles as long as they did not confront leading officials too bluntly. For example, it is usually acceptable to disagree with the effectiveness of a given policy, but not acceptable to call politburo standing committee members idiots for foolishly proposing the policy. One technique which authors employ is to position heterodox thoughts in the center of their articles, wedged between ideologically correct introductions and conclusions. Academic journals, with their fairly limited readerships, are not normally carefully scrutinized by official censors.

By the 1990s, efforts to cleanse the media of tasteless shows that audiences liked had ceased. Chinese television now has game shows and variety programs similar to those found in other consumer-oriented societies. Programs which critics regard as tacky serve to divert popular attention from society's more serious problems. There are parallels with the bread-and-circuses techniques used by Roman emperors. Fantasy novels featuring dragons, treasure hunters, and ghosts are popular, as are the adventures of Harry Potter. Whereas in 1989 the Chinese government had to make great efforts to erase the internationally known dissident Wei Jingsheng's name from the Chinese information environment, today very few people know who Wei is because their attentions are focused on Hollywood starlets and the NBA championships. Although this tactic was almost certainly stumbled upon rather than consciously planned, it has proven very effective.

Nonetheless, in 1997, more than 10 percent of the PRC's newspapers, as well as several hundred journals, were shut down. Party officials explained that the decision had been taken to avoid redundancy and upgrade quality. The surviving publications were grouped into media conglomerates or syndicates in order to maximize publishing efficiency and cut costs. Officials had legitimate concerns about journalistic ethics: there were documented instances of reporters refusing to cover stories unless paid by the people or businesses they were to write about. In one well-publicized case, a favorable story about a company persuaded many people to invest in it: The company, which had bribed reporters to praise it, was actually financially weak. When it failed, investors lost hundreds of millions of dollars. Moreover, some artists really did seem to be pandering to the lowest standards of their audiences.

Liberals, however, argued that the press and journal cuts fell disproportionately on those who were critical of party and government policies. They point out that investigative reporting can be hazardous to the health of the investigators. For example, public security personnel have threatened reporters to make them surrender a videotape showing police abusing their power. Artists and journalists are sued for producing critical works. Liberals suspected that the real motive behind the establishment of media syndicates was to enhance official control rather than, as stated, to save money and improve journalistic ethics. Syndicates can operate only print media: they are forbidden to own television or radio outlets and cannot cross provincial borders. Their establishment reinforces the hypothesis that post-Mao China is more apt to resemble the communist neo-traditional model than a civil society.

Those who had hoped that Hu Jintao and Xi Jinping would allow more tolerance than their predecessors were disappointed. Critics charged that Hu's campaign to achieve a harmonious society was an excuse to suppress any information that could be construed as implying that society was anything less than harmonious. Fears that the "color revolutions" in Eastern Europe could spread to the PRC may have reinforced Hu's desire to monitor expressions of dissent more closely. In October 2004, authorities told the media not to report on officials seizing land from farmers and not to follow up on land-seizure cases they had been investigating. Since the government had previously pledged to protect farmers' land rights, the presumed reason behind banning news on the seizures was fear that reports would stoke anti-government protests, or even more drastic action, by the dispossessed. In 2005, the government banned dozens of newspapers and confiscated almost a million unregistered or improperly registered publications. A year later, it ordered several art galleries in Beijing to remove a number of paintings whose themes could be interpreted as political. One of the objectionable works depicted Mao's famous swim, save that the Yangtze is blood red. Another showed Tiananmen Square with tanks visible. The censors also closed a weekly supplement to *China Youth Daily* after the newspaper published a university professor's article that criticized textbooks for their biased treatment of historical events. Interestingly, two separate groups of influential individuals, including retired party and government officials, openly protested. They accused the Central Propaganda Department of manipulating and controlling the range of speech and of making itself the sole judge of truth.

New rules introduced in 2007, purportedly aimed at creating a healthy environment by banning violence, pornography, and false information, have been used to restrict access to topics that have nothing to do with these categories. There are also more subtle forms of coercion that induce people to censor themselves. The charges which police bring against those they arrest tend to be vague.

Often, they will say, "you yourself know what you did," and imply that they have sufficient evidence to back up their claims. The individual is advised to confess immediately and beg for lenient treatment. Not knowing what the rules are, most people choose to err on the side of caution: they self-censor. Chinese literature expert Perry Link compares the plight of the outspoken to coping with an anaconda in the chandelier. Although the anaconda rarely stirs, those below it are aware of its presence and move carefully, since they are unsure about what actions will cause the snake to strike.

Filmmakers have less to complain about. Now able to obtain independent funding, they are freer from government restrictions than before, although their movies may be banned from Chinese theaters. Filmmakers report that it is now possible to argue with the censors about what portions they want to cut. One of the PRC's most famous directors, Zhang Yimou, several of whose films had been censored and banned, was chosen to orchestrate the lavish ceremonies of the 2008 Beijing Olympics. Nonetheless, and in direct contravention of promises made to the International Olympic Committee as a condition of Beijing being awarded the 2008 games, media censorship was tightened rather than loosened.

A few authors have also published books that would have been banned a few years previously. Jiang Rong, whose bestselling novel *Wolf Totem* is set in Inner Mongolia, describes his work as a metaphorical critique of the sheep-like mentality of the Han Chinese. However, Yang Jisheng's *Tombstone* cannot be sold in the PRC: it concerns the still-taboo topic of the famine brought about by the foolhardy policies of the Great Leap Forward 60 years ago. Ma Jian's *Beijing Coma*, a fictionalized treatment of the pro-democracy movement that was cut off by the events at Tiananmen Square in 1989, is banned as well. In fall 2008, there was an eerie echo of Cultural Revolution charges that authors were using the past to criticize the present. A magazine was censured for a seemingly innocuous article reporting that forensic analysis on the hair of the Guangxu emperor (see Chapter 3) confirmed long-standing beliefs that he had been poisoned. On closer scrutiny, the article could also be read allegorically as praise for former leader Zhao Ziyang. Both Guangxu and Zhao tried to change the system from within; both were deposed by the real power holders behind them: the former by Empress Cixi and the latter by Deng Xiaoping.

News, as opposed to variety shows or interviews with or about celebrities, is carefully monitored. Certain topics, such as criticism of, or speculation about, China's leaders, are always off-limits. Attitudes toward other issues may change according to circumstances. Logging on to their computers each day, journalists for state television find guidance on how to treat specific issues. The media are warned not to report on such topics as violent attacks in Chinese schools, on "incidents" that might occur during important gatherings, and on the risk of a real estate bubble. Critics refer to these warnings as "directives from the Ministry of Truth." According to a professor of journalism, the state news agency produces three versions of the news. The first, for government officials, is straightforward and factual. The second, for the public, is a more sanitized account. The third, targeted at foreign audiences, typically covers events in greater and more factual detail than the second so as to create the illusion of openness in the Chinese media.

International rating agencies give low marks to press freedom in the PRC: In 2017, the Paris-based non-governmental organization Reporters Without Borders rated China 176th among 180 countries in press freedom, with North Korea in last place and the U.S. in 43rd.

An underground publishing industry manages to exist despite pervasive censorship, and interested parties can buy many banned books from unlicensed publishers and retailers. Several newspapers continue the "edge ball" tradition begun by the *World Economic Herald*. Those who overstep the invisible line of the censors have seen personnel dismissed and been reorganized in order to deter future journalistic activism. But some have re-emerged undaunted, and other papers and journals have become more active. The editor of one such magazine compared her technique to that of a woodpecker: to hammer the tree constantly, with the intent of helping it to grow better rather than to destroy it.

The advent of the internet has been accompanied by the simultaneous growth of grassroots activism and authoritarianism. Those who blog, twitter, and otherwise use the internet are harder to control than reporters, despite strenuous efforts to do so. In 2010, internet service provider Google created a sensation when it announced that it had been the target of a sophisticated attack on its corporate infrastructure that resulted in the theft of intellectual property as well as the surveillance of the gmail accounts of Chinese human rights activists. The company subsequently removed its operations from China. Authorities hope that more easily controlled domestic internet providers like sina.com and QQ will fill the gap. Under Xi Jinping's administration, the government has sought to become a partner with major internet providers by purchasing shares in them, thereby giving it a voice in the companies' decision making.

When rules are tightened, the rationale is given as the need to crack down on pornography or false advertising, which do indeed exist but could be targeted more selectively. Party and government find the internet useful as a safety valve for outraged public opinion, and sometimes as a source of information on misdeeds by officials and their children—as long as public anger does not lead to the dreaded social instability. Some online postings have been extremist and abusive, verging toward a decidedly uncivil society. A legitimate fear is that such postings may lead to mob violence. In what has been called a human flesh-eating search engine, cyber-vigilantes may seek out, and often find, the identities of people deemed to have committed offensive acts and urge vengeance against them and even their families.

The authorities have responded in various ways. One is using censors. Although numerous, they have a difficult job: For example, a children's group ostensibly singing about a grass mud horse doing battle with an evil river crab circulated widely before regulators realized that it was actually code for an obscene act which the horse, written with different characters that are pronounced the same, commits on the river crab, a homonym for Hu's harmonious society. Anonymous cartoonists regularly post scathing criticisms on the internet: these are removed, though often not before thousands of people have seen and remarked on them. The PRC is considered to be the world's most advanced country in internet filtering, much of it carried out using equipment bought from companies in Western states that pride themselves on freedom of expression.

Although a number of bloggers have been arrested for their comments, a small number of high-profile individuals seem to be immune despite their very pointed criticisms. Still, fame is no guarantee against official retaliation. Outspoken artist Ai Weiwei, creator of Beijing's celebrated Bird's Nest stadium, spent 81 days in prison in 2011, charged with tax evasion and barred from leaving the country. Supporters threw packets of money over the wall around his home to help Ai pay what the government said he owed. It is believed that the proximate cause for his apprehension was the government's fear that Ai would encourage the Arab Spring unrest then gripping the Middle East to spread to China.

Another technique to control the internet involves paying people a small amount to post messages supportive of party and government policies. Referred to contemptuously by dissidents as "the 50 cent party," they are estimated to number about two million. A third effort is the requirement for real-name registration. Beginning in 2012, internet users, though able to post with pseudo-names, must register their real names, as linked to their national identity cards or mobile phone numbers, with the authorities. The unregistered can view microblogs, but can neither pass them along nor post for themselves.

Yet another method of control is a 2013 law announcing jail sentences of up to three years for posting rumors that are shared 500 times or seen 5,000 times. There is no clear definition of what constitutes a rumor, which may simply be a story that authorities are displeased with. One can receive jail time for rumors that are true.

Chinese hackers have devised ways to circumvent internet blockages—substituting "1" for "i" to access the banned word Tibet, for example, or using a proxy server in a different country. These prompt countermoves by officialdom to re-block them by other means. Falun Gong members have, on occasion, succeeded in inserting their own messages onto government websites and in hijacking satellite signals. It is not clear who will win these cat-and-mouse games, although officialdom would seem to have the more difficult task. Since 2008, China has had the world's largest number of netizens. According to a 2016 report, they exceeded 738 million, or more than 53 percent of the population.

Hopes that Xi Jinping's administration would usher in a more liberal atmosphere received a setback when, soon after assuming office Xi announced the "seven unmentionables" (see Chapter 6). Shortly thereafter, several university professors lost their jobs, and restrictions on news media were tightened. Following the publication of a compendium of Xi's thoughts, bookstores throughout China featured them prominently, often gift-wrapped, and centers for the study thereof opened at universities. This does not guarantee how faithfully people will adhere to the new orthodoxy. A government app offering rewards to citizens who report problems ranging from traffic violations to subversive activities has not been a success. Since people must reveal their locations and identities to claim their prizes, many are reluctant to do so.

Conclusions

By the 1990s, despite the efforts of party and government to retain control over literature, the arts, and journalism, China had achieved a degree of cultural pluralism that appears to be irreversible. Critics believe that although there is more variety and a greater range in these areas now than existed a decade ago, this does not equate to liberalization. Repressive periods alternate with periods of greater freedom, although generally speaking restrictions have tightened progressively since the Tiananmen demonstrations of 1989. Artists and journalists continue to test the limits of the leadership's toleration. Pressures for self-censorship indeed deter many would-be critics, but courageous individuals and publications who wish to make their views known continue to come forth. A human rights activist describes the current situation as one of high walls, but with spaces existing within the walls. When, in late 2010, imprisoned dissident Liu Xiaobo was awarded the Nobel Peace Prize, the news spread almost instantly, as did news of his death in prison in 2017. Although censorship efforts are not completely successful, the authorities have so far been able to balance internet growth with what may be called networked authoritarianism.

Whether increased activism will be able to bring about a fundamental change in the system, as predicted by the civil society hypothesis, or whether it will be shaped and co-opted by the system, as proponents of the communist neotraditionalist theory predict, remains to be seen. It should be remembered that not all of the activists are proponents of democracy: Some are advocates of a return to Maoist or traditional Chinese values; others urge the government to take a stronger stand internationally.

It is possible that fundamental modifications in the system can be achieved gradually. Neither party nor government is monolithic, and influential segments in both are aware that listening to the criticisms of the PRC's literati and accommodating their suggestions are important to the country's social stability.

Party and government want to use the media to achieve certain goals, such as unearthing corruption, but do not want to have their own legitimacy undermined in the process. Since a great deal of corruption involves party and government officials, this puts participants in a difficult position. In the words of a popular slogan that may be heard all over China, "If we do not root out corruption, the country will perish; if we do root out corruption, the party will perish." Xi Jinping's vigorous campaign against corruption has claimed more than a million alleged perpetrators, though cynics see it as a tool against his opposition that has not touched what they believe to be the comparable behavior of his supporters and their families.

Suggestions for Further Reading

2017 Human Rights Report: China (Washington, DC: United States Department of State, March 3, 2017).

Jacques deLisle et al., *The Internet, Social Media, and a Changing China* (Philadelphia, PA: University of Pennsylvania Press, 2016).

Gary King, Jennifer Pan, and Margaret Roberts, "How the Chinese Government Fabricates Social Media Posts for Strategic Distraction, Not Engaged Argument," *American Political Science Review*, Vol. 111, No. 3 (2017): 484–501.

Yingjin Zhang, *A Companion to the Chinese Cinema* (Hoboken, NJ: Wiley Blackwell, 2012).

Ying Zhu, *Two Billion Eyes: The Story of China Central Television* (New York: The New Press, 2012).

CHAPTER 13

Ethnic Minorities and National Integration

China's Minority Peoples

In 1949, when the communist government first came to power, China's minorities probably numbered less than 6 percent of the country's total population. Even now, after years of government pressure on the Han Chinese majority to practice family planning while applying far less stringent restrictions to the minorities, minorities constitute slightly over 8 percent of the population of the People's Republic of China (PRC). Moreover, there are 55 officially recognized minority groups, and although there is great variation in the sizes of the different groups, no single minority is especially large (Table 13.1).

In spite of this relatively insignificant minority population, party and government have spent a great deal of time and energy, as well as money, on the minorities and the areas in which they live. There are five basic reasons for this. The first is strategic. Most minorities live on or near China's land frontiers (see Map 13.1). Frequently, the border divides a group arbitrarily: Kazakhs live in both China and Kazakhstan, which was formerly part of the Soviet Union; Miao in China, Thailand, Vietnam, Laos, and Burma; Mongols in China and Mongolia; and so forth. Hostile foreign powers might wish to make use of their own minority nationals to infiltrate the PRC and cause problems. There is also the problem of irredentism to consider: Mongolia could decide to claim the parts of China inhabited by Mongols, or Kazakhstan to include the PRC's Kazakhs in their state. Constant vigilance, as well as certain efforts to keep the minorities happy with their lives in the PRC, have seemed to be wise courses of action.

Second, most minority areas are sparsely populated relative to areas inhabited by Han Chinese. They therefore have the potential to absorb immigrants from overcrowded areas. Minority areas comprise well over 60 percent of the PRC's total land area. Third, a number of minority areas possess rich natural resources. Oil, coal, gold, and other minerals are located in different parts of the country inhabited by minorities. Eighty percent of China's meat-, milk-, and wool-supplying animals are also found there. Proper exploitation of these resources is important to raising standards of living and economic development in general.

Fourth is the propaganda factor. During the Mao era, the Chinese Communist Party (CCP) maintained that its model of socialism was applicable to other areas of the developing world besides Han China. If the PRC could showcase

TABLE 13.1 Population of China According to Ethnic Group in Censuses, 1953–2010

Ethnic Group	Language Family	1953	%	1964	%	1982	%	1990	%	2000	%	2010	%
Han	Chinese	547,283,057	93.94	651,296,368	94.22	936,703,824	93.30	1,039,187,548	91.92	1,137,386,112	91.53	1,220,844,520	91.60
Minority groups		35,320,360	6.06	39,883,909	5.78	67,233,254	6.67	90,570,743	8.01	105,225,173	8.47	111,966,349	8.40
Zhuang	Tai-Kadai	6,611,455	1.13	8,386,140	1.21	13,441,900	1.32	15,555,820	1.38	16,178,811	1.28	16,926,381	1.27
Hui	Chinese	3,559,350	0.61	4,473,147	0.64	7,207,780	0.71	8,612,001	0.76	9,816,802	0.78	10,586,087	0.79
Manchu	Tungusic	2,418,931	0.42	2,695,675	0.39	4,299,950	0.43	9,846,776	0.87	10,682,263	0.84	10,387,958	0.78
Uyghurs	Altaic (Turkic)	3,640,125	0.62	3,996,311	0.58	5,917,030	0.59	7,207,024	0.64	8,399,393	0.66	10,069,346	0.76
Miao	Miao-Yao/Hmong-Mien	2,511,339	0.43	2,782,088	0.40	5,017,260	0.50	7,383,622	0.65	8,940,116	0.71	9,426,007	0.71
Yi	Tibeto-Burman	3,254,269	0.56	3,380,960	0.49	5,492,330	0.54	6,578,524	0.58	7,762,286	0.61	8,714,393	0.65
Tujia	Tibeto-Burman					284,900	0.03	5,725,049	0.51	8,028,133	0.63	8,353,912	0.63
Tibetans	Tibeto-Burman	2,775,622	0.48	2,501,174	0.36	3,821,950	0.38	4,593,072	0.41	5,416,021	0.43	6,282,187	0.47
Mongols	(Altaic Mongolic)	1,462,956	0.25	1,965,766	0.28	3,402,200	0.34	4,802,407	0.42	5,813,947	0.46	5,981,840	0.45
Buyei	Tai-Kadai	1,247,883	0.21	1,348,055	0.19	2,103,150	0.21	2,548,294	0.22	2,971,460	0.23	2,870,034	0.22
Korean	Korean	1,120,405	0.19	1,339,569	0.19	1,783,150	0.18	1,923,361	0.17	1,923,842	0.15	1,830,929	0.14
Dong	Tai-Kadai Miao-Yao/Hmong-					1,446,190	0.14	2,508,624	0.22	2,960,293	0.24	2,879,974	0.22
Yao	Mien					1,414,870	0.14	2,137,033	0.19	2,637,421	0.21	2,796,003	0.21

(Continued)

TABLE 13.1 Population of China According to Ethnic Group in Censuses, 1953–2010 *(Continued)*

Ethnic Group	Language Family	1953	%	1964	%	1982	%	1990	%	2000	%	2010	%
Bai	Sino-Tibetan					1,147,360	0.11	1,598,052	0.14	1,858,063	0.15	1,933,510	0.15
Hani	Tibeto-Burman					1,063,300	0.11	1,254,800	0.11	1,439,673	0.12	1,660,932	0.12
Kazakh	Altaic (Turkic)					878,570	0.09	1,110,758	0.10	1,250,458	0.10	1,462,588	0.11
Li	Tai-Kadai					882,030	0.09	1,112,498	0.10	1,247,814	0.10	1,463,064	0.11
Dai	Tai-Kadai					864,340	0.09	1,025,402	0.09	1,158,989	0.09	1,261,311	0.09
She	Miao-Yao/Hmong-Mien					379,080	0.04	634,700	0.06	709,592	0.06	708,651	0.06
Lisu	Tibeto-Burman					466,760	0.05	574,589	0.05	634,912	0.05	702,839	0.05
Gelao	Tai-Kadai					59,810	0.01	438,192	0.04	579,357	0.04	550,746	0.05
Dongxiang	Altaic (Mongolic)					—	—	373,669	0.03	513,805	0.03	621,500	0.04
Gaoshan	Austronesian					1,750	0.00	2,877	0.00	4,461	0.00	4,009	0.00
Lahu	Tibeto-Burman					320,350	0.03	411,545	0.04	453,705	0.04	485,966	0.04
Sui	Tai-Kadai					300,690	0.03	347,116	0.03	406,902	0.03	411,847	0.03
Va	Mon-Khmer					271,050	0.03	351,980	0.03	396,610	0.03	429,709	0.03
Nakhi	Tibeto-Burman					248,650	0.02	277,750	0.02	308,839	0.02	326,295	0.02
Qiang	Tibeto-Burman					109,760	0.01	198,303	0.01	306,072	0.02	309,576	0.02

Tu	Altaic (Mongolic)	148,760	0.01	192,568	0.01	241,198	0.02	289,565	0.02
Mulao	Tai-Kadai	91,790	0.01	160,648	0.01	207,352	0.01	216,257	0.02
Xibe	Tungusic	77,560	0.01	172,932	0.01	188,824	0.02	190,481	0.01
Kyrgyz	Altaic (Turkic)	108,790	0.01	143,537	0.01	160,823	0.01	186,708	0.01
Daur	Altaic (Mongolic)	—	—	121,463	0.01	132,143	0.01	131,992	0.01
Jingpo	Tibeto-Burman	100,180	0.01	119,276	0.01	132,143	0.01	147,828	0.01
Maonan	Tai-Kadai	37,450	0.00	72,370	0.00	107,106	0.01	101,192	0.01
Salar	Altaic (Turkic)	68,030	0.01	82,398	0.01	104,503	0.01	130,607	0.01
Blang	Mon-Khmer	—	—	87,546	0.01	91,882	0.01	119,639	0.01
Tajik	Indo-European (Iranian)	27,430	0.00	33,223	0.00	41,028	0.00	51,069	0.00
Achang	Tibeto-Burman	31,490	0.00	27,718	0.00	33,936	0.00	39,555	0.00
Pumi	Tibeto-Burman	18,860	0.00	29,721	0.00	33,600	0.00	42,861	0.00
Ewenki	Tungusic	19,440	0.00	26,379	0.00	30,505	0.00	30,875	0.00
Nu	Tibeto-Burman	25,980	0.00	27,190	0.00	28,759	0.00	37,523	0.00
Gin (Vietnamese)	Mon-Khmer	12,140	0.00	18,749	0.00	22,517	0.00	28,199	0.00
Jino	Tibeto-Burman	11,260	0.00	18,022	0.00	20,899	0.00	23,143	0.00
De'ang	Mon-Khmer	—	—	15,461	0.00	17,935	0.00	20,556	0.00

(Continued)

TABLE 13.1 Population of China According to Ethnic Group in Censuses, 1953–2010 (Continued)

Ethnic Group	Language Family	1953	%	1964	%	1982	%	1990	%	2000	%	2010	%
Bonan	Altaic (Mongolic)					6,620		11,683	0.00	16,505	0.00	20,074	0.00
Russian	Indo-European (Slavic)					2,830		13,500	0.00	15,609	0.00	15,393	0.00
Yugur	Altaic (Turkic)					7,670		12,293	0.00	13,719	0.00	14,378	0.00
Uzbek	Altaic (Turkic)					13,810		14,763	0.00	13,370	0.00	10,569	0.00
Monba	Tibeto-Burman					1,040		7,498	0.00	8,923	0.00	10,561	0.00
Oroqen	Tungusic					2,280		7,004	0.00	8,196	0.00	8,659	0.00
Derung	Tibeto-Burman					4,250		5,825	0.00	7,426	0.00	6,930	0.00
Chinese Tatars	Altaic (Turkic)					7,510		5,064	0.00	4,890	0.00	3,556	0.00
Hezhen	Tungusic					670		4,254	0.00	4,640	0.00	5,354	0.00
Lhoba	Tibeto-Burman					1,030		2,322	0.00	2,965	0.00	3,682	0.00
Unrecognized						3,370,880		3,498	0.33	734,379	0.00	640,101	0.05
Unknown						4,720		752,347	0.00	735,379	0.07	—	0.06
Foreigners						—		—		941		1,448	0.00
Total mainland China		582,603,417		694,581,759		1,008,175,288		1,133,682,501		1,242,612,226		1,332,810,869	

Source: Chinese census data, 2010.

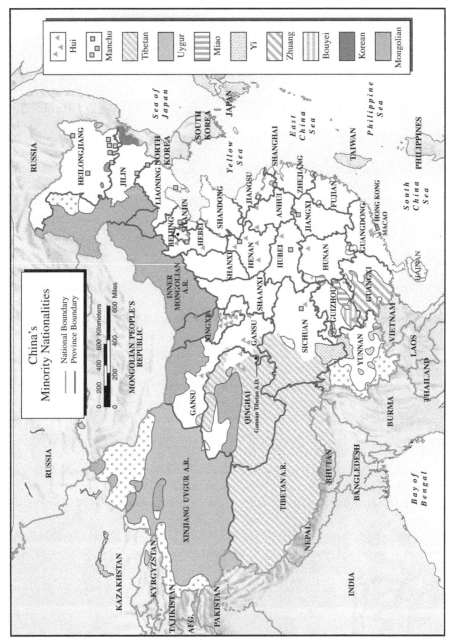

MAP 13.1 China's Minority Nationalities

its minorities as prosperous and contented, they could serve as living proof of the successes that the Chinese model of socialism would have for non-Han peoples. Conversely, having discontented and rebellious ethnic populations would be, and continues to be, an embarrassment for the PRC. Ethnically based discontent could also compound China's strategic problems in that dissident minorities would be more receptive to subversive influences from foreign powers.

A fifth reason is more recent: tourism. The post-Mao era has included both an opening to the outside world and ambitious plans for economic development. Many minorities wear colorful costumes of exquisite workmanship and possess rich artistic traditions. Some live in areas of breathtaking scenery. Thus, visiting minority areas has been popular with tourists, and provides a pleasant contrast with the somewhat drab appearance of many of the PRC's major cities. It has become an important source of foreign exchange for the government.

Finally, even though minorities may total only 8.4 percent of the PRC's population, this amounts to approximately 112 million people. Their numbers thus exceed the populations of most of the countries in the world, including France, Germany, and Great Britain. Hence, in spite of being a small part of the total population of the PRC, what China's media refer to as "the minorities problem" has occupied an important place in Chinese policy making. Essentially, the minorities problem is one of *integration*: For reasons of defense, economic and social well-being, and national pride, the Chinese communist elite has attached considerable importance to, first, assuming jurisdiction over minority peoples and, second, obtaining their loyalties. This chapter examines the steps taken by the party and government to achieve integration and attempts to assess the success of these efforts.

There are many different methods by which to bring about the assertion of administrative authority and reorientation of loyalties. These may be conceptualized as a continuum ranging from *assimilation* at one end to *pluralism* at the other. Assimilation involves minorities being absorbed into the dominant group. In the process, they lose their languages and other distinguishing characteristics, being, in essence, indistinguishable from the majority group. At the other end of the spectrum, in a pluralist system, minorities retain their languages as well as large parts of their culture and traditional ways of behavior. They accept the administrative authority of the government of the dominant group, and even participate in it. But they remain distinct from the majority group. Minorities' policy in post-1949 China has vacillated between an emphasis on pluralism and an emphasis on forced assimilation. During Mao's lifetime, these shifts were sudden and violent; in the Deng era and thereafter, there have been moves toward greater and lesser restrictions on the exercise of minorities' freedoms, with an underlying acceptance of a degree of pluralism, albeit with the end goal of their being firmly under party and government control.

Past Chinese governments have tried each of these extremes. Although there were wide variations over the long course of Chinese history, and even several non-Han dynasties, the dominant pattern in traditional China was pluralistic. It was also quite condescending. The Ming dynasty philosopher-statesman Wang

Yangming compared the administration of barbarians to dealing with wild deer: if invited into one's home, they would destroy the ancestral tablets, but if left alone, they would trample crops. In essence, Wang was advocating supervision and control; he believed that efforts to force minority groups to behave like Han would be counterproductive.

Ethnicity in Communist Ideology

Initially, the most important factor conditioning Chinese communist policy toward minorities was ideology. Karl Marx believed that what appeared to be ethnic or nationality characteristics were actually just manifestations of the bourgeois–capitalist phase of society. After the dictatorship of the proletariat was established, these manifestations of bourgeois society would wither away, and a homogeneous proletarian culture would evolve.

No coercion would be necessary to bring about this homogeneous culture. Some resistance from a few die-hard remnants of the aristocratic or bourgeois classes of the old society might have to be dealt with forcefully, but would be a relatively minor problem. The homogeneous society would come about almost automatically as levels of socialism and communism increased. It would blend the best of all nationalities' customs and habits. Given this favorable ideological prognosis, a lenient policy toward minority cultures and ethnic identities was called for. After the new communist government eliminated the die-hard types, time and the increasing communization of the economy and society would take care of the rest.

Minorities Policy in Practice
The Early Years: 1949–1957

Ideology was reinforced by the practical situation in which the Chinese communists found themselves in 1949. There was a great deal of hostility between minorities and Han Chinese. The CCP had taken over most minority areas through military victory or because minority leaders perceived armed resistance to be futile. The party elite was well aware that the hearts and minds of most minority peoples had yet to be won.

The party had trained a small group of minority cadres who were also communists, but there were not nearly enough of them to take care of the administrative and other work that the CCP felt it needed to do in minority areas. The leadership was aware that it knew too little about the various minorities to understand how to deal with them. Ignorance of specific ethnic groups' customs could cause grievous insult—for example, it might be extremely important to know whether a guest should sit to the right or the left of his host's campfire. Breaches of etiquette, however unintentionally committed, could cause lasting harm to the party's image and complicate the process of integration. Lack of knowledge about the minorities meant that the party had little sense of what their problems were; conversely, possessing such knowledge would allow the party to approach them with suggestions for solutions.

The people who were best equipped to enlighten the party's representatives, or cadres, and who could also be most influential in winning the trust of the minorities' masses for the party, were typically the pre-1949 leadership elite of the minorities. Particularly in the case of the smaller and more primitive minority groups, headmen were the interpreters of the outside world to their constituencies and sometimes the only ones of their group who could speak Chinese. To approach the "exploited masses" directly, as the party had done in Han areas, was more apt to cause confusion and rejection than to achieve the desired results. The fact that the party needed to work with traditional pre-1949 elites was also conducive to a policy of tolerance and accommodation of differences.

Hence, the Chinese communists fashioned a minorities policy that resembled a pluralistic model of integration. Many of its elements were borrowed from the Soviet Union; a number of Soviet ethnologists served as advisers to the Chinese and assisted in research and data collection in minority areas. However, the PRC's situation differed from that of the USSR in some important ways: Nearly half of the USSR's population was non-Russian, and a much higher proportion of the USSR's minorities were educated and economically developed to a level equal to, or higher than, that of Russians.

In accordance with Soviet doctrine, minorities were given so-called autonomous areas. Depending on the concentrations of minority populations involved, these areas could be created at province, prefecture, county, or township level. The areas provided certain accommodations for the customs of the host nationality and preferential treatment for them in the selection of official positions. Minorities received the right to use their own languages, both spoken and written. In the case of those minorities who did not have a written language, the party promised to help them to devise one. Minorities were guaranteed the right to keep their traditional costumes and customs so long as these did not interfere with production. In the majority of cases, they could even keep their traditional leaders, so long as those leaders did not actively oppose socialism. This policy fitted well with the idea of a united front of cooperation with "patriotic" bourgeois upper strata in general, which was prevalent in the early days of the PRC.

The party organization most closely connected with minorities work was, and remains, the United Front Work Department (UFWD) of the party central committee. Originally set up in Yan'an in 1944, the UFWD has been responsible for shaping the broad outlines of policy in minority areas in accordance with the party line. It is also in charge of other aspects of united front work concerned with the implementation of the People's Democratic Dictatorship, which Mao had deemed appropriate for China in this transition period from "new democracy" to socialism. The UFWDs also exist as sections of the party apparatus on the provincial level. At lower levels where no UFWD exists, the Rural Work Department of the local party organization may fill the task of political guidance for minorities.

At the central government level, broad guidelines from the UFWD are sent to the Nationalities Affairs Commission (NAC) of the State Council, which has the responsibility for implementing them. Major pronouncements on minorities' affairs are drawn up by the commission, and then approved and promulgated by the State Council. The NAC is then charged with implementing them. Despite its subordination to the UFWD, the NAC, meeting every day and functioning as a regular ministry, has considerable powers. NACs also exist at provincial, prefectural, and county levels in areas with substantial minority populations (Figure 13.1). Where minority populations are not large and their problems are deemed uncomplicated, they may be handled by a department of civil affairs at the relevant level, with an office or a particular cadre designated as responsible.

The National People's Congress (NPC) has a nationalities' committee. Comprising all ethnic minority delegates to the NPC, it has no real power, being confined to discussion and approval of measures decided upon elsewhere. However, delegates' speeches may include important information about problems in minority areas, even though the delegates themselves have little ability to effect solutions. In addition, the members' selection as NPC delegates provides an index of the party's assessment of their prestige in their own respective areas.

Minorities were initially given assurances that socialist reforms would not be introduced until the minority masses wanted them. In addition, they received exceptions from certain other rules imposed upon the Han. For example, animals killed in connection with a ritual sacrifice were exempt from the slaughter tax. Muslim minorities, whose customs included polygamy, and Tibetans, whose culture encouraged multiple husbands, were allowed to continue these practices. Where early marriage was a tradition, it could remain. The Yi could even continue to own slaves.

Meanwhile, the party made various efforts to speed up the transition period into socialism and the homogenization of proletarian culture. A network of nationalities' institutes was established in order to educate minorities, and some Han Chinese, to carry out the party's work in minority areas. They were trained as teachers, administrative cadres, veterinarians, and entertainers. All courses of study, even entertainment, carried a pro-communist message.

Research teams, which included anthropologists and linguistics experts, among others, were sent out to live with the minorities and learn their languages and customs. Health teams also visited minority areas, as did work teams, which were generally staffed by People's Liberation Army (PLA) members. These visits had propaganda motives in addition to their overt functions. Doctors and paramedics dispensed pills and salves as gifts from the CCP and Chairman Mao; work teams dug irrigation ditches and reclaimed wasteland with the same message. They focused on unity and patriotism. The teams also tried to build a positive image of the party and socialism. They did not emphasize ideology or sweeping social or economic reforms.

Pleased with the results of these early efforts at social mobilization, the party moved on to the next step: setting up so-called people's governments in minority areas. These were established at different times in different minority areas during

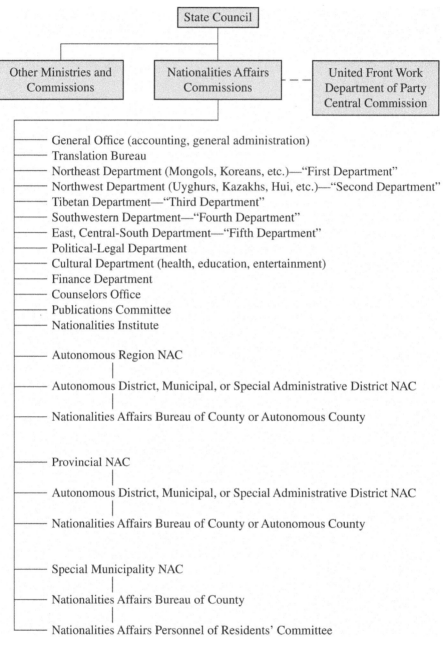

FIGURE 13.1 The Administration of Minorities Work in China

the early 1950s, consonant with the party's estimate of the receptivity of the target group. Such governments generally included a fair sprinkling of traditional minorities' leaders. In Tibetan and Mongolian areas, lamas were included; in the southwest, tribal heads participated.

Also included were as many minority group activists as the party had been able to train. Some of these actually were from the stratum of society that the party considered exploited: children of serfs or slaves who were bright, personable, and quick to absorb the party's message. Quite a few others, however, were scions of the traditional elite, for whom cooperation seemed the best way to ensure their survival. For example, the numerous offspring of the Tibetan nobleman and arch collaborator Ngapo Ngawang Jigme were trained at the Central Nationalities Institute in Beijing and given various positions of responsibility when they graduated. Han Chinese administrators constituted a third group in the memberships of the new people's governments. Nearly always party members and sometimes PLA members as well, they were the decisive elements of decision making, whether or not they held the top positions.

Including the more cooperative and prestigious members of the traditional minority elite in the new people's governments gave the party a way to allow traditional governmental structures to wither out of existence without actually abolishing them. Many of the traditional leaders themselves, and their prestige, remained intact. The party's motive seems to have been to maintain traditional symbols of power, thereby minimizing their resistance to change while gradually modifying the power structure they had represented. Another attempt at symbol manipulation was the granting of the title *bator*, a Mongolian word meaning hero. It had been used by Uyghurs and Kazakhs as well as Mongols to honor outstanding individuals among them, usually for valor on the battlefield. Henceforth, it was to be given to heroes of socialist labor.

Certain other gestures were made to accommodate minority sensitivities. For example, the names of many minority groups had been rendered into Chinese using characters containing the dog radical, the obvious intent being to disparage the humanness of the particular group. Other groups were called not by the name they commonly called themselves but by a pejorative term, such as Lolo for the group that knew itself as Yi. The party ordered an end to such practices although, of course, changing long-standing attitudes was a more difficult task. Offensive place names were also changed; these had typically been given to commemorate Han conquests of so-called barbarian areas or the suppression of rebellion therein. For example, Dihua, the capital of Xinjiang, was changed to its Uyghur name, Urumqi.

The goal of introducing socialist reforms had not been forgotten; it was simply postponed until after the preliminary work had been done. Land reform in minority areas began only around 1952/1953, by which time it had been almost completed in Han Chinese areas. Research efforts helped decide whether an area's level of development was suitable for the introduction of reforms. Target areas were chosen as test cases, with reforms generalized to surrounding locations only after they had been judged successful in the target area. The result was a relatively flexible reform process that was responsive not only to differences between one minority group and another but also to differences within minority groups. For example, Mongols whose main occupation was fixed agriculture, termed "sedentary Mongols," were judged ready for reforms, while Mongols who were nomadic herdsmen, termed "pastoral Mongols," were not. The Yi of Yunnan were ordered to emancipate their slaves, whereas the Yi of Sichuan, who were found to be "less culturally advanced"—meaning less sinicized—were not. Tibetan areas east of the Jinsha River underwent land reform in 1954, whereas land reform was not attempted west of the Jinsha.

In 1956, there was a speed-up in agricultural collectivization in minority areas similar to that which had occurred in Han areas in mid-1955. But it, too, was based on an assessment of what a given minority would be receptive to: minorities who had already undergone land reform were moved up to mutual aid teams, those already at the stage of mutual aid teams were raised to lower level cooperatives, and so forth. In other words, the 1956 collectivization effort did not remove the differences between Han and non-Han areas; it simply raised them to a loftier level in the hierarchy of socialism.

Dissatisfaction with this flexible system began to grow when, in 1956 and 1957, as part of a routine investigation of minorities' work and also in connection with the Hundred Flowers campaign (see Chapter 4), ethnic minorities were asked to express their opinions about party and government. What they said proved shocking. Some wanted to secede from China. Others said that they thought the party's policies amounted to thinly disguised plans for assimilation. A third group pointed out that the party was violating its own promise to allow dispensations from certain policies that ran counter to minorities' special characteristics. Collectivization and socialism in general, they argued, were incompatible with their customs and religions. The party's policy of autonomy was denounced as a sham, "as useful as ears on a basket," since, in actuality, they had no rights. Moreover, critics expressed the attitude that minorities who had joined the party or become cadres were traitors to their fellow ethnics, "jackals serving the Han."

The party responded much as it had to the Han Chinese who had been overly frank during the Hundred Flowers campaign. Some efforts were made to deal with certain grievances that minorities critics had raised: For example, where there were complaints of arrogance on the part of Han cadres, or where it could be shown that the language of the minority had been suppressed, there were attempts at redress. However, just as in Han areas, an anti-rightist campaign was carried out in minority areas. There, its main target was "local nationalism," which was equated with antisocialism. The chief victims were certain traditional leaders whom the party viewed as stumbling blocks on the road to the reforms that the party wanted to introduce in minority areas. A number of traditional leaders were replaced by young minority activists whom the party had trained. Nonetheless, the campaign against local nationalism was far from a thoroughgoing purge. The united front continued in both theory and practice.

The Great Leap Forward and Its Aftermath: 1959–1965

The outpouring of grievances during 1956 and 1957 disabused the party leadership of its idea that a policy of toleration toward minorities' special characteristics would end in the atrophy of those special characteristics. This reassessment fed into a general mood of impatience with the pace of China's progress in other spheres as well, culminating in the massive social and economic upheaval of the Great Leap Forward. The Leap's goals of increasing production, simplifying administration, eliminating bureaucratism and red tape, and achieving pure communism seemed ill served by the congeries of special arrangements the party had made in minority areas. The existence of a number of different levels of collectivization, the issues of the timing of the introduction of reforms, the policies of cooperation with the traditional upper strata, respect for special characteristics, and encouragement of local languages were now seen as standing squarely in the way of progress.

Hence, in 1958 and 1959, areas that had widely different levels of socialist reforms were hurriedly organized into communes. Often, several different nationalities, including some that had very different economic levels and cultures, were combined in these communes. The mere mention of "special characteristics" was dangerous: it was regarded as equivalent to opposing socialism. Likewise, the policy of tolerating, and even encouraging, minorities' languages changed, and a hitherto unnoticed high tide of enthusiasm for studying the Chinese language was suddenly discovered.

All kinds of customs the party had tolerated became regarded as "decadent." What had been promised, the media pointed out, was that customs not detrimental to production could be kept. Festival days were now deemed detrimental to production, since people did no work on those days. So also was the ritual killing of animals, because it reduced the food supply. Traditional turbans were counterproductive: They were a waste of cloth. Moreover, many turbans were very heavy and apt to cause headaches for wearers who were engaged in hard physical labor. A cloth cap or straw sun hat was superior. Colorful sashes were also declared counterproductive. Like turbans, they wasted material. Many sashes were intricately embroidered, a process that wasted time that could have been spent in producing more necessary items. In addition, wearing sashes prevented one from bending over freely while working in the fields. A belt would keep one's trousers on just as well, at less cost and greater convenience.

Research projects into minorities' languages, history, and cultures were terminated. Castigated as "bourgeois scientific objectivism," they, too, were considered a waste of time and money that could better be devoted to increasing production levels. For example, a dictionary compilation project that had amassed 50,000 words was ridiculed, since a few hundred words, mostly relating to production, were all that were really needed. In their zeal to raise production, officials also took land that had been promised to herders for pasture and reclassified it as crop land. The people thus affected were reported to be very pleased with the changes. Even the Hui, who are Muslims, were said to be enthusiastic about joining communal mess halls, despite the fact that dishes containing pork were served there.

The Great Leap Forward produced a fiasco in minority areas, just as it had in Han China, but with one crucial difference: ethnic minorities, unlike Han, perceived the Leap as being imposed on them by outsiders in an attempt to destroy their culture and ways of life. The party's abrupt swing to blatantly assimilationist policies contradicted its previous pronouncements that reforms would not be carried out except according to the desires of the minority masses, and by minorities themselves. It also ran counter to the role the party had set for itself as protector of minorities' cultures.

Beginning in early 1959, official publications started to admit that the gap between the party's promises and its performance in minorities' areas had caused it to "lose the trust of the masses," and that "production had suffered to a certain extent." Minorities' resentment and resistance took many forms, ranging from passive resistance and small-scale sabotage to open revolt. The latter occurred in Tibet and Xinjiang, and among the Hui and Yi. In the case of the revolts in Tibet and Xinjiang, large numbers of refugees crossed the borders into India and the Soviet Union, respectively. This created two hostile émigré communities on two different borders, both of them vigorously denouncing China's minorities' policy as forced assimilation.

India, whose own relations with the PRC were strained by a bitter border dispute, tried to persuade the refugees to take a low profile. The Soviet Union, on the other hand, encouraged them to publicize their experiences, even providing more radio programming in native languages and setting up a separate newspaper for the refugees. The newspaper was published in Arabic script, even though the USSR had forced its own members of the same minority group to use the Cyrillic alphabet.

The Great Leap Forward's drive for unity through uniformity of language, dress, and lifestyle backfired, creating a heightened sense of awareness on the part of minorities of the differences between them and the Han, and an increasingly stubborn desire among many of them to retain their separate natures. China was in very bad shape in 1959 as a result of the Leap, and the government had to concentrate on policies that would enable people to simply survive. In both Han and minority areas, these focused on repairing the damage done by the Great Leap. Ideology was a luxury that had to be foregone, at least temporarily. Land that had been taken from herders was returned: Most of it had been found unsuitable for cultivation anyway, just as the locals had pointed out in 1958 when the campaign started. Unfortunately, there were far fewer animals to graze on it: Many herders had killed their livestock rather than turn the animals over to communes.

Communes that were set up in minority areas were typically disbanded in fact though not in name, just as in Han areas. In a few areas, however, communes had created such problems that even the name was discarded. These included those of the Dai (Thai), Yi, Lisu, and Tibetans outside the Tibetan Autonomous Region (TAR). Tibetans who lived within the boundaries of the TAR had not had communes imposed on them. Rumors that the harsh policies imposed in other Tibetan areas during the Great Leap Forward were about to be applied to them were one but not the only important cause of the March 1959 revolt.

In the case of communes that comprised several different ethnic minorities, the reorganization specified that members of the more prosperous group would be guaranteed the income level they had before entering the commune.

Considerable resentment was engendered when minorities with better farming skills had been combined with those of lesser abilities and the total incomes averaged. Hui were no longer obliged to eat in mess halls where pork was served.

Other accommodations made in the wake of the Great Leap Forward included the rehabilitation of some members of the traditional elite who had been purged in the anti-rightist campaign. Research projects that were canceled at the beginning of the Leap were revived. The media explained that "careful research and investigation has *always* been the basic method of Marxism–Leninism." The concept of respect for minorities' special characteristics was also reinstated.

This backtracking on the rigid ideological positions that had been prevalent during the Great Leap Forward was similar to what was being done in Han areas, but the extent of backtracking was greater in minorities' areas. The years 1959 and 1960 saw a return to the pluralistic policies that characterized the period from 1949 through 1957. Some attempts to tighten up a few of the more lenient manifestations of this in Han China occurred during what is known as the socialist education campaign from 1962 to 1965, but do not seem to have had much of an effect on policies in minority areas.

The Cultural Revolution: 1966–1971

Although the period of the Cultural Revolution is officially 1966–1976, this periodization does not apply well to minorities' policy. The major changes in minorities' policy began in 1966, as elsewhere in China, but were substantially modified in 1971. Hence, the period from 1966 to 1971 is a more accurate time frame for the Cultural Revolution as it concerns minorities. As seen in Chapter 5, the Great Proletarian Revolution was a massive effort to wrench China away from the ideological laxity that had been induced by the failure of the Great Leap Forward and to return it to the path of orthodoxy. For minority areas, this meant a return to radical assimilationist policies.

Radicals demanded, and often got, the purge of many of the administrators who had favored gradualism and pluralism. One party leader, a Han, was accused of actively seeking to disband minorities' communes; another, also a Han, was purged for "surrendering to" the upper classes of the ethnic minorities. It was apparently a shock to discover that "seventeen years after liberation, minority chiefs and slaveowners are still riding roughshod over the peasants." The party leader of Inner Mongolia, Ulanhu, a Mongol who had been a CCP member since his youth in the 1920s, was accused of having encouraged the study of the Mongolian language and cultural heritage. He had thus promoted "national splittism" and impeded the development of unity among all nationalities. It will be remembered that encouraging the study of minority languages and cultures was party policy at the time the accused individuals were allegedly committing their heinous crimes.

Some of the charges seemed preposterous. For example, Ulanhu was also accused of plotting to make himself emperor of an independent, reunified Mongolian state. Since the Mongolian People's Republic was firmly under the protection of the much more powerful Soviet Union and, moreover, had evinced no interest whatsoever in reuniting with its fellow Mongols in China, it is difficult to see how even the most imaginative plotter could have intended to proceed.

Radical assimilationists aided by Red Guards used an earlier statement of Mao on the minorities problem—"The nationalities problem is in essence a class problem"—as their rallying cry and interpreted it in the most extreme way possible. Since nationalities' problems were class problems, they reasoned, and since class differences were to be abolished, nationality differences must also disappear. Consonant with this logic, Red Guards attacked the "four olds" in minority areas. They called for an end to the united front, which they regarded as "class capitulationism," and demanded that concessions to minorities' special characteristics be terminated. Class struggle, they argued, must be introduced into minority areas; autonomous areas themselves should be abolished.

Radical assimilationists had some successes during the Cultural Revolution. For example, communes were begun in the TAR where they had never existed before, and were re-imposed in other minority areas where they had been disbanded. Many of those to whom the radicals referred as "entrenched power holders" in minority areas were removed from office. But the net result of the Cultural Revolution fell far short of radicals' hopes. Quite a few of the old guard in minority areas, including nobles, headmen, and respected religious leaders known as Living Buddhas, were retained. Some of the minorities' special characteristics also remained, and the autonomous areas were never abolished. Members of minority groups continued to be identified as such in the press.

Part of this failure to achieve assimilationist goals was the fear that pushing minorities too hard would jeopardize border defense. Another was simply that the goal was essentially unrealizable. In areas where radical supervision was strong, ethnic feelings went underground. For example, Xinhua news agency proudly reported that in Lhasa, the capital of Tibet, pictures of Mao Zedong had replaced pictures of the Dalai Lama in local homes. However, Mao had not replaced the Dalai Lama in the residents' esteem. As soon as the pressure was off, Mao's picture came off the walls and the Dalai Lama's went back up. Where radical supervision was sporadic or nonexistent—which was often the case, since a number of minorities lived in remote, not easily accessible areas—the changes that were ordered could be, and were, ignored.

From 1968 through mid-1971, however, minorities were a low-key presence in the PRC. On the fairly rare occasions when they were mentioned at all by the mass media, they were treated as Han by any other name. Individuals with noticeably non-Han names were regularly included among the chorus of praise for the party line of the moment. For any problems of livelihood and production, studying the works of Mao was the recommended solution.

Return to Pluralism: 1971–1977

This situation changed markedly after mid-1971. It is impossible to prove causality, but the return to pluralism closely coincided with the decline from power of

Lin Biao, heretofore regarded as Mao Zedong's heir apparent, and key members of his Fourth Field Army. From May to November 1971, several regional broadcasting stations resumed the programming in minority languages that had ceased in 1966/1967. In addition, the media began to encourage people, both minorities and Han, to study minorities' languages.

Books in minorities' languages began to be printed again. Party propaganda boasted that they sold for less than the same book in Han Chinese, because the party subsidized the costs. The party also took credit for saving the Mongolian language from dying out. This was ironic in view of the Inner Mongolian party secretary having been purged during the Cultural Revolution for, among other crimes, urging people to study Mongolian. Ulanhu was soon rehabilitated and cleared of all charges, including, presumably, his plans to make himself emperor. The media announced that the government was making special consumer goods available to the minorities, and restrictions were eased on religious practices.

There were some problems with minorities during this period. For example, in 1975, a directive that forced people to work on Fridays was issued. This being the Muslim holy day, riots among Muslims were reported from Xinjiang to Yunnan. Frictions continued to exist between various minorities and Han, occasionally escalating into violence triggered by some essentially minor incident. But basically, the years after mid-1971 saw a return to pluralistic policies, and minority–Han relations began to improve.

Post-Mao Minorities' Policy

Deng Xiaoping extended this policy of toleration, with some innovations that had profound consequences for ethnic minority areas. This was more an indirect result than a conscious design. As seen in Chapter 7, Deng believed that his paramount goal of creating prosperity could best be achieved by investing capital where it had the highest multiplier effect. In general, this meant investing in coastal cities like Shanghai and Guangzhou or major river ports like Wuhan. Certain areas, such as Shenzhen and Zhuhai, received tax breaks and other perquisites designed to draw in foreign capital. None of these was in minority areas, whose inhabitants were told that they would have to adjust to the market economy: subsidies were replaced with loans. Just as in Han rural areas, minorities received the right to sell their goods on the free market.

The policy of nationalities problems being class problems was officially repudiated, with the explanation being that Mao had been "misunderstood." Differences between minorities and Han were henceforth to be understood as a function of income inequalities between the two groups. As living standards equalized, tensions would disappear. Overt differences between minorities and Han, such as language, dress, and customs, should not be expected to disappear in the near future, if at all. This went beyond the Mao era's periods of willingness to temporarily accommodate minorities' special characteristics and toward a pluralist model of long-term acceptance of these characteristics. To help reduce tensions between Han and non-Han, minorities were exempted to various degrees from the one-child policy imposed upon the Han. Their children also enjoyed easier access to higher education.

Reform Produces Problems

New problems arose. Han complained about the unfairness of special treatment for minorities; some solved this by re-registering as an ethnic minority in order to take advantage of the ability to have additional children and the preference these children would receive on university entrance exams. Although at first the government explained this increase in the country's minority population, it soon realized the reasons and attempted to curb the re-registration process. Puzzlingly, the 2010 census showed a drop in the proportion of China's population of ethnic minorities relative to Han (see table 13.1); no official explanation has been given.

Other issues arose from economic policies that favored China's most productive areas. With investment capital from both domestic and foreign sources flowing into selected enclaves, these already relatively prosperous areas became still wealthier, while minority areas lagged behind. New rural policies increased food supplies in minority areas, but simultaneously re-established the class inequities the CCP had come to power promising to abolish. Those who were disadvantaged by the reforms felt that the party was breaking faith with the masses. A study of Tibetan herders indicated that the newly prosperous families were precisely those who had prospered under the pre-communist system. When a policy change replaced subsidies ("blood transfusions") with measures designed to encourage local initiative ("blood creation") by requiring matching funds, these proved disadvantageous for different reasons. Two-thirds of minority areas were so poor that they could not raise the necessary sums.

Moreover, the inflation that accompanied the upsurge of production in coastal areas proved disproportionately hurtful to minority areas. Typically, they had been the suppliers of raw materials to the manufacturing areas of the coast. Finished products were then made available for minorities to purchase at value-added prices. When these prices rose sharply, minorities' sense that they were being exploited by the Han—a feeling that long predated the communist era—was reinforced. At one point, the Xinjiang Uyghur Autonomous Region (XUAR) actually banned no less than 48 kinds of products, including soap, bicycles, and color television sets, from entering the XUAR.

There was unrest in Xinjiang; in Tibet, a famine. Crops failed after a party policy that forced people to plant wheat, which proved to be unsuitable to the soil, rather than the traditional barley. Transport aircraft were sent to evacuate Han. In Xinjiang, Han cadres were quietly withdrawn from the grass roots, a fact not revealed until late May 1998, when the withdrawal was linked to the rise of subversive religious activities there. In Yunnan, there were disputes over land and water rights. Minorities' land and rubber trees were illegally appropriated when plantations were established.

Efforts were made to deal with these problems. Hu Yaobang made an inspection visit to Yunnan and Tibet to try to soothe problems. Tibetans were again allowed to cultivate the barley they preferred; state subsidies were increased. Tibet was also exempted from certain taxes. Border minorities in general were encouraged to develop their economies through trade with neighboring countries. Hence, Tibetans began to trade with Nepal and India; Yunnan minorities with Laos, Burma, and Thailand; Xinjiang minorities with the then-Soviet Union; and Inner Mongolians with the Mongolian People's Republic and the former USSR. Tourism to minority areas began to be encouraged. The government also announced that it would welcome foreign investment in minority areas. Although the investment potential was not as great as in coastal areas, the government hoped that foreigners would invest for essentially noneconomic reasons. For example, wealthy Saudis or Malaysians might wish to aid their co-religionists in China.

Well meant as these efforts were, they had serious side effects. Borders became more porous. Calls for increased trade, tourism, and foreign investment in minority areas coincided with an upsurge of fundamentalist sentiments in the Islamic world. Potential Muslim investors were interested in how their fellow Muslims were treated, and often asked to tour mosques and religious schools. Spies could pose as businesspeople or tourists. Given that few Han administrators in minority areas had learned the local languages, foreign visitors could often converse freely with minorities while their guides remained oblivious to what was being said. Subversive materials, weapons, and explosives could be smuggled in, and letters and tapes alleging or documenting atrocities smuggled out. Yunnan's border trade included an upsurge of traffic in the Golden Triangle's most famous export product: opium.

Dai minorities were impressed with the affluent lifestyles of their fellow Thai who came as tourists to Yunnan. The cultural and economic lure of Bangkok was apparently strong enough that when Thailand's state airline suggested opening a direct route from Chiang Mai to Jinghong, the capital of the Xishuangbanna Dai Autonomous Prefecture, Beijing initially refused. Visitors from the Republic of Korea (ROK) similarly impressed their fellow Koreans in the PRC. Until the authorities began to keep close watch on them, Chinese Korean "tourists" simply disappeared after checking into their Seoul hotel rooms, and sought jobs in the vibrant South Korean economy. Chinese Koreans tried to enter the ROK on undocumented boats as well. The ROK police also discovered a thriving marriage-of-convenience market involving elderly ROK males and young Chinese Korean women.

In addition, there were complaints that the policies devised to develop the economies of minority areas primarily benefited the Han residents thereof. This was an especially sore point in Tibet, where the aforementioned tax exemptions resulted in a flood of Han migrants into the TAR in order to take advantage of them. Most of the peddlers in the tourist areas of Lhasa were Han from Sichuan. Western guests at the Lhasa Holiday Inn who spoke Tibetan to waitresses wearing traditional Tibetan clothing discovered that the young women were likewise

Han. To make matters worse, workers brought in under government auspices to work at jobs that included weaving traditional Tibetan carpets received higher wages than did the Tibetans who worked alongside them. The authorities argued that these skilled workers would not have wanted to relocate to Tibet's harsh climate had they not been enticed by higher wages, and that they were enhancing economic benefits for all. Tibetans, however, felt that they were being treated as second-class citizens in their own country, and that any Han who were brought in were taking jobs away from Tibetans.

Construction workers building pseudo-Dai structures in Jinghong, presumably for the benefit of tourists, were Han migrant workers. In northwest China, Uyghurs and Kazakhs complained that Han received preference for better jobs in "their" oilfields and elsewhere. The central government itself admitted that Han migrants had caused ecological damage in Xinjiang through careless land use. Environmental damage from Han misuse of the land has been an ongoing complaint among the Mongols of Inner Mongolia, dating at least as far back as the Great Leap Forward. As concerns about the environment in general have grown, so have the complaints from minorities.

Whether the benefits of these new economic policies were going primarily to the minorities in minority areas or to the Han in minority areas, the income gap between minority regions and Han China continued to grow. The average industrial and agricultural output in ethnic minority areas had dropped to 47.9 percent of the national average by 1989; more than two decades and many policy initiatives later, official sources admitted that the gap continued to widen. Only the Guangxi Zhuang Autonomous Region managed to perform at a level comparable to Han China. The Zhuang had accommodated well to Han culture long before 1949, and Guangxi also benefited from its geographic location bordering on booming Guangdong province. The four remaining autonomous regions—Tibet, Ningxia, Xinjiang, and Inner Mongolia—plus three other provinces—Gansu, Guizhou, and Qinghai, which have large minority populations—lagged far behind. Authorities in Tibet complained that once having lifted the poorest of its poor out of poverty, it was difficult to prevent them from slipping back. Some areas experienced declines in minority education rates.

In any case, and contrary to the assumptions of party policy, narrowing the income and educational gap between minorities and Han will not necessarily end internationality tensions. People who are less focused on sheer survival may have more leisure to indulge their antigovernment feelings, and more money to finance the purchase of weapons. Better educational levels may stimulate interest in one's indigenous culture and enhance one's ability to learn more about it. A number of the Inner Mongolian dissidents who were arrested on splittist charges were graduates of the party's own nationalities' institutes, where they had become interested in going beyond the officially sanctioned versions of Mongolian culture. The existence of tensions in a number of minority areas notwithstanding, serious disturbances have been reported in recent years only from Xinjiang, Tibet, and to a lesser extent, Inner Mongolia.

External Factors

As for the effects of tourism, while some members of minorities profited from the presence of the outsiders and welcomed them, others believed that the central government was exploiting them on behalf of its desire for more foreign exchange. In effect, minorities are being exoticized in pursuit of profit. There are also complaints that the government is perverting and trivializing their culture. Many of the handicrafts marketed as minority-made are not authentic in style and not made by minorities. So-called "minority villages," in which foreign visitors are shown how several different minority groups live, strike outsiders as more like human zoos than authentic representations of minority life.

Western views of minorities were also influenced by the increased concern with human rights that began in the 1980s. Tibet, in particular, captured the imagination of large numbers of people. Buddhism became the fastest-growing religion in the West, and adherents to its Tibetan variant spanned a range that included eminent scholars and prominent entertainers. Hollywood produced several films sympathetic to the Tibetan cause, and a U.S. congressman slipped into Tibet disguised as a tourist, later charging that the local culture was being systematically destroyed. Some genuine tourists readily complied with Tibetans' requests to send in pictures of the Dalai Lama—possession of which is intermittently banned by the Chinese government—and to take out documents detailing abuses.

These difficulties were compounded by the disintegration of the Soviet empire and the rise of Islamic fundamentalism. States governed by ethnic groups with kin in China, several of them predominantly Muslim, appeared on the PRC's borders. The Mongolian People's Republic, whose government had discouraged any "greater Mongolia" sentiments, was replaced by a noncommunist republic that found it more difficult to repress such feelings. Adherence to Tibetan Buddhism, which had been the religion of most Mongols before communism, revived. This was accompanied by an upsurge of interest in studying the Tibetan language. Despite Chinese protests, the Dalai Lama was invited to Mongolia and warmly received.

Repression Increases

The years 1988 through 1990, while these events were unfolding externally, were particularly difficult for Beijing's relations with its most restive minorities. In June 1988, the Dalai Lama addressed the European Parliament in Strasbourg. There, he offered Beijing a compromise under which the PRC would have responsibility for Tibet's foreign policy, while the TAR would have a popularly elected legislature and its own legal system. Beijing rejected the proposal, lashing out at the European community for hosting the Dalai Lama and at the Dalai Lama for internationalizing what it saw as a domestic issue.

At this point, the central government decided to add the stick of increased repression to the carrot of its post-1979 policy of economic development as a solution to its minorities problem. Police and military forces in the TAR were augmented with personnel sent in from outside the region. Monasteries were searched, and persons believed to be sympathetic to the Dalai Lama were arrested. Antigovernment demonstrations took place in December 1988. In January 1989, the normally placatory Panchen Lama stated publicly that although there had been progress in Tibet since the communists arrived, it had exacted too high a price. Four days later, the heretofore healthy 51-year-old was reported to have died of a heart attack. Many assumed he had been killed for speaking out, and there were more protests. Martial law was declared in Lhasa in the spring, and continued for more than a year. During this time, the Dalai Lama was awarded the Nobel Peace Prize, indicating that the Tibet issue had indeed been internationalized.

Also in the spring of 1989, Uyghurs and Kazakhs attacked communist party headquarters in Urumqi with rocks and steel bars. The publication in Shanghai of a book containing defamatory statements about Islam was the proximate cause of the protest, though other ongoing grievances were expressed as well. At the same time, Chinese Muslims (Hui) were causing problems in neighboring Gansu and Qinghai provinces over other Islam-related issues. Their activities included attacks on rail lines, causing several suspensions in service. A government investigation produced evidence of collusion among Muslim groups in different provinces, as well as foreign support for their activities. Han settlers who had been moved into Xinjiang's border with the former Soviet Union to provide a buffer against movements of minorities back and forth provided a further irritant in that area. Major protests occurred in Inner Mongolia as well, probably influenced by the growth of anticommunist sentiment in neighboring Mongolia.

Following the Tiananmen disturbances and the fall of the Soviet Union, there were sharp crackdowns in all these areas. Inner Mongolia's leadership group was reorganized. Teams investigated monasteries in Tibetan areas as well as mosques and religious schools in Islamic enclaves. There were many arrests, some for matters that might have been considered relatively trivial a few years before. For example, members of two organizations to promote research into Mongolian culture, both of which had tried to register themselves legally with the government, were accused of subversive and splittist intentions.

A "strike hard" campaign against crime that began in the mid-1990s was used in minority areas to target separatism. Human rights advocates charged that the government was equating any expression of disagreement with government policies, no matter how innocuous, with separatism, and using the campaign to make arrests accordingly. Repression in Xinjiang became still more severe after the September 11, 2001 attacks on the World Trade Center and Pentagon. PRC sources claimed that over 1,000 Taliban-trained Uyghurs had infiltrated Muslim communities in China to disseminate fundamentalism and terrorist propaganda. Foreign experts placed their numbers from four to thirteen, some of whom were from the Uyghur exile community in Pakistan who had left Xinjiang in the 1930s.

Official propaganda stresses that the problems are caused by a small handful of malcontents who are deceiving others. Most people are happy and appreciate the many benefits which party and government have brought to their previously "backward" areas. Han and minorities are interdependent, part of the same family of the PRC; each must help the other for the good of the country as a whole. Although the central government does extract resources from minority areas, it pays a fair price for these materials. Moreover, it also subsidizes the economies of many minority areas to a significant degree and fosters the development of their cultures.

There are differences of opinion between party and government on the one hand and certain members of minorities on the other about what constitutes fostering the development of minority languages, cultures, and traditions—which party and government publicly favor—and what constitutes undermining the unity of the state and engaging in splittist activities. Most parties to these disputes understand that languages and cultures are not frozen in time but rather adapt to changing circumstances and changing perceptions of what is appropriate. The point at issue is that the central leadership reserves for itself the right to determine these changes. In actual practice, cultural development carried out by party and government *on behalf of* minorities seems to be acceptable, whereas cultural development carried out by minorities *on their own behalf* is not. Ethnic minority culture under the direct control of party and government is celebrated; all other manifestations thereof are regarded with utmost suspicion.

The issue of control is starkly evident in party/government attitudes toward local efforts to deal with alcoholism, heroin, and the HIV/AIDS problem that accompanies drug use. In 1997, Uyghur students in Ili, one of Xinjiang's more secular areas, organized a campaign to persuade people to limit their consumption of liquor, and stores to limit sales to those with drinking problems. The government, assuming that fundamentalist Islam, which prohibits drinking alcohol, was behind the campaign, clamped down on the organizers. An estimated 5,000 students demonstrated against this, with an estimated 300 Uyghurs killed when police moved against the demonstrators. During the previous year, Rebiya Kadeer, a successful Uyghur businesswoman, was arrested for subversive activities. She had campaigned for women's rights and AIDS education, and against heroin use. Rebiya was released from prison in 2005, but only after a major international campaign for her release. Subsequently, two of her children were convicted of tax evasion, and a third was charged with "attempting to split the state." Now living in the United States, Rebiya has found it difficult to travel, since the Chinese government warns other countries against allowing her to enter.

In contrast to the marked shifts between pluralist and assimilationist policies that characterized the early years of the PRC, a model has evolved that is pluralist in form but assimilationist in function. For example, as plans for a conference on Tibetan literature were being finalized in Beijing and the party was taking credit for rescuing lamaist ritual dances from extinction, one of the last neighborhoods of traditional Tibetan homes in central Lhasa was being destroyed. Visitors remarked that only the Potala Palace now distinguished the city from one that might be seen anywhere in Han China. Another case in point was the presentation of an allegedly Tibetan opera as part of the 2008 Olympics festivities. Basically a Chinese opera with some Tibetan clothing added, it told the story of a Chinese princess sent to marry a Tibetan leader, implying not quite accurately that China's control of Tibet was of long standing. In a third event, a huge Chinese flag carried into the opening ceremony of the same Olympics by children, each wearing the costume of one of the PRC's ethnic minorities, was meant to symbolize the unity of all nationalities. However, critics found a different symbolism when it was discovered that all the children were Han.

In Inner Mongolia, the central government proudly reported that it was refurbishing the mausoleum of Chinggis Khan only weeks after rejecting the appeal of sentences meted out to Mongols who were active in a cultural organization. In 1998, Xinjiang's party head, a Han, stated, "We say the constitution provides that all nationalities have the freedom to use and develop their spoken and written languages, but this in no way means advocating the use of their own spoken and written languages." Since, he opined, it was impossible to properly translate many things into minority languages, it was urgent that minorities' cadres have a good command of Chinese. At the same time, Xinjiang University began to phase out instruction in the Uyghur language. In 2000, the Han party secretary of Sichuan complained about having to teach minorities in their own languages, saying, "The whole world is learning English. Why bother so much?"

Cultural organizations may, of course, have agendas that are more subversive than they seem, cloaking what the Chinese government would call splittist intentions with language classes, dancing lessons, or marriage celebrations. The government charges that Tibetan monasteries have been used to store weapons, Islamic schools for preaching fundamentalist messages, and Uyghur festivals as meeting places for subversives. In the absence of definitive evidence, judgment calls must be made. Is an Uyghur story about a pigeon king who commits suicide rather than continue to live in captivity a call to action against CCP rule? Is a Tibetan song of longing for the return of a precious bird that has flown away a coded call for the return of the Dalai Lama? The author of the former was arrested; the singer of the latter was not.

Minorities can also practice dissimulation. A study of Yunnan's ethnic groups revealed that, while outwardly conforming to the officially sanctioned narrative of their culture, minorities are quietly developing their language, music of both traditional and pop genres, and computer projects to publish their own versions of ancient epics and modern literature.

In 1996, Beijing declared that religion would have to adapt itself to socialism rather than vice versa. It underscored this point by rejecting the Dalai Lama's candidate for the reincarnation of the Panchen Lama. The child simply disappeared and was replaced by a candidate approved by Beijing. The government also stated explicitly that the areas under control of the state, where religion must not intrude, included education, family planning, burial arrangements, and the legal system.

The central leadership sought as well to enlist the cooperation of border states in curbing dissident activities. This was one motive behind the founding of the Shanghai Cooperation Organization, whose first meeting, in April 1996, was hosted by Jiang Zemin. Members have pledged mutual support against national separatism and religious extremists. Burma has complied with Chinese demands to return Uyghurs to the PRC, and the Nepalese government has turned over Tibetans, although its border guards can often be evaded or bribed. In 2007, Chinese border guards fired on an unarmed group of would-be refugees, at least one of whom died. The incident was filmed by Western mountain climbers, thus disproving the government's version of what had happened.

As government repression increases, dissident forces develop countermeasures. For example, one government effort involved sending work teams into rural areas, where they were instructed to set up "joint-defense" teams to ensure public security. The teams were to apprehend not only dissidents but also those who harbored suspects; both would be punished. Dissidents struck back by assassinating not only those who joined the teams but also their family members. Even religious leaders who appeared to tolerate government supervision were targets of assassination, as were their family members.

Party and government expressed concern that lower levels were simply indifferent to their wishes. There were repeated complaints that primary organizations showed "weak political sensitivity" and had "not exerted themselves in the struggle against national separatism and illegal religious activities." Worse, some officials actively sided with the dissidents. Contrary to the policy that party members should be atheists, they openly practiced their religious beliefs. Tibetan officials maintained lavish shrines in their homes and kept pictures of the Dalai Lama in plain view. A number of cadres whose children attended schools in India run by the Dalai Lama refused a party directive to bring them back.

Officials in Muslim areas proved similarly recalcitrant. In mid-1996, the Xinjiang regional party committee called for:

> [S]ternly dealing with party members and cadres, especially leading cadres, who continue to be devout religious believers despite repeated education; instill separatist ideas and religious doctrines into young people's minds; publish distorted history; [issue] books or magazines advocating separatism and illegal religious ideas; or make audio or video products propagating such ideas.

Tighter post-9/11 efforts by the Chinese government notwithstanding, incidents continue to occur. They are typically triggered by a local grievance such as a car accident involving a Han and a minority, anger over being discriminated against for jobs, or lack of payment for services rendered. But the disproportionate response indicates an underlying degree of hostility between the groups. In Inner Mongolia, for example, numerous people were arrested for distributing leaflets protesting against the sale of Chinggis (Genghis) Khan's mausoleum to a Han company which planned to replace it with a larger building in order to accommodate more tourists. Curfews were imposed on Inner Mongolian campuses, and a local webmaster was ordered to close his site.

In March 2008, and again in October 2010, demonstrations broke out in several widely separated Tibetan areas, the former resulting in the arrest of nearly 1,000 people and the latter of several hundred. Another demonstration occurred in Xinjiang in 2008, followed by four separate terrorist attacks in August that killed more than 30 people. Violence again erupted in Xinjiang during the following year, after a rumor, later proved false, that Uyghur workers in a Guangdong factory had raped a Han woman led Han to attack Uyghurs. Hundreds died—as usual, there is a wide discrepancy between official figures and those from local sources—and ten times that many were injured.

There is an apparent paradox of sending Uyghurs to work in south China when the jobs in Xinjiang they believe are rightfully theirs are going to Han: Uyghurs have reported being forced to designate a family member to send to Guangdong, and Han factory managers report being surprised to find their new workers accompanied by a police officer. The government's motive is integration or, as some would argue, assimilation. For example, young Uyghur women surrounded by Han Chinese will hopefully form friendships, adopt Han customs, and not be tempted to wear veils. Following the riots, the two groups were separated by dormitory and production line. While reducing the possibility for ethnic violence, this segregation also defeated the purpose of sending the young people away in the first place. In the aftermath of both the Tibet and Xinjiang uprisings, the government allocated large aid packages to the areas and pledged to raise income levels to approximately those of the national average by 2020. More worried about Xinjiang than Tibet, judging from the higher ranking central government figures who were sent to the XUAR to inspect, Beijing also removed Xinjiang's long-serving first party secretary. He had been regarded as head of a corrupt Shandong gang that dominated politics in the XUAR to the exclusion of not only minorities but also groups of Han who had emigrated there from other provinces.

However, the central government clearly also intended to maintain the repressive policies. Those suspected of involvement in the demonstrations were executed or sentenced to lengthy prison terms. Police made house-to-house sweeps checking for residence registration permits and anything that could be construed as suspicious behavior. Internet access to Xinjiang was cut for ten months. While presumably inhibiting activists from communicating with each other, it also caused hardship for commerce, and the Uyghur area of Kashgar, a way station on the Silk Road from China to Central Asia of enormous cultural value, was bulldozed. Although the government stated that its aim was to replace unsafe old houses with more modern ones, it was widely believed that the true motive was punishment and yet another move to erode the vestiges of Uyghur culture. More than 100 Tibetans have publicly burned themselves to death in protest against restrictions on their way of life. Mongols have protested about being forcibly settled and repeated insults to both their culture and nomadic lifestyles. A new countryside stability maintenance structure that adds a grid system to neighborhood communities is most stringently applied in these areas. "Convenience police posts" have also been set up. Ostensibly for the benefit of residents, since they include first-aid and other amenities, the convenience posts also include surveillance cameras and anti-riot equipment. State-of-the-art artificial intelligence techniques, first tested in Xinjiang, are being introduced elsewhere: security checkpoints with identification scanners guard train stations and roads; facial scanners track those who enter and leave hotels, shopping malls, and banks. Police with handheld devices search smartphones for such suspicious content as encrypted chat apps and videos with political messages. In Xinjiang, permits are needed to purchase even a single kitchen knife, and drivers who wish to fill their cars' tanks must first swipe their identification cards and be photographed. Surveillance at gas stations in Tibet is particularly tight due to concerns about self-immolation.

Participation of minorities in meaningful political decision making has also been very limited. Most minority officials are found at the lower levels of government, becoming sparse at mid-levels, and in the case of the more important party, as opposed to government, positions, often nonexistent. In 2014, although all of the governors of the five autonomous regions are of the eponymous ethnic group, none of the party heads are. The heads of the public security bureaus in Tibet, Inner Mongolia, and Xinjiang are all Han Chinese. Representation in the National People's Congress is slightly over 14 percent, well in excess of ethnic minorities' share of the PRC's population as a whole, but the NPC has very little power. Sixteen members of ethnic minorities were named to the Nineteenth Party Congress in 2017, constituting 7.8 percent of the total; up from ten, or 4 percent, at the Eighteenth congress five years before. However, there is no ethnic minority representation on the inner sanctum of the 7-member politburo standing committee; nor in the 25-member politburo.

This lack of meaningful participation means that minorities find it difficult to transmit their concerns about projects that affect their areas. One angry Mongol complained that although his area had been protesting against ecologically damaging policies since the mid-1950s, it was only after huge sandstorms threatened Beijing in the early twenty-first century that the central government appeared to take notice. Tibetans have been concerned about the increase in sandstorms as well. Xinjiang residents have issued similar warnings about the water taken from underground reservoirs to feed intensive cotton cultivation. There have been severe environmental costs to past development projects. Dam construction has displaced several minority groups in the southwest and eroded the grasslands in Qinghai. New and larger scale projects are liable to have still worse effects.

Genuine Autonomy as a Possible Solution

It has been suggested that granting true autonomy to autonomous areas—that is, simply implementing existing laws—would blunt the appeal of separatists. The

Dalai Lama has often indicated that this would be sufficient for him to return to Tibet, and several Inner Mongolian dissidents have said so as well. Noting that repressive policies which do not address the underlying causes of hostilities will simply breed more hostility, a Han who is sympathetic to minorities has compared the central government's situation to chair acrobatics, wherein chairs are piled progressively one on top of another while the acrobats twirl ever more precariously as each new layer is added. Sooner or later, the tower will fall. Although he advocates not independence but simply granting true autonomy to autonomous areas, he has had to go into hiding periodically.

A Uyghur professor who is also a party member makes similar arguments: phasing out minority languages when the law says they are to be encouraged is not only illegal, it is counterproductive. There is also a glaring contradiction between the CCP's stated goal of bringing enlightenment to minorities and shutting down their internet access. He has been arrested several times.

A law on regional autonomy was enacted in 1984 as part of Deng Xiaoping's reforms. When discussions on it began in 1979, there were immediate complaints from party members that "some communist party members hardly sound like Marxists on the question of minority nationalities." The law required that the administrative head of an autonomous region be a citizen of the nationality or nationalities exercising regional autonomy in the area, and gave autonomous areas the power to administer local finances. However, it said nothing about appointing ethnic minorities to leadership positions in the party hierarchy, which is far more powerful. In addition, since the economies of many minority areas depend on state subsidies, which come under the purview of the State Council, there are limits on how financially autonomous they can be.

Three years after the law was passed, there were complaints that Han chauvinism was blocking its implementation and that leaders were unwilling to actually grant autonomy. Minorities worried that their areas could be overrun by Han migrants whom they had no power to keep out. The lack of implementation of the autonomy law, or its partial implementation, was termed "quite serious;" with "some leading cadres" accused of never even having read it. Only a more liberal and better enforced autonomy law could hope to blunt separatist demands.

The national autonomy law was revised in 2001 in order to bring it into line with the campaign to develop the west: Officials described it as providing higher levels of support for minority regions in terms of policy, infrastructure, and finance than its predecessor. Critics, noting that the revisions enhanced the central government's involvement in all these areas, charged that the development program is based on the wider needs of the Chinese market rather than on local needs or interests. They questioned whether development that is against the wishes of the local population should be considered development.

Adding to these grievances, long-standing plans to write more explicit guidelines on the practice of autonomy into law were postponed as unrest increased in some minority areas. As of 2018 there had been little devolution of authority to the autonomous region level. Even legislation on autonomous regions' self-governance must be reviewed by the central government: none of the five has been able to implement any regulations, because the NPC standing committee has yet to endorse the draft legislation submitted by them. The Guangxi Zhuang Autonomous Region, where separatist activity has not occurred, submitted 18 drafts to the standing committee; all were returned to local people's congresses for revision. Ordinary provinces are required only to report to the NPC: paradoxically, therefore, they are more autonomous, at least legislatively, than are autonomous regions. Party and government fear that granting more autonomy would generate still more demands. Their concern is that acceding to what appear to be reasonable calls for devolution of decision making will be the slippery slope toward gradual erosion of all government control and de facto independence. The risks of liberalization are regarded as greater than those of continued repression.

It has been argued that allowing Tibet, with its meager resources, forbidding climate, and hostile population, to go its own way except for its foreign relations—an accommodation the Dalai Lama has already proposed—would end a huge financial drain out of the central government treasury as well as eliminate a festering human rights problem. From Beijing's point of view, however, this would be foolish. Tibet has undoubted strategic value, which must seem all the more important in view of intermittently strained relations with India. It also contains the headwaters of most of Asia's major rivers, which is increasingly important as competition for water supplies grows. Western sympathy for Tibet aside, there have been few actual adverse consequences for Beijing as a result of its conduct there. Sustained attention from the international community is unlikely: there will be other causes to attract its attention. In talks with representatives of the Dalai Lama in fall 2008, Beijing officials were intransigent: the talks failed. The Dalai Lama is in his mid-eighties; when he dies, Beijing will install a successor, as it has with the Panchen Lama, and take great care to imbue him with its values.

Moreover, to give Tibet real autonomy would surely stimulate demands for comparable treatment from other areas. Xinjiang has important natural resources as well as a strategic location, and its more vocal dissidents remain unwilling to accept anything short of complete independence. Demands for the creation of an East Turkestan Republic (ETR) hark back to ETRs that had brief existences under the Qing dynasty and the Chinese republic; they are unlikely to disappear with the current generation of dissidents. Some Inner Mongolian dissidents have said explicitly that they would be open to the idea of autonomy for the moment, but would not necessarily be satisfied with it in the long term.

Beijing would also need to confront the problem of what to do with the Han in minority areas should those areas gain true autonomy. This would not be a great problem in the TAR. However, the TAR is surrounded by autonomous areas belonging to other provinces, but with substantial Tibetan populations. Tibetan dissidents claim these areas as well, though numerous Han now live there. In Xinjiang, Han comprise nearly half the population; in Inner Mongolia, they are the majority by perhaps 7:1. The trend has been to move in more Han to preserve stability and aid in economic development. Minorities have complained that such practices amount to "ethnic swamping," in which Han are resettled in their areas to dilute the voice of minorities. Critics also believe that Hu Jintao's quest for a harmonious society was, like the campaign against terrorism, a pretext to suppress requests for true autonomy.

Ending the Current System as a Solution

In light of recent unrest, several Chinese academics have argued that stability would be better ensured by ending the system of special arrangements for ethnic minorities, i.e., proposing that less autonomy would be preferable to more. They state that the USSR's ethnic policies led to its disintegration and that continuation of these policies will lead the PRC to a similar fate, and contrast the failed Soviet model with America's successful melting pot. These arguments overlook the fact that the USSR's population was half ethnic minorities *vis-à-vis* China's 8.4 percent, and that the educational and economic levels of more of the Soviet Union's ethnic minorities were at levels equal to or higher than that of the dominant Russian group. Moreover, there were other factors in the disintegration of the USSR, such as its weak economy, that do not apply to the PRC. In addition, the United States maintains an active affirmative action system. The weaknesses of their arguments notwithstanding, these scholars argue for the elimination of group-differentiated rights so that all citizens are equal. State aid should be allocated on the basis of need rather than ethnicity. Ethnicity should be removed from all official documents, including national identification cards.

Possibly in response to such sentiments, the state statistical bureau has in recent years not reported the population of ethnic minority groups in its annual yearbook; hence there have been no updates to the numbers that appear in Figure 13.1. The hope is to creating a collective civic identity and culture: There should be increased economic interaction between minority and non-minority areas of the country and intermarriage should be encouraged. Such measures would surely be resisted by vested interests who profit from the current system—those Han and non-Han who "eat ethnic rice." Even if implemented, critics argue, they could sharpen rather than mitigate tensions.

Conclusions

At present, it does not seem likely that the central government intends to deviate from its current policy of encouraging economic development while suppressing expressions of dissent in ethnic minority areas. Tensions appear to cluster around three interrelated factors: first, minorities' limited and ineffectual participation in the power structure of the PRC; second, inequitable and discriminatory development; and third, inadequate protection of cultural identity. The gap between income levels in minority areas and Han China, particularly coastal Han China, continues to grow. Although economic growth reports from Tibet and Xinjiang are higher, these are the results of massive infusions of capital from outside. There is consensus that few of the minorities who live there have benefited from the preferential policies.

Discrimination is an acknowledged fact. For many minorities, religion is an integral part of their ethnic identity, whereas party and government tend to see religion and other manifestations of a non-Han identity as breeding grounds for separatism. To be fair to the central government, it is in a difficult position: Leaving the areas alone risks widening the gap in living standards relative to Han China, while bringing in development opens it to charges of exploitation of resources and the destruction of local cultures. Nonetheless, whether good or bad, many of the projects seem to have been carried out with unnecessary insensitivity to local feelings. Political institutions provide few opportunities for minorities to influence decision making at either central or lower levels of party and government. Yet modernization projects are liable to fail if they do not address the concerns of those whose lives are directly affected by them. Although the stated policy is development and stability, the way in which development has been carried out has fostered instability, while efforts to suppress dissent seem to breed more instability.

Party and state have made genuine efforts to accommodate ethnic minorities within the framework of the PRC, and a degree of mutual accommodation has evolved in certain areas. For example, Hui use the term *minjian*, literally "among the people," to refer to people, places, and things, such as clerics, mosques, and tombs, that are not registered or sanctioned by state law. This is a realm not dominated by the state, is practiced according to the minority's tradition, and is apt to exist where the law is silent. When it is not, for example, in property transactions, compromises can be worked out. Basic-level courts have sometimes referred to the minority's traditions in making decisions. Negotiation, subterfuge, evasion, and collaboration are common. These adjustments notwithstanding, the fundamental nature of the nationalities problem is little changed: Minorities who were content to be part of imperial China have not been disruptive under the PRC; those who were unhappy continue to be so. Neither pluralist nor assimilationist policies have succeeded in solving the nationalities problem.

Dissident minorities do not have the strength to force the government to accept their demands for separatism or true autonomy. They will in all likelihood continue to press their demands through remonstrations and demonstrations. But in the absence of some fundamental change in the system as a whole, which would include pressure from important segments of the Han majority, such as peasants, workers, and intellectuals, it seems unlikely that minority unrest can win anything more than token concessions from the central government. The integration of ethnic minorities into the PRC is far from complete, yet those minorities who are discontented have little hope that there will be disintegration.

Suggestions for Further Reading

Matthew Erie, *China and Islam: The Prophet, the Party, and Law* (London: Oxford University Press, 2016).

Ben Hillman and Gray Tuttle, eds, *Ethnic Conflict and Protest in Tibet and Xinjiang: Unrest in China's West* (New York: Weatherhead Institute/Columbia University Press, 2016).

Lin Le, "China's Perception of External Threats and Its Current Tibet Policy," *China Journal* No. 76 (2016): 103–123.

James Leibold, "Toward a Second Generation of Ethnic Policies?," *China Brief*, July 6, 2012.

John Powers, *The Buddha Party: How the People's Republic of China Works to Define and Control Tibetan Buddhism* (New York: Oxford University Press, 2017).

CHAPTER 14

Foreign Policy

Determinants

In China, as elsewhere, many factors interact to influence the country's foreign policy. Among the major determinants in the conceptual framework of the Chinese leadership are tradition, ideology, and their perception of China's capabilities.

Tradition

As mentioned in Chapter 1, the traditional Chinese worldview saw the country as the Middle Kingdom: the center of the world and the hub of civilization. The concept of the nation-state system, with sovereign states interacting as theoretical equals, was unknown. Rulers of culturally inferior lands or their envoys were expected to appear in the Chinese capital, make the ceremonial kowtow of obeisance to the emperor, and present tribute. This consisted of costly gifts of local products—for example, lacquerware, incense, or exotic animals native to their areas. In return, the rulers received confirmation of their leadership over their own people as well as expensive gifts of Chinese workmanship. Reflecting its view of all other states as inferior, imperial China did not have a foreign ministry, but dealt with non-Chinese groups through its Board of Rites or Court of Colonial Affairs. The Chinese believed that their culture was superior in all respects—morally, materially, and aesthetically—and that it had universal validity.

There have been certain resonances of these views in post-1949 China. Particularly during the 1960s, the reverence accorded to Mao Zedong reminded observers of that paid to the emperor. Mao's claim of a world communist movement based in Beijing, with himself and his close associates as arbiters of what constituted true Marxism and who had committed the heresy of revisionism, is another case in point. So were the claims by Mao's disciples that he had raised Marxist–Leninist thought to a higher level of validity, and their contention that it was suitable for the rest of the Third World. Richard Nixon's February 1972 visit to Beijing, during which Mao received the U.S. president in a formal state audience and presented him with a pair of panda bears, struck some Western observers as uncomfortably reminiscent of the tribute system, with Nixon unwittingly performing a symbolic kowtow. Most recently, countries that are irked when Beijing orders them not to invite certain individuals to visit or what weapons systems not to acquire have complained that the People's Republic of China (PRC) continues to practice kowtow diplomacy.

However, the differences from tradition are at least as important as the parallels. Even at the height of the PRC's devotion to orthodox communism, the most fanatic pro-Maoist would have had to acknowledge that the universal belief system—the one at which their great leader stood at the apex—had its origins outside China: neither Marx nor Lenin was a Chinese. The PRC's efforts to establish diplomatic recognition with other countries of the world on a reciprocal basis, and to participate in the United Nations (UN) and other world organizations, seem to indicate an acceptance of the multistate system. A persistent theme of Chinese foreign policy has been to win back the territories that were lost during the country's time of internal disintegration and humiliation by other powers. In this view, rather than re-creating the previous universal order of the Middle Kingdom, the traditionalist element of the PRC's foreign policy has aimed at placing the country in a position of international respect *within* a multistate order, thereby reversing the previous century's experience when it occupied a position of inferiority therein.

China has, moreover, become a zealous defender of the concept of sovereign rights, the latter being an important underpinning of the multistate system. Ironically, this happened at a time when many of the originators of that system had begun to move away from strong views on state sovereignty. In the mid-1980s, the PRC appeared to be softening its view of absolute sovereignty, as exemplified by its acceptance of limitations on its sovereignty over Hong Kong. However, China moved back toward a position of absolute sovereignty following the Tiananmen demonstrations, the disintegration of the Soviet Union, and the Gulf War of 1991. The Chinese saw U.S. actions against Iraq as a big power bullying a small one. America's forcing Iraq to disavow its conquest of neighboring Kuwait had obvious parallels to the PRC's claims over Taiwan: this was not a precedent with which Chinese authorities were comfortable. They were still more uncomfortable with U.S. efforts to force the Yugoslav government to end its policy of ethnic cleansing in Kosovo in 1999: the United States bypassed the UN, working through the North Atlantic Treaty Organization (NATO) instead. Moreover, Kosovo, unlike Kuwait, was not even a sovereign state. Chinese analysts worried that America could use the argument it employed in the Yugoslav case—that human rights concerns took precedence over sovereign rights—to intervene in its restive ethnic minority regions, or if the PRC attempted to take over Taiwan, since Beijing considers the Taiwan issue to be a domestic dispute rather than one between two sovereign states. The authorities' fears were exacerbated when, unable to obtain UN Security Council authorization, American and British forces invaded Iraq in 2003 to bring about a change in government there.

A law passed by the National People's Congress (NPC) in early 1992 unilaterally declared sovereignty over a number of territories claimed by the PRC as well as several neighboring states, and declared that the People's Liberation Army (PLA) would enforce these claims. China's media also became more strident in rejecting foreign criticism of its human rights policy, arguing that it is an unjustifiable interference in the internal affairs of a sovereign state.

Both the soft and hard lines on sovereignty may be viewed as situational: The PRC's acceptance of limits on sovereignty was strongly conditioned by its desire to enter the U.S. capital market and to make the prospect of unification with the mainland more attractive to Taiwan. In the early 1990s, the PRC's immediate concern was to assert itself against what it perceived as foreign bullying. And, despite rejecting other countries' human rights policies, Beijing has criticized those of other countries.

More recently, China's assertive actions toward areas it claims in East and Southeast Asia, plus efforts that seem to be aimed at making China the fulcrum of an international economic system in which it dictates the rules, have led to speculation that, while paying lip service to the idea of a multinational state system, Xi Jinping is attempting to establish a modern-day tribute system with himself as ruler of *tianxia*, all under heaven.

Ideology

The analysis of international politics found in the works of Marx and Lenin forms one facet of the prism through which the Chinese leadership has interpreted world events. The Marxist–Leninist view of rapacious capitalist–imperialist states that colonized other nations to exploit their resources and workers resonated with the founders of the Chinese Communist Party (CCP): they saw China in exactly that position. Mao Zedong's worldview was heavily influenced by his desire to further the cause of international communism even when, as in the Korean conflict, it harmed more immediate Chinese interests such as rebuilding the economy and conquering Taiwan. Later in the 1950s, when the USSR seemed to have abandoned the revolutionary cause, Mao asserted China's right to lead the international communist movement. However, Mao was not rigidly constrained by Marxist–Leninist categories. In 1970, in a classic balance of power-influenced decision, he opted to move closer to the capitalist United States when he believed that the PRC was threatened by the socialist Soviet Union. Post-Mao leaders have followed pragmatic rather than ideologically based foreign policies.

Although communist ideology has greatly declined in importance, it is not dead. Marxist–Leninist thought categories remain. For example, the United States is frequently denounced as a "hegemonic power bent on a desire for world conquest." This has clear implications for Beijing's interpretations of U.S. actions which Americans might view as more benignly motivated. In general, however, communist ideology has become less a guide for policy formulation than an instrument for after-the-fact rationalization of actions taken on the basis of other criteria. As the influence of ideology declined, nationalism came to the fore. Party and government may have consciously fostered it to shore up their declining legitimacy after the suppression of the Tiananmen demonstrations and a decade of decidedly unsocialist economic reforms. Nationalism served to unify the citizenry behind the authorities while focusing on external threats to the

PRC as opposed to divisive internal questions. Regardless of the leadership's motivation, nationalism struck a responsive chord with many people.

Capabilities

The PRC has the world's largest military force, backed by a still larger reserve/militia component. Since it also possesses the world's largest population, China has the ability to call up more reinforcements than any other state. The navy has developed a blue-water capability that has become worrisome to neighboring states with which the PRC has territorial disputes. New missiles give it the ability to attack ships, including aircraft carriers, from great distances. China now has two aircraft carriers and stealth fighter planes, and has advanced from catching up to leaping ahead in military and dual-use technology. However, logistics remains a weak link, and since the military has no recent combat experience it is not battle-tested. Moreover, the country's economy would be severely strained by a major confrontation. Since most of China's domestically produced food is raised in three river basins, a nuclear attack on those areas could have devastating effects, for both the long and short term, on the country's ability to feed itself. This is, however, unlikely to happen.

Since no state currently has such intentions, this is a moot point. China's military is capable of causing significant disruption and anxiety to its neighbors and their allies. Military capabilities are rapidly improving, as are the incidence and sophistication of cyber hacking into other countries' security establishments.

Diplomacy and intelligence operations, though less visible than military capabilities, are equally important components of the PRC's foreign policy apparatus. The PRC's diplomacy is generally regarded as relatively effective. Its intelligence services, however, receive less high marks. A foreign intelligence agent describes the PRC's operations as inefficient, mired in red tape, and unable to keep secrets. There have indeed been successes. In one case, a Chinese employee of the U.S. Central Intelligence Agency, arrested in 1981, was found to have been passing secrets to CCP sources since 1944. In another, a French diplomat who fell in love with a performer in the Beijing opera was persuaded to provide classified information to the PRC for over 15 years. He was eventually allowed to marry his love, who presented him with a son. Only after the couple's arrest by French counterintelligence did the diplomat learn that he had been set up: His "wife" was male, and the child was not his. The publicity surrounding this bizarre episode inspired the Broadway show *M. Butterfly*, a Hollywood movie, and a bestselling book.

Another factor contributing to the success of PRC intelligence operations is lax security in many of the areas it targets. Foreign experts believe that their sheer numbers rather than their quality enable a portion of Chinese intelligence operations to succeed, since target countries' counterintelligence and law enforcement agencies are simply overwhelmed. In addition, because many of the PRC's collection activities concern mid-level technology, they are not a major focus of concern for the foreign governments affected.

Goals

China's foreign policy has shown underlying continuities, despite tactical shifts taken in response to international and domestic factors. These goals may be summarized as:

- preservation of China's territorial integrity;
- recovery of lost territories considered to be part of China;
- recognition of the PRC as the sole legitimate government of China;
- enhancement of China's international stature.

The Formulation of Foreign Policy

As with other aspects of high-level decision making in the PRC, the precise methods of formulating foreign policy are unknown. Newspapers do not discuss the merits and demerits of responses to the latest crisis in the Middle East. Intra-leadership debates on whether to invade one country or extend diplomatic recognition to another are not made public. Although there are many reasons for the Chinese leadership's reluctance to discuss the mechanics of foreign policy formation, the most important is probably the most obvious: there is little to be gained from revealing to potential international rivals anything that does not have to be revealed. It is also regarded as useful to present an image of a nation and leadership united behind a foreign policy decision, however dissonant with reality this image of harmony may be.

Certain information is known. Ultimately, the responsibility for foreign policy decision making rests with the supreme leader. Under Mao, the party's politburo and its standing committee were the principal loci of foreign policy making. During the 1980s, however, they were superseded by the party secretariat and the State Council. From late 1987 on, the politburo standing committee again came to the fore. While consensual decision making within this group seemed to be evolving, Xi Jinping reversed that process, in effect centralizing decision-making power under himself. Such changes indicate that at the elite level of policy making it is not so much institutions as individuals that are important.

These individuals are relatively few in number, and simultaneously bear heavy responsibilities in a number of other areas. Since most foreign policy decisions cannot be intelligently made without reference to a wide variety of specialized information—for example, trade-flow statistics, knowledge of the power structure of another country, or information on the military capabilities of a potential enemy or ally—leaders must rely on other individuals and organizations for information and guidance.

A variety of support groups exists to provide this information and guidance. On important matters, a "leading small group" of senior party and government leaders may be formed to devise and consider various policy options. Within the party structure, the party central committee has an international liaison office to provide data on foreign communist parties. On the government side, the most important organ concerned with foreign policy is the foreign ministry of the State Council. This ministry is divided into departments responsible for the study and analysis of given geographic areas of the world. It also has departments for other specialized functions, including consular affairs, foreign press information, international organizations, and treaties (Figure 14.1). While in theory the international liaison department had responsibilities for relations between the CCP and other communist parties whereas the foreign ministry was in charge of state-to-state matters, there was a great deal of overlap between them. Not surprisingly, the relationship had its frictions.

Externally, tensions also surrounded the use of the communist party-to-communist party channel. Where China had formal diplomatic relations with a non-communist state, the latter was understandably concerned about PRC support for subversive movements aimed at overthrowing that government. These tensions lessened when, in the 1980s, Beijing greatly reduced its support for insurgent communist parties in foreign countries. Following the collapse of communism abroad, the international liaison department began to host delegates from other countries' political parties regardless of ideological affiliation. Thus, it might sponsor visits by members of the British Labour Party or Japan's Liberal Democratic Party. The party-to-party channel is particularly useful when relations between China and a foreign country are strained: opposition parties are invited to Beijing and cultivated with the hope that they may come to power and prove more sympathetic to Chinese positions.

Other organizations subordinate to the State Council, such as the defense ministry, the finance ministry, the People's Liberation Army, and the People's Bank, are concerned with foreign relations to varying degrees. A mass organization, the Chinese People's Association for Friendship with Foreign Countries, is responsible for a semi-official channel, "people's diplomacy." This involves exchanges of sports teams as well as professional groups like surgeons, archaeologists, nuclear physicists, and businesspeople. Theoretically, these activities take place between nongovernmental groups, although in practice they are closely monitored by the PRC leadership and, to varying degrees, by the leadership of the other countries involved. People's diplomacy aims to create goodwill for the PRC and is a means to influence domestic public opinion in a foreign country.

Decision makers also receive information relevant to foreign policy making through other channels. Personnel of the official news agency, Xinhua (New China), who are stationed in foreign countries, are one such conduit. Intelligence operatives, some of whom may use embassy or Xinhua employment as cover, are another. Chinese who study or travel abroad or who maintain contacts with foreign sources may also provide information. Several research institutes may be called upon for facts and analysis. These include the Chinese Academy of Social Sciences (CASS), the Shanghai Institute for International Studies (SIIS), and the China Institute of Contemporary International Relations (CICIR). The personnel thereof are typically well informed and able to express their opinions frankly to policy makers. As in other governments, however, policy makers may choose not to act on their advice, and the analysts therein do not necessarily speak with one voice. While precisely how these individuals and organizations impact the foreign policy decision-making process is not known, we are at least able to analyze the differing strategies which the PRC has pursued to effect its goals.

Departments within the Ministry of Foreign Affairs

General Office

Department of Policy Planning

Department of Asian Affairs

Department of West Asian and North African Affairs

Department of African Affairs

Department of European-Central Asian Affairs

Department of European Affairs

Department of North American and Oceanian Affairs

Department of Latin American Affairs

Department of International Organizations and Conferences

Department of Arms Control

Department of Treaty and Law

Information Department

Protocol Department

Department of Consular Affairs

Department of Hong Kong, Macao and Taiwan Affairs

Department of Translation and Interpretation

Department of Foreign Affairs Management

Department of External Security Affairs

Department of Personnel

Bureau for Retired Personnel

Administrative Department

Department of Finance

Bureau of Archives

Department of Supervision

Bureau for Chinese Diplomatic Missions Abroad

Department of Services for Foreign Ministry Home and Overseas Offices

FIGURE 14.1 Organization of the Ministry of Foreign Affairs

Source: Adapted from Chinese Ministry of Foreign Affairs chart.

Chinese Foreign Relations: An Overview
The "Lean to One Side" Policy: 1949–1954

In 1949, the sweeping international changes desired by China's ambitious leaders seemed far off. Although many of the more distasteful provisions of the so-called unequal treaties forced on China during the nineteenth century had been abrogated in the course of two world wars, others remained. Hong Kong was still in the hands of the British; Macao was held by Portugal. The Soviet Union occupied many thousands of kilometers of land that Chinese patriots considered part of their country. Mongolia, effectively independent since 1911, had received international recognition after a plebiscite in 1947. Tibet retained de facto independence. And the island of Taiwan was held by the defeated Kuomintang (KMT) government under Chiang Kai-shek.

China's leaders began the task of restoring their country's greatness with limited resources. Exhausted by nearly 20 years of war and opposed by numerous hostile powers, the country could ill afford an adventuristic foreign policy. Claims to Mongolia, though not forgotten, had to be postponed, since the Mongolian People's Republic was a client state of the Soviet Union. Tibet was invaded only after a year of careful preparation. Subsequently, an agreement was signed that, though extremely distasteful to Tibetan nationalists, nonetheless promised a significant degree of autonomy to the area.

The CCP's initial tendency was to seek normal diplomatic relations with other countries, but on the condition that those nations agree to break relations with the KMT government. Predictably, all of the communist countries immediately recognized the PRC. Britain, anxious to forestall Chinese claims to its lucrative Hong Kong colony, also quickly recognized the Beijing government. So did the Scandinavian countries, Switzerland, Israel (not reciprocated by the PRC), and six Asian states: India, Pakistan, Sri Lanka, Afghanistan, Burma, and Indonesia.

In February 1950, with the United States having adopted a policy of "letting the dust settle," expecting that the PRC would soon take over Taiwan, Beijing signed a Treaty of Peace, Friendship, and Mutual Assistance with the Soviet Union. The negotiations that preceded the conclusion of the treaty required Mao Zedong's presence in Moscow for two months, indicating that intense bargaining was taking place between Mao and Soviet leader Joseph Stalin. Stalin had the better bargaining position, and the treaty granted significant concessions to the USSR in return for Soviet financial and technical assistance to China. These concessions gave Moscow substantial leverage over the PRC government. Subsequent events in Korea were to strengthen China's dependence on the Soviet Union.

In January 1950, U.S. secretary of state Dean Acheson defined a defense perimeter for America, excluding South Korea from U.S. responsibility. This convinced North Korean premier Kim Il-Sung that the United States would not actively intervene to prevent a North Korean takeover of the south, and he obtained Stalin's agreement to back the invasion. The assessment that America would not intervene proved to be erroneous. Domestic critics of the Truman administration's China policy pointed to the Korean invasion as fresh proof of the same unbridled expansionism that had caused the Chinese mainland to be absorbed by the communist camp, and they demanded immediate action. U.S. resistance, channeled through the UN, ended America's "let the dust settle" policy in favor of a policy of protecting Taiwan. Since a Chinese communist takeover of Taiwan would complicate the logistical problems of U.S. forces fighting in Korea, President Truman ordered the Seventh Fleet to "neutralize" the Taiwan Strait, thereby preventing the CCP government from invading the island. Chinese research into Soviet archives has found evidence that Stalin drew Mao into the Korean conflict to weaken his ability to invade Taiwan. He reasoned that, should communist forces succeed in unifying Korea under Kim, the peninsula would surely become a client state of the USSR. However, were the PRC able to absorb Taiwan, China would rival the USSR for primacy in the communist world. Presumably, Mao did not anticipate that intervention in Korea would doom his efforts to deal a final blow to Chiang.

In addition to blocking the PRC from attaining one of its major foreign policy goals and, moreover, one that had seemed within easy reach, the Korean war hardened attitudes between the United States and China. U.S.–PRC animosity increased when, in October 1950, Chinese "volunteers" began crossing into North Korea to aid their fellow communists in fighting U.S. and UN forces. Direct confrontation between U.S. and Chinese troops in Korea resulted in the war becoming a stalemate. In the course of prosecuting the conflict, the United States increased its aid to Chiang Kai-shek's government on Taiwan. A vigorous effort by the PRC in 1954 to take Taiwan, including shelling the offshore island of Quemoy (Jinmen), stiffened U.S. determination to protect the island. In late 1954, the Eisenhower administration signed a mutual defense treaty with Chiang's government, thus delaying Mao's plans indefinitely.

The failure of the United States and China to create sufficient common ground for the establishment of diplomatic relations increased China's reliance on the Soviet Union. In part, this resulted from the circumstances described previously, and in part it was a response to Stalin's personality. Becoming more paranoid with advancing age, the Soviet leader exacted fanatic loyalty from his followers, proclaiming that "whoever is not with us is against us." In general, the Soviet Union's allies conducted their foreign policies accordingly.

China's trade and other relations during this period were overwhelmingly with other communist bloc countries. While the military strength evinced by Chinese forces in Korea increased international respect for the PRC, this was not necessarily accompanied by international diplomatic recognition. The United States, reminding the UN that China had fought UN troops in Korea, was able to block the PRC's bid to unseat the KMT government from membership in that body. On a state-to-state level, most nations continued to recognize Chiang Kai-shek's Taiwan-based government as being the legitimate representative of China.

In addition to its intervention in Korea, the PRC also strongly supported Ho Chi Minh's struggle against the French in Indochina, sending arms and supplies to his Viet Minh. When accused by Western sources of being one-sided in his policies, Mao replied, "Exactly! . . . All Chinese without exception must lean to the side of imperialism or to the side of socialism. Sitting on the fence will not do, nor is there a third road."

The Bandung Spirit: 1954–1957

Several events conspired to moderate the "lean to one side" policy. First, the death of Stalin in 1953 removed the principal force in favor of a monolithic communist bloc arrayed against the outside world. Stalin's successors held a somewhat less confrontational view of the international scene. They favored a reduction of tensions, both within the communist bloc and between the communist countries and the noncommunist world.

Second, soon after Stalin's death, several causes of tension appeared to be resolved. In July 1953, a cease-fire was signed in Korea, thus stabilizing the situation in Northeast Asia, and in 1954, the Geneva Conference met to determine the Indochina question. PRC diplomats, led by Premier Zhou Enlai, played a major role in devising a truce that led to the partition of Vietnam and the inclusion of its northern half within the communist bloc.

Third, in the years following World War II, a number of colonies either became independent or received firm promises that independence would be granted in the near future. This made imperialism seem less menacing. In addition, most newly liberated colonies were concerned to avoid entanglement with either power bloc, announcing that they would pursue neutralist foreign policies. Rather than ignore or antagonize so many countries who chose not to lean to one side, it seemed wisest to move away from rigid insistence that whoever was not on the side of the communist bloc was against it.

In asserting this more outward-looking foreign policy, a primary focus of China's interest was its Asian neighbors. India, the largest of the Asian states espousing a neutral foreign policy, was an immediate recipient of Chinese attention. In June 1954, Zhou Enlai met with Indian prime minister Nehru to work out a basis for continuing relations between the two countries. From this meeting emerged the *Pancha Sheela*, or Five Principles, which were to be the cornerstone of Chinese diplomacy during the 1954–1957 period and are regularly reiterated in current PRC policy statements. These are:

- mutual respect for each other's territorial integrity;
- nonaggression;
- noninterference in each other's internal affairs;
- equality and mutual benefit;
- peaceful coexistence.

Relations between China and India during this period were relatively harmonious, despite a border dispute between the two countries and the distaste of many Indians for China's forcible occupation of Tibet. Ties with Burma, which also had a territorial dispute with the PRC, improved as well. A Sino–Burmese border agreement soon followed.

Both India and Burma agreed to remain aloof from the Cold War and to maintain friendly relations with China. In return, the PRC agreed to refrain from aggression on the Indian and Burmese borders—both countries had problems with independence-minded ethnic groups who inhabited border areas—and to negotiate on the delicate issue of the people of Chinese ancestry who live abroad.

Known as overseas Chinese, they are an important presence in most Southeast Asian countries. Overseas Chinese typically have higher income levels than the indigenous population, and often control important sectors of the economy of these countries. They tend toward clannishness; educating their children in separate Chinese-language schools; and remitting substantial portions of the profits from their businesses back to China rather than allowing the capital to remain in the countries where it was earned. In consequence, they are frequently much resented by the local population.

The sentiments symbolized by the *Pancha Sheela* and given concrete expression by China's improving relations with Burma and India led to the convening of an Asian–African conference at Bandung, a resort city in Indonesia. There, in April 1955, the PRC's emissaries renewed acquaintances with Asian diplomats and made contact with representatives of African states. Most of the latter were on the verge of becoming independent from the European states which had colonized them. Zhou Enlai held extended talks with Egypt's president Nasser, which became the basis for closer relations between the two countries in later years. A number of other contacts were made that would prove useful in future years.

Bandung came to symbolize a political vision: that African and Asian states, since they shared common social and economic problems, should work together for the solution of these problems. Guided by the *Pancha Sheela* and based on mutual respect and opposition to colonialism, "have-not" countries with dissimilar social systems could not only coexist peacefully but even prosper. Later, the PRC added Latin American and Middle Eastern states to this vision as well. Despite its limited resources, China began a modest foreign aid program to encourage progress toward unity and prosperity.

China's conciliatory posture even extended to expressing willingness to discuss outstanding issues with the United States. The PRC won considerable goodwill during this period, and a number of countries broke relations with the Taiwan government to recognize the mainland regime. Beijing frequently invoked the Bandung spirit to encourage Third World states to support policies that China favored. However, its lofty principles were never translated into effective institutions for coordination or implementation of these policies, and few actual problems were solved on the basis of the *Pancha Sheela*. Still, the Bandung spirit came to represent a striving for unity among Third World countries in an atmosphere of relaxed tension. As such, it demarcates an important period in the development of Chinese foreign policy.

Resurgent Nationalism and Isolation: 1957–1969

In emphasizing peaceful coexistence with Third World countries, China had muted rather than abandoned its revolutionary message. In 1957, the Chinese leadership reassessed its view of the international situation and decided that circumstances again favored revolutionary forces. The factors precipitating this reassessment included major scientific and technological breakthroughs on the part of the Soviet Union: the successful testing of an intercontinental ballistic missile in August 1957, and the launching of Sputnik, the world's first man-made satellite in October of the same year.

In November 1957, Mao Zedong delivered a famous speech signifying the change in his worldview. Asserting that an international turning point had been reached, he warned:

> There is a saying in China: "If the East wind does not prevail over the West wind, then the West wind will prevail over the East wind." I think that the characteristic of the current situation is that the East wind prevails over the West wind: that is, the strength of socialism exceeds the strength of imperialism.

Mao's metaphorical message was meant to prod the Soviet Union into a more militant stance: the communist states, led by the USSR, should take advantage of their momentum over the capitalist world and pursue more aggressive revolutionary policies. Not to take advantage of this momentum might result in serious damage to the communist camp. His efforts, however, were unsuccessful. Khrushchev, who had assumed Stalin's leadership position after the latter's death, was faced with growing demands from the Soviet populace for better living standards. Adopting a more aggressive foreign policy would mean diverting funds from consumer goods to military purposes. The post-Stalin Soviet leadership was also more wary of the dangers of a confrontation with capitalism than were the Chinese. While the PRC pursued peaceful coexistence with Third World countries, Khrushchev went even further, evincing willingness to coexist peacefully with capitalist countries as well.

Annoyed by the USSR's reluctance to capitalize on its revolutionary advantage, China assumed a more militant posture on its own initiative. Annoyance turned to anger when the Soviet Union refused to support its ally's more aggressive stance. For example, in 1958/1959, China adopted a harder line on Taiwan and resumed bombardment of the offshore island of Quemoy. Another disputed offshore island, Matsu, was also shelled. Khrushchev, visiting Beijing, countered with a metaphor of his own. In a speech criticizing adventurism, he mentioned Brest-Litovsk—an allusion to the Treaty of Brest-Litovsk, under the terms of which the newly founded, weak USSR had agreed to cede a large area of formerly czarist territory to Germany. The term became synonymous with a policy of trading space for time: Hence, Khrushchev was unsubtly telling China to bide its time with regard to Taiwan. Mao was reportedly livid.

In another instance, the PRC decided to put pressure on India to resolve a complicated border dispute between the two countries. The Soviet Union not only refused to back China, but also sought openly to improve relations with the Nehru government. Khrushchev's position was all the more irritating in that the weight of evidence tended to support China's position that the border had not been legally demarcated, vis-à-vis the Indian government's contention that it had.

These and other accumulated disagreements between the PRC and the Soviet Union culminated in an open break between the two countries, permanently rupturing communism as a monolithic entity. The Sino–Soviet dispute had many causes. First, czarist Russia had incorporated a large amount of territory that the PRC claimed as Chinese, building cities, railroads, and ports on it. The USSR, despite promises to end the unequal treaties of its predecessor government, had never returned these lands.

Second, the Soviet government had ordered the infant Chinese communist movement to pursue policies that many CCP members felt to be unwise, and that had resulted in the deaths of many of their comrades, including Mao's wife and their two children.

Third, Stalin had consistently supported CCP members other than Mao during Mao's drive for leadership of the party. He had also publicly criticized Mao's movement as little more than agrarian reform, describing the CCP as "margarine communists," or "radish communists," the latter epithet implying that they were red on the surface but white inside.

Fourth, the Soviet Union had taken large quantities of material from northeastern China during the USSR's occupation of that area following World War II. The Chinese saw this as being looted by an ally. Moreover, the USSR continued to negotiate with Chiang Kai-shek long after it was clear that the CCP was winning its battle to control China. Stalin sought to sell arms to Chiang in return for concessions in Xinjiang and elsewhere.

The Sino–Soviet Treaty of 1950 had granted aid to China when the PRC could not expect aid from elsewhere. Nonetheless, the terms of the agreement were hardly generous by international standards, and included concessions to the Soviet Union in Xinjiang, Dalian (Port Arthur), and on the Chinese Eastern Railway. These concessions were canceled by Khrushchev in 1954, but Chinese pride had already been hurt. The Chinese leadership was also annoyed by the terms under which the Soviet Union had supplied the PRC with weapons to pursue the Korean War. They saw China as fighting on behalf of the socialist world in a war that would, moreover, protect the Soviet Union. Yet, the USSR not only supplied China with weapons that were obsolescent but required the PRC to pay for them as well.

The Chinese were shocked when, at the Twentieth Congress of the Communist Party of the Soviet Union (CPSU) in 1956, Khrushchev delivered a biting denunciation of Stalin. Khrushchev had not consulted them beforehand, and, to the intense embarrassment of the Chinese leadership, the Chinese delegate to the CPSU had just finished a speech eulogizing Comrade Stalin. The PRC leadership also believed that Khrushchev had acted recklessly. Although they had excellent reasons for disliking Stalin, they were concerned that to publicly destroy the reputation of this symbol of the unity of the communist bloc might cause the bloc's unity to disintegrate. Mao may also have feared that Khrushchev's denunciations of the cult of Stalin would subsequently be used to put pressure on Mao to eliminate his own personality cult.

To compound these other dissatisfactions with the Soviet Union, Chinese planners became increasingly convinced that the Soviet developmental model was not adequately serving the PRC's needs. When they adopted a radically different developmental scheme, the Great Leap Forward, Khrushchev publicly ridiculed it. Sino–Soviet differences were expressed in rather muted form at first, but reached a major turning point by early 1960, when the PRC's media began to imply that since Khrushchev had betrayed the most fundamental beliefs of Marxism–Leninism, China must now assume leadership of the communist world. Monolithic communism was henceforth dead, in both theory and practice.

The immediate consequences of this declaration were not to China's benefit. The Soviet Union, having already reneged on promises to help China develop nuclear weapons, abruptly withdrew its technicians and much of its aid, thereby hindering the PRC's economic development. Most communist states tended to side with the Soviet Union. In states where communist parties existed but did not govern, the communist party often split over the issue of the Sino–Soviet dispute, thus weakening its chances of coming to power. In general, the larger portion of these bifurcated parties remained loyal to the USSR, while the smaller splinter was pro-PRC. With Khrushchev's removal from office in October 1964, public Sino–Soviet polemics abated, but the ideological differences between the two countries remained.

In the noncommunist world, China appeared threatening because of its diatribes against peaceful coexistence, insistence that wars were inevitable so long as imperialism remained, and denial of the possibility of peaceful roads to communism. Chinese actions exacerbated the fears aroused by its propaganda. In 1962, the PRC used military force against India with regard to the border dispute between the two countries. Its decisive victory appeared to arouse more fear than admiration in world public opinion.

Other Chinese foreign policy actions were less successful. Although definitive proof is lacking, the PRC is likely to have been involved in an attempted coup d'état by the Communist Party of Indonesia (PKI) in 1965. The Indonesian coup was put down by a coalition of generals; a bloodbath followed in which not only members of the PKI were massacred, but many thousands of noncommunist overseas Chinese as well. Thousands more Indonesian Chinese were herded into detention camps and eventually deported to the PRC. The formerly pro-PRC government of Indonesia was replaced by one distinctly cool toward China, and diplomatic relations between the two countries were suspended.

In the Middle East, China's support for the activities of the Palestinian Liberation Organization (PLO) annoyed the Egyptian government, as did China's efforts to wean Egypt away from its alliance with the Soviet Union. In Kenya, the popular nationalist leader Jomo Kenyatta resented Chinese support for his opposition party and declared, "It is naive to think that there is no danger of imperialism from the East . . . this is why we reject communism." And in Latin America, Fidel Castro complained of Chinese interference in Cuban affairs, asserting that he had not liberated his country from U.S. imperialism only to endure similar treatment from the PRC.

A final rebuff occurred when China's efforts to exclude the Soviet Union from a projected Afro–Asian conference in 1965 failed. The PRC announced that it would not attend a conference convened in disregard for China's views, and the gathering was postponed indefinitely. Chinese sources acknowledged these reversals, stating that "temporary setbacks" to the world revolution were to be expected. Because truth was on its side, the PRC, though presently outnumbered by the forces of imperialism—that is, the United States and its allies—would yet triumph.

China's isolation reached an extreme during the Cultural Revolution from 1966 to 1969. During this period, radical leftists criticized the PRC's foreign policy for giving insufficient weight to world revolution. The PRC increased its encouragement of subversive movements in several countries, and groups of Chinese militants, most of them students, caused disruptive incidents in a number of foreign states. As a result, the PRC's diplomatic relations with more than 30 countries were damaged. In addition, China's foreign policy-making apparatus was attacked by radicals who claimed that it had succumbed to subversive bourgeois influences from the foreigners with whom they interacted. Red Guards attacked foreign embassies, terrorizing their personnel and causing at least one death. They also sacked their own country's foreign ministry. With organs of decision making near paralysis, the PRC recalled all its ambassadors save that to Cairo. The importance China attached to the Middle East, and to Egypt's importance within the Middle East, is the most probable explanation for this exception. It also suggests that, despite the feverish ideological pronouncements of this era, some modicum of pragmatism remained.

Chinese leftists' feelings against the Soviet Union ran especially high. Militant extremists believed that China was in danger of contamination from Soviet "revisionism" and the USSR's tolerance of various invidious heterodox forms of capitalism. Thus, it is not surprising that Soviet diplomats were a special target of extremist attacks, and that polemics against the Soviet government increased. The USSR's media responded by denouncing the turmoil within China as the product of insanity among the CCP elite. The Sino–Soviet dispute, quiescent since Khrushchev's fall in October 1964, became increasingly bitter. China denounced the Soviet invasion of Czechoslovakia in 1968 as a "monstrous crime," and there were rumors that the USSR was planning a pre-emptive strike against the PRC's nuclear installation in Xinjiang, its only nuclear facility at the time.

Border tensions heightened, and there were minor incidents involving border guards and civilians on both sides throughout 1968 and early 1969. In March 1969, on a small island in the Ussuri River that formed one part of the territorial disputes between the two countries, Chinese soldiers opened fire on a Soviet patrol. The Soviets retaliated. Other clashes then followed on the border between China's Xinjiang and the Soviet Union's Kazakh SSR, far to the west of the Ussuri incident. China's isolation from the international community was virtually complete, and even its territorial integrity seemed in jeopardy.

Global Power Politics: 1969–Present
Triangular Politics: 1969–1989

China's actions on the Ussuri puzzled many foreign observers. To provoke hostilities against its more powerful neighbor at a time of domestic weakness over a long-standing claim to a tiny piece of land of no great value—the island is actually under water a great deal of the time—seemed absurd. Moreover, even if, as the PRC claimed, the démarche aimed to demonstrate that China would not be "bullied," the scenario seemed ill conceived. Soviet troops were well trained and showed themselves fully competent to deal with the PLA. Finally, it seemed pointless to provoke a major foreign policy crisis just a few weeks before the CCP's Ninth Congress was scheduled to open.

Some Western analysts believed the clash to be a natural outgrowth of the foreign policy excesses of the Cultural Revolution; others suggested that a local commander had simply exceeded his orders. A third explanation is that one faction of the highest echelon of the party's decision-making elite ordered the PLA to attack Soviet troops to force another faction of that elite to agree to a startling change in China's foreign policy: rapprochement with the United States.

In this scenario, Mao and Zhou Enlai interpreted the Soviet invasion of Czechoslovakia and the USSR's subsequent enunciation of the Brezhnev doctrine—that other socialist countries had the right to interfere when events within a socialist country were endangering the socialist community as a whole—as threatening the security of China. At the same time, the United States began to look less threatening. The Paris peace talks on Vietnam had begun, and a new president, Richard Nixon, had been elected. Part of Nixon's campaign rhetoric had included promises to reduce America's presence in Asia. Since the Soviet Union was far more menacing to the PRC than the United States, and since the United States was hostile to the Soviet Union while being approximately equal to it in strength, conciliatory moves toward the United States were indicated.

However, according to this line of analysis, the Mao–Zhou group was prevented from improving relations with the United States because they were opposed by Cultural Revolution radicals led by Defense Minister Lin Biao. Lin's group preferred to try to improve relations with the Soviet Union, reasoning that, despite its many faults, the USSR was still preferable to a capitalist state. Lin would in any case not have wanted to agree with a policy alternative suggested by Zhou Enlai, since Zhou was his principal rival for power.

In this interpretation, then, the Ussuri clash was contrived to discredit those members of the Chinese elite who believed that a rapprochement with the Soviet Union was possible and to open the way for better relations with the United States. Chinese media, of course, described the clash as having been instigated by the Soviet Union. Lin Biao's demise in 1971, as he was allegedly fleeing to the Soviet Union, and the rapprochement with the United States that actually occurred in that same year, have been adduced as further evidence for this scenario. Whatever the truth of this hypothesis, and although Chinese propaganda continued to regularly denounce the machinations of both the United States and the USSR, the dominant faction of the post-1971 Chinese leadership clearly indicated that it considered the USSR to be the more dangerous of the two superpowers. However, the issue of U.S. support for Taiwan remained outstanding, inhibiting PRC moves toward better relations with the United States.

China responded favorably to President Nixon's relaxation of restrictions on trade and travel with the PRC, and in April 1971 Mao Zedong invited an

American table tennis team to tour China. With enthusiastic approval from Washington, the team accepted. Their widely publicized trip, which included meetings with high-ranking Chinese officials, was dubbed "ping-pong diplomacy." It formed the antecedent to President Nixon's own trip to Beijing in 1972.

Nixon's visit brought a further advance in the rapprochement process. After extensive talks, in February 1972 the two sides issued the Shanghai Communiqué, which affirmed their mutual desire to normalize diplomatic relations. It finessed the Taiwan issue by stating that "All Chinese on either side of the Taiwan Strait maintain that there is but one China and that Taiwan is a part of China. The U.S. government does not challenge that position." However, the United States did not go so far as to state that it *agreed* with that position. There were awkward ethical and legal considerations for the United States to deal with. To break relations with its loyal Taiwan ally might call into question the sincerity of America's commitments to other allies. There was also the question of what to do about the U.S.–ROC Mutual Security Treaty. Moreover, a large number of native-born Taiwanese did *not* consider the island part of Chinese territory or consider themselves to be ethnically Chinese, and were vehemently opposed to unification with a mainland to which they felt no ideological or emotional affinity.

With the question of Taiwan temporarily in abeyance and the Shanghai Communiqué as a basis, relations between the United States and the PRC improved. In lieu of regular diplomatic representation, each side established a liaison office in the capital of the other. Bilateral trade increased, and contacts and exchanges took place in a number of areas, including technology, sports, and culture. Eventually, on January 1, 1979, Beijing and Washington began full diplomatic relations. America agreed to end formal ties with the Republic of China on Taiwan while declaring its intention to maintain cultural, commercial, and other unofficial relations with what it would henceforth refer to only as Taiwan. The 1954 defense treaty was abrogated in accordance with its own provisions, which gave either party the option of termination after giving one year's notice. The Taiwan Relations Act, passed by Congress in April 1979, attempted to provide for the security of the island by declaring that the United States would provide its government with such defensive weapons as were deemed necessary to maintain a balance of power in the Taiwan Strait.

At the same time that Mao Zedong began seeking better relations with the United States, China's attitudes toward countries other than the Soviet Union also became a great deal more conciliatory. Ambassadors began to return to their posts in 1970, and the PRC not only formally apologized to foreign countries for what had happened to their embassies in Beijing during the Cultural Revolution but agreed to make restitution as well. This more accommodative posture enabled China both to re-establish relationships that had been broken off during the Cultural Revolution and to win new supporters. The PRC's acceptance as a legitimate member of the international community received formal endorsement in October 1971, when the country was admitted to membership in the United Nations and made a permanent member of the UN Security Council.

Agreement on the PRC's right to UN membership was far from unanimous. Critics, citing the irresponsible acts of the Cultural Revolution period and quoting militant Chinese propaganda, predicted that the PRC would disrupt UN functions. These fears proved to be groundless: observers agree that China has been a responsible member of both the UN's main bodies and its specialized agencies. Beijing has used its UN membership to back causes important to the less developed countries, including support for regulating multinational corporations, obtaining better control over technology transfers from advanced countries, and setting more favorable terms for repaying foreign debts. However, the PRC did not join the nonaligned bloc or, despite briefly being an oil exporter, the Organization of Petroleum Exporting Countries (OPEC). While giving rhetorical support to the New International Economic Order, a favorite project of developing countries, China joined the World Bank, the International Monetary Fund, and the World Trade Organization—all institutions of the old international economic order. The PRC's large size, abundant natural resources, and relatively well-educated population make it unique among developing countries. While frequently declaring its solidarity with the less developed world, the PRC votes in favor of its own interests, which often run counter to those of the so-called Third World. One observer described China's voting record at the UN as constituting "a Gang of One."

Post-Mao Foreign Policy

After Mao's death in 1976, Chinese foreign policy became more unabashedly pragmatic in theory, as it had been in practice for several years previously. There were significant gains for China. Acceptance of certain generally agreed-upon norms in international law made it easier for the PRC to obtain loans and attract foreign investment. The existence of a number of tension-inducing issues notwithstanding, China was able to obtain substantial help from Japan to bolster its economic development plans. In 1978, the two sides ratified a Sino–Japanese Treaty of Peace and Friendship. The PRC also began to use its Muslim minorities to persuade wealthy Islamic states to invest in China. Settlements were negotiated with Britain to return Hong Kong in 1997 and with Portugal to rescind Macao in 1999. The process of negotiations was helped by the less militant rhetoric emanating from Beijing, and also by the PRC's willingness to grant a quasi-autonomous status to the two areas in light of their unique historical and developmental situations. The category of special administrative region (SAR), granting some powers of self-government while Beijing would take over the SAR's foreign and defense functions, was written into the PRC's 1982 constitution. The SAR's creators also saw it as a mechanism through which Taiwan could be absorbed.

China's efforts to contain the Soviet Union suffered a setback when Vietnam, finally unified under a communist government, decided to lean toward the USSR. The historical animosities between China and Vietnam that had been muted during Vietnam's struggle with the United States were rekindled. Vietnam's expropriation of the assets of its wealthiest citizens, a disproportionate number of whom were overseas Chinese, brought charges of ethnic discrimination from the PRC. Vietnam replied that it was doing just what one should expect a communist state to do: destroying capitalism. Vietnam's December 1978 invasion of the PRC's ally, tiny Cambodia, proved to be the last straw. In February 1979, the PLA attacked across the two countries' disputed border, aiming to force Vietnam to withdraw its troops from Cambodia and "teach it a lesson." Neither aim was fulfilled. Chinese casualties were heavy, and the cost of the attack temporarily hindered the PRC's modernization program.

Deng Xiaoping had anticipated that the Soviet Union would aid its Vietnamese ally and made preparations against such an attack. Armed Soviet intervention proved unnecessary, though Vietnam welcomed the USSR's moral support and material aid. Chinese propaganda put a positive spin on Moscow's decision not to join the hostilities, boasting that the PRC had "touched the tiger's backside" with impunity. Nonetheless, soon after the confrontation, Vietnam rewarded the Soviet Union by granting it basing rights at strategically located Cam Ranh Bay. The USSR now had easy access to a warm-water port located not far from China.

Shortly after its strike against Vietnam, the PRC abrogated the Sino–Soviet Treaty of 1950, accurately describing the agreement as having been a dead letter for nearly two decades. China argued that the treaty had been drawn up with the PRC in an inferior position, which was not only insulting but also no longer consonant with reality. Its leaders declared themselves willing to negotiate a new treaty on the basis of equality between the contracting partners. Talks, which began in an atmosphere characterized by neither trust nor harmony, were suspended by the Chinese after the USSR invaded Afghanistan in December 1979. The PRC then announced preconditions for future negotiations: Soviet troops were to be withdrawn from Afghanistan, from the Sino–Soviet border, and from Mongolia, and the USSR was to cease support for Vietnam's occupation of Cambodia.

Since neither past Soviet behavior nor the attitudes of the then-current Moscow leadership gave evidence that these conditions might be agreed to, prospects for better Sino–Soviet relations did not seem bright. However, by late 1981, Beijing had begun to reassess its position. Irritants in its relations with the United States had accumulated, including the amount of textiles the PRC was allowed to export to the United States, the pace of American technology transfer, how U.S. officials had handled the defection of a Chinese tennis player, and continued U.S. support for Taiwan. In 1982, Beijing was able to pressure Washington into agreeing to gradually reduce its sales of arms to Taiwan, but since the communiqué said nothing about ending the transfer of military technology to the island, the United States was able to use this omission to help Taiwan design and build high-quality fighter planes and warships of its own.

At the very least, Chinese officials reasoned, the threat of better PRC–USSR relations could be used as a lever to influence American policies in ways that would benefit China. Stressing that more cordial relations in no way modified the PRC's insistence that its preconditions be met, China employed "people's diplomacy," exchanging sports and professional delegations with the USSR. Cross-border trade, which had almost ceased after 1960, picked up rapidly. After Mikhail Gorbachev came to power in the Soviet Union, he did actually comply with all of the Chinese demands. Trade continued to grow, and Gorbachev announced his intention to visit China, making him the first Soviet head of state to do so in over 30 years. In terms of media attention, the drama of Gorbachev's May 1989 visit to Beijing was upstaged by the student demonstrations in Tiananmen Square, but in terms of putting a symbolic end to the Sino–Soviet dispute it was significant indeed.

At the same time, however, China's ability to play the Soviet Union off against the United States was waning. Gorbachev's policies included not only conciliatory gestures toward the PRC but also increasing accommodation to U.S. positions. This resulted in much better relations between the two superpowers. The brutality of the PRC leadership's actions against unarmed demonstrators at Tiananmen Square and elsewhere in China caused many people, including many Americans, to become disillusioned with the PRC. While Gorbachev's Soviet Union appeared less menacing and more deserving of American support than it had in the past, Deng's China now appeared less benign, and less worthy of American support.

Counterbalancing the Sole Superpower

The disintegration of the Soviet Union into 15 successor states made it far more difficult for the PRC to practice triangular diplomacy, confronting Beijing with a single superpower, the United States. This was not a situation the leadership was comfortable with, particularly in the years following the Tiananmen incident, when American sermonizing on human rights and the need for representative democracy intensified. Chinese sources predicted that a multipolar international order would be the eventual outcome of the realignment of power caused by the USSR's collapse, and the country's leaders set about trying to aid its emergence. They envisioned a decline in American power, with the country then being balanced off by Japan, an increasingly integrated European Union (EU), India, Russia, and the PRC itself. Chinese diplomacy thus encouraged greater distance between Japan and the United States, highlighted issues on which European countries disagreed with the United States, and courted good relations with various Middle Eastern, African, Latin American, and Central Asian states.

Beijing's attempts to form a multilateral coalition against American hegemony while the PRC's economy boomed and its military expenditures increased produced mixed results. Some policy makers in neighboring states viewed China as an unstoppable juggernaut and concluded that placatory policies were likely to achieve more than confrontational ones. This attitude did not necessarily rule out tactics that involved resistance to Chinese expansion, nor efforts to form countervailing coalitions of their own against the PRC. Placatory policies included regular reciprocal visits by officials at various levels of importance, cultural exchanges, and the signing of commercial treaties. The Association of Southeast Asian Nations (ASEAN) agreed to give the PRC, along with Japan and South Korea, dialogue partner status, and Beijing began to explore the feasibility of a free trade agreement with ASEAN. China also established close relations with Russia, which soon became its leading supplier of advanced weaponry and an important trading partner.

Although concerned to counter American hegemony, Beijing's attitude toward the United States was not overtly hostile. American policy seemed premised on the belief that a prospering China enmeshed in the world trading system would be a peaceful China that would favor global or at least regional stability.

Moves by regional neighbors that involved deterring the PRC from aggression included Indonesia's holding, in 1996, its largest air, land, and sea military maneuvers in four years. Symbolically, they were held in Indonesia's Natuna Islands, which had recently appeared on Chinese maps as part of the PRC's exclusive economic zone. Jakarta invited foreign military attachés to attend; China's attaché declined to do so. Other Southeast Asian states took similar actions. Some of these efforts to stem perceived Chinese expansion were, however, undone by the Asian currency crisis, which severely impacted several of the countries, and by internal turmoil in Indonesia.

Japan's reaction was more worrisome to Chinese leaders, who either did not see, or did not wish to acknowledge, the reasons for Tokyo's anxieties. In 1995/1996, in response to the United States granting a visa to Taiwan's president Lee Teng-hui so that he could receive an award from his alma mater, the PLA began nearly a year of war games and missile tests in the Taiwan Strait. Taiwan had been a Japanese colony for 50 years until the end of World War II, and Japanese companies still hold extensive investments on the island. Should China take over Taiwan, PLA naval patrols into what Japan considers its territorial waters, already a concern, would become more intrusive. Tokyo approached Washington for an upgrade in the security relationship between the two, resulting in an agreement to cooperate in "dealing with situations in the areas surrounding Japan which would have an important influence in the peace and security of Japan." Beijing demanded Tokyo's assurances that the phrase "areas around Japan" did not include Taiwan; Japanese diplomats replied that since the definition of areas surrounding Japan was situational rather than geographic, they could not give such assurances.

This, plus Japan's decision to join American efforts to establish a Theater Missile Defense system, led Beijing to reassess its opinion of the U.S.–Japan alliance. Heretofore, it had seen Washington as mitigating Japanese impulses toward a revival of militarism by including Japan under U.S. military protection. After these developments, however, it saw Washington as fostering the revival of militarism by encouraging Japan to become a partner in its plans to dominate the world.

Perceptions of the United States as determined to bring the world under its control were reinforced when an American-led NATO coalition began bombing the Yugoslav Republic in an effort to prevent it from slaughtering an ethnic minority there. When one of the bombs landed on the Chinese embassy in Belgrade, Beijing refused to believe Washington's explanation that it was accidental. Angry mobs hurled rocks at the American embassy in Beijing, and the Chinese government publicly repudiated the idea of a strategic partnership between the two countries.

Only weeks after the signing of the agreement strengthening the U.S.–Japan alliance, Jiang Zemin convened the leaders of Russia and three Central Asian states in Shanghai to form a countervailing organization. Initially called the Shanghai Five, the group was renamed the Shanghai Cooperation Organization (SCO) when another Central Asian member joined. Among the issues discussed were border demarcations, border security, and "a long-term convergence of strategic aims" which was generally interpreted as aimed at resisting undue U.S. influence. China regularly referred to Russia as its strategic partner. In July 2002, the two countries concluded a treaty—the first since the 1950 agreement between Mao Zedong and Joseph Stalin. Other potential allies were not neglected: there were proposals, never acted upon, that the Sino–Russian partnership be expanded to include Iran and even India. Beijing argued for ending UN sanctions against Iraq, and helped upgrade Baghdad's air defenses.

Post-9/11 Developments

Events set in motion by Muslim fundamentalists' attacks on the World Trade Center and Pentagon on September 11, 2001 led to yet another realignment of power, although in a direction that the PRC perceived as hostile to its interests. Although Beijing pledged to assist Washington in its efforts to deal with terrorists, the result was a deepening of Chinese concerns that the United States was using the war against terrorism to expand its hegemonic designs rather than as a united front against terrorism. After several SCO members offered support, including basing rights, to Washington, Beijing became concerned that the U.S. presence in Central Asia might become permanent, to the detriment of Chinese interests there. Moreover, Russian president Vladimir Putin also moved closer to the United States; in 2002, Washington and Moscow signed an arms reduction treaty and issued a joint declaration on the establishment of a new strategic relationship between them. Against Chinese wishes, Putin acquiesced in the abrogation of the Anti-Ballistic Missile Treaty, and Russia became a participant, though not an actual member, of NATO—an alliance that was originally established to contain the Soviet Union. Chinese analysts assessed this as signifying "the complete assimilation of Russia into the American orbit," thereby upsetting the balance between the hegemonic and anti-hegemonic forces in the world. Beijing saw U.S. plans to replace Saddam Hussein as an attempt to impose its notions of liberal democracy on yet another area of the world, as well as to take over Iraq's oilfields in order to benefit America.

Beijing was likewise unhappy when President Bush's vow to pursue terrorists and whatever countries harbored them led to American military advisers being sent to several Southeast Asian states. More anxiety was generated by the mending of relations between India and the United States. These had been strained since India carried out nuclear tests in 1998. India's defense minister made it clear at the time that fear of China had been behind his country's decision to develop a nuclear arsenal. Consonant with its policy of opposing proliferation, Washington initially responded by levying sanctions on India. By early 2002, however, Washington and New Delhi had agreed to conduct joint military training, and India's president had made a speech to the U.S. Congress declaring that the two states were natural allies.

International opposition to the U.S. decision to invade Iraq in search of weapons of mass destruction gave Beijing an opportunity to redress these trends. China courted the EU countries, lobbying strongly for the EU to lift an arms embargo which it had imposed against the PRC following the Tiananmen incident in 1989. Free trade agreements were signed with ASEAN states. Relations with India, though remaining wary, improved as the two Asian giants discovered the benefits of an information-technology partnership between India's impressive software and China's computer hardware industries.

The search for oil and raw materials to fuel the PRC's rapidly growing economy also led it further afield in the early twenty-first century. While sellers in many countries welcomed these new customers, others worried about the toll on their environments. Southeast Asian rain forests were being depleted because of growing Chinese demand for lumber. Wildlife was also adversely affected: according to international conservation organizations, the demand for ivory, most of it from the PRC, would, if sustained, result in the extinction of the world's elephant population.

Chinese companies and high-ranking leaders visited Latin America and Africa in search of resources needed to sustain the PRC's rapid economic growth. Energy and geopolitical concerns converged in Venezuela as China signed an agreement for oil with then-president Hugo Chavez. Chavez, who had been criticized by Washington for human rights violations, welcomed an additional buyer for his country's crude oil, and Beijing was happy to have made a friend in America's backyard. China's need for oil also led it to support a far more serious human rights violator, the government of Sudan.

Relations with Japan were economically warm but politically tepid. Japanese appreciated that trade with China accounted for much of their country's recent economic growth, but considerable friction existed between the two countries over a range of issues. These included territorial disputes, matters related to Japan's conduct in China during World War II, Tokyo's concerns with the PRC's rapidly increasing military expenditures, and what each side regarded as highhanded treatment by the other. Accumulated tensions erupted into anti-Japanese violence in several Chinese cities in April 2005. Although these tensions calmed down for a time, a 2010 incident in which the Japanese government arrested the captain of a Chinese fishing ship that rammed two Japanese coastguard vessels set off another round of anti-Japanese demonstrations in the PRC.

With regard to Taiwan, Beijing's decision to ignore the country's incumbent, anti-unification president in hopes that he would be replaced with a more amenable individual received a setback when, in March 2004, the objectionable president was re-elected. The NPC then passed an anti-secession law (ASL), presumably as a warning. Since both of Taiwan's major political parties agree that because the island is already an independent sovereign state there is no need to declare independence, the passage of an ASL would seem superfluous. The ASL, however, aroused enough anxiety elsewhere that the EU decided to postpone lifting the embargo against military sales to the PRC which had been in effect since the Tiananmen incident.

The victory of Beijing's preferred candidate, the KMT's Ma Ying-jeou, in Taiwan's 2008 presidential election began a period of more cordial cross-strait relations. Ma stated that he did not oppose eventual unification, though adding that the PRC would have to become a democracy first. Under his administration, commercial and transportation ties increased Beijing's economic control over the island, to the displeasure of many Taiwanese. When Ma used an irregular tactic to force a controversial agreement through the legislature, anger erupted into a huge, though peaceful, protest movement. The KMT suffered a devastating defeat in the 2016 election, with new president Tsai Ing-wen taking a cautious attitude toward Beijing while seeking other trade and investment partners.

The rapid growth of the PRC's economy caused both developed and developing countries to worry that their economies might be swallowed by the Chinese behemoth. In many cases, goods from the PRC could be marketed more cheaply than domestically produced items, leading to job losses in the industries that undergird their economic systems. At first, Beijing countered by explaining that China was "peacefully rising," but discovered that the slogan, when coupled with the country's rapidly increasing military budgets, had an ominous ring. "Peaceful rising" was replaced by "peaceful development." Spokespersons emphasize that a rising tide will raise all boats: join with the PRC, and one will prosper; remain aloof, and suffer the consequences.

This has been coupled with a good neighbor policy. Among other manifestations thereof, Beijing has sought to use soft power. Confucius Institutes have been founded in many countries to help teach the Chinese language, create goodwill for the PRC, and popularize knowledge about the great sage and Chinese culture in general. One area of emphasis is the Confucian concept of a Great Harmony, with obvious applicability to world peace. Chinese leaders have also made various goodwill gestures, including increasing foreign aid to and canceling the debt obligations of several African states.

Overcoming its long-standing opposition to UN peacekeeping operations in 1990, the PRC had contributed over 30,000 troops by 2017, the largest number among the permanent members of the Security Council. Becoming economically engaged with so many countries around the globe has nonetheless opened China to criticisms similar to those that Beijing leveled at capitalist countries only a few decades before. A South African leader encapsulated views in many countries when he described the PRC as both a tantalizing opportunity and a terrifying threat. In Zambia, there has been a backlash against Chinese influence, fueled by concerns over poor working conditions and low pay in Chinese-run copper and iron mines and resentment over an influx of Chinese traders into the retail clothing industry. In Nigeria, Chinese workers have been kidnapped. Latin American concerns are strikingly similar. From the inception of Chinese control of the Hierro Peru iron complex in 1992, there have been strikes centering on allegations of substandard wages and failure to live up to promises made to workers. Both African and Latin American countries have also complained that the Chinese typically prefer to bring in their own workers rather than hire local people, and that their factories and infrastructure projects show no concern for the environment.

Beijing was put in an awkward position when North Korea torpedoed a South Korean navy ship in March 2010, and again when the DPRK military forces shelled a ROK island in November of the same year. It was unable to placate both sides. Similarly, Beijing's agreement to attenuated sanctions against Iran in the UN Security Council irked officials in Tehran while falling short of the measures hoped for by the United States and Europe.

Recent Developments

With China becoming stronger economically and militarily, the PRC's leadership seems to have decided that the time has come to move beyond Deng Xiaoping's advice that China should observe international events calmly, take a firm stance while hiding its accomplishments, and bide its time: by the second decade of the twenty-first century, Beijing's more assertive stance was undeniable. Beijing strongly asserted the PRC's claim to the so-called nine-dotted line or "cow's tongue" that encompasses the numerous dispute areas within the East China and South China seas. Beijing has designated certain entities "core areas," presumably meaning that, if challenged, China will fight to control them. When, in 2010, the U.S. secretary of state suggested at an ASEAN foreign ministers' meeting that territorial disputes be settled through peaceful negotiations, the PRC foreign minister reacted angrily. Looking pointedly at the Singaporean representative, he remarked that China was a big country and other countries would have to understand that they were small. In 2012, Beijing established a new prefecture, Sansha, to back up its South China Sea claims. When Vietnam and the Philippines attempted to take their territorial disputes with China to ASEAN, Beijing put pressure on host government Cambodia to prevent the item from being included on the agenda.

As for Japan, after imposing economic sanctions that forced Japan to release the fishing boat captain (see p. 349), Beijing announced that its ships would patrol the area around the disputed islands, and did so. In response to this increased pressure, Tokyo's nationalistic governor declared his intention to buy the islands on behalf of the municipality from the Japanese family that owned them. Hoping to forestall a diplomatic crisis, the Japanese premier arranged to purchase the islands on behalf of the nation instead. Beijing reacted angrily nonetheless: there were unruly demonstrations in several of the PRC's cities, and China stepped up its patrols in the area. In 2013, China announced an Air

Defense Identification Zone (ADIZ) that overlapped territories disputed with Japan and South Korea, creating tensions with both countries.

India has become concerned with PLA incursions past the line of actual control in disputed areas of the Himalayas as well as over increased Chinese naval activities in the Indian Ocean that include deep-sea mining. In Europe, which has no territorial disputes with the PRC, EU economies which were experiencing extreme financial difficulties welcomed Chinese investment. PRC businesses concluded contracts with the port of Piraeus in Greece and with Ireland to construct a trade hub in Athlone. They also purchased millions of euros of Spanish bonds, and a stake in a major Portugal-based European power provider. What influence these investments will have in the PRC in Europe remains to be seen. Concerns about trade imbalances with China cause friction, and the PRC's human rights record remains a thorny issue.

Uncooperative countries, wherever located, could face economic sanctions, as when Norwegian fish imports were banned when its government stood behind the Nobel Peace Prize committee's decision to award the honor to imprisoned Chinese dissident Liu Xiaobo. Until it released the fishing boat captain, sanctions against Japan included a ban on the shipment of the rare earths that are critical to the Japanese automobile manufacturing industry. The Philippines were threatened with a ban of fruit exports to the PRC. Imports of Argentine soya were halted after Buenos Aires brought an anti-dumping action against Beijing in the WTO. All parties realize that they have important reasons for cooperation with China that may transcend other concerns.

Even soft power has been shown to have hard edges: since box-office sales in China account for an increasingly large proportion of Hollywood's profits and, since censors will demand changes to or even ban films that portray China negatively, scripts now accommodate them. Beijing has also ordered long-established Western academic journals to remove articles from their websites, albeit with mixed results.

Conclusions

In terms of achieving major foreign policy goals, China's record contains several successes and a few failures. The PRC's territory has remained free from attacks, and the humiliating concessions made to foreign powers within China in the past have been abolished. China's international prestige has been restored. The country has attained membership in the UN, holds a permanent seat on the UN Security Council, and participates actively in major international financial organizations, such as the International Monetary Fund, the World Bank, and the World Trade Organization. It enjoys observer status in ASEAN and the Arctic Council. The PRC has the second-largest economy in the world.

All but 19 nations recognize the CCP as the legitimate government of China, and even those few count the PRC as an important force in international politics. China no longer aspires to a position of leadership over the Third World; since it occupies such an anomalous position in the Third World, some have argued that it should not even be classified therein. From a position of abject weakness during the century preceding 1949, China has come to be regarded as one of the more important powers in the world. Particularly when considered in light of the PRC's until recently modest military capabilities, this is an impressive achievement.

As for recovering the territories which China claims, the record is mixed. The PRC has regained Tibet, Hong Kong, and Macao. It has achieved border settlements with several countries, including Burma and Nepal, and established de facto control over substantial segments of its disputed borders with India and Vietnam. There has been a peaceful resolution of contending claims on the Sino–Russian border.

Taiwan remains independent, with polls indicating that a large majority of its population does not want to be part of the PRC. Many schemes for unification, such as a "one country, two systems" idea, have been proposed but found to be unacceptable. Beijing has rejected the idea of federation or confederation. Taiwan's citizens reject the status of SAR, pointing out that provisions for the self-government of SARs are ultimately dependent on China's voluntary acquiescence, and that Hong Kong's experience has proved that China's promises cannot be trusted. Moreover, the island's residents enjoy one of the highest living standards in Asia, including a per capita income level far higher than that of the mainland. They also have a functioning democratic political system and a free press. Mongolia seems unlikely to be recovered. The freer intellectual climate in Mongolia has included a revival of the area's traditional lamaist Buddhist religion. Since this is the faith of most of Tibet's population as well, Mongols' sympathies are likely to lie with the Tibetans in their ongoing conflict with Chinese rule. Many Mongols are also apprehensive lest their country become an economic colony of China.

The more recent goal of establishing a multipolar world to counter American influence has also proved elusive. The Atlantic alliance has held firm. With Britain leaving the EU, many of its members recovering only slowly from the financial crisis of 2007/2008, and democratic values having more in common with the United States than with China, Europe does not currently seem capable of constituting a pole. Japan has added a quasi-security alliance with the U.K. to its strengthened cooperation with the U.S., India, and Australia.

Ties with Russia continue to the extent that some Westerners worry about the rise of an "authoritarian internationale" replacing the former Sino–Soviet alliance. But at the same time, a reassertive Russia is apt to have differences with the PRC on many issues. With regard to Georgia, for example, Beijing has misgivings about Russia aiding the separatist ambitions of South Ossetians and Azerbaijanis, seeing dangerous precedents for its control of restive areas, such as Tibet and Xinjiang. And Russia worries about Beijing's one-belt-one-road initiative encroaching on its influence in Central Asia.

Changes in the PRC's foreign policy since 1949 have been described as China moving from being a "shaker" of the world order from 1949 through the early 1970s to being a "taker"; that is, accommodating to its principles, in the 1980s and 1990s, to being a more assertive "shaper" and even "maker" of international norms in the twenty-first century. Its foreign policy makers have shown considerable skill and flexibility in bringing about relatively smooth shifts in strategy in response to perceived changes in the international climate. In contrast to rhetoric that has often been militant and pro-revolutionary, China's international actions have generally been rather circumspect, indicating careful forethought and shrewd calculation of both adversary capabilities and foreign public opinion. Exceptions to this are associated with the periods of the Great Leap Forward and the Cultural Revolution, and with certain aspects of the 1978/1979 dispute with Vietnam. Over the 65 years since the founding of the PRC, many of its initial goals have been attained. In the process, foreign policy has evolved in a manner in which the PRC's international responses may be fairly described as pragmatism with Chinese characteristics.

Suggestions for Further Reading

June Teufel Dreyer, *Middle Kingdom and Empire of the Rising Sun: Sino–Japanese Relations Past and Present* (Oxford: Oxford University Press, 2016).

François Godemont and Abigaël Vasselier, *China at the Gates: A New Power Audit of EU–China Relations* (Paris: European Council on Foreign Relations, 2017).

John Pomfret, *The Beautiful Country and the Middle Kingdom: America and China, 1776 to the Present* (New York: Henry Holt, 2016).

David Shambaugh, *China Goes Global: The Partial Power* (Princeton, NJ: Princeton University Press, 2013).

Robert G. Sutter, *Chinese Foreign Relations: Power and Policy since the Cold War*, 4th edition (Lanham, MD: Rowman & Littlefield, 2016).

CHAPTER 15

Conclusions

Any assessment of how successful the Chinese communist political system has been presents problems of what weight to assign to the various criteria of success. Those who place high value on the criterion of a government's ability to keep the peace, or that of satisfying its citizens' minimal needs for existence, will make a very different judgment from those whose greatest concerns are issues such as human rights and freedom of the press. In addition, since every political system has both its backers and detractors, one would normally want to consult the opinions of Chinese themselves as to how successful they feel the system has been. Carefully read opinion polls can tell us much about changes in citizens' views of their government over time. Only within the last 20 years, however, has the People's Republic of China (PRC) begun to use opinion polls, and there are limitations on what may be concluded from local samples. Although respondents' trust in the anonymity of their answers to pollsters has increased, researchers have noticed that replies tend to reflect what the respondents perceive to be "correct" answers based on their understanding of official policy. Moreover, no data are available for the past. Therefore, both we and, for that matter, the country's leaders are deprived of the guidance such data might provide.

Party and government preside over the feeding and clothing of nearly a quarter of the world's population on a mere 7 percent of the world's arable land. The average Chinese has a life span of 73 years, putting the PRC on the level of more developed nations and well ahead of many developing areas. Although one can question the claimed literacy rate of over 90 percent, there is no doubt that a markedly higher proportion of China's population is literate today than prior to 1949. Thousands of miles of railroads and highways have been built, and the country's industrial base has been greatly expanded. The PRC has developed a nuclear deterrence capability and sells a variety of military equipment to Third World countries. It is regarded as a major actor in international affairs. China is a respected member of the United Nations and a permanent member of its Security Council.

All of these are important achievements. On the other hand, in the 1950s, economic conditions in China, Japan, Korea, Taiwan, and Southeast Asia were relatively similar. Since then, living standards in many of these countries have exceeded those of the PRC. Moreover, compared to citizens in most of these states, the average Chinese is far more constrained in what he or she can say and to whom. Freedom to associate with whom one wishes, to state one's grievances, and to practice one's religion is also restrained in various ways, constitutional guarantees notwithstanding. So is the right to a fair trial.

The Chinese Communist Party (CCP) came to power with clearly articulated goals of equality and prosperity for the society it wished to create. For a time, the party enjoyed relatively solid support from the people in whose interests it claimed to rule. Since the best path to the goals the CCP espoused was not preordained, there was a great deal of social and economic experimentation. Loyalty to the party, to Marxism–Leninism, and to Mao Zedong's interpretation of Marxism–Leninism, was not merely encouraged but demanded. There was a tendency for all of these to be subsumed into a demand for absolute and unswerving loyalty to the person of the supreme leader himself. While Mao's desire for self-aggrandizement was certainly a factor in the growth of his personality cult, it was also a way to smooth over the strains of modernization and industrialization. There appeared to be a genuine belief that however difficult the problems of the present, the emergence of a classless society was inevitable: the communist cause would triumph in the end. Meanwhile, peasants and workers were regarded as the most worthy classes, and loyalty both to the person of Mao and to communist doctrine was rigidly enforced.

The cult of personality that developed around Mao and the style of rule that characterized his leadership seem to fit the eminent German sociologist Max Weber's description of charismatic rule. According to Weber, the norms and practices developed under this leader, who generally eschews past practices and makes his own rules, will gradually become accepted ways of behavior and decision making. Hence, the stage of government after charismatic leadership is called the transition to institutionalization. In Weber's paradigm, bureaucracies will grow up to enforce these norms and staff the institutions. The third, and final, stage described by Weber is that of rational rule legitimization, a process he called the routinization of charisma. The result is a modern, bureaucratic state.

Most social scientists assumed that China would follow the path outlined by Weber in its quest for modernity. However, Mao strenuously resisted the routinization and bureaucratization of his revolution. Fearing a return to everything he had disliked about the mandarinate of his childhood, Mao was concerned to keep society from settling into comfortable rules and routines.

They would undermine progress toward creating the type of society that had been his life's work. The best way to prevent this was, in Mao's own words, to have the country in a state of permanent revolution until the advent of the classless society. Periodic economic and social upheavals, most notably the Great Leap Forward and the Great Proletarian Cultural Revolution, were designed to further this end.

Unfortunately, the widespread economic and social disruptions they caused also led many Chinese to have doubts about the party's ability to govern them and to improve living standards. Mao's death was followed not by the routinization of charisma, as in Weber's paradigm, but by what has been termed a transitional crisis system. In such a system, conflict may not be expressed openly, but can be discerned through differences in terminology among members of the elite, removal of leaders from office, expulsions from the party, and, occasionally, an open rift within the party. The period of Deng Xiaoping's de facto leadership was characterized by a pragmatic reworking of communism. "Socialism with Chinese characteristics" was defined as including a definite commitment to modernization and to the raising of living standards, as well as an acceptance of the need for laws and regulations to govern conduct. The PRC seemed well on its way to Weber's stage of rational rule legitimization. Particularly in the first few years after Deng's plans began to be implemented, there were marked improvements in living standards.

However, these were accompanied by rapidly increasing differences between rich and poor in terms of both individual persons and geographic regions. If Deng Xiaoping's reforms made some people and areas wealthier, they made others poorer by comparison. In his efforts to achieve industrialization through energizing enthusiasm for production, Deng dismantled the welfare state. The expectation of protection from insecurity, inequality, and uncertainty had been an important factor in the ordinary person's support for the communist party. In essence, Deng gambled on being able to compensate these individuals with greater prosperity in exchange for this erosion of security, equality, and certainty. Thus far, this has not happened, and the ordinary person's faith in party and government has also eroded. Escalating inflation, corruption, arguments within the leadership elite, and uncertainty about the future of reform undermined stability and further weakened many people's faith in their government and leadership. These phenomena indicated that China continued to resemble a transitional crisis system.

Abolition of the communes and decentralization of economic decision making, although good for raising production, led to a diminution in the capabilities of central-level institutions. Generally, no compensatory mechanisms emerged to fulfill the important services they had provided. The system appeared to be becoming less, rather than more, capable of coping with problems. In a number of areas, political development was replaced by political decay. There was a resurgence of traditional forms and patterns of authority. This retraditionalization included the revival of the power of clans, religious figures, and secret societies as well as that of village leaders, who were chosen by consensus within the village rather than by the party. The position of women, whom Mao metaphorically described as "holding up half the sky," deteriorated in a number of ways. When economic restructuring occurred, for example, females were disproportionately likely to be among the first workers to be laid off. Local and regional protectionist tendencies in the economy and even in the court system caused problems for the further development of a nationwide market directed by the party from the capital city. Decentralization and market reforms also strengthened centrifugal forces in ethnic minority areas.

Individuals, groups, and regions became increasingly assertive *vis-à-vis* party and central government. Sometimes, as in the cases of tax assessment and mandatory retirement ages, they engaged in extensive bargaining, thereby causing significant modifications in the policies. Occasionally, meaningful proportions of the citizenry were able to passively resist, or completely ignore, the central government's directives. The one-child policy is the best-known example of a widely evaded directive that was frequently circumvented by various means and has now been modified into a two-child policy. Party and government's inability to extract compliance with its directives is especially striking in the case of the nearly 250 million people who comprise the floating population.

On several occasions, Deng attempted to determine the succession to the highest offices of government and party, but his first two choices proved unable to maintain their positions. He forced a number of other high-ranking people to retire, but many of them, like Deng himself, were able to exercise considerable influence without benefit of formal position. In effect, power became divorced from responsibility. The advent of a classless society was no longer seen as inevitable. In fact, it seemed less attainable than ever and, except for a minority of individuals, so did the prospect of the good life. As the Deng era progressed, large numbers of people became convinced that however much the new system differed from Mao's, it was no better in its ability to produce equality and prosperity.

By the mid-1980s, widespread disaffection with the status quo began to permeate various sectors of society: peasants, workers, professionals, students, and members of the military expressed their grievances in disparate and, at least initially, disconnected ways. Many, particularly the students and intellectuals, demanded what amounted to a broadening of political participation. They had come to regard the guardianship of the elite as inadequate. This situation has many similarities to that described by Harvard social scientist Samuel Huntington as praetorian society: a politicized society in which not just the military but other social forces, such as students, bureaucrats, workers, and farmers, participate as well. Political institutions lack effectiveness; power is fragmented; and groups disagree on the legitimate and authoritative methods for resolving conflict. By contrast, in institutionalized polities, most political actors agree on the procedures to be used for the resolution of political disputes, such as the allocation of offices and the determination of policies. For example, offices may be assigned through election, heredity, examination, drawing lots, or some combination thereof. Policy issues may be resolved by hierarchical processes, petitions, hearings, appeals, majority votes, or consensus. The crucial factors are, first, the existence of general agreement on what those means are; second, that groups participating in the political process recognize their obligation to employ those means.

In a praetorian society, each group employs the means at its command: those who have enough money bribe, students riot, mobs demonstrate, and the military uses force. In the absence of accepted procedures, all these forms of direct action are found in the political scene of a praetorian society. *Radical* praetorianism, says Huntington, has its social roots in the gap between the city and the countryside. The city replaces rural areas as the main focus of political action and becomes the continuing source of political instability. The stronger influence of the city in the political life of the society leads to greater political turbulence. In a radical praetorian society, the city cannot furnish the basis for governmental stability. The extent of the instability depends on the extent to which the government is able, and willing, to use the countryside to contain and pacify the city. If the government can build a bridge to the countryside—if it can mobilize support from the rural areas—it can contain and ride out the instabilities of the city.

This characterization seemed to accurately describe the PRC at the time of the 1989 demonstrations. Rather than being mobilized in *support* of the government, however, the rural areas simply gave the leadership the margin of *passivity* it needed to ride out the crisis caused by widespread demonstrations. Since then, China's rapid industrialization has resulted in city dwellers now outnumbering those in rural areas. Moreover, rural areas have their own problems: it cannot be assumed that they will remain passive in a future confrontation. Deng Xiaoping's educational reforms concentrated almost wholly on the large cities, allowing the countryside to go its own way so long as it produced sufficient food to nourish the population and support the government's modernization programs. The number of rural semi-literates and school dropouts increased. Since coastal cities rather than the rural hinterland garnered most of the benefits of Deng's reform programs, resentments sharpened.

As a result of efforts to restructure and rationalize the economic structure, workers have fared little better than peasants. The alliance between the party and China's new entrepreneurs, symbolized by Jiang Zemin's Three Represents, is yet another indication that the twenty-first-century CCP no longer accords the workers and the peasants the same degree of respect as the party's founders. Although the country's leaders would disagree, many Chinese feel that in its quest for modernization and industrialization, the CCP has betrayed the interests of the workers and peasants who brought it to power.

Despite a proliferation of small-scale protests, there have been no large anti-government demonstrations in the 20 years since the Tiananmen incident: The PRC no longer resembles a praetorian society. Jiang Zemin's assumption of office as a result of the Tiananmen upheaval rather than through regularly established selection processes is an example of the transitional crisis system. Yet the smooth transfer of power after Deng Xiaoping's death and the transitions from Jiang to Hu Jintao and from Hu to Xi Jinping seemed to indicate that routinization is occurring—despite evidence of considerable maneuvering beforehand, as well as Jiang's holding on to military power for an extended period and attempts by both Jiang and Hu to pack the standing committee of the politburo with their supporters even though they were retiring. An orderly transition to the fourth and fifth generations of post-1949 leaders does not, however, mean leadership consensus on how China should, and will, evolve in the future. The disruptions that preceded the Eighteenth Party Congress in 2012, and the re-centralization of power under Xi Jinping that were consolidated in the Nineteenth Party Congress five years later have been interpreted as a regression back to the Maoist era.

In the analysis of Pei Minxin, the PRC may be trapped in a different problem of transition: as a consequence of Deng's opting for a gradual transformation of the economy from state-controlled to market-driven, China is caught in a partial reform equilibrium where partially reformed economic and political institutions support a hybrid neo-authoritarian order that caters mostly to the needs of a small ruling elite. The power of the state is used to defend the privileges of the ruling elite and to suppress societal challenges to those privileges rather than to advance the broader goals of development. Since this small ruling elite cannot effect further reform without adversely affecting its own privileges, it will not do so, leaving China in a partial reform equilibrium trap.

China's current dilemma has been compared to that existing in the late Qing dynasty. There is a crisis of meaning very similar to that of a century ago, except that now it is Marxist orthodoxy that has collapsed rather than Confucian orthodoxy. This threatens the social order and causes economic, political, and cultural problems that are exacerbated by contact with the West. And, as in the past, this sense of crisis and urgency has led to quick-fix proposals for radical and extreme change. These reflect only limited consideration of practical realities and have very little hope of success. Ironically, the leadership has turned back to Confucianism, albeit in a carefully modified form that supports its vested interests, for guidance.

In a country as large and diverse as the PRC, with changes occurring at all levels of society, it is difficult to distinguish linear movements from cyclical movements and trends from counter-trends. One can find evidence for whatever conclusion that one's hopes or biases conduce toward. Among the commonly heard scenarios are that:

- party and government will re-impose Beijing's control over society.
- the present government will be overthrown and replaced by a popularly chosen, reformist regime.
- there will be an evolution toward a more liberal regime that is market oriented and tolerant of a variety of political views.
- party and government will remain in a kind of paralysis as power continues to devolve to provinces and regions, with a range of variations within each.

Historical prediction is always difficult and fraught with errors. Thirty years ago, anyone who predicted the dismantling of the Berlin Wall and the fall of the Soviet empire would have been thought a misguided idealist. China, as the PRC government frequently points out, is very different from the Soviet Union, or from Europe, and one cannot assume that it will replicate developments in either. This said, certain developments seem more likely than others.

The first scenario resembles the neo-authoritarian paradigm that Chinese media began to publicize around 1988. With party and state firmly in control again, mechanisms will be established to substitute for those functions that were lost after Deng Xiaoping's reforms were introduced. System decay, to use Huntington's terminology, will be halted. Economic development, adherents of neo-authoritarianism argue, needs a firm guiding hand. Market reforms must be introduced gradually and closely monitored by the central government in order to correct for such unwanted side effects as inflation and maldistribution. This guided economic development and, ultimately, the country as a whole could only be hurt by disruptive demonstrations and calls for pluralistic decision making. Therefore, demands for political liberalization must be firmly rejected.

There is some evidence that this has been happening. Although China, after the Tiananmen incident, had a ruling elite that appeared unstable, politically backward-looking, and internationally isolated, Jiang Zemin was able to maintain the leadership position for which Deng Xiaoping had chosen him, even after the patriarch's death. The PRC's economy grew rapidly, and the country quickly reintegrated into the global system. Analysts who espouse this scenario find other indications that party and government have been re-legitimated, including:

- the routinization of leadership succession;
- an increase in meritocratic criteria for social mobility;
- the co-optation of groups such as prosperous entrepreneurs and intellectuals into the party;
- institutions that have become more specialized in their functions and are therefore able to perform their responsibilities more effectively;
- the growth of mechanisms for political participation—for example, village elections—that have strengthened the party's appeal to the public.

In short, some believe, state capacity is actually on the rebound. Party and government leaders do not seek to resuscitate the all-powerful Maoist state and are aware of the need to reform. While rejecting multi-party democracy and the separation of powers, they hope to improve state–society relations and become more responsive to the people through intra-party democracy and by establishing more transparency in government operations. They envision what might be called consultative Leninism, whose major characteristics include:

- a strong focus on staying in power;
- ongoing reforms in governance designed to blunt public demands for democracy;
- efforts to improve the party's ability to determine public opinion and to channel it so as to avoid social instability;
- pragmatic management of the economy;
- promoting nationalism.

Performance-based criteria have replaced ideology as the basis for the legitimization of the party's rule. A major overriding goal, in addition to keeping the party in power, is to provide stability within which economic development can continue. The CCP will institutionalize checks and balances within its leadership, meaning that there will be intra-party democracy, not liberal democracy. Efforts are being made to improve the effectiveness of organs of government. Restructured fiscal and tax systems have given central authorities a stronger revenue base. Regulatory institutions are being improved, and attempts made to curb bureaucratic abuses of power. If used vigilantly, the central government's ability to appoint officials to posts and rotate them at will may prevent the emergence of personal fiefdoms.

Other scholars see this as overstating what has happened. For example, Jiang Zemin's ability to retain military power for a period after his resignation as president and party head, and to arrange for the appointment to the politburo standing committee of persons known more for their loyalty to him than for their competence, indicates that there are limitations on the routinization of leadership succession and the application of meritocratic criteria for promotion. Such aberrations are not, these scholars point out, isolated phenomena. Princelings occupy high positions that are disproportionate to their numbers.

Moreover, increased functional specialization of bureaucracies does not necessarily mean better government, as shown by the miscarriages of justice that occurred during the "strike hard" campaign. There is no guarantee that the groups participating in intra-party checks and balances will cooperate with each other to maintain the overall stability of the society: They could collude with each other to conceal malfeasance or, on the other hand, indulge in conflictual factional behavior that disrupts stability. Furthermore, although a fair and predictable legal system is recognized as important to the maintenance of stability, leaders have not accepted that the party itself should be bound by this system. Xi Jinping has been able to centralize power in his person while carrying out a major purge that, although nominally directed only against corruption, has fallen hardest on his opponents. This hardly seems like intra-party democracy.

Finally, while village elections have often improved governance in rural areas, the party will not tolerate any actions there that contravene its policies. It has invalidated the election results of candidates who it believes might challenge party authority, and has resorted to a variety of methods to impose, or re-impose, its control. There has been no change in the fundamental values of party and government. Repression has not been mitigated; it has simply become more subtle and therefore better able to operate below the scrutiny of international monitoring agencies or, in the manner of the "anaconda in the chandelier" metaphor described in Chapter 12, to induce individuals to exercise self-censorship. As seen in the arrest and sentencing of petitioners, of the signatories of Charter 08, and of those who sought to defend the rights of earthquake victims, when self-censorship fails, party and government quickly resort to harsher measures. This scenario may be termed authoritarian stability: the leadership will make such adjustments as it deems necessary to preserve its hold on power. China 20 years from now may be economically more prosperous, but its form of government will not be more liberal. Artificial intelligence is being used to oversee the population in ways that Mao Zedong could not have imagined.

The second scenario, namely that the present government will be overthrown, is predicted by those who believe that an accumulation of problems is causing pressures which will lead to an explosion of anger against the current form of government. They do not agree with proponents of the first scenario that the authoritarian government is stable. Protests by farmers and displaced workers will escalate; runs on banks will cause the fragile economic system to collapse. Democracy will follow. Unfortunately for proponents of this scenario, however unpopular the party and state leaders may be, they have effectively prevented the articulation of alternative formulations of government, at least in any organized and aggregated form. In other words, it is conceivable that the government will be overthrown, but more difficult to imagine that those who overthrow it will be able to replace the basic social structure of society. This is not to say that a group with a more democratic agenda could not seize power, as it did in parts of Eastern Europe, the Soviet Union, and the Middle East. But many of these leaders are having trouble holding their countries together while maintaining a degree of pluralistic decision making in the midst of economic chaos and tendencies toward political anarchy on the one hand and authoritarianism on the other. These problems would be compounded for a similar group trying to seize control in the PRC, which has many more people and, despite its enclaves of dazzling affluence, is even poorer than many of them.

A prominent Chinese economist, He Qinglian, describes the situation in today's PRC as volcanic stability. Underground fires, deriving from labor unrest, displaced peasants, and a rapidly deteriorating environment, are smoldering dangerously just below the surface. They could erupt and rage out of control at any time. While nearly all Chinese may feel the heat, none are more sensitive to it than the elite, whose privileged positions are threatened by these forces. They believe that maintaining the status quo through repression is the best way to cope. Eventually, however, the leadership's fire brigade techniques will prove inadequate, and the CCP's rule will be consumed in the resultant conflagration. Ms. He does not believe that democracy will be the necessary outcome of this cleansing by fire.

The third scenario, that of an evolution toward a more liberal regime, has great appeal. In this view, the economic pluralism that market reforms have encouraged will generate pressures for political pluralism and eventually lead to liberal democracy. Analysts who are hopeful that the process of evolution is underway point to signs that a civil society has been developing in the PRC. As noted in Chapter 1, this term refers to the sphere of independent activity outside the structure of the state and party. Marxist–Leninist systems aspire to total control of a society, aiming at comprehensive domination of all aspects of economic, political, and social life. Groups such as labor unions, youth organizations, and medical associations are to be controlled by party and state and subsumed under them. In a civil society, by contrast, these and other groups have their own agendas, which may differ from those of party and state, and exert influence on parties and governments to implement their proposals.

The past two decades have indeed seen a proliferation of new forms of association, which the party state has sought to co-opt or, in some cases, declared to be illegal. The PRC's several hundred thousand nongovernmental organizations are carefully monitored and have little or no autonomy, although certain forms of accommodation occur. These organizations may be described as corporatist with a Chinese form, and more closely resemble Walder's communist neo-traditionalist paradigm than a civil society. Although official control over them could gradually decline, the opposite seems to be happening: control is becoming tighter.

Despite the increasing disparities of income between rich and poor, a middle class has developed: in time, it may demand an increase in civil liberties. Nonetheless, in the near term, the evolutionary process is likely to be accompanied by a great deal of economic and social disruption. This will cause great discomfort within the ruling elite, who will be strongly tempted to crush it.

Moreover, even if an evolution toward civil society occurs despite government attempts to stifle it, the result may not be liberal democracy: the illegal autonomous groups are divided among themselves on the issue of political reform. Some do want liberal democracy, but others want to return to Maoist politics or espouse militantly nationalistic agendas. Ethnic separatists may advocate the dissolution of the current political system but do not necessarily advocate democracy, even for their own areas. There are a variety of positions within all of these groups, and little discourse among the holders of these positions.

Certain key counter-elites who could potentially challenge the current communist leadership, most notably the new private entrepreneurial class, show little concern for meaningful political change. Their interests are closely tied to the stability of the process of market reform under the auspices of the current authoritarian government. Pro-democracy dissidents argue that the two groups—political and economic elites—have a common interest in exploiting and repressing the peasants and workers. Hence, market forces tend toward an incorporation of society rather than a liberation of society. In this view, it is not simply party/government repression that prevents economic freedom from generating political freedom; it is the type of capitalism that has developed in the PRC, which does not lend itself to generating demands for freedom. China has developed relation-based capitalism, in which the interests of entrepreneurs are protected not by institutions but by special relationships with those in power. Hence, entrepreneurs not only do not demand autonomy but may actually fear it, since their persons and their business activities will no longer be protected.

The result could be what has been called the Latin Americanization of China. Those who make this argument realize that China is different from Latin America, where both the military and the church have traditionally exercised far more influence than in the PRC. They focus on the development of a collusive relationship between business and political elites, particularly at the local level, that functions to create prosperity for them at the expense of workers and farmers. This has spawned class conflict that could pit the have-not class against the entitled business/bureaucratic elite in the sort of ongoing and economically costly low-level disputes that have characterized much of Latin American politics.

Those who espouse the fourth scenario—paralysis within the central government as power devolves to lower levels—see state capacity continuing to deteriorate. Leaders from Deng Xiaoping through Xi Jinping have strongly backed continued reform and announced ambitious plans to effect it, but their view of reform is relatively narrow and, essentially, instrumental: political reform must serve the needs of economic modernization while simultaneously supporting the party's hold on power. The gradual transition from communism begun by Deng has helped entrench the party state, which now thwarts efforts to deepen market reforms and ease the transition into democracy. The emergence of an increasingly collective leadership would actually reduce the likelihood that thoroughgoing reforms will even be attempted, much less implemented, since the need for consensus makes bold moves improbable. Gradualism allows the ruling elites to make selective withdrawals from the centrally planned state that maintain their control of the most lucrative, high-profit rent sectors of the economy. Control over sectors with rich financial yields also facilitates the emergence of political alliances with stakes in the semi-reformed system but no interest in political reform. The ruling elites use their control to co-opt emerging social elites into a collusive network of rent-sharing, which pre-empts political challenges. Initial reform efforts buy the regime a temporary lease on life, but high economic growth rates cannot compensate indefinitely for weak political institutions. Because of the problem of dissipation of rents among so many groups, party and government's ability to extract compliance with their directives continues to erode. Each incremental reform step must be carefully negotiated and will therefore necessitate compromises that permit the continuation of local protectionism as well as the expansion of existing economic inefficiencies. Ultimately, these will take a toll on growth rates.

Authoritarian power, already fragmented, will become more so. Advocates of this position describe the PRC as in a crisis of governance, and note that an intrusive state is not necessarily an effective state. Among other factors:

- grassroots party organizations have deteriorated markedly;
- lawlessness, including the incidence of violent crime, is increasing;
- public finances are in chaos, most markedly at local government level;
- the central government has insufficient regulatory capacity;
- issues of identity are not fully resolved, particularly in certain ethnic minority areas, thus posing a threat to territorial integrity.

Local forces continue to gain strength and, so long as they do not directly challenge the central authorities, are rarely challenged by those central authorities. For the time being at least, the clientelist networks that arose from the institutional framework established by the party are functioning sufficiently well to bind state and society together, albeit not in the manner originally envisaged by the CCP leadership. In this analysis, China is trapped in a transition state that is ultimately unsustainable.

What this means for the future is problematic. Broadly speaking, there is a debate between those who feel that the current authoritarian government can reform itself—that is, the autocracy is resilient—or that it cannot withstand the pressures which partial reform has created and hence must democratize or disintegrate. In other words, will China continue in the neo-traditional paradigm or is the emergence of civil society a necessity for continued modernization?

Those who believe that China's best interests are served by the former acknowledge that the PRC has serious problems, but point out that party and government have shown themselves capable of reforms, which include returning the fiscal system to more firm central control, implementing a rotation system for officials to avoid localism, and imposing mandatory retirement ages to intro-duce circulation within the bureaucracy. Meritocracy has become an important criterion in official promotions; millions of people have been lifted out of pov-erty. Policy experiments continue at the local level, are modified on the basis of experience, and, where appropriate, introduced more widely. Evolution and innovation will continue within the current structure.

Under Xi Jinping, however, there has been a reversal of what seemed to be a trend toward collective leadership. The capacity of the party-state has increased; power is less fragmented. Polls indicate that the citizenry accepts the legitimacy of party and government. Democracies, too, have problems with corruption and pollution, with an autocratic government perhaps better positioned to deal with them. Repression is needed to deal with the small minority who wish to top-ple the system; the current economic slowdown is cyclical, not structural. The leadership will consolidate the one-party model, challenging the Western world's democratic paradigm with a post-democratic one.

Those who believe that only democracy can solve China's problems scoff at data indicating that the majority of citizens accept the CCP's rule as legitimate: in a country without free speech, such polls are similar to giving a single-choice examination. Rather than being confined to a small minority of the perpetually dissatisfied, calls for democratic reform continue to gain strength despite repres-sion. The PRC is not a meritocracy, since patronage, not ability, is the chief crite-rion for promotion. Some highly capable people do manage to rise through the system, just as patronage and princeling-like connections allow some less capable people to rise to power in democracies. But in neither case are they the norm. A Bo Xilai simply could not have gone so far as he did in the West.

The current system's ability to innovate should not be underestimated, and is one reason why the PRC's political system has not crumbled sooner. But many more promising reforms have been stifled by apparatchiks who fear threats to their vested interests or the wrath of their superiors. The party has indeed pre-sided over impressive economic growth, but it has been ineffective at distributing it equitably and providing the social services the economic growth would enable. At the same time, it devotes immense sums to the military, even though China has no external enemy. Expenditures for domestic security are even higher, not so much against crime as because party and government feel they must pro-tect themselves against the Chinese people. In this analysis, a democratic China might not exceed the economic growth rate of previous decades, but at least the growth would be more inclusive, flowing to the majority of the population rather than, as at present, to party/government functionaries and a small number of well-connected capitalists. Since 1989, the party has not adopted any genuine political reforms, with high economic growth rates providing an emollient to many discontents, but, as the World Bank has pointed out, these growth rates cannot be sustained without fundamental reforms to the system. If these are not forthcoming, existing discontents will be magnified. Past economic gains have provided a cushion for the implementation of such reforms, thereby providing an opportunity for liberalization which party and government must not squander.

Oxford don Stein Ringen characterizes the PRC as a "controlocracy." The use of techniques like artificial intelligence has enabled a degree of surveillance that would have been unimaginable in the Mao era. While a few dissidents continue to advocate liberal reform, resistance is both dangerous and futile. Aware that the party state is able to track their movements and comments, written or verbal, most do not care to try. The regime's legitimacy is based not on ideology or loyalty but on controls: If the controls should fail, so will its claims to rule. China, Ringen argues, has not become a softer totalitarian government but a more subtle one.

Following this line of analysis, Ringen believes that Xi's anti-corruption campaign should be seen as his war against the "barons": people on whom the top leader must depend to implement his orders but who use their powerful positions to become, in essence, economic warlords. Siphoning wealth from the central treasury into their families' accounts, they ultimately form centers of resistance to him that weaken the power of the top authority. In essence, Xi's anti-corruption campaign aims at enhancing state capacity, making the party state a more efficient machine. However, at the same time, it alienates the people he must depend on to carry out the work of administration and therefore undermines state capacity. Slowing economic growth rates compound these problems.

Currently, however, the PRC's rapid development in a relatively peaceful manner since the Tiananmen disturbances, and the country's rapid recovery from the global economic crisis of 2008/2009, has reinforced the leadership's argument that an authoritarian government can best guide the country. There is considerable skepticism about the economic efficiency of democracy. For now, China more nearly represents the communist neo-traditional model than that of an emerging civil society. There is a fair degree of consensus on the problems that the PRC faces. The real question on which analysts differ is whether the reforms described here will be sufficient to ameliorate social tensions, or whether they will prove to be too little and too late. There is a great deal of inertia in the Chinese system, and party and government have shown themselves resilient in the face of challenges. The CCP has survived predictions of cataclysm and collapse before and may yet muddle through again.

Thus far, the leadership's efforts to make minor adjustments to the system while portraying chaos as the alternative to its rule and itself as the standard bearer of Chinese nationalism have proved persuasive enough to a sufficient number of people to keep the party in power. Should the strategy of maintaining one-party rule through limited market reform prove sustainable, the PRC will have evolved a new variant of development that may fairly be called modernity with Chinese characteristics. This is far from a foregone conclusion, however. At the time of Mao's death, no one could predict the momentous changes that were to ensue; similarly unpredicted was the degree to which Xi Jinping was able to re-centralize power within the top leadership. Further unprecedented events cannot be ruled out. In China, as elsewhere in the world, the future is unpredictable.

Suggestions for Further Reading

William Callahan, "China 2035: From the China Dream to the World Dream," *Global Affairs,* Vol. 2, Issue 3 (Fall 2016): 1–12.

Yasheng Huang "Democratize or Die: Why China's Communists Face Reform or Revolution," and Eric X. Li, "The Life of the Party," *Foreign Affairs* (January–February 2013): 34–46; 47–54.

Minxin Pei, "Transition in China? More Likely Than You Think," *Journal of Democracy*, Vol. 27, No. 4 (October 2016): 5–19.

Stein Ringen, *The Perfect Dictatorship: China in the 21st Century* (Hong Kong: Hong Kong University Press, 2016).

Steve Tsang, "Consultative Leninism," *Journal of Contemporary China* (November 2009): 865–880.

USEFUL WEBSITES

The following list is not meant to be definitive, but only to suggest likely avenues for further research. Many of the sites contain links to other sites of interest.

http://english.mep.gov.cn—State Environmental Protection Ministry website.

www.cecc.gov—commission established by the U.S. Congress which sponsors hearings and round-table discussions on major issues of human rights, legal developments, and related topics.

www.chinadaily.com.cn—the PRC's official English-language daily newspaper.

www.chinadigitaltimes.net—summary website compiled by researchers at the University of California, Berkeley. Reports on commentaries by PRC netizens.

http://chinaspc.wordpress.com—Supreme People's Court Monitor.

www.chinatoday.com—*China Today*, a compendium of news items with links to major newspapers and wire services.

www.chrdnet.com—China Human Rights Defenders, weekly briefings on developments; comprehensive archives; annual report on human rights in the PRC.

http://ecfr.eu/programmes/china—China analysis by European experts.

www.fmprc.gov.cn—the PRC's Ministry of Foreign Affairs.

http://globaltimes.cn—livelier coverage than its parent paper, *People's Daily*.

www.hoover.org/publications/clm—*China Leadership Monitor*, in-depth analysis of current political and economic topics, published three times a year.

www.jamestown.org/china_brief/—biweekly brief analyses of current political and economic topics.

www.pbc.gov.cn/english—People's Bank of China.

www.peopledaily.com.cn/english/index.htm—*People's Daily (Beijing)*, in English translation. Official paper of the CCP's Central Committee.

www.probeinternational.org—specializes in environmental issues.

www.sina.com—Sina.com, a Chinese news service with English translations.

www.stats.gov.cn/english—the PRC's State Statistical Bureau.

www.taipeitimes.com—*Taipei Times*, Taiwan's leading English-language daily.

www.undp.org.cn—United Nations Development Program/China; focus on poverty reduction, energy, climate change.

www.uscc.gov—website of commission established by the U.S. Congress that sponsors hearings and discussions on economic and security matters.

www.xinhuanet.com/english—the PRC's official news agency.

INDEX